Utilizing Information Technology Systems Across Disciplines:
Advancements in the Application of Computer Science

Evon M. O. Abu–Taieh
Civil Aviation Regulatory Commission, Jordan

Asim A. El–Sheikh
The Arab Academy for Banking and Financial Sciences, Jordan

Jeihan Abu–Tayeh
The World Bank, USA

INFORMATION SCIENCE REFERENCE

Hershey · New York

Director of Editorial Content:	Kristin Klinger
Senior Managing Editor:	Jamie Snavely
Managing Editor:	Jeff Ash
Assistant Managing Editor:	Carole Coulson
Typesetter:	Chris Hrobak
Cover Design:	Lisa Tosheff
Printed at:	Yurchak Printing Inc.

Published in the United States of America by
Information Science Reference (an imprint of IGI Global)
701 E. Chocolate Avenue, Suite 200
Hershey PA 17033
Tel: 717-533-8845
Fax: 717-533-8661
E-mail: cust@igi-global.com
Web site: http://www.igi-global.com/reference

and in the United Kingdom by
Information Science Reference (an imprint of IGI Global)
3 Henrietta Street
Covent Garden
London WC2E 8LU
Tel: 44 20 7240 0856
Fax: 44 20 7379 0609
Web site: http://www.eurospanbookstore.com

Library of Congress Cataloging-in-Publication Data

Utilizing information technology systems across disciplines : advancements in the application of computer science / Evon Abu-Taieh,

Asim A. El-Sheikh, and Jeihan Abu-Tayeh, editors.

p. cm.

Includes bibliographical references and index.

Summary: "This book provides all aspects of information resources management, managerial and organizational applications, as well as implications of information technology"--Provided by publisher. ISBN 978-1-60566-616-7 (hardcover : alk. paper) -- ISBN 978-1-60566-617-4 (ebook : alk. paper) 1. Information technology. 2. Information resources management. 3. Management information systems. I. Abu-Taieh, Evon, 1966- II. El-Sheikh, Asim A, 1956- III. Abu-Tayeh, Jeihan, 1980- T58.5.U88 2009 004--dc22

2008052437

British Cataloguing in Publication Data
A Cataloguing in Publication record for this book is available from the British Library.

Editorial Advisory Board

Table of Contents

Detailed Table of Contents

Chapter I

    K. Ganesh, Manufacturing ISU, Tata Consultancy Services Limited, Mumbai, India
    R. Dhanlakshmi, D-Link India Ltd, Bangalore, India
    A. Thangavelu, Vellore Institute of Technology, Vellore, India
    P. Parthiban, National Institute of Technology, Tiruchirappalli, India

Chapter I, *Hybrid Artificial Intelligence Heuristics and Clustering Algorithm for Combinatorial Asymmetric Traveling Salesman Problem*, develops a set of meta-heuristics genetic algorithms (GA), simulated annealing (SA) and hybrid GA-SA to solve a variant of combinatorial optimization problem called asymmetric traveling salesman problem. The set of met heuristics is compared with clustering based heuristic and the results are encouraging.

Chapter II

    Sameh Ghwanmeh, Yarmouk University, Jordan
    Ghassan Kanaan, The Arab Academy for Banking and Financial Sciences, Jordan
    Riyad Al-Shalabi, The Arab Academy for Banking and Financial Sciences, Jordan
    Ahmad Ababneh, The Arab Academy for Banking and Financial Sciences, Jordan

Chapter II, *An Enhanced Text-Classification-Based Arabic Information Retrieval System*, presents enhanced, effective and simple approach to text classification. The approach uses an algorithm to automatically classifying documents. The effects of the Arabic text classification on Information Retrieval have been investigated.

Chapter III, *Landmark-Based Shape Context for Recognition of Handwritten Digits*, introduces a new handwriting methodology based on landmark shapes. The primary contribution is a robust and simple algorithm for finding correspondence between handwritten digits using a variant of shapes. In this chapter, an approach to recognizing *handwritten digits* based on shape similarity computed through landmark-based shape context is presented. Shape context based object recognition being an iterative process; the reduction in the number of sample points provides a basis for faster recognition.

Chapter IV, *Enhanced Information Retrieval Evaluation between Pseudo Relevance Feedback and Query Similarity Relevant Documents Methodology Applied on Arabic Text*, introduces an enhanced information retrieval evaluation between pseudo relevance feedback and query similarity relevant documents methodology applied on Arabic text. The new method uses global feedback information for query expansion in contrast to local feedback information.

Chapter V, *New Technique to Detect CNP Fraudulent Transactions*, presents comprehensive frameworks that mines and detect fraudulent transactions of Card-Not-Present (CNP) in the e-payment systems with a high degree of accuracy. The motivation for a comprehensive framework is that money in the e-commerce network is really bits and bytes. Which in turn, make digital crime within banking and financial systems happen very fast and may cost billions of dollars each year-undetected and unreported.

Chapter VI, *Key Topics in the Ethics and Economics of Cyber Security*, studies key topics in a nascent literature on a cyber security. The chapters first concentrate on how inducements influence the major topics in information security. Three significant topics pertinent for a cyber security concerns are: an exterior security, the internet consequence and information sharing which make effect in the information security. The budding literature has started to study the relationships between vulnerability revelation, patching, manufactured goods prices and profits.

Chapter VII

Asim El-Sheikh, The Arab Academy for Banking and Financial Sciences, Jordan
Husam A. Abu Khadra, The Arab Academy for Banking and Financial Sciences, Jordan

Chapter VII, *Using Maturity Model to Govern Information Technology*, introduces the COBiTs' maturity model as a mean of studying the information technology (IT) governance and its affect on the perceived security threats. It argues that IT governance using the maturity model offers a probable influence on the level of security breaches frequency; such evidence would be extracted through a complex quantitative and qualitative approach, offers a better understanding of intricate relationships between different factors. Moreover, the authors aimed at understanding the influence of using the maturity model will not only inform the researchers of a better design for IT governance and defining implementation pitfalls, but also assist in the understanding of IT governance practices trend in the Jordanian environment.

Chapter VIII

Saad Ghaleb Yaseen, Al-Zaytoonh University of Jordan, Jordan
Khaled Saleh Al Omoush, Al-Zaytoonh University of Jordan, Jordan

Chapter VIII, *The Critical Success Factors of Web-Based Supply Chain Collaboration Adoption: An Empirical Study,* identify the critical success factors (CSFs) and outcomes of Web-based supply chain collaboration (SCC). The study is conducted on seven manufacturing firms in Jordan that use Web systems to collaborate with supply chain members. The results showed that top management support, IT infrastructure, training and education, business processes reengineering, trust among partners, open information sharing, and performance measurement are critical factors for Web-based SCC implementation success. In addition, this study revealed that Web-based SCC implementation is positively related to supply chain relationship quality, performance effectiveness, and performance efficiency.

Chapter IX

Haroon Altarawneh, Albalqa' Applied University, Jordan
Asim El-Sheikh, The Arab Academy for Banking and Financial Sciences, Jordan

Chapter IX, *Web Engineering in Small Jordanian Web Development Firms: An XP Based Process Model,* proposes a theoretical model for small Web project development and its special features in the context small Web firms, which are capable of being 'tailor able' to the particular stage of organizational development of small Web firms.

Chapter X

Sattam Alamro, Albalqa' Applied University, Jordan
Asim El-Sheikh, The Arab Academy for Banking and Financial Sciences, Jordan

Chapter X, *A Proposed Theoretical Framework for Assessing Quality of E-Commerce Systems,* suggests framework for assessing quality of e-commerce systems. The proposed framework consisted of new indicators that are clear, measurable, and flexible to the possibility of its application on all sites and services, regardless of the nature of the company or institution. Consequently, the proposed framework can be applied easily to evaluate the quality of any system.

Chapter XI

Evon M. O. Abu-Taieh, The Arab Academy for Banking and Financial Sciences, Jordan

Chapter XI, *Information Technology and Aviation Industry: Marriage of Convenience,* pinpoints the affects of information technology on the aviation industry, specifically on the Airline ticket prices. The chapter first introduces the different costs that comprise the airline ticket. Then the chapter introduces the different information technology systems that are used in the aviation industry which in turn reduces the price of the airline ticket.

Chapter XII

Hussein Al-Bahadili, The Arab Academy for Banking and Financial Sciences, Jordan
Arafat Abu Mallouh, The Hashemite University, Jordan

Chapter XII, *Dynamic Channel Allocation Scheme in Cellular Communication Networks,* presents a description and performance evaluation of an efficient distributed dynamic channels allocation (DDCA) scheme, which can be used for channel allocation in cellular communication networks (CCNs), such as the global system for mobile communication (GSM). The scheme utilizes a well known distributed artificial intelligence (DAI) algorithm, namely, the asynchronous weak-commitment (AWC) algorithm, in which a complete solution is established by extensive communication among a group of neighboring collaborative cells forming a pattern, where each cell in the pattern uses a unique set of channels. To minimize communication overhead among cells, a token based mechanism was introduced.

Chapter XIII

Maha T. El-Mahied, The Arab Academy for Banking and Financial Sciences, Jordan
Firas Alkhaldi, The Arab Academy for Banking and Financial Sciences, Jordan
Evon M. O. Abu-Taieh, The Arab Academy for Banking and Financial Sciences, Jordan

Chapter XIII, *Discovering Knowledge Channels in Learning Organization: Case Study of Jordan,* aims to discover the knowledge channels in the learning organization in Jordan. The research studied three aspects of the trusted knowledge channels: first studied the worker perspective and understanding of the

TRUST issue. Second the research studied the worker perspectives of the knowledge channels, finding that the worker consider boss, colleague, and assistant as the most important sources of knowledge in the organization. Third the research studied how the organization by providing the right environment will encourage knowledge sharing.

Chapter XIV
Ali Al-Haj, Princess Sumaya University for Technology, Jordan
Aymen Abu-Errub, The Arab Academy for Financial and Banking Sciences, Jordan

Chapter XIV, *Performance Optimization of DWT-Based Image Watermarking Using Genetic Algorithms*, applies Genetic algorithms to locate the optimal discrete wavelet transform (DWT) sub-band and the corresponding watermark amplification factor that will lead to maximum imperceptible and robustness. The motivation for such researcher is the widespread of the Internet and the continuous advancements in computer technology have facilitated the unauthorized manipulation and reproduction of original digital multimedia products. The audio-visual industry has been the main victim of such illegal reproduction, and consequently, the design and development of effective digital multimedia copyright protection methods have become necessary more than ever.

Chapter XV
Farrukh Amin, Institute of Business Management, Pakistan

Chapter XV, *Internet Banking System in South Asian Countries: Preliminary Findings*, studies internet banking systems in South Asian Countries and concentrates on Pakistan as an example. The preliminary results indicate that Pakistani banks have been successful in the introductory phase of web based banking. The authors suggest that Pakistani web based banking to move forward with a view of conducting real financial transactions and improving electronic customer relationship. The results and recommendations can be generalized to banks in developing economies, which can no longer ignore the internet as a strategic weapon and distribution channel for their services. The study had are threefold: Examine the extent to which web based banking is practiced in Pakistan; Identify barrier to Internet banking and Offer future directions for both practice and research.

Chapter XVI
Kasthurirangan Gopalakrishnan, Iowa State University, USA
Naga Shashidhar, Corning Inc., USA

Chapter XVI, *Computer Simulation of Particle Packing in Bituminous Concrete*, applies particle packing simulation concepts to study aggregate structure in asphalt pavements, in conjunction with the recent advances in nondestructive imaging techniques and discrete element method simulations have tremendous potential to help develop a deeper understanding of the aggregate structure in asphalt concrete, develop and optimize the various parameters that describe the aggregate structure and relate them to the performance of pavements in a scientific way. Which in turn provide s the foundations to building more durable and long-lasting pavements.

Chapter XVII

In Chapter XVII, *Information Technology as a Service*, the discussion focuses on IT as a service. The author, presents IT development, research, and outsourcing as a knowledge service; on the other hand, argues that IT as a service helps enterprises align their business operations, workforce, and technologies to maximize their profits by continuously improving their performance. Numerous research and development aspects of service-enterprise engineering from a business perspective will be briefly explored, and then computing methodologies and technologies to enable adaptive enterprise service computing in support of service-enterprise engineering will be simply studied and analyzed. Finally, future development and research avenues in this emerging interdisciplinary field will also be highlighted.

Chapter XVIII

In Chapter XVIII, *The Impact of Sociocultural Factors in Multicultural Communication Environments: A Case Example from an Australian University's Provision of Distance Education in the Global Classroom*, by providing insight on the impact multiple sociocultural and communicative norms have on virtual communication, this research uses qualitative discursive analysis of case examples to examine how variance in the structure and delivery of virtual communication environments at a leading distance education university in Australia affects student satisfaction, perception, and learning outcomes. Whereas previous research fails to include a theoretical or conceptual framework, this work draws upon interdisciplinary work from the fields of sociology, education, and science and technology studies. How "cyberspace" changes interaction rituals, masks cultural norms, and alters entrenched social expectations by creating new sensitivities is discussed, along with the ramifications of variation in technological availability, competence, and expectations in global classrooms. In sum, ideas for informing change in policy, administration, and the delivery of distance education and virtual communication in global environments are discussed to equip leaders and participants with skills to foster effective communicative and interaction strategies.

Chapter XIX

Chapter XIX, *Adaptive Computation Paradigm in Knowledge Representation: Traditional and Emerging Applications*, is survey article discusses the new paradigm of the algorithmic models of intelligence, based on the adaptive hierarchical model of computation, and presents the algorithms and applications utilizing this paradigm in data-intensive, collaborative environment. Examples from the various areas include references to adaptive paradigm in biometric technologies, evolutionary computing, swarm intelligence, robotics, networks, e-learning, knowledge representation and information system design. Special topics related to adaptive models design and geometric computing are also included in the survey.

Preface

In the information technology age coupled with computer advances, information systems have become an integral part of many disciplines; accordingly, business, marketing, medicine, communication, banking, geography, physics, chemistry, aviation, pilots, forensics, agriculture, and even traffic lights have one thing in common called computers. Interdisciplinary information technology systems are called different names: Decision support systems (DSS), geographic information systems (GIS), knowledge management systems (KM), management information systems (MIS), data mining (DM), simulation and modeling (SM), artificial intelligence (AI), etc. All the aforementioned systems are based on computer science whether that may be in terms of hardware, software, software engineering, and hardware engineering.

The goal of this book is not to look at computer science from traditional perspectives, but to illustrate the benefits and issues that arise from the application of computer science within other disciplines. This book focuses on major breakthroughs within the technological arena, with particular concentration on accelerating principles, concepts and applications.

The book caters to the needs of scholars, PhD candidates, and researchers as well as graduate level students of computer science, operations research, and economics. The target audience for this book also includes academic libraries throughout the world that are interested in cutting edge research. Another important segment of readers are students of Master of Business Administration (MBA) and Master of Public Affairs (MPA) programs, which include information systems components as part of their curriculum. To make the book accessible to all, a companion website was developed that can be accessed through the link (http://www.computercrossroad.org/).

Computer science has aligned with many disciplines, including geography, linguistics, hand writing, security and the web industry, communications, Knowledge management and simulation. Within this context, this book is organized in 19 chapters. On the whole, the chapters of this book fall into five categories, while crossing paths with different disciplines. The first section concentrates on artificial intelligence technology; the second section concentrates on security: interior, exterior, and security standards; the third section concentrates on Web based industry: assessing quality, Web engineering, and critical success factors; the fourth section that sheds light on computer science implementation in the business arena: aviation industry, learning organizations, multimedia, communications, banking, construction; and the fifth section is suggested readings of different authors, aiming to enrich this book with others' knowledge, experience, thought and insight.

Chapter I, *Hybrid Artificial Intelligence Heuristics and Clustering Algorithm for Combinatorial Asymmetric Traveling Salesman Problem*, develops a set of meta-heuristics genetic algorithms (GA), simulated annealing (SA) and Hybrid GA-SA to solve a variant of combinatorial optimization problem called asymmetric traveling salesman problem. The set of meta heuristics is compared with clustering based heuristic and the results are encouraging.

Chapter II, *An Enhanced Text-Classification-Based Arabic Information Retrieval System*, presents enhanced, effective and simple approach to text classification. The approach uses an algorithm to automatically classifying documents. The effects of the Arabic text classification on Information Retrieval have been investigated.

Chapter III, *Landmark-Based Shape Context for Recognition of Handwritten Digits*, introduces a new handwriting methodology based on landmark shapes. The primary contribution is a robust and simple algorithm for finding correspondence between handwritten digits using a variant of shapes. In this chapter, an approach to recognizing *handwritten digits* based on shape similarity computed through landmark-based shape context is presented. Shape context based object recognition being an iterative process; the reduction in the number of sample points provides a basis for faster recognition.

Chapter IV, *Enhanced Information Retrieval Evaluation between Pseudo Relevance Feedback and Query Similarity Relevant Documents Methodology Applied on Arabic Text*, introduces an enhanced information retrieval evaluation between pseudo relevance feedback and query similarity relevant documents methodology applied on arabic text. The new method uses global feedback information for query expansion in contrast to local feedback information.

The second section concentrates on security: interior, exterior, and security standards, where it is covered in chapter five through seven as follows.

Chapter V, *New Technique to Detect CNP Fraudulent Transactions*, presents comprehensive frameworks that mines and detect fraudulent transactions of Card-Not-Present (CNP) in the e-payment systems with a high degree of accuracy. The motivation for a comprehensive framework is that money in the e-commerce network is really bits and bytes. Which in turn, make digital crime within banking and financial systems happen very fast and may cost billions of dollars each year-undetected and unreported.

Chapter VI, *Key Topics in the Ethics and Economics of Cyber Security*, studies key topics in a nascent literature on a cyber security. The chapters first concentrate on how inducements influence the major topics in information security. Three significant topics pertinent for a cyber security concerns are: an exterior security, the internet consequence and information sharing which make effect in the information security. The budding literature has started to study the relationships between vulnerability revelation, patching, manufactured goods prices and profits.

Chapter VII, *Using Maturity Model to Govern Information Technology*, introduces the COBiTs' maturity model as a mean of studying the information technology (IT) governance and its affect on the perceived Security Threats. It argues that IT governance using the maturity model offers a probable influence on the level of security breaches frequency; such evidence would be extracted through a complex quantitative and qualitative approach, offers a better understanding of intricate relationships between different factors. Moreover, the authors aimed at understanding the influence of using the maturity model will not only inform the researchers of a better design for IT governance and defining implementation pitfalls, but also assist in the understanding of IT governance practices trend in the Jordanian environment.

The third section of the book concentrates on web based industry: assessing quality of, web engineering, and critical success factors. The chapters *eight through ten* cover this as follows.

Chapter VIII, *The Critical Success Factors of Web-Based Supply Chain Collaboration Adoption: An Empirical Study*, identify the Critical Success Factors (CSFs) and outcomes of Web-based supply chain collaboration (SCC). The study is conducted on seven manufacturing firms in Jordan that use Web systems to collaborate with supply chain members. The results showed that top management support,

IT infrastructure, training and education, business processes reengineering, trust among partners, open information sharing, and performance measurement are critical factors for Web-based SCC implementation success. In addition, this study revealed that Web-based SCC implementation is positively related to supply chain relationship quality, performance effectiveness, and performance efficiency.

Chapter IX, *Web Engineering in Small Jordanian Web Development Firms: An XP Based Process Model*, proposes a theoretical model for small web project development and its special features in the context small web firms, which are capable of being 'tailor able' to the particular stage of organizational development of small web firms .

Chapter X, *A Proposed Theoretical Framework for Assessing Quality of E-Commerce Systems,* suggests framework for assessing quality of e-commerce systems. The proposed framework consisted of new indicators that are clear, measurable, and flexible to the possibility of its application on all sites and services, regardless of the nature of the company or institution. Consequently, the proposed framework can be applied easily to evaluate the quality of any system.

The fourth section of this book sheds light on computer science implementation in the business arena: aviation industry, learning organizations, multimedia, communications, banking, construction. The chapters eleven through sixteen will cover such topics.

Chapter XI, *Information Technology and Aviation Industry: Marriage of Convenience,* pinpoints the affects of information technology on the aviation industry, specifically on the Airline ticket prices. The chapter first introduces the different costs that comprise the airline ticket. Then the chapter introduces the different information technology systems that are used in the aviation industry which in turn reduces the price of the airline ticket.

Chapter XII, *Distributed Dynamic Channel Allocation Scheme in Cellular Communication Networks*, presents a description and performance evaluation of an efficient distributed dynamic channels allocation (DDCA) scheme, which can be used for channel allocation in cellular communication networks (CCNs), such as the global system for mobile communication (GSM). The scheme utilizes a well known distributed artificial intelligence (DAI) algorithm, namely, the asynchronous weak-commitment (AWC) algorithm, in which a complete solution is established by extensive communication among a group of neighboring collaborative cells forming a pattern, where each cell in the pattern uses a unique set of channels. To minimize communication overhead among cells, a token based mechanism was introduced.

Chapter XIII, *Discovering Knowledge Channels in Learning Organization: Case Study of Jordan,* aims to discover the knowledge channels in the learning organization in Jordan. The research studied three aspects of the trusted knowledge channels: first studied the worker perspective and understanding of the TRUST issue. Second the research studied the worker perspectives of the knowledge channels, finding that the worker consider boss, colleague, and assistant as the most important sources of knowledge in the organization. Third the research studied how the organization by providing the right environment will encourage knowledge sharing.

Chapter XIV, *Performance Optimization of DWT-Based Image Watermarking Using Genetic Algorithms,* applies Genetic algorithms to locate the optimal discrete wavelet transform (DWT) sub-band and the corresponding watermark amplification factor that will lead to maximum imperceptible and robustness. The motivation for such researcher is the widespread of the Internet and the continuous advancements in computer technology have facilitated the unauthorized manipulation and reproduction of original digital multimedia products. The audio-visual industry has been the main victim of such illegal reproduction, and consequently, the design and development of effective digital multimedia copyright protection methods have become necessary more than ever.

Chapter XV, *Internet Banking System in South Asian Countries: Preliminary Findings*, studies internet banking systems in South Asian Countries and concentrates on Pakistan as an example. The preliminary results indicate that Pakistani banks have been successful in the introductory phase of web based banking. The authors suggest that Pakistani web based banking to move forward with a view of conducting real financial transactions and improving electronic customer relationship. The results and recommendations can be generalized to banks in developing economies, which can no longer ignore the internet as a strategic weapon and distribution channel for their services. The study had are threefold: Examine the extent to which web based banking is practiced in Pakistan; Identify barrier to Internet banking and Offer future directions for both practice and research.

Chapter XVI, *Computer Simulation of Particle Packing in Bituminous Concrete*, applies particle packing simulation concepts to study aggregate structure in asphalt pavements, in conjunction with the recent advances in nondestructive imaging techniques and discrete element method simulations have tremendous potential to help develop a deeper understanding of the aggregate structure in asphalt concrete, develop and optimize the various parameters that describe the aggregate structure and relate them to the performance of pavements in a scientific way. Which in turn provide s the foundations to building more durable and long-lasting pavements.

The fifth section of this book is made of 3 chapters as suggested readings. In chapter XVII, *Information Technology as a Service*, the discussion focuses on IT as a service. The author, presents IT development, research, and outsourcing as a knowledge service; on the other hand, argues that IT as a service helps enterprises align their business operations, workforce, and technologies to maximize their profits by continuously improving their performance. Numerous research and development aspects of service-enterprise engineering from a business perspective will be briefly explored, and then computing methodologies and technologies to enable adaptive enterprise service computing in support of service-enterprise engineering will be simply studied and analyzed. Finally, future development and research avenues in this emerging interdisciplinary field will also be highlighted.

In Chapter **XVIII**, *The Impact of Sociocultural Factors in Multicultural Communication Environments: A Case Example from an Australian University's Provision of Distance Education in the Global Classroom*, by providing insight on the impact multiple sociocultural and communicative norms have on virtual communication, this research uses qualitative discursive analysis of case examples to examine how variance in the structure and delivery of virtual communication environments at a leading distance education university in Australia affects student satisfaction, perception, and learning outcomes. Whereas previous research fails to include a theoretical or conceptual framework, this work draws upon interdisciplinary work from the fields of sociology, education, and science and technology studies. How "cyberspace" changes interaction rituals, masks cultural norms, and alters entrenched social expectations by creating new sensitivities is discussed, along with the ramifications of variation in technological availability, competence, and expectations in global classrooms. In sum, ideas for informing change in policy, administration, and the delivery of distance education and virtual communication in global environments are discussed to equip leaders and participants with skills to foster effective communicative and interaction strategies.

Chapter **XIX**, *Adaptive Computation Paradigm in Knowledge Representation: Traditional and Emerging Applications*, is survey article discusses the new paradigm of the algorithmic models of intelligence, based on the adaptive hierarchical model of computation, and presents the algorithms and applications utilizing this paradigm in data-intensive, collaborative environment. Examples from the various areas include references to adaptive paradigm in biometric technologies, evolutionary computing, swarm intelligence, robotics, networks, e-learning, knowledge representation and information system design. Special topics related to adaptive models design and geometric computing are also included in the survey.

As mentioned earlier, this book is not meant to look at computer science from traditional perspectives, but to illustrate the benefits and issues that arise from the application of computer science within other disciplines. This book focuses on major breakthroughs within the technological arena, with particular concentration on the accelerating principles, concepts and applications.

As such, through this book, the reader will conclude that computer science crosses paths with many disciplines: geography, linguistics, hand writing, security and the web industry, communications, Knowledge management and simulation. Generally the chapters of this book fall into four categories while intersecting with different disciplines. The first section of the book, chapters one through four, concentrates on Artificial Intelligence technology. The second section, chapters five through seven, concentrates on security: interior, exterior, and security standards. The third section of the book, chapters eight through ten, concentrates on web based industry: assessing quality of, web engineering, and critical success factors. The fourth section, chapters eleven through sixteen, discusses computer science implementation in the business arena: aviation industry, learning organizations, multimedia, communications, banking, construction. The fifth sectin of the book, chapters seventeen to nineteen, include suggested readings.

Acknowledgment

The editors would like to acknowledge the relentless support of the IGI Global team, as their help and patience have been infinite and significant. Moreover, the authors would like to extend their gratitude to Mehdi Khosrow-Pour, Executive Director of the Information Resources Management Association and Jan Travers, Vice President. Likewise, the authors would like to extend their appreciation to the Development Division at IGI-Global; namely Julia Mosemann, Development Editor, Rebecca Beistline, Assistant Development Editor, and Christine Bufton- Editorial Assistant.

In this regard, the authors would like to express their gratitude to their respective organizations and colleagues represented by: The Arab Academy for Banking & Financial Science, World Bank Group, and Civil Aviation Regulatory Commission, for the moral support and encouragement that have proved to be indispensable.

In the same token, the editors would like to thank the reviewers for their relentless work and for their constant demand for perfection.

More importantly, the authors would like to express their sincere gratefulness to their family for their love, support, and patience. The editors would like to devote this work for the loving memory of the late Eng. Akef Abu-Tayeh for his relentless support and infinite encouragement extended to each one of them throughout his life.

Editors
Evon Abu-Taieh, PhD
Asim A. El-Sheikh, PhD
Jeihan Abu-Tayeh, MBA

Chapter I
Hybrid Artificial Intelligence Heuristics and Clustering Algorithm for Combinatorial Asymmetric Traveling Salesman Problem

K. Ganesh
Manufacturing ISU, Tata Consultancy Services Limited, Mumbai, India

R. Dhanlakshmi
D-Link India Ltd, Bangalore, India

A. Thangavelu
Vellore Institute of Technology, Vellore, India

P. Parthiban
National Institute of Technology, Tiruchirappalli, India

ABSTRACT

Problems of combinatorial optimization are characterized by their well-structured problem definition as well as by their huge number of action alternatives in practical application areas of reasonable size. Especially in areas like routing, task allocation, or scheduling, such kinds of problems often occur. Artificial Intelligence Heuristics, otherwise called Meta-heuristic techniques that mimic natural processes, can produce 'good' results in reasonable short runs for this class of optimization problems. Even though those bionic heuristics are much more flexible regarding modifications in the problem description when being compared to classical problem specific heuristics, they are often superior in their results. Those bionic heuristics have been developed following the principles of natural processes. In that sense, Ge-

netic Algorithms (GAs) try to imitate the biological evolution of a species in order to achieve an almost optimal state whereas Simulated Annealing (SA) was initially inspired by the laws of thermodynamics in order to cool down a certain matter to its lowest energetic state. This paper develops a set of meta-heuristics (GA, SA and Hybrid GA-SA) to solve a variant of combinatorial optimization problem called Asymmetric Traveling Salesman Problem. The set of met heuristics is compared with clustering based heuristic and the results are encouraging.

1. INTRODUCTION

Supply chain management (SCM) is now at the center stage of manufacturing and service organizations. Supply Chain is the network of suppliers, manufacturing, assembly, distribution and logistics facilities that perform the function of procurement of materials, transformation of these materials into intermediate and finished products and distribution of these finished products to the customers. The task of managing the entire supply chain constitutes the core of the supply chain Management.

1.2. Distribution Logistics Management

Logistics is that part of the supply chain process that plans, implements and controls the efficient, effective flow and storage of goods, services and related information from the point of origin to the point of consumption in order to meet consumer's requirements.

A major component of supply-chain system is Distribution, which involves delivery of goods and services to the customers. Efficient distribution of goods and services is of great importance in

Figure 1.1.Supply chain structure

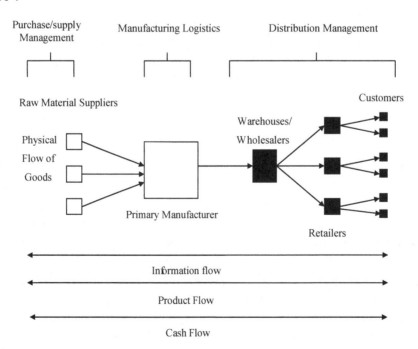

today`s competitive market, because transportation cost constitutes a considerable portion of the purchase price of most products or services. A broad range of decisions, ranging from warehouse location to distribution of goods falls under distribution logistics management. This study addresses the routing aspect of Distribution Logistics in SCM. A wide range of decisions is taken under distribution logistics management.

Distribution facility: The aspects pertaining to the types of distribution facilities such as warehouses, cross-docks and dropouts are examined with respect to the requirements and a choice is made.

Location and allocation: The location of distribution facilities and the assignment of facilities to individual customers are to be decided.

Facility configuration: The choice of an appropriate facility for each product, the earmarking of products and their quantities to be stocked at each facility and the replenishment strategy are some of the required decisions.

Transportation: The type of vehicles and the route to be followed by each vehicle to service customer's demands, decisions related with transportation aspect of logistics management are an important part of supply chain decisions. This study addresses the transportation of distribution logistics in SCM. The problem has been modeled as a classical routing problem.

1.3. Transportation and Vehicle Routing in Supply Chain Management

One of the central problems of supply chain management is the coordination of product and material flows between locations. A typical problem involves bringing products located at a central facility to geographically dispersed facilities at minimum cost. For example, a supply of product is located at a plant, warehouse, cross-docking facility or distribution center and must be distributed to customers or retailers. A fleet of vehicles under direct control or not of the firm often performs the task. Transportation is an area that absorbs a significant amount of the cost in most firms. Therefore, methods for dealing with the important issues in transportation as mode selection, carrier routing, vehicle routing and scheduling and shipment consolidations are of need in most companies.

One important aspect in transportation management is the coordination with the remaining activities in the firm, especially within warehouse and customer service. In some cases the transport is the last contact with the customer, and therefore, the companies should pay attention to fulfill the customer expectations and use this relationship to improve their sales. The transport coordination of the different elements of a supply chain, that can evolve different companies, can be very important since all of them most likely benefit by having a fast delivery to a specific customer. Therefore, many issues in the integration of transportation with other activities in the network can be a challenge to the academic and industrial communities.

One basic and well-known problem in transportation is the vehicle scheduling and routing. A vehicle scheduling system should output a set of instructions telling drivers what to deliver, when and where. An "efficient" solution is one that enables goods to be delivered when and where required at least cost, subject to legal and political constraints. The legal constraints relate to hours of work, speed limits, vehicle construction and use regulations, and restrictions for unloading, and so on. With the growing of sales by Internet, this problem is gaining enormous importance, since the delivery times are usually very short, the customers can be dispersed in a region, every day there is a different set of customers and also with very short time-windows to deliver the product.

1.4 Motivation for study

Transportation comprises a significant fraction of the economy of most developed nations. It has been estimated that transportation cost contributes to 15% of U.S gross national product. The economic importance has motivated both private companies and academic researchers to pursue the use of Operations Research and Management Science tools to improve the efficiency of transportation.

A bird's eye view of major decision issues in the design and operation of supply chain management (SCM) is provided in (Narahari and Biswas, 2000) who have indicated the part played by distribution management in SCM. Earlier researchers have modeled the distribution problem as Travelling Salesman Problem (TSP) (Lenstra and Rinnooy, 1981) and if there is more than one vehicle, it was interpreted as Vehicle Routing Problem (VRP). TSP belongs to a class of non polynomial (NP) complete problems. The solution methods for TSP can be classified broadly as classical heuristics and meta heuristics. Classical heuristics perform limited exploration of search space and yield good solutions with moderate computational effort.

Meta heuristics often combine sophisticated neighbourhood search rules, memory structures and recombination of solutions. These methods generally yield better solutions than classical heuristics but require computing time. Among the well-known meta heuristics are Tabu Search, SA, GAs and Artificial Neural Networks. Among these, GA has proved to be most successful tool for solving the TSP. However the application of GA with uniform crossover and double operated crossover hybrid with SA algorithm remains unexplored. Moreover the application of K Means Clustering Algorithm to solve TSP along with hybrid algorithm remains unexplored. The current study seeks to fill this research gap by considering the K Means Cluster based heuristic hybrid with GA and SA algorithm.

2. VARIANTS OF TRAVELING SALESMAN PROBLEM

2.1 Introduction to Travelling Salesman Problem

A salesman has to visit n cities and return to his city of origin. Each city has to be visited exactly once, and the distance (or more generally the cost) of the journey between each pair of cities is known. The problem is to do the **tour** at minimum total cost. This forms one of a class of problems known as NP-complete problems, which are believed to require a computation time exp(kn), where k is a constant of the problem, and n is the number of cities for an exact solution. Precisely, TSP can be interpreted as follows: given a finite number of "cities" along with the cost of travel between each pair of them, find the cheapest way of visiting all the cities and returning to your starting point. A common special case of the TSP is the metric TSP, Where the distances between cities satisfy the triangle inequality. It means that there is little hope for us to solve it in polynomial time unless P=NP.

The TSP has been studied with much interest within the last three to four decades. The majority of these works focus on the static and deterministic cases of vehicle routing in which all information is known at the time of the planning of the routes. In most real-life applications though, stochastic and/or dynamic information occurs parallel to the routes being carried out. Real-life examples of stochastic and/or dynamic routing problems include the distribution of oil to private house holds, the pick-up of courier mail/packages and the dispatching of buses for the transportation of elderly and handicapped people. In these examples the customer profiles (i.e. the time to begin service, the geographic location, the actual demand etc.) may not be known at the time of the planning or even when service has begun for the advance request customers. Two distinct features make the planning of high quality routes in this environment much more difficult than in its deterministic counterpart; firstly, the constant change, secondly, the time horizon. A growing number of companies offer to service the customers within a few hours from the time the request is received. Naturally, such customer service oriented policies increase the dynamism of the system and therefore its complexity. During the past decade the number of published papers dealing with dynamic transportation models has been growing.

2.2 The Conventional Travelling Salesman Problem

The most fundamental and well-studied routing problem is without doubt the TSP, in which a salesman is to visit a set of cities and return to the city he started. The objective for the TSP is to minimize the total distance traveled by the sales-man. The VRP is a generalization of the TSP in that the VRP consists in determining *m* vehicle routes, where a route is a tour that begins at the depot, visits a subset of the customers in a given order and returns to the depot. All customers must be visited exactly once and the total customer demand of a route must not exceed the vehicle capacity. The objective of the VRP is to minimize the overall distribution costs. In most real-life distribution contexts a number of side constraints complicate the model. These side constraints could for instance be time constraints on the total route time and time windows within which the service must begin. The latter problem is referred to as the VRP with Time Windows (VRPTW). Furthermore, having to deal with aspects such as multiple depots and commodities complicates the models further. Solution methods include exact methods such as mathematical programming, but custom designed heuristics and meta heuristics such as Genetic Algorithm (GA), tabu search and Simulated Annealing (SA) have also been applied to the VRP.

2.3. Variants of Travelling Salesman Problem

There are different variants of TSP, among with Asymmetric TSP (ATSP) is considered for this project and the remaining variants are described as follows:

a. Symmetric TSP (STSP)

Given a set of n nodes and distances for each pair of nodes, find a round trip of minimal total length visiting each node exactly once. The distance from node i to node j is the same as from node j to node i. For STSP, the number of possible paths to consider is given by (N-1)!/2. It is obvious that we can't solve it in polynomial time. There are some algorithms to approximate it. The best know algorithm is Lin-Kernighan 2-opt. It is suitable for any symmetric TSP.

b. Asymmetric TSP (ATSP)

Given a set of n nodes and distances for each pair of nodes, find a round trip of minimal total length visiting each node exactly once. In this case, the distance from node i to node j and the distance from node j to node i may be different.

c. Hamiltonian Cycle Problem (HCP)

A Hamiltonian cycle is a *path* through a *graph*, which starts and ends at the same *vertex* and includes every other vertex exactly once. HSP is a special case for TSP wih the distance of each city be 1.

d. Sequential Ordering Problem (SOP)

This problem is an asymmetric TSP with additional constraints. Given a set of n nodes and distances for each pair of nodes, find a Hamiltonian path from node 1 to node n of minimal length, which takes given precedence constraints into account. Each precedence constraint requires that some node i have to be visited before some other node j. A lot of real-world problems that can be modelled as a SOP, such as

- Routing applications where a pick-up has to precede the delivery,
- Scheduling applications where a certain job has to be completed before other jobs can start.

e. Capacitated VRP (CVRP)

We are given n-1 nodes, one depot and distances from the nodes to the depot, as well as between nodes. All nodes have demands, which can be satisfied by the depot. For delivery to the nodes, trucks with identical capacities are available. The problem is to find tours for the trucks of minimal total length that satisfy the node demands without violating truck capacity constraint. The number of trucks is not specified. Each tour visits a subset of the nodes and starts and terminates at the depot.

f. Prize-Collecting TSP (PCTSP)

In the standard TSP problem there is a map and a starting point and would like a route that visits all the cities in as short a total distance as possible. But, the need is to visit, say, k out of the n cities? In this case, before even deciding on the route, there is the more fundamental question that which k cities do visit in the first place. This is the most basic case of the PCTSP.

g. The Euclidean Traveling Salesman Selection Problem (TSSP)

The problem is restricted to the Euclidian case where the TSP can be formulated as follows: Given n cities in the plane and their Euclidian distances, the problem is to find the shortest TSP-tour, i.e.

a closed path visiting each of the n cities exactly once. In addition to that the TSSP specifies a number $k < n$ of cities and the shortest TSP--tour through any subset of k cities shall be found. Existing heuristics are based on approximations for the k-Minimal Spanning Tree to find the node cluster containing the shortest k-tour. Unlike many related problems, the TSSP does not include a depot that has to be visited by the k-tour

h. Circulant TSP (CTSP)

This is the problem of finding a minimum weight Hamiltonian cycle in a weighted graph with circulant distance matrix. The computational complexity of this problem is not known. In fact, even the complexity of deciding Hamiltonicity of the underlying graph is unknown.

i. Online TSP (OTSP)

The online TSP requests for visits to cities (points in a metric space) arrive online while the salesman is traveling. The salesman moves at no more than unit speed and starts and ends his work at a designated origin. The objective is to find a routing for the salesman, which finishes as early as possible.

2.3 Literature Survey

The TSP is a typical example of a very hard combinatorial optimization problem. The problem is to find the shortest tour that passes through each vertex in a given graph exactly once. Problems of this type arise in various applications, such as VRPs, integrated circuit board chip insertion problems, printed circuit board punching sequence problems, and a wing-nozzle design problem in the aircraft design. The TSP has received considerable attention over the last two decades and various approaches are proposed to solve the problem, such as branch-and-bound, cutting planes, 2-opt, SA, neural network, and tabu search (Chiung Moon *et al.* 2002]. Some of these methods are exact algorithms, while the others are near-optimal or approximate algorithms. The exact algorithms include the integer linear programming approaches with additional linear constraints to eliminate infeasible sub-tours (Dantzig and Ramser, 1959). On the other hand, network models yield appropriate methods that are flexible enough to include the precedence constraints. More recently, GA approaches are successfully implemented to the TSP. Potvin (1996) presents survey of GA approaches for the general TSP.

Symmetric TSP

Many researchers have studied the symmetric version of the TSP, in which bi-directional distances between a pair of cities are identical, and the understanding of the polyhedral structure of the problem has made it possible to optimally solve large size problems. Nonetheless, efforts to develop good heuristic procedures have continued because of their practical importance in quickly obtaining approximate solutions of large size problems. Good heuristic procedures are also important in designing an efficient implicit enumeration method for the problem and its variants. Heuristic methods such as the k-opt heuristic by Lin and Kernighan and the Or-opt heuristic by Or are well known for the symmetric TSP. There also have been a few attempts to solve it by various meta-heuristics such as tabu searches and GAs (Choi *et al.* 2003).

Routing problems arise in many contexts and in general they are very difficult to solve to optimality. Therefore a main concern for scientists and practitioners is to develop approximation algorithms yielding provably good solutions; yet for some intractable problems no polynomial-time approximation algorithm is known. The ATSP is the problem of finding a shortest Hamiltonian cycle on a weighted digraph, that is a cycle visiting each node of the graph once; it belongs to the

class of NP-hard routing problems (Righini and Trubian, 2004), that is no algorithm is known to find an optimal solution in time polynomial in the size of the instance. The ATSP does not seem to be more tractable from the viewpoint of approximation either. Sahni and Gonzales proved that finding a solution to the symmetric TSP within a constant worst-case approximation bound is NP-hard, if the triangle inequality can be violated, and their result obviously applies to the ATSP too. But even when the triangle inequality holds, no polynomial-time algorithm is known to provide a constant worst-case approximation bound to the ATSP.

Some of the researchers examined certain algorithms for the ATSP with triangle inequality, proving worst-case bounds that depend on the number of cities or other parameters of the instance. Though computational complexity theory classifies problems, not instances, a useful approach to NP hard problems consists of the identification of particular classes of instances, whose special properties make them easier to optimize or to approximate. The characterization of such instances is as important as the development of optimization or approximation algorithms. For instance, some classes of ATSP instances can be optimized in polynomial time; unfortunately the conditions that must hold are very restrictive and in some cases no algorithm is known to check them.

ATSP

This problem appears frequently in the context of the scheduling problems involving setup times although the problem can be easily seen in the two-dimensional space in which the distance is replaced with traveling time. Some heuristic procedures for solving the symmetric version of the problem can be easily modified for the asymmetric versions, but others are not. In general, the heuristic procedures developed for the former are not well suited for the latter because of shifts in arc orientations. Interestingly, heuristic algorithm has been reported, based on 'arbitrary insertion', performs remarkably well on benchmark test problems in terms of both solution quality and computation time. Several branch and bound algorithms are available in the literature for the asymmetric TSP. Brief literature has been reported in (Choi *et al.* 2003) which emphasis on branch and bound algorithm for the asymmetric TSP by considering a simple bounding scheme based on the opportunity cost of excluding an arc, branch and bound with a bounding procedure based on the assignment relaxation of the problem and branch and bound algorithm implementation under the parallel computing environment. New separation algorithms for some classes of facet-defining cuts for the asymmetric TSP and also a branch and bound algorithm has been reported. And it has been reported computational results that show superior performance of their algorithm over the branch and bound algorithm based on the assignment relaxation. On theoretical sides, a compact formulation of the asymmetric TSP and a small subset of disjunctive inequalities has been reported.

The earlier studies using the GA to solve TSP were those of Goldberg (1989) and Lingle and Grefenstette et al. since then, TSP has become a target for the GA community. The studies on GA/TSP provide rich experiences and a sound basis for combinatorial optimization problems. Roughly speaking, major efforts have been made to achieve the following:

1. Give a proper representation to encode a tour
2. Devise applicable genetic operators to keep building blocks and avoid illegality.
3. Prevent premature convergence.

2.4 State of the Art

Most of the approaches in the literature treat the TSP with single crossover type and does not

deal with the uniform crossover type and there has been less research in application of Hybrid algorithm in solving TSP. Moreover, few of the researchers proposed heuristics for solving TSP, but the application of K Means Cluster with hybrid algorithm remains unexplored. So, there is a scope for developing K Means Cluster based heuristic hybrid with GA and SA search algorithms to solve this type of problem. So, GA, SA, a hybrid algorithm called Hybrid GA-SA, Hybrid K-Means Cluster based heuristic-GA, Hybrid K-Means Cluster based heuristic-GA-SA is proposed in this project along with GA and SA.

3. PROBLEM DEFINITION

3.1. Description of the Asymmetric Travelling Salesman Problem

The TSP is one of the widely studied combinatorial optimization problems. Its statement is deceptively simple: a salesman seeks the shortest tour through n cities. Many aspects of the problem still need to considered, and questions are still left to be answered satisfactorily. The study of this problem has attracted many researchers from various fields, for example, mathematics, operations research, physics, biology, or artificial intelligence. This is because TSP exhibits all aspects of combinatorial optimization and has served, and continues to serve, as the benchmark problem for new algorithms like SA, tabu search, neural networks and evolutionary methods.

Consider an asymmetric TSP with n cities to visit. Let Cij be the distance from city i to city j. Moreover, let Xij be 1 if the salesman travels from city i to city j and 0, otherwise. Then, the asymmetric TSP can be formulated as seen in Box 1

We set up the problem by numbering each of the *n* cities as $C_1,..., C_n$; a tour is then just a permutation, say $(k_1, k_2, k_3,..., k_n)$ of $(1,..., n)$. We interpret this as the tour which starts at C_{k1},

Box 1.

$$\min \sum_{i=1}^{n} \sum_{j=1}^{n} CijXij$$

$$s.t. \ (1) \quad \sum_{i=1}^{n} Xij = 1 \qquad where \ j = 1,......,n.,$$

$$(2) \quad \sum_{i=1}^{n} Xij = 1 \qquad where \ i = 1,........,n,$$

$$(3) \quad Xij \in \{0,1\} \qquad where \ j = 1,.........,n, \ i = 1,..........,n.$$

then goes to C_{k2} and so on, running through the remaining cities up to and including C_{kn} before finally completing the tour back at C_{k1}. It is thus clear than we can permute the permutation cyclically without changing the tour. There is no loss of generality then in assuming that $C_{k1} = C_1$; it is then clear that there are $(n-1)!$ different tours. This also shows that solving the problem by exhaustive enumeration is infeasible unless there are very few cities. However this does not capture the problem exactly; as it stands a pair of disjoint subtours will be acceptable. To cope with this we introduce $n-1$ new variables *integral* $u_2, u_3,...,u_n$ with $u_i \leq 0$ and $(n-1)^2 - (n-1)$ new constraints: $u_i - u_j + nx_{ij} \leq n-1$ for $i, j = 2, 3,...n$ and $i \neq j$

3.2. Problem Objective

The objective of this research is to find the minimum distance traveled for covering all the given 'n' cities from a single depot and to return back to the same. The issue is many kind of operations management problem such as scheduling problem can be easily converted into the TSP matrix type and those problem can be solved nearer optimally using considered algorithms namely GA, SA, Hybrid GA-SA, K-Means Cluster based heuristic, Hybrid K-Means Cluster based heuristic-GA-SA.

3.2. Assumptions

The assumptions considered are

1. Each city is visited once.
2. There is only one vehicle for distribution.
3. The problem is an asymmetric TSP.

4. INTRODUCTION TO OPTIMIZATION ALGORITHMS

4.1. Optimization Algorithms

In nature, individuals best suited to competition for scanty resources survive. Evolving to keep adapted to a changing environment is essential for the members of any species. Although evolution manifests itself as changes in the species' features, it is in the species' genetical material that those changes are controlled and stored. Specifically evolution's driving force is the combination of natural selection and the change and recombination of genetic material that occurs during reproduction (Goldberg, 1989).

Evolution is an astonishing problem solving machine. It took a soup of primordial organic molecules, and produced from it a complex interrelating web of live beings with an enormous diversity of genetic information. Enough information to specify every characteristic of every species that now inhabits the planet. The force working for evolution is an algorithm, a set of instructions that is repeated to solve a problem. The algorithm behind evolution solves the problem of producing species able to thrive in a particular environment.

Placement and routing are two search intensive tasks. Even though agent objects use knowledge to reduce search time, a great deal of searching is still necessary. A good proportion of this search time will be spent optimizing the components' placement in the layout. In searching for optimum solutions, optimization techniques are used and can be divided into three broad classes, as shown in Figure 4.1.1

Numerical techniques use a set of necessary and sufficient conditions to be satisfied by the solutions of an optimization problem. They subdivide into direct and indirect methods. Indirect methods search for local extremes by solving the usually non-linear set of equations resulting from setting the gradient of the objective function to zero. The search for possible solutions (function peaks) starts by restricting itself to points with zero slope in all directions. Direct methods, such as those of Newton or Fibonacci, seek extremes by "hopping" around the search space and assessing the gradient of the new point, which guides the search. This is simply the notion of "hill climbing", which finds the best local point by climbing the steepest permissible gradient. These techniques can be used only on a restricted set of "well behaved" functions.

Enumerative techniques search every point related to the function's domain space (finite or discretized), one point at a time. They are very simple to implement but usually require significant computation. These techniques are not suitable for applications with large domain spaces. Dynamic programming is a good example of this technique.

Guided random search techniques are based on enumerative techniques but use additional information to guide the search. Two major subclasses are SA and evolutionary algorithms. Both can be seen as evolutionary processes, but SA uses a thermodynamic evolution process to search minimum energy states. Evolutionary algorithms use natural selection principles. This form of search evolves throughout generations,

Figure 4.1.1. Classes of search techniques

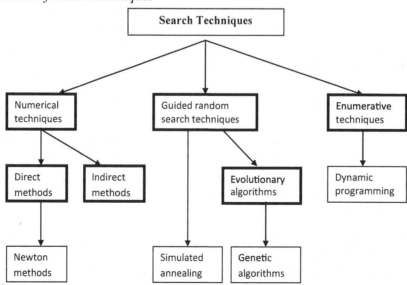

improving the features of potential solutions by means of biological inspired operations. GAs and SA are a good example of this technique.

Calculus based techniques are only suitable for a restricted set of well-behaved systems. Placement optimization has a strong non-linear behaviour and is too complex for these methods. The set of possible layouts for a circuit can be enormous, which rules out the enumerative techniques.

These assumptions leave out only the guided random search techniques. Their use of additional information to guide the search reduces the search space to manageable sizes. There are two subclasses to this technique, SA and evolutionary algorithms.

4.2. Introduction to Genetic Algorithms

A key element of what is assumed to be intelligences the capability to learn from past experience. Especially when things are done repeatedly, intelligent behavior would avoid doing a mistake more than once and would prefer making advantageous decisions again. For optimization a class of today's most popular heuristic approaches is known as GAs. Due to its widespread use and vast amount of literature dealing with GAs, a comprehensive review of research activities is doomed to failure; thus we stick to outline of the fundamental ideas. The adjective genetic reveals the roots of these algorithms. Adapting the evaluation strategy from natural life forms, the basic idea is to start with a set of (feasible) solutions and to compute a set of new solutions by applying some well defined operations on the old ones. Then, some solutions (new and/or solutions) are selected to form a new set with which another is started, and so on until some stopping criterion is met. Solutions are represented by sets of attributed, and different solutions are met by different collections of attribute values. The decision that solutions are dismissed and which is taken over to form a new starting

point for the next iteration is made on the basis of priority rule. GAs are adaptive heuristic search algorithm premised on the evolutionary ideas of natural selection and genetic. The basic concept of GAs is designed to simulate processes in natural system necessary for evolution, specifically those that follow the principles first laid down by Charles Darwin of survival of the fittest. As such they represent an intelligent exploitation of a random search within a defined search space to solve a problem. First pioneered by John Holland in the 60s, GAs has been widely studied, experimented and applied in many fields in engineering worlds. Not only does GAs provide alternative methods to solving problem, it consistently outperforms other traditional methods in most of the problems link. Many of the real world problems involved finding optimal parameters, which might prove difficult for traditional methods but ideal for GAs. However, because of its outstanding performance in optimization, GAs has been wrongly regarded as a function optimizer. In fact, there are many ways to view GAs. Perhaps most users come to GAs looking for a problem solver, but this is a restrictive view.

GA can be used as problem solvers, challenging technical puzzle, basis for competent machine learning, computational model of innovation and creativity, computational model of other innovating systems and guiding philosophy. Many scientists have tried to create living programs. These programs do not merely simulate life but try to exhibit the behaviors and characteristics of real organisms in an attempt to exist as a form of life. Suggestions have been made that a life would eventually evolve into real life. Such suggestion may sound absurd at the moment but certainly not implausible if technology continues to progress at present rates.

Nearly everyone can gain benefits from GAs, once he can encode solutions of a given problem to chromosomes in GA, and compare the relative performance (fitness) of solutions. An effective GA representation and meaningful fitness evaluation are the keys of the success in GA applications. The appeal of GAs comes from their simplicity and elegance as robust search algorithms as well as from their power to discover good solutions rapidly for difficult high-dimensional problems. GAs is useful and efficient when

- The search space is large, complex or poorly understood.
- Domain knowledge is scarce or expert knowledge is difficult to encode to narrow the search space.
- No mathematical analysis is available.
- Traditional search methods fail.

The advantage of the GA approach is the ease with which it can handle arbitrary kinds of constraints and objectives; all such things can be handled as weighted components of the fitness function, making it easy to adapt the GA scheduler to the particular requirements of a very wide range of possible overall objectives. GAs has been used for problem solving and for modeling. GAs are applied to many scientific, engineering problems, in business and entertainment, including: optimization, automatic programming, machine and robot learning, economic models, immune system models, ecological models, population genetics models, interactions between evolution and learning and models of social systems (Goldberg, 1989).

4.3. Procedure of Genetic Algorithms

The algorithm operates through a simple cycle:

1. Creation of a population of strings.
2. Evaluation of each string.
3. Selection of the best strings.
4. Genetic manipulation to create a new population of strings.

Figure 4.3.1 shows how these four stages interconnect. Each cycle produces a new generation of possible solutions (individuals) for a given problem. At the first stage, a population of possible solutions is created as a start point. Each individual in this population is encoded into a string (the chromosome) to be manipulated by the genetic operators. In the next stage, the individuals are evaluated, first the individual is created from its string description (its chromosome) and its performance in relation to the target response is evaluated. This determines how fit this individual is in relation to the others in the population. Based on each individual's fitness, a selection mechanism chooses the best pairs for the genetic manipulation process. The selection policy is responsible to assure the survival of the fittest individuals.

The manipulation process applies the genetic operators to produce a new population of individuals, the offspring, by manipulating the genetic information possessed by the pairs chosen to reproduce. This information is stored in the strings (chromosomes) that describe the individuals. Two operators are used: Crossover and mutation. The offspring generated by this process take the place of the older population and the cycle is repeated until a desired level of fitness in attained or a determined number of cycles is reached.

Crossover

Crossover is one of the genetic operators used to recombine the population genetic material. It

Figure 4.3.1. The reproduction cycle

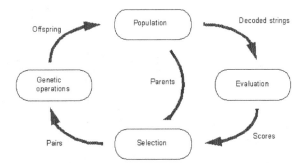

takes two chromosomes and swaps part of their genetic information to produce new chromosomes. This operation is similar to sexual reproduction in nature. As Figure 4.3.2. shows, after the crossover point has been randomly chosen, portions of the parent's chromosome (strings) **Parent 1** and **Parent 2** are combined to produce the new offspring **Son**.

The selection process associated with the recombination made by crossover assures that special genetic structures, called building blocks, are retained for future generations. These building blocks represent the most fit genetic structures in the population.

Mutation

The recombination process alone cannot explore search space sections not represented in the population's genetic structures. This could make the search get stuck around local minima. Here mutation goes into action. The mutation operator introduces new genetic structures in the population by randomly changing some of its building blocks, helping the algorithm escape local minima traps. Since the modification is totally random and thus not related to any previous genetic structures present in the population, it creates different structures related to other sections of the search space.

As shown in Figure 4.3.3. mutation is implemented by occasionally altering a random bit from a chromosome (string), the figure shows the operator being applied to the fifth element of the chromosome.

A number of other operators, other than crossover and mutation, have been introduced since the basic model was proposed. They are usually versions of the recombination and genetic alterations processes adapted to constraints of a particular problem. Examples of other operators are: inversion, dominance and genetic edge recombination.

Figure 4.3.2. Crossover process

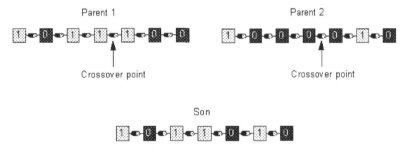

Figure 4.3.3. Mutation

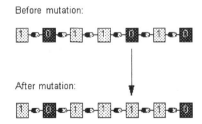

Problem Dependent Parameters

This description of the GAs' computational model reviews the steps needed to create the algorithm. However, a real implementation takes account of a number of problem-dependent parameters. For instance, the offspring produced by the genetic manipulation (the next population to be evaluated) can either replace the whole population (generational approach) or just its less fitted members (steady-state approach). Problem constraints will dictate the best option. Other parameters to be adjusted are the population size, crossover and mutation rates, evaluation method, and convergence criteria.

Encoding

Critical to the algorithm performance is the choice of underlying encoding for the solution of the optimization problem (the individuals on the population). Traditionally, binary encoding have being used because they are easy to implement. The crossover and mutation operators described earlier are specific to binary encodings. When symbols other than 1 or 0 are used, the crossover and mutation operators must be tailored accordingly. A large number of optimization problems have continuous variables. A common technique for encoding them in the binary form uses a fixed-point integer encoding, each variable being coded using a fixed number of bits. The binary code of all the variables can then be concatenated in the strings of the population. A drawback of encoding variables as binary strings is the presence of Hamming cliffs: large Hamming distances between the codes of adjacent integers. For instance, 01111 and 10000 are integer representations of 15 and 16, respectively, and have a Hamming distance of 5. For the GA to change the representation from 15 to 16, it must alter all bits simultaneously. Such Hamming cliffs present a problem for the algorithm, as both mutation and crossover can not overcome them easily.

It is desirable that the encoding makes the representation as robust as possible. This means that even if a piece of the representation is randomly changed, it will still represent a viable individual. For instance, suppose that a particular encoding scheme describes a circuit by the position of each of its components and a pointer to their individual descriptions. If this pointer is the description's memory address, it is very unlikely that, after a random change in its value, the pointer will still point to a valid description. But, if the pointer is a binary string of 4 bits pointing into an array of 16 positions holding the descriptions, regardless of the changes in the 4 bit string, the pointer will always point to a valid description. This makes the arrangement more tolerant to changes, more robust.

The Evaluation Step

The evaluation step in the cycle, shown in Figure 4.3.1.is the one more closely related to the actual system the algorithm is trying to optimize. It takes the strings representing the individuals of the population and, from them, creates the actual individuals to be tested. The way the individuals are coded in the strings will depend on what parameter one is trying to optmize and the actual structure of possible solutions (individuals).

However, the resulting strings should not be too big or the process will get very slow, but should be of the right size to represent well the characteristics to be optimized. After the actual individuals have been created they have to be tested and scored. These two tasks again are very related to the actual system being optimized. The testing depends on what characteristics should be optimized and the scoring, the production of a single value representing the fitness of an individual, depends on the relative importance of each different characteristic value obtained during testing.

4.4. Applications of Genetic Algorithms

1. GA on optimization and planning: TSP
2. GA in Business and Their Supportive Role in Decision Making

GAs have been used to solve many different types of business problems in functional areas such as finance, marketing, information systems, and production/ operations. Within these functional areas, GAs has performed a variety of applications such as tactical asset allocation, job

scheduling, machine-part grouping, and computer network design.

If the conception of a computer algorithms being based on the evolutionary of organism is surprising, the extensiveness with which this algorithms is applied in so many areas is no less than astonishing. These applications, be they commercial, educational and scientific, are increasingly dependent on this algorithms, the GAs.

Its usefulness and gracefulness of solving problems has made it the more favorite choice among the traditional methods, namely gradient search, random search and others. GAs are very

Figure 4.5. Flow chart for genetic algorithms

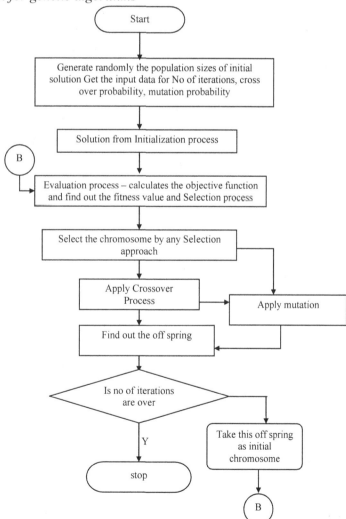

helpful when the developer does not have precise domain expertise, because GAs possess the ability to explore and learn from their domain.

4.6. Introduction to Simulated Annealing

SA is a generalization of a Monte Carlo method for examining the equations of state and frozen states of n-body systems. The concept is based on the manner in which liquids freeze or metals recrystalize in the process of annealing. In an annealing process a melt, initially at high temperature and disordered, is slowly cooled so that the system at any time is approximately in thermodynamic equilibrium. As cooling proceeds, the system becomes more ordered and approaches a "frozen" ground state at T=0. Hence the process can be thought of as an adiabatic approach to the lowest energy state. If the initial temperature of the system is too low or cooling is done insufficiently slowly the system may become quenched forming defects or freezing out in metastable states (ie. trapped in a local minimum energy state).

The original Metropolis scheme was that an initial state of a thermodynamic system was chosen at energy E and temperature T, holding T constant the initial configuration is perturbed and the change in energy dE is computed. If the change in energy is negative the new configuration is accepted. If the change in energy is positive it is accepted with a probability given by the Boltzmann factor exp -(dE/T). This processes is then repeated sufficient times to give good sampling statistics for the current temperature, and then the temperature is decremented and the entire process repeated until a frozen state is achieved at T=0.

By analogy the generalization of this Monte Carlo approach to combinatorial problems is straightforward. The current state of the thermodynamic system is analogous to the current solution to the combinatorial problem, the energy equation for the thermodynamic system is analo-

gous to at the objective function, and ground state is analogous to the global minimum. The major difficulty (art) in implementation of the algorithm is that there is no obvious analogy for the temperature T with respect to a free parameter in the combinatorial problem. Furthermore, avoidance of entrainment in local minima (quenching) is dependent on the "annealing schedule", the choice of initial temperature, how much iteration are performed at each temperature, and how much the temperature is decremented at each step as cooling proceeds.

The method itself has a direct analogy with thermodynamics, specifically with the way that liquids freeze and crystallize, or metals cool and anneal. At high temperatures, the molecules of a liquid move freely with respect to one another. If the liquid is cooled slowly, thermal mobility is restricted. The atoms are often able to line themselves up and form a pure crystal that is completely regular. This crystal is the state of minimum energy for the system, which would correspond to the optimal solution in a mathematical optimization problem. However, if a liquid metal is cooled quickly i.e. quenched, it does not reach a minimum energy state but a somewhat higher energy state corresponding, in the mathematical sense, to a sub optimal solution found by iterative improvement or hill-climbing.

In order to make use of this analogy with thermo dynamical systems for solving mathematical optimization problems, one must first provide the following elements:

- A description of possible system configurations, i.e. some way of representing a solution to the minimization (maximization) problem, usually this involves some configuration of parameters that represent a solution.
- A generator of random changes in a configuration; these changes are typically solutions in the neighborhood of the current configuration, for example, a change in one of the parameters.

- An objective or cost function E(X) (analog of energy) whose minimization is the goal of the procedure.
- A control parameter T (analogue of temperature) and an annealing schedule which indicates how is lowered from high values to low values e.g. after how many random changes in configuration is T reduced and by how much?

There are two aspects of the SA process that are areas of active research. The first is the cooling schedule and the second is determining how many Monte Carlo steps are sufficient at each temperature. If the temperature is decreased too slowly, CPU-cycles will be wasted. On the other hand, if the cooling is too rapid, the search will be trapped in a sub optimal region of search space. Two different cooling schedules are generally used in practice. The first reduces the temperature by a constant amount in each phase, while the second reduces the temperature by a constant factor (e.g. 10%). The first method allows the simulation to proceed for the same number of Monte Carlo steps in the high, intermediate and low temperature regimes, while the latter causes the simulation to spend more time in the low temperature regime than the high one.

A simulation at a fixed temperature can be run before the full simulation and the expectation value determined as a function of the number of Monte Carlo steps. An understanding of this behavior is used to estimate the number of attempts that should be made at each temperature.

As stated for many of the other methods described earlier, SA is a computational methodology, not a fixed algorithm, or program. This means that the the problem should dictate which variables should be changed at each Monte Carlo step, the magnitude of their change, the number of Monte Carlo attempts at each temperature and the cooling schedule. As such, a "canned" program that is not sufficiently flexible should not be used for more than educational purposes. SA has

been used in various combinatorial optimization problems and has been particularly successful in circuit design problems.

SA, first suggested by Kirkpatrick *et al.* (1983) is a multi purpose heuristic for the solution of combinatorial optimization problems. A neighborhood structure is superimposed on the usually finite but large space of feasible solutions (configuration or in this context production schedules). Given current feasible configuration, say in this context, current sequence (σ_{cur}) a candidate solution (σ_{can}) is drawn randomly from the corresponding neighborhood. This new configuration will be accepted subjected to either improvement of the objective function or another random experiment with acceptance probability given by $e^{-\Delta c/y}$, where $\Delta C = C(\sigma_{can}) - C(\sigma_{cur})$ is the difference of the cost function values of the candidate and the current configuration. γ is the control parameter corresponding to temperature in the original physical analogue in thermodynamics. Infinite repetition of this procedure with a fixed value of control parameter γ can be viewed as one realization of a homogenous Markov chain where the current state of the Markov chain is the last accepted configuration. Iterative reduction of the temperature (i.e., γ) yields a sequence of such Markov chains. The main advantage of SA related to tailored methods is its general acceptability. Solving a specific problem with SA requires only determination of a cooling schedule (i.e., choice of the sequence of control parameters γ and number and length of finite approximation of the homogeneous Markov chains) and a neighborhood structure. Different cooling structures are also discussed. The neighborhood choice is usually based on the set of feasible configurations only.

4.8. Hybrid Genetic Algorithm – Simulated Annealing

The motivation behind the GA-SA combination is the power of GA to work on the solution in a global sense while allowing SA to locally optimize

Figure 4.7. Flow chart for simulated annealing

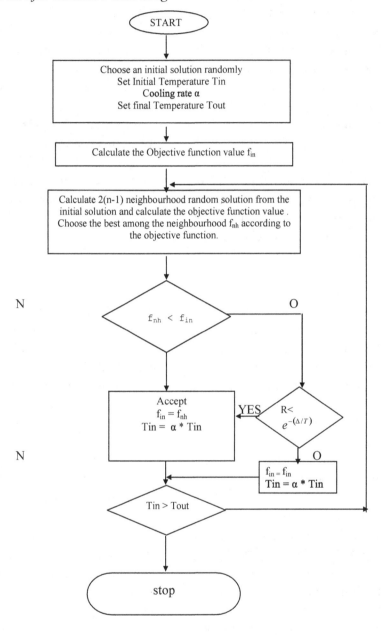

each individually solution. The Hybrid GA-SA algorithm is explained in the following section.

Concept of Hybrid GA-SA

Many researchers have proposed the concept of joining the two powerful optimization techniques namely GA and SA. The steps followed are given as follows

Initialize the parameters of the GA.
Generate the initial population.
Execute GA for one generation.
For each of the chromosomes do the following:
Initialize the parameters of the SA.
Improve the quality of solution using SA and the string with the best solution is returned to the new population of GA.

Repeat the steps 3 and 4 for required number of generations.

The hybrid algorithm executes in two phases, the GA and SA. In the first phase, the GA generates the initial solutions (only once) randomly. The GA then operates on the solutions using selection, crossover and mutation operators to produce new and hopefully better solutions. After each generation the GA sends each solution to the SA (second phase) to be improved. The neighborhood generation scheme used in SA is a single insertion neighborhood scheme. Once the SA is finished for a solution of GA, another solution GA is passed to SA. This process continues until all solutions of GA in one generated are exhausted. Once the SA is finished for all solutions in one generation of GA, the best of solutions of population size obtained from SA are the solutions of GA for the next generation. The GA and SA exchange continues until the required number generations are completed.

4.9. General structure of hybrid genetic algorithm – simulated annealing

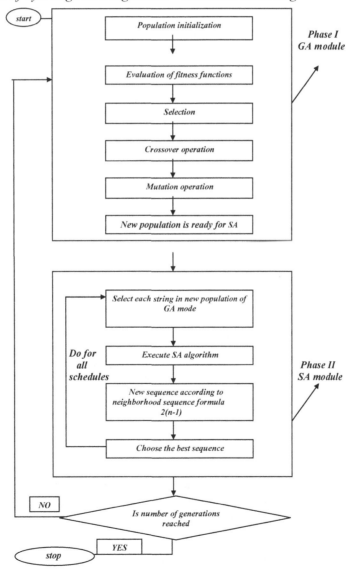

4.10. K Means Cluster Analysis

A clustering algorithm attempts to find natural groups of components (or data) based on some similarity. Also, the clustering algorithm finds the centroid of a group of data sets. To determine cluster membership, most algorithms evaluate the distance between a point and the cluster centroids. The output from a clustering algorithm is basically a statistical description of the cluster centroids with the number of components in each cluster.

Raw Data ⟶ Clustering Algorithm ⟶ Clusters of Data

The centroid of a cluster is a point whose parameter values are the mean of the parameter values of all the points in the clusters. Generally, the distance between two points is taken as a common metric to assess the similarity among the components of a population. The commonly used distance measure is the Euclidean metric which defines the distance between two points p= (p1, p2, ...) and q = (q1, q2, ...) is given by:

$$d = \sqrt{\sum_{i=1}^{k} (p_i - q_i)^2}$$

Distance-Based Clustering

Assign a distance measure between data. Find a partition such that distance between objects within partition (i.e. same cluster) is minimized and distance between objects from different clusters is maximised.

K-Means Clustering

This method initially takes the number of components of the population equal to the final required number of clusters. In this step itself the final required number of clusters is chosen such that the points are mutually farthest apart. Next, it examines each component in the population and assigns it to one of the clusters depending on the minimum distance. The centroid's position is recalculated every time a component is added to the cluster and this continues until all the components are grouped into the final required number of clusters. The basic ideas are using a cluster centre (means) to represent cluste, assigning data elements to the closet cluster (centre). The main goal is to minimise square error (intra-class dissimilarity). The variations of K-Means is Initialisation (select the number of clusters, initial partitions), Updating of center and Hill-climbing (trying to move an object to another cluster).

K-Means Clustering Algorithm

1. Select an initial partition of k clusters
2. Assign each object to the cluster with the closest center:
3. Compute the new centers of the clusters:

$$\vec{C}(S) = \sum_{i=1}^{n} \vec{X}_i / n, \vec{X}_1, ..., \vec{X}_n \in S$$

4. Repeat step 2 and 3 until no object changes cluster.

5. GENETIC ALGORITHM (GA), SIMULATED ANEALING (SA), HYBRID GA-SA AND K MEANS CLUSTER BASED HEURISTIC FOR TRAVELLING SALESMAN PROBLEM

5.1 Genetic Algorithms for Asymmetric Travelling Salesman Problem

In this section the design of proposed modified GA for ATSP is explained. The details are explained with an example in this chapter. These are important components that are to be completely described by GA are:

- The representation format used by the GA,
- The operators of crossover, mutation and reproduction,
- The fitness evaluation function,
- The various parameters like the population size, the number of generations, the probability of applying the operators, etc., and,
- A method for generating the initial population.

Evolution Program

GA evolution program for ATSP is presented. It includes representation structure, initialization process, evaluation function, selection, mutation and crossover operations.

Representation Structure

Traditionally, chromosomes are a simple binary string. This simple representation is not suitable for TSP and other combinatorial problems. During the past decade, several representation schemes have been proposed for TSP. Among them, permutation representation and random keys representation have an appeal not only for the TSP but also for other combinatorial optimization problems.

Permutation Representation

This representation is perhaps the most natural representation of a TSP tour, where cities are listed in order in which they are visited. The search space for this representation is the set of the permutations of the cities. For example, a tour of a 9-city TSP 3-2-5-4-7-1-6-9-8 is simply represented as [3 2 5 4 7 1 6 9 8]. This representation is also called a path representation. This representation may lead to illegal tours if the traditional one-point crossover operator is used. Many crossover operators have been investigated for it. We proposed a new crossover namely Uniform Crossover and double operated uniform versus swap crossover for the modified GA.

Random Keys Representation

Random keys representation was first introduced by bean. This representation encodes a solution with random numbers from (0,1). These values are used as sort keys to decode the solution. For example, a chromosome to a 9-city problem may be [0.23 0.82 0.45 0.74 0.87 0.11 0.56 0.69 0.78] where position i in the list represents city i. The random solutions in position i determines the visiting order of city i in a TSP tour. We sort the random keys in ascending order to get the following tour: 6-1-3-7-8-4-9-2-5. Random keys eliminate the infeasibility of the offspring by representing solutions in a soft manner. This representation is applicable to a wide variety of sequencing optimization problems including machine scheduling, resource allocation, vehicle routing, quadratic assignment problem, and so on.

An integer n and a vector V is used as a chromosome to represent solution $(y_1, y_2, ..., y_n)$ to ATSP, i.e.,

$$z(t) = \left\{ \begin{array}{l} y_i, \quad where \;\; i = 1, 2, \cdots, n. \end{array} \right\}$$

Initialization

The initial population for the GA is generated based on the given 'n' number of cities. All the resulting schedules produced are therefore feasible in terms of meeting the constraints, after experimenting with different value; the following probability values were used for the operators. A sensitivity analysis is done by varying the parameters and the values were fixed as follows. The crossover operators are applied with a probability of 0.8. The mutation operators are applied with a probability of 0.02. The number of generations for the GA was fixed at 100. The population size was fixed as 10. Population sizes (popsize) of chromosomes can give as user input but the speciality is random initialization. So, Popsize chromosomes will be randomly initialized by the following way.

To determine a chromosome, we firstly determine its dimension, i.e., the number of capacity expansions. Usually, the range for possible n can be given by some priori knowledge. So we can generate a random integer n in that range, then n random numbers according to the number of cities on the interval [Lower Bound, Upper Bound]. Repeat these processes pop size times and produce pop size initial feasible solutions.

Evaluation Function

Let u denote the original fitness, i.e., the objective value. Usually, the original fitness proportionate-reproduction scheme frequently causes two significant difficulties: premature convergence termination at early generations, and stalling at late generations. To overcome these two problems, Goldberg (1989) suggests a linear-fitness scaling scheme, $u^l = au + b$. Lee and Johnson ( ) suggests a modified linear-fitness scaling scheme, i.e., for the lower-fitness strings, the minimum original fitness u_{min} maps to 1; for the higher-fitness strings, the maximum original fitness u_{max} maps to $f_{multiple}$; the average fitness u_{avg} maps to 1. Researchers suggested the power law scaling scheme, $u^l = u^k$, where k is a real number which is close to one. Here we employ the well-known rank-based evaluation function, i.e.,

$$eval(V) = a(1 - a)^{rank - 1}$$

where rank is the ordinal number of V in the rearranged series. We mention that rank = 1 means the best individual, rank = pop size the worst individual, and, of course,

$$\sum_{j=1}^{popsize} eval(V_j)$$

For the aforementioned evaluation function, the chromosome with higher fitness can have more chance to produce offsprings.

Selection Process

The selection process is based on spinning the roulette wheel pop size times and each time we select a single chromosome for a new population in the following way:

1. Calculate the cumulative probability qi for each chromosome Vi

$$q_0 = 0$$
$$q_i = \sum_{j=1}^{i} eval(V_j), \quad i = 1, 2, \cdots, pop\ size.$$

2. Generate a random real number r in [0, 1].
3. Select the i-th chromosome Vi ($1 \leq i \leq pop$ size) such that $q_{i-1} < r \_ q_i$.
4. Repeat steps (2) and (3) pop size times and obtain pop size copies of chromosomes.

Crossover Operation

A parameter Pc of an evolution system as the probability of crossover is defined. This probability gives us the expected number Pc · pop size of chromosomes, which undergo the crossover operation.

1. Generate a random real number r in [0, 1].
2. Select the given chromosome for crossover if r < Pc.
3. Repeat this operation pop size times and produce Pc · pop size parents, averagely.
4. For each pair of parents (vectors V1 and V2), if they have the same dimension, the crossover operator on V1 and V2 will produce two children X and Y as follows:

$$X = c1 \cdot V1 + c2 \cdot V2 \ \&$$
$$Y = c2 \cdot V1 + c1 \cdot V2$$

where $c1 + c2 = 1$ and c1 is a random number on the interval [0, 1]. Otherwise, skip the crossover operation. Since the constraint set is convex, this arithmetical crossover operation ensures that both children are feasible if both parents are.

Two different crossovers have boon used for solving ATSP. From the literature it was identified that uniform crossover haven't been used as a crossover operator for solving ATSP. So there is a scope of using uniform crossover operator to improve the solution better. Moreover it was identified that the scope of using the combination of two-crossover operator in solving ATSP using GA received less attention. So an attempt has been made to solve the ATSP using GA with the impact of uniform crossover and the combination of two different crossover operator namely uniform and swap crossover operator.

The solution has been tested using the uniform crossover, swap crossover, combination of uniform and swap crossover with the effect of uniform crossover as the first and combination of swap and uniform crossover with the effect of swap crossover as the first.

The example of uniform crossover is described as follows:

    1 2 3 4 5 6 7
    3 5 7 6 4 2 1

There are two chromosome strings to be crossover should be taken. According to crossover probability, pc, the string set is randomly chosen in the first chromosome. In the given example, the string set chosen is **3 4 5**. Compare the string set with the second chromosome and generate the new offspring by keeping the string bit **3 4 5** constant and arrange the remaining gene through matching process of two chromosomes.

The offspring of the two parents is

    7 6 3 4 5 2 1

Swap crossover is described as follows:

Swap the randomly chosen gene according to crossover probability and swap the genes between the chromosomes feasibly.

An example for swap crossover is shown as follows

Before crossover

    1 2 3 4 5 6 7 8
    2 3 4 5 6 7 1 8

After crossover

    1 2 4 5 6 7 3 8
    2 7 3 4 5 6 1 8

Mutation Operation

Two different types of mutation namely swap and insertion mutation is used.

The example of swap mutation is described as follows:

Before mutation

    1 2 3 4 5 6 7 8
    2 3 5 4 6 7 8 1

After mutation

    1 2 3 4 5 7 6 8
    2 3 5 4 7 6 8 1

The example of insertion mutation is described as follows:

Before mutation

    1 2 3 4 5 6 7 8
    1 6 2 3 4 5 7 8

After finding the better combination of crossover the mutation process should be carried out. It was found that that the sequence uniform-swap crossover was better when compared with the other single and combined effect of crossovers. So test these two types of mutations with the sequence of crossovers.

First swap mutation was tested with sequence uniform-swap crossover and then with insertion mutation. From both of these the sequence, Uniform crossover-swap crossover-insertion mutation was found better in yielding the solution.

The performance of crossover and mutation operator is shown as follows

Algorithm for the Process
The evolution program for ATSP is as follows.

Step 0. Set parameters
Input
max gen; //numbers of generations
pop size; //population size
Pc; // probability of crossover
Pm; // probability of mutation
a; // parameter in rank-based evaluation function

Step 1. Initialization process
for i = 1 to pop size do
produce a random integer n;
produce n random real numbers $y_1, y_2, \ldots, y_n$ on $[\varepsilon,$ up bound];
$V_i = (y_1, y_2, \ldots, y_n)$;
Endfor

Step 2. Evaluation
for i = 1 to pop size do
compute the objectives u_i for V_i;
endfor
for i = 1 to pop size do
compute the rank-based fitness u_i ;
endfor
for i = 1 to pop size do
compute the cumulative probabilities
qi =
endfor

Step 3. Selection operation
for i = 1 to pop size do
if(q_{i-1} <=random( ) < = q_i) then
select V_i;
endif
endfor

Figure 5.

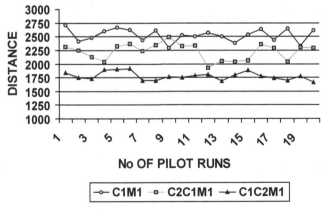

No OF PILOT RUNS

—◦— C1M1 —◻— C2C1M1 —▲— C1C2M1

C1 – UNIFORM CROSSOVER
C2 – SWAP CROSSOVER
M1 – INSERTION MUTATION

Step 4. Crossover operation
for i = 1 to pop size/2 do
if(random() < Pc) then
int j = random(pop size);
int k = random(pop size);
perform the uniform crossover, swap crossover
and combination of uniform crossover, and swap
crossover on j-th and k-th chromosomes;
endif
endfor

Step 5. Mutation operation
for i = 1 to pop size do

r=random();
if(r <= Pm1) then
Insertion mutation(); /
swap mutation();
endif
endfor

Step 6. Termination test
if(number of iterations < max gen) then
goto step 2;
else
stop;
endif

Figure 6. Flow chart for genetic algorithms

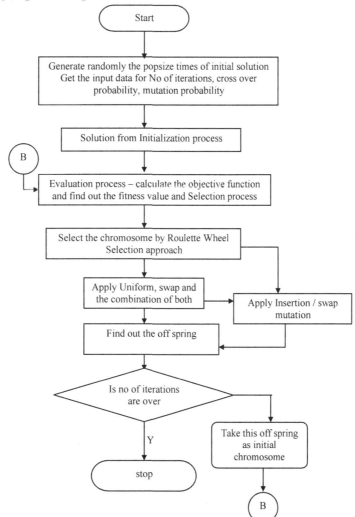

6.2 Simulated Annealing for Asymmetric Travelling Salesman Problem

The SA algorithm along with the parameters is presented. The classical concept of generating a sequence of solutions for a particular temperature T is used in the algorithm. A new solution is generated as a slight perturbation of the current state by using a single insertion neighborhood creation scheme by creating $2(n-1)$ neighborhoods. If the difference in the total cost, δ between the current state and the slightly perturbated one is negative, then the process is continued from the new state. If $\delta >= 0$, then the perturbation of acceptance of the perturbated state is given by the Metropolis oracle.

Parameters used

σ_0 – initial sequence of the schedule

δ – improvement in the objective function value.

$Z(\sigma_0)$ – objective function value of the sequence σ_0.

α - the temperature reduction coefficient set to 0.7.

τ^0 - The initial temperature given the value of 475

r_t^{max} – the maximum number of repetitions at a given temperature $= \beta * t$,

where β is a constant set 5 and t denotes the value of

the temperature change counter.

ε – termination condition set to 1.

NEIGHBORHOOD GENERATION

The neighborhood creation scheme proposed by Quenichie et al. (1999) is used in the model. For a given sequence σ, this neighborhood is defined as the set of sequences obtained by moving any product from its actual position in σ^1 to any other position. Thus to generate a neighbor solution,

denoted σ, first we chose, at random, two positions in σ, say k_1 and k_2 ($k_1 \neq k_2$). Then we move the product in position k_1, say product I, to the position k_2. . Ouenniche et.al, (1999) conducted a test to evaluate few neighborhood generation schemes and they concluded that the single insertion neighborhood always lead to better results than other neighborhoods. The number of neighborhood depends upon the application and the common formula used is $2(n-1)$ number of neighborhoods. From those neighborhoods the best one is selected according to the objective function.

Algorithm

Start with an initial sequence σ_0 and set $\sigma^* = \sigma_0$

Choose an initial temperature τ^0 and set $\tau = \tau^0$

Set temperature change counter t $=0$

REPEAT until $\tau < \varepsilon$

Set repetition counter r $= 0$

REPEAT until $r = r_t^{max.}$

Generate $2(n-1)$ neighborhood sequences of the current sequence σ_0

Choose the minimum among all neighborhood sequence σ'

Calculate $\delta = Z(\sigma_0) - Z(\sigma^1)$, the improvement in the objective function value if σ' is retained.

IF $\delta > 0$ OR Random $(0,1) < e^{-\delta/t}$ THEN set $\sigma_0 = \sigma_1$

IF $z(\sigma^1) < z(\sigma^*)$ THEN set $\sigma^* = \sigma^1$ and $z(\sigma^*) = z(\sigma^1)$.

R $= r + 1$

END REPEAT

T $= t + 1$

$\tau = \alpha * \tau$

END REPEAT

K Means Cluster Based Heuristic Algorithm

In this heuristic, the sequencing of the cities is based upon the distances between them. The idea of K-Means heuristic is to cluster the cities into groups and then travel between the clusters

Figure 6.1 Flow chart for simulated annealing

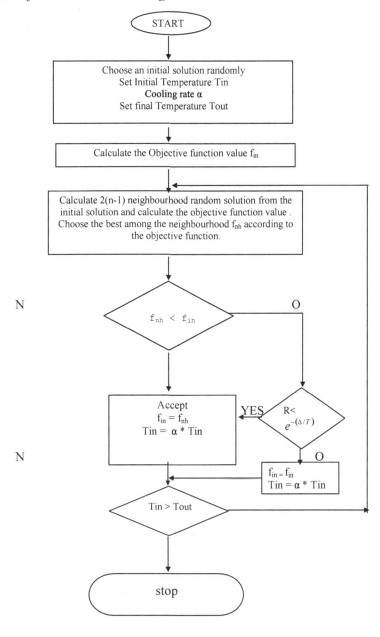

there by reducing the search space considerably. Initially sets of centroid points are selected randomly around which cluster is to be made. A distance matrix is formed between the centroid cities and the rest of the cities with the centroid cities as the x-axis and the rest of the cities as the y-axis. The minimum distance is marked for each of the rest of the cities to the centroid cities. When all the minimum cities have been marked, the minimum marked against the centroids are taken as its cluster. In each of the clusters the cities are sorted in ascending order according to the distance between the centroids and the rest of the cities. Thus sets of sequence of cities are formed equal to the number of centroid cities.

The initial sequence is selected by considering the distance between the depot and the centroid cities. The least distant centroid from the depot is taken as the initiator of the solution to be fed to the genetic algorithm. Once the initiating centroid city is fixed the last city in that sequence is compared with the rest of the centroid cities. The minimum distant centroid city sequence is attached to the initial sequence and the process is continued to get the initial solution.

The procedure of k-means cluster based heuristic is as follows:

1. Fix the number of centroids for proceeding with K-Means Cluster analysis
2. By fixing the centroids, calculate the distance by Euclidean distant method from centroid to the other cities and tabulated in matrix form.
3. Choose the minimum distance in each row and mark it.
4. Compare the marked cells with centroids and keep those cells as the element of a new cluster with the respective centroid.
5. After choosing the cluster of cities along with the centroid, rearrange the sequence of the city cluster according to the minimum distance traveled.
6. Choose the city which is nearer to the central single depot and find out the next sequence by comparing the distance between the last city in the first sequence and the other centroid chosen
7. Then arrange all the cities in sequence and the final sequence to be the new string of the cities. Find out the distance traveled for the sequence of cities chosen and compare the results with other optimization algorithms.

Hybrid K Means Cluster Based Heuristic-GA and Hybrid K Means Cluster based Heuristic-GA-SA Algorithm

When K-Means Cluster based heuristic hybrid with optimization algorithms like GA, Hybrid-GA-SA, there is a possibility of yielding better solutions. So, K-Means Cluster based heuristic is hybrid with GA, Hybrid –GA –SA. The initial solution is generated by this method to feed the genetic algorithm instead of being generated by the genetic algorithm, which generates the initial solution randomly. The Initial population chromosome for the GA process and Hybrid-GA-SA is chosen from the results of K-Means Cluster based heuristic and further proceed the process of GA algorithm and Hybrid-GA-SA algorithm for yielding better solutions.

6. RESULTS AND DISCUSSIONS

The performance of the algorithms GAs, SA, Hybrid search algorithm combining GA and SA called Hybrid GA-SA algorithm, K-Means Cluster based heuristic, Hybrid K-Means Cluster based heuristic-GA, Hybrid K-Means Cluster based heuristic-GA-SA for ATSP are evaluated by considering 50 pilot test problems. The problem data set is generated randomly for 80 numbers of cities and comparing with different optimization techniques validates the data set. The performance of the different algorithm is compared. GA is compared with SA and Hybrid GA-SA, K-Means Cluster based heuristic is compared with GA, Hybrid GA-SA, Hybrid K-Means Cluster based heuristic-GA and Hybrid K-Means Cluster based heuristic-GA-SA and Hybrid K-Means Cluster based heuristic-GA is compared with Hybrid K-Means Cluster based heuristic-GA-SA.

General GA process has been modified by incorporating the new crossover operator uniform crossover operator and by applying the methodology of double operated crossover operator namely uniform and swap crossover operator. The different combination of crossover operator has been tested using pilot runs. The modified GA has been tested with uniform crossover operator, swap operator, insertion mutation, swap mutation and the combination of two crossover operator along with one mutation operator namely the combination uniform crossover-swap crossover-insertion mutation, uniform crossover-swap crossover-swap mutation, swap crossover-uniform crossover-insertion mutation, swap crossover-uniform crossover- swap mutation. The results are compared and it was found that the sequence of uniform crossover-swap crossover-insertion mutation operation sounds better than other combination. The results are shown in the Figure 6.1.

The percentage improvement of GA over SA and Hybrid GA-SA, K-Means based heuristic over GA, Hybrid GA-SA, Hybrid K-Means Cluster based heuristic-GA over K-Means Cluster based heuristic, Hybrid K-Means Cluster based heuristic-GA-SA over K-Means Cluster based heuristic, Hybrid K-Means Cluster based heuristic-GA over Hybrid K-Means Cluster based heuristic-GA-SA is given in Table 1

The performance measure employed in the numerical study is mean percentage improvement from SA for comparison of GA with the SA, mean percentage improvement from Hybrid GA-SA for comparison of GA with the Hybrid GA-SA, mean percentage improvement from GA for comparison of K-Means Cluster based heuristic with GA, mean percentage improvement from GA-SA for comparison of K-Means Cluster based heuristic with Hybrid GA-SA, mean percentage improvement from K-Means Cluster based heuristic for comparison of Hybrid K-Means Cluster based heuristic-GA-SA with K-Means Cluster based heuristic, mean percentage improvement from Hybrid K-Means Cluster based heuristic-GA-SA for comparison of Hybrid K-Means Cluster based heuristic-GA with Hybrid K-Means Cluster based heuristic-GA-SA.

Percentage improvement of GA over SA

$$= \frac{(Total\ cost)_{SA} - (Total\ cost)_{GA}}{(Total\ cost)_{SA}}$$

Percentage improvement of GA over Hybrid GA-SA

$$= \frac{(Total\ cost)_{GA-SA} - (Total\ cost)_{GA}}{(Total\ cost)_{GA-SA}}$$

Percentage improvement of Hybrid GA-SA over SA

$$= \frac{(Total\ cost)_{SA} - (Total\ cost)_{GA-SA}}{(Total\ cost)_{SA}}$$

Percentage improvement of K-Means over GA

$$= \frac{(Total\ cost)_{GA} - (Total\ cost)_{K-MEANS}}{(Total\ cost)_{GA}}$$

Percentage improvement of K-Means over Hybrid GA-SA

$$= \frac{(Total\ cost)_{GA-SA} - (Total\ cost)_{K-MEANS}}{(Total\ cost)_{GA-SA}}$$

Percentage improvement of K-Means-GA over K-Means

$$= \frac{(Total\ cost)_{K-MEANS} - (Total\ cost)_{K-MEANS-GA}}{(Total\ cost)_{K-MEANS}}$$

Percentage improvement of K-Means-GA-SA over K-Means

$$= \frac{(Total\ cost)_{K-MEANS} - (Total\ cost)_{K-MEANS-GA-SA}}{(Total\ cost)_{K-MEANS}}$$

Percentage improvement of k-Means-GA over K-Means-GA-SA

$$= \frac{(Total\ cost)_{K-MEANS} - (Total\ cost)_{K-MEANS-GA-SA}}{(Total\ cost)_{K-MEANS}}$$

Table 1. Comparative results of ASTP for GA, SA, Hybrid GA-SA, K-Means, K-Means-GA, K-Means-GA-SA with % improvement with each other

| SL. No | K-Means | GA | SA | GA-SA | K-GA-SA | K-GA | GA over | | GA-SA over SA | K-Means over | | K-Means GA over | | K-Means-SA over K-means |
							SA	GA-SA		GA	GA-SA	K-Means	K-Means-GA-SA	
1	13830	17360	31240	21480	15890	16040	44.4	19.2	31.2	20.3	35.6	-16.0	-0.9	-14.9
2	13960	21070	33560	20230	15350	15470	37.2	-4.2	39.7	33.7	31.0	-10.8	-0.8	-10.0
3	14260	21340	33160	20850	15120	16670	35.6	-2.4	37.1	33.2	31.6	-16.9	-10.3	-6.0
4	14580	20250	30510	22110	14560	16270	33.6	8.4	27.5	28.0	34.1	-11.6	-11.7	0.1
5	14710	21270	31810	20700	14490	14150	33.1	-2.8	34.9	30.8	28.9	3.8	2.3	1.5
6	14780	20950	30840	21320	15130	15540	32.1	1.7	30.9	29.5	30.7	-5.1	-2.7	-2.4
7	15270	19960	32580	19090	15500	13750	38.7	-4.6	41.4	23.5	20.0	10.0	11.3	-1.5
8	15480	20940	33490	21220	14010	15700	37.5	1.3	36.6	26.1	27.0	-1.4	-12.1	9.5
9	15530	22490	33470	21780	14080	15010	32.8	-3.3	34.9	30.9	28.7	3.3	-6.6	9.3
10	15550	18450	32070	21810	13970	15040	42.5	15.4	32.0	15.7	28.7	3.3	-7.7	10.2
11	15570	21470	32850	21990	15510	14630	34.6	2.4	33.1	27.5	29.2	6.0	5.7	0.4
12	15600	20800	32360	19490	15820	15090	35.7	-6.7	39.8	25.0	20.0	3.3	4.6	-1.4
13	15620	20210	33400	22250	15320	14330	39.5	9.2	33.4	22.7	29.8	8.3	6.5	1.9
14	15660	21610	33360	21170	16690	14350	35.2	-2.1	36.5	27.5	26.0	8.4	14.0	-6.6
15	15700	21500	33120	21120	15760	15200	35.1	-1.8	36.2	27.0	25.7	3.2	3.6	-0.4
16	15720	21410	31940	20960	14400	15270	33.0	-2.1	34.4	26.6	25.0	2.9	-6.0	8.4
17	15810	22010	34200	19830	15060	15780	35.6	-11.0	42.0	28.2	20.3	0.2	-4.8	4.7
18	15820	18560	31180	19840	15670	15650	40.5	6.5	36.4	14.8	20.3	1.1	0.1	0.9
19	15840	21000	33310	20960	19320	15600	37.0	-0.2	37.1	24.6	24.4	1.5	19.3	-22.0
20	15990	19590	32260	21080	15900	15430	39.3	7.1	34.7	18.4	24.1	3.5	3.0	0.6

Percentage Difference of

Table 2. Comparative results of ASTP for GA, SA, Hybrid GA-SA, K-Means, K-Means-GA, K-Means-GA-SA with % improvement with each other

SL. No	K-Means	GA	SA	GA-SA	K-GA-SA	K-GA	Percentage Difference of							
							GA		GA-SA over SA	K-Means over		K-Means GA over		K-Means-SA over K-means
							SA	GA-SA		GA	GA-SA	K-Means	K-Means-GA-SA	
21	16110	20040	31630	20660	14540	14970	36.6	3.0	34.7	19.6	22.0	7.1	-3.0	9.7
22	16290	20340	32030	21060	16350	15380	36.5	3.4	34.2	19.9	22.6	5.6	5.9	-0.4
23	16650	19280	33190	20330	13750	14720	41.9	5.2	38.7	13.6	18.1	11.6	-7.1	17.4
24	16760	20400	32810	21000	14120	15430	37.8	2.9	36.0	17.8	20.2	7.9	-9.3	15.8
25	16760	19720	33000	19170	14240	15930	40.2	-2.9	41.9	15.0	12.6	5.0	-11.9	15.0
26	16820	21740	33720	19860	14560	13960	35.5	-9.5	41.1	22.6	15.3	17.0	4.1	13.4
27	16830	20400	33300	21640	15930	17110	38.7	5.7	35.0	17.5	22.2	-1.7	-7.4	5.3
28	16850	20270	32010	21300	15070	14830	36.7	4.8	33.5	16.9	20.9	12.0	1.6	10.6
29	16860	19400	31550	21330	17000	15360	38.5	9.0	32.4	13.1	21.0	8.9	9.6	-0.8
30	17040	21760	33890	20570	15560	15080	35.8	-5.8	39.3	21.7	17.2	11.5	3.1	8.7
31	17190	18700	32780	21380	14950	16590	43.0	12.5	34.8	8.1	19.6	3.5	-11.0	13.0
32	17260	18080	38580	21630	16020	14630	53.1	16.4	43.9	4.5	20.2	15.2	8.7	7.2
33	17330	20630	33210	20000	14630	15420	37.9	-3.2	39.8	16.0	13.4	11.0	-5.4	15.6
34	17350	19010	33630	19760	14560	16560	43.5	3.8	41.2	8.7	12.2	4.6	-13.7	16.1
35	17370	20120	33570	20670	15130	15240	40.1	2.7	38.4	13.7	16.0	12.3	-0.7	12.9

continued on following page

Table 2. continued

SL. No	K-Means	GA	SA	GA-SA	K-GA-SA	K-GA	Percentage Difference of							
							GA over		GA-SA over SA	K-Means over		K-Means GA over		K-Means-SA over K-means
							SA	GA-SA		GA	GA-SA	K-Means	K-Means-GA-SA	
36	17430	20200	32020	21010	15800	13150	36.9	3.9	34.4	13.7	17.0	24.6	16.8	9.4
37	17640	21420	31960	19820	14680	14460	33.0	-8.1	38.0	17.6	11.0	18.0	1.5	16.8
38	17690	20080	33230	20750	13750	14070	39.6	3.2	37.6	11.9	14.7	20.5	-2.3	22.3
39	17740	21430	32690	22260	14500	14100	34.4	3.7	31.9	17.2	20.3	20.5	2.8	18.3
40	17770	22630	33380	20090	16240	14480	32.2	-12.6	39.8	21.5	11.5	18.5	10.8	8.6
41	17950	22440	33710	22850	16010	15470	33.4	1.8	32.2	20.0	21.4	13.8	3.4	10.8
42	18080	22550	33220	22770	16080	15500	32.1	1.0	31.5	19.8	20.6	14.3	3.6	11.1
43	18220	19520	33370	21680	16020	14630	41.5	10.0	35.0	6.7	16.0	19.7	8.7	12.1
44	18400	20280	33140	20680	14710	15370	38.8	1.9	37.6	9.3	11.0	16.5	-4.5	20.1
45	18860	21450	32580	18770	16170	16210	34.2	-14.3	42.4	12.1	-0.5	14.1	-0.2	14.3
46	18860	21130	31090	20890	15410	15290	32.0	-1.1	32.8	10.7	9.7	18.9	0.8	18.3
47	18900	18830	32500	20570	15980	15080	42.1	8.5	36.7	-0.4	8.1	20.2	5.6	15.4
48	19070	20760	31850	20640	15330	14310	34.8	-0.6	35.2	8.1	7.6	25.0	6.7	19.6
49	19400	21060	33050	21760	14770	15280	36.3	3.2	34.2	7.9	10.8	21.2	-3.5	23.9
50	20550	21680	32280	20690	16780	16260	32.8	-4.8	35.9	5.2	0.7	20.9	3.1	18.3
Avg	16706	20552	32794	20897	15324	15197	37.3	1.5	36.2	18.5	19.9	8.3	0.5	7.6

From the results it is concluded that the GA performs better than SA and Hybrid GA-SA , K-Means Cluster based heuristic performs better than GA and Hybrid GA-SA, Hybrid K-Means Cluster based heuristic-GA performs better than GA and K-Means Cluster based heuristic. Hybrid K-Means Cluster based heuristic-GA-SA performs better than GA and K-Means Cluster based

Figure 6.1. Comparison of combined crossover operator with the mutation operator

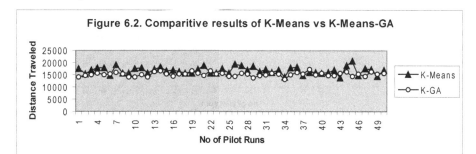

Where C1 – UNIFORM CROSSOVER
C2 – SWAP CROSSOVER
M1 – INSERTION MUTATION

heuristic, Hybrid K-Means Cluster based heuristic-GA performs better than Hybrid K-Means Cluster based heuristic-GA-SA. The comparative results are presented in Figures 6.2 to 6.9.

Interpretation analysis of GA is provided in Figure 6.11 and 6.12.

8. CONCLUSION

A simple but effective algorithms GA, SA, Hybrid GA-SA, K-Means Cluster based heuristic, Hybrid K-Means Cluster based heuristic-GA and Hybrid K-Means Cluster based heuristic-GA-SA

Figure 6.2 to 6.9: Comparative results

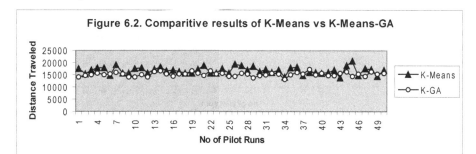

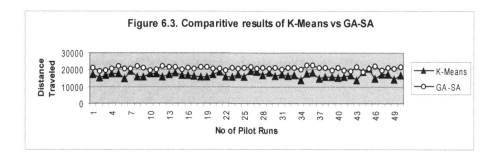

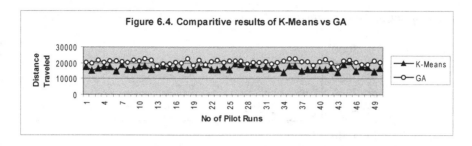

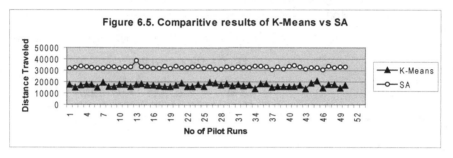

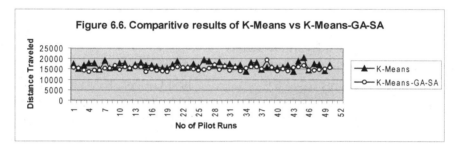

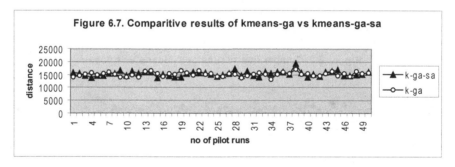

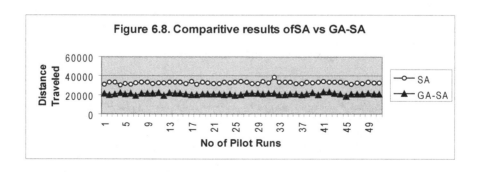

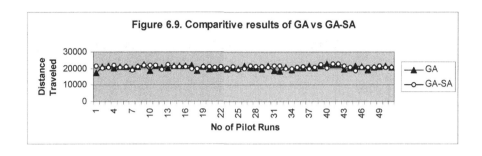

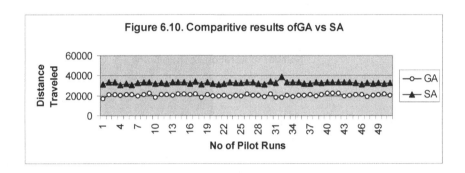

for ATSP is proposed in this thesis. The problem of minimizing the distance traveled from center single depot to all given 'n' cities is considered as the objective function for ATSP. GA has been modified by incorporating the uniform crossover operator and double operated crossover operator namely uniform crossover operator and swap crossover operator in the crossover process. The modified GA is compared with general GA and the modified is proved better in obtaining nearer optimal solutions for ATSP. When comparing the different sequence of crossover and mutation operator, the uniform crossover-swap crossover-insertion mutation sequence process sounds better than the other sequence process. The proposed Hybrid GA-SA algorithm consists of two phases. GA is used in first phase and SA is used in second phase. Merging of these powerful techniques has the strength of exploring the search space and accepting the inferior solution. The results

Figure 6.11. Objective function vs. Iterations

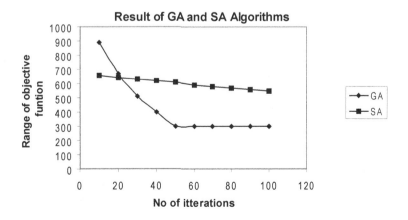

Figure 6.12. Objective function vs population size

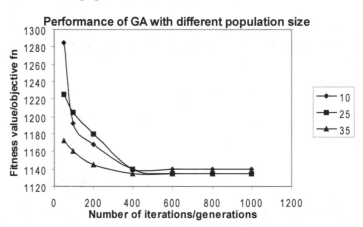

obtained from GA and Hybrid GA-SA algorithm are encouraging over SA. Out of which, GA outperforms Hybrid GA-SA. When comparing the K-Means Cluster based heuristic with all optimization technique algorithms, it is evident that K-Means Cluster based heuristic performs better than GA. When K-Means Cluster based heuristic hybrid with GA-SA, it performs better than K-Means Cluster based heuristic. But, as a whole, when K-Means Cluster based heuristic hybrid with GA, it outperforms the Hybrid K-Means Cluster based heuristic-GA-SA.

REFERENCES

Chiung Moon, Kim, J., Choi, G., & Seo, Y., (2002). An efficient genetic algorithm for the traveling salesman problem with precedence constraints. European Journal of Operational Research, *140*(3), 606-617.

Dantzig, B.G. & Ramser, J.H. (1959). The truck dispatching problem. Management Sciences, *6*(1), 80-91.

Righini, G., & Trubian, M., (2004), A note on the approximation of the asymmetric traveling sales-man problem. *European Journal of Operational Research, 153*(1), 255-265.

Goldberg D.E. (1989) *Genetic algorithms in search optimization and machine learning.* Addison-Wesley Publishers.

Choi, I.C., Kim, S.I., & Kim, H.S. (2003). A genetic algorithm with a mixed region search for the asymmetric traveling salesman problem. *Computers & Operations Research, 30*(5), 773–786

Kirkpatrick, S., Gelatt, Jr., C.D., & Vecchi, M.P. (1983). Optimization by Simulated Annealing. *Science, 220*(4598), 671-680.

Lenstra, J. & Rinnooy, K.A., (1981). Complexity of vehicle routing and scheduling problems. *Networks, 11*, 221-227.

Narahari, Y., & S. Biswas. S., (2000), Supply Chain Management: Modeling and Decision Making. Invited paper. International Conference on Flexible Autonomous Manufacturing Systems, Coimbatore Institute of Technology. Coimbatore, January 2000.

Potvin, J.Y. (1996). Genetic Algorithms for the traveling salesman problem, *Annals of Operations Research, 63*, 339–370.

Chapter II
An Enhanced Text–Classification–Based Arabic Information Retrieval System

Sameh Ghwanmeh
Yarmouk University, Jordan

Ghassan Kanaan
The Arab Academy for Banking and Financial Sciences, Jordan

Riyad Al-Shalabi
The Arab Academy for Banking and Financial Sciences, Jordan

Ahmad Ababneh
The Arab Academy for Banking and Financial Sciences, Jordan

ABSTRACT

This chapter presents enhanced, effective and simple approach to text classification. The approach uses an algorithm to automatically classifying documents. The main idea of the algorithm is to select feature words from each document; those words cover all the ideas in the document. The results of this algorithm are list of the main subjects founded in the document. Also, in this chapter the effects of the Arabic text classification on Information Retrieval have been investigated. The goal was to improve the convenience and effectiveness of information access. The system evaluation was conducted in two cases based on precision/recall criteria: evaluate the system without using Arabic text classification and evaluate the system with Arabic text classification. A chain of experiments were carried out to test the algorithm using 242 Arabic abstracts From the Saudi Arabian National Computer Conference. Additionally, automatic phrase indexing was implemented. Experiments revealed that the system with text classification gives better performance than the system without text classification.

INTRODUCTION

Information-retrieval systems process files of records and requests for information and identify and retrieve from the files certain records in response to the information requests. The retrieval of particular records depends on the similarity between the records and the queries, which in turn is measured by comparing the values of certain attributes of records and information requests. An Information Retrieval System is capable of storage, retrieval, and maintenance of information. Information in this context can be composed of text (including numeric and date data), images, audio, video, and other multi-media objects (Jingho and Tianshun, 2002; Salton, 1989).

Classification is the mean whereby we order knowledge. Classification is fundamentally a problem of finding sameness. When we classify, we seek for group things that have a common structure or exhibit a common behavior. Text classification mainly uses information retrieval techniques. Traditional information retrieval mainly retrieves relevant documents by using keyword-based or statistic-based techniques (Jingho and Tianshun, 2004). A standard approach to text categorization makes use of the classical text representation technique that maps a document to a high dimensional feature vector, where each entry of the vector represents the presence or absence of a feature (Lodhi, 2002).

Text Classification is the problem of assign documents to predefine classes or categories. The approaches to topic identification can be summarized in groups: statistical, knowledge-based, and hybrid. The statistical approach infers topics of texts from term frequency, term location, term co-occurrence, etc, without using external knowledge bases such as machine readable dictionaries. The knowledge-based approach relies on a syntactic or semantic parser, knowledge bases such as scripts or machine readable dictionaries, etc., without using any corpus statistics.

The hybrid approach combines the statistical and knowledge-based approaches to take advantage of the strengths of both approaches and thereby to improve the overall system performance (Jingho and Tianshun, 2002).

This chapter presents enhanced, effective and simple approach to text classification. The approach uses an algorithm to automatically classifying documents. The main idea of the algorithm is to select feature words from each document; those words cover all the ideas in the document. The results of this algorithm are list of the main subjects founded in the document. Also, in this chapter the effects of the Arabic text classification on Information Retrieval have been investigated. The goal was to improve the convenience and effectiveness of information access. The system evaluation was conducted in two cases based on precision/recall criteria: evaluate the system without using Arabic text classification and to evaluate the system with Arabic text classification. A series of experiments were carried out to test the algorithm using 242 Arabic abstracts From the Saudi Arabian National Computer Conference. Additionally, automatic phrase indexing was implemented. The system was evaluated for the two cases based on precision/recall evaluation as shown before. Experiments reveal that the system with text classification gives better performance than the system without text classification.

GENERAL APPROACHES TO CLASSIFICATION

Classical Categorization

In this approach all entities that have a given property or a collection of properties in common form a category. Classical categorization comes to us from Plato, then from Aristotle through his classification of plants and animals (Joachims, 1999).

Prototype Theory

A category is represented by a prototypical object, an object is considered to be a member of this category if and only if it resembles this prototype in significant ways.

Conceptual Clustering

Can be defined as more modern variation of the classical approach, in which, we generate categories as follows:

- Formulate conceptual description of these categories.
- Classify the entities according to the description.

For example, we may state a concept such as "love song" this is a concept more than property, if we decide certain song is more of a love song than not, we place it in category. How often have you failed to find what you wanted in an online search because the words you used failed to match words in the material that you needed? Concept-based retrieval systems attempt to reach beyond the standard keyword approach of simply counting the words from your request that occur in a document. The Conceptual Indexing is developing techniques that use knowledge of concepts and their interrelationships to find correspondences between the concepts in your request and those that occur in text passages. The central focus of Conceptual index is the "paraphrase problem," in which the words used in a query are different from, but conceptually related to, those in material that you need (Ghani, 1999).

In conceptual clustering, we group things according to distinct concepts. In prototype theory, we group things according to degree of their relationship to concentrate prototype (Joachims, 1999). In Text Classification the main task is to choose the correct category for each text document in the corpus. It might be needed to categorize sports by types; or to divide sentences into questions and statements. Two main types of text classification, consider single-category text classification problems, in which; there are a predefined set of categories, and each text belongs to exactly one category. In multi-category text classification, each text can have zero or more categories (nltk, 2007).

APPLICATIONS OF TEXT CLASSIFICATION

E-Mail Filtering

In which we can use text classification to filter emails into folders set up by user, this helps us to search our e-mails.

Knowledge-Based Creation

Company web sites provide large amounts of information about products, marketing contact persons, etc. Categorization can be used to find companies' web pages and organize them by industrial sector.

E-Commerce

Users locate products in two basic ways: search and browsing. Browsing is best when user doesn't know exactly what he/she wants. Text classification can be used to organize products into a hierarchy according to description.

Information Extraction

In which we can extract information from talk announcements (room, time, date, title, speaker, etc).

CLASSIFICATION ALGORITHMS

The classification algorithm can be described as per the main steps shown in Figure 1. In the following sections the main system elements will be explained in details.

Building the Feature Dictionary

The feature dictionary is mainly used to store some terms that can illustrate the topic feature concept.

Figure 1. System architecture.

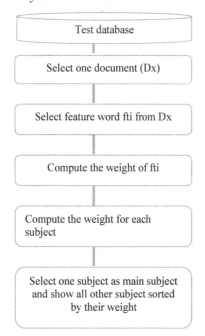

The data structure of the feature dictionary is consisting of word or phrase, document number, Frequency, Title Frequency, End Frequency and field attribute, frequency (number of times of the feature term occurring in the document), title frequency (number of times of the feature term occurring in the document), end frequency (number of times of the feature term occurring in the first sentence of a document). Table 1 shows examples of the feature dictionary.

Computation of Topic Feature Distribution

According to the field attributes, frequencies and positions of Feature terms, we could compute topic feature distribution. According to the frequency and position of a feature term fti, we could compute the weight of the term fti. The computing formula is described as follows (Jingho and Tianshun, 2002).

$$p(ft_i) = \frac{freq(ft_i) + N_{title} + 0.5 \times N_{end}}{\sum freq(ft_i)}$$

Where, p (fti) is the weight of the feature term fti. Freq (fti) is frequency of the feature term fti. N_{title} is number of times of the feature term fti occurring in the title, N_{end} is number of times of the feature term fti occurring at the end sentence

Table 1. Examples of the feature dictionary

Phrase	Word1	Word2	Doc. #	Freq	Title_F	End_F	Field
الاشتقاق الآلي	الاشتقاق	الآلي	1	5	1	0	تاغل
نص عربي	نص	عربي	1	7	1	1	تاغل
قرآن كريم	كريم	قرآن	1	1	0	0	علوم الدين
مفردات قياسية	مفردات	قياسية	1	5	0	2	تاغل
حاسب آلي	آلي	حاسب	1	4	1	0	حاسب آلي

paragraph. freq (fti) is total frequency of the all feature terms in the text.

The weight p(fi) computing formula of a topic feature fi is described as follows:

$$p(f_i) = \sum_{f_{t_j} \in f_i} p(ft_j) \qquad (2)$$

Where: p (fi) is the weight of the topic feature fi. p (ftj) is the weight of the feature term ftj. Ftj_fi shows feature term set illustrating the same topic feature fi (Jingho and Tianshun, 2002).

Traditional Information Retrieval System

To conduct the necessary comparison, the traditional Information Retrieval System (IR) has been used, in which we use simple information retrieval techniques based on simple word and phrase matching. We have used a table in which we store with each phrase its components words and the number of documents in which this phrase appears. The steps involved in this algorithm are as follows:

Exact Match: In this step the system retrieves the documents which have exact match between user query and phrases in the table and rank them as the top of the answer.

Partial Match: Partial match based on number of words matched. For example if the query was "الذكاء الاصطناعي" (Artificial Intelligence Approaches), the document that appear on it "الذكاء الاصطناعي" (Artificial Intelligence) will be ranked before the document which include just the word "الذكاء" (Artificial) . The results of this step are ranked in the middle of the answer set.

One word match: For example if the query was "الذكاء الاصطناعي" (Artificial Intelligence Approaches) we search for each individual

Figure 2. Phrase index

Phrase	Word1	Word2	Document#

Table 2. Phrase index for the query "الذكاء الاصطناعي" (Artificial Intelligence)

Phrase	Word1	Word2	Doc. #
الذكاء الاصطناعي Artificial Intelligence	الاصطناعي Artificial	الذكاء intelligence	10

word in the query. The results of this step are ranked in the bottom of the answer set. The two words phrase index built is shown in Figure 2.

Enhanced IR System Supported by Text Classification

The traditional IR system has been enhanced and upgraded. After we retrieve the document that have exact match between the query and the phrase, we must look at the subjects of these document. The steps involved in this algorithm are as follows:

Exact Match: In this step the system retrieves the documents which have exact match between user query and phrases in the table and rank them as the top of the answer. Use the subjects of the returned documents to search and return the document which have the same subjects.

Ranking: Rank the documents that have exact match at the top of the answer set. Rank the documents that have the same subject as the subjects of the document on the top rank (that have exact match).

Table 3 shows an example of the queries used and system output for each query and the subject for both query and system output.

The system begins the searching process by exact match between the user query الذكاء الاصطناعي"" (Artificial intelligence) and the

41

Table 3. Example of system output

Query	Subject	System Output	Subject
قرآن كريم	علوم الدين	قرآن كريم,سنن مطهره, طريق السلامية,علوم الشريعة	علوم الدين
الحاسب الآلي	و حاسب معلوماتية	الحاسب الآلي يهندس الحاسب,وحاسب شخص يعم بالجاتمع معلوماتية, طباعتبارتفيات قاعده بيانات	و حاسب معلوماتية

phrases in the feature dictionary then the system search again by using the subjects of the returned document الذكاء الاصطناعي"""" (Artificial intelligence). The system retrieved phrases whose subject is الذكاء الاصطناعي"""" (Artificial intelligence) for example ("اللغات الطبيعية") (Natural Languages) مظن الخبرة", ,"(Expert Systems) , "قواعد المعرفة" (Knowledge Bases).

SYSTEM IMPLEMENTATION

The first component of the system is the building of Feature Dictionary. In this step we use automatic phrase each phrase consists of two words and compute the necessary frequencies. The subject field of the feature dictionary has been filled manually. In main form window the user can enter or select a query. After the user type his query as needed; the system retrieves the relevant documents to this query automatically. The system is constructed in Visual Basic running on a Windows PC, and makes use of an Access database to manage the feature dictionary contents.

PERFORMANCE EVALUATION

The performance of the system has been evaluated by run the system and observes the results (relevant retrieved documents) to each query. From these runs, we calculate precision and recall evaluation measures for each query in two cases with text classification and without text classification.

Precision/Recall Measurements

The following Formulas have been used in calculating Precision–recall measurements (Mihalcea, 2004).

Precision = No. of Relevant retrieved docs / No. of Total Retrieved Docs
Recall = No. of Relevant retrieved docs / No. of Relevant Exist Docs, and the average recall precision has been calculated using the following formula.

$$P(r) = \frac{\sum Pi\ (r)}{Nq}$$

where, $P(r_j) = Max\ r_j <= r <= r_{j+1}\ P(r)$

P(r) is the average precision at the recall level r; N_q is the number of queries used, and Pi (r) is the precision at recall level r for each of the queries.

To measure the differences and observes the enhancements, a comparison is made between both cases for the system runs (i.e. without text classification and with text classification) from the precision–recall evaluation measurements calculations. The system has been tested using a set of 242 Arabic abstracts from the proceedings of the Saudi Arabian National Computer Conferences. A total of 59 Arabic queries have been used in the tests and made relevance judgments automatically and manually for each query.

Experiments and Results

The testing process involved 40 queries. These queries applied in two cases: with and without text classification. Table 4 shows the recall/precision resulted from a relevant document with query" "اللغة العربية" (Arabic Language).

Based on the resulted values of precision and recall, It can be shown that the average precision/recall for the system without Arabic text classification is (Precision=31% and Recall=78%) and with

Table 4*. Recall /Precision as seen relevant document for query* ةيبرعلا ةغللا. *(Arabic Language)*

Doc.#	R or Not R	Relevant Retrieved Counter	Retrieved Counter	Precision	Recall
2	1	1	1	1.00	0.01
4	1	2	2	1.00	0.02
8	1	3	3	1.00	0.03
9	1	4	4	1.00	0.04
242	1	5	5	1.00	0.05
198	1	6	6	1.00	0.06
86	1	7	7	1.00	0.07
26	0	7	8	0.88	0.07
18	0	7	9	0.78	0.07
42	0	7	10	0.70	0.07
41	0	7	11	0.64	0.07
22	0	7	12	0.58	0.07
39	1	8	13	0.62	0.08
87	1	9	14	0.64	0.09
88	1	10	15	0.67	0.10
89	1	11	16	0.69	0.11
92	1	12	17	0.71	0.13
93	1	13	18	0.72	0.14
101	0	13	19	0.68	0.14
102	1	14	20	0.70	0.15
103	1	15	21	0.71	0.16
106	1	16	22	0.73	0.17
107	1	17	23	0.74	0.18
108	1	18	24	0.75	0.19
110	1	19	25	0.76	0.20
114	1	20	26	0.77	0.21
121	1	21	27	0.78	0.22
122	1	22	28	0.79	0.23
123	1	23	29	0.79	0.24
124	0	23	30	0.77	0.24
125	0	23	31	0.74	0.24
126	1	24	32	0.75	0.25
127	1	25	33	0.76	0.26
128	1	26	34	0.76	0.27
129	0	26	35	0.74	0.27
130	0	26	36	0.72	0.27
131	1	27	37	0.73	0.28
132	0	27	38	0.71	0.28
133	1	28	39	0.72	0.29
134	0	28	40	0.70	0.29

Table 5. Recall /Precision table with and without Arabic text classification

	without TC		with TC	
Intervals	Precision	Recall	Precision	Recall
0 - 0.1	0.765	0.0560	0.7529	0.0562
0.1 - 0.2	0.4937	0.1522	0.5325	0.1525
0.2 - 0.3	0.4296	0.2522	0.4384	0.2515
0.3 - 0.4	0.3879	0.3470	0.3890	0.3518
0.4 - 0.5	0.3451	0.4405	0.3596	0.4556
0.5 - 0.6	0.2910	0.5263	0.31781	0.5525
0.6 - 0.7	0.2224	0.6067	0.2734	0.6521
0.7 - 0.8	0.2010	0.6874	0.2603	0.7531
0.8 - 0.9	0.1744	0.7518	0.2343	0.8503
0.9 - 1	0.1279	0.8091	0.1815	0.9290

Figure 3. Recall/precision with text classification and without text classification

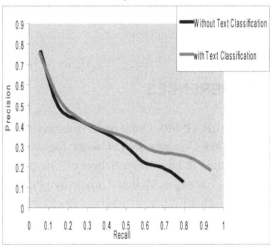

Arabic text classification is (Precision=37% and Recall=93%). Figure 3 shows the performance of the system for both cases and the affects of the Arabic text classification on the retrieval process. It can be noted that the performance of the system is better with Arabic text classification.

CONCLUSION

An Arabic information retrieval system has been explained, in which specific documents within a collection of documents are retrieved in response to a query and then ranked these documents. It can be concluded that the system performance and the Arabic information retrieval efficiency with text classification is better than the same system without using text classification by calculating precision/recall measures for both situations. The affects of text classification on the system performance has been observed. The results of the experiments show that good precise and recall measures are achieved. The system key benefits can be summarized as follows:

a. Specific **passage retrieval**: finds specific passages of Information.
b. Intuitive ranking of hits: produces a scored list of specific Passages within documents.
c. Conceptual navigation: structured taxonomy is suitable for efficient browsing and navigation of concepts found documents.

REFERENCES

Ghani, R. (1999). *Using Error-Correcting Codes for Text Classification*. Center for Automated Learning & Discovery, School of Computer Science, Carnegie Mellon University, Pittsburgh, PA.

Jingho Z., & Tianshun, Y. (2004). *A knowledge-based Approach to text classification*.

Joachims, T. (1999). Making large–scale SVM learning practical. In B. Sch⁄olkopf, C. J. C. Burges, and A. J.

Lodhi, H. (2002). *Text Classification using String Kernels*. Department of Computer Science, Royal Holloway, University of London, Egham, Surrey TW20 0EX, UK.

Mihalcea, R. (2004). Information Retrieval and Web Search Instructor.

Ricardo, B., & d Berthier, R. (1999). Addison Wesley *Modern Information Retrieval Textbook*, ACM Press.

Salton, J. (1989). *Automatic Text Processing: The Transformation: Analysis and Retrieval of Information by Computer*. Mass: Addison-Wesley, Reading

Smola, editors, *Advances in Kernel Methods —Support Vector Learning*, (pp. 169–184), Cambridge, MA: MIT Press.

Search Engine, NLTK Tutorial: Text Classification, nltk.sourceforge.net/tutorial/classifying/ (visited Jan, 2008).

Web Site, www.dcs.gla.ac.uk/keith/chapter.1/ch.1.html (visited Jan, 2008)

Web Document, Haav, H., &, Lubi, T. (2007). A Survey of Concept-based Information Retrieval Tools, Institute of Cybernetics at Tallinn Technical University.

Chapter III
Landmark–Based Shape Context for Handwritten Digit Recognition

Shyamanta M. Hazarika
Tezpur University, India

ABSTRACT

This chapter introduces landmark-based shape context. Standard shape context computation samples at regular interval on the contour of an object. Corner points of an object being landmarks on the contour; set of corner points is a good descriptor of shape. Landmark-based shape context is computed by sampling a reduced set of points based on such landmarks. In this chapter, an approach to recognizing handwritten digits based on shape similarity computed through landmark-based shape context is presented. Shape context based object recognition being an iterative process; the reduction in the number of sample points provides a basis for faster recognition.

INTRODUCTION

Over last three decades, character recognition has been an active research area. The potential of being used in various applications such as developing reading aid for the blind, office automation, language processing and multi-media design makes Optical Character Recognition (OCR) popular. OCR focuses on the recognition of machine printed output. The goal of OCR is automatic reading of optically sensed document text so as to translate human-readable characters to machine readable codes. OCR focuses on the recognition of machine printed output where special fonts can be used and variability between characters and digits with similar font size and font attributes is reasonably small. On the contrary, variability of handwritten characters and digits is surprisingly high. This makes handwriting recognition far more challenging.

Handwritten digit recognition is important for automating bank cheque processing, postal mail sorting, job application form sorting, and automatic scoring of tests containing multiple choice questions as well as other applications where numeral recognition is necessary. Further, with the development of miniaturized, portable and wireless equipment, *Calligraphic User Interface* based on handwriting recognition has become an essential part in the next generation of human-computer interaction (Hansmann, Merk, Nicklous, & Stober, 2001). Consequently, handwriting recognition has seen much active research in the past decade. The thrust is to push recognition rates to those near human performance (Wierer & Boston, 2007a). The ultimate objective of handwriting recognition is high-speed recognition, which has zero error rate and low rejection rate. Recognition of isolated handwritten digits continues to be of interest for the research community. Numerous approaches have been proposed for pre-processing, feature extraction, learning as well as classification. For a comprehensive survey see (Plamondon & Srihari, 2000).

Handwritten digit recognition can be classified into two categories: offline recognition and online recognition (Liu, Nakashima, Sako, & Fujisawa, 2003). Offline recognition process and recognize the user input handwritten digit based on images (the scanned images of handwritten digit). A number of methods have been proposed to solve offline recognition (Plamondon & Srihari, 2000). Offline recognition has a number of hurdles. The algorithm for image processing is complex and poses a high resource requirement. Moreover, the recognition clues available are few. For many applications, off-line handwritten recognition suffices. Inversely, the on-line recognition technology, which has emerged in recent years, uses the geometry and temporal dynamic information of the users' input (Jiang, Sun, Yuan, Zheng, & Xu, 2006). The methods for online recognition relatively pose low resource and processing requirement, and may effectively use many kinds of clues to capture users' input customs. They are effective with good user adaptation. The major issue of

applying online recognition methods is how to effectively model handwritten digit and implement user adaptation.

Many systems and classification algorithms have been proposed in the past years for handwritten digit recognition. Liu et al. (2003) does a bench-marking of the different techniques in the field including major feature sets, learning algorithms and datasets. Suan and Tan (2005) present an analysis of state-of-art classifiers for recognition of handwritten digits. Most approaches involve statistically based methods, due to their relative ease of implementation as compared to semantic methods. Techniques ranging from statistical methods such as nearest neighbour classification (Aradhya, Kumar, & Noushath, 2007) and shape matching (Belongie, Malik, & Puzicha, 2002) have been applied. Machine learning techniques like neural networks (Hu, Zhu, Lv, & Zhang, 2006) and support vector machines (DeCoste & Schölkopf, 2002) have been used. Lately, hybrid (Gorgevik, 2004) as well as non-traditional classifiers (Xiu-fang, Tian and Xue-song, 2007) has been explored.

The feature description of handwritten digit has critical role in recognition. The traditional feature description of handwritten digit can be mainly categorized into two sorts: global features and structural features. The global features mainly refer using statistical methods to obtain the features such as the pixel destiny, rectangular, feature point, mathematical transform and so on. These features are hard to be extracted and the computation requirement is expensive. The structural features are the basic features about the character shape, which are extracted from the outline or skeleton of character, including the circle, the vertex, the pitch point, the arc, breaks out, hollowly, the stroke and so on. These features are suitable for syntax analysis, because they are easy to be extracted and discriminated. However, the descriptions for them are too complex.

Selection of a feature extraction method is probably the single most important factor in achieving high recognition performance. Overview of feature extraction methods for off-line recognition of segmented characters have been proposed by (Trier, Jain, & Taxt, 1996). The paper reviewed feature extraction methods based on template matching, deformable templates, unitary image transforms, graph description, projection histograms, contour profiles, zoning, geometric moment invariants, Zernike moments, Spline curve approximation, and Fourier descriptors. Jain, Duin and Mao (2000) summarize and compare some of the well-known methods used in various stages of a pattern recognition system and identify research topics and applications which are at the forefront of this exciting and challenging field.

Lauer, Suen and Bloch (2007) focus on the problem of feature extraction and subsequent recognition. A trainable feature extractor based on convolutional neural network is introduced. Classification is through support vector machine to enhance the generalization ability. Lauer et al. (2007) achieve results that out perform both support vector machines and convolutional neural networks, while providing performances comparable to the best performance on the MNIST database. Aradhya et al (2007) propose a novel system based on radon transform for handwritten digit recognition. They have used radon function which represents an image as a collection of projections along various directions. The resultant feature vector by applying this method is the input for the classification stage. Wierer & Boston (2007a) propose to use a genuinely two-dimensional hidden Markov model (2D HMM) to extract features from unclassified digit images, which are drawn from the MNIST database. Distances between unclassified digit images and prototypes are computed hierarchically, that is, distance computations become finer as the algorithm enters later stages and as prototypes with large distances from the unclassified image are removed from consideration. Wierer and Boston (2007a) are the first to use powerful

techniques from the emerging mathematical fields of tropical geometry and algebraic statistics (Pachter & Sturmfels, 2005) to perform digit recognition. Another novel technique is that of Sadri, Suen and Bui (2007) exploiting contextual knowledge for segmentation and recognition of unconstrained handwritten numeral string using genetic algorithms.

The challenge of handwritten digit recognition involves 2-D shape matching. Shape matching can be either feature-based or brightness-based. Brightness based methods make use of pixel brightness. Feature-based approaches involve the use of spatial arrangements of extracted features. One of the most striking feature-based object descriptor is *shape contexts*. Objects are treated as a point set with the underlying motivation that the shape of an object can be captured by a finite subset of its points. Shapes are represented by a set of points sampled from the shape contours. The shape context method by Belongie et al. (2002) samples a large number, typically 100 or so pixel locations from the output of an edge detector to compute the shape contexts.

Typically, *shape context* computation samples at regular interval on the contour without regard to *landmarks*. In contrast, qualitative representation of shape relies on *landmarks* on the contour (Meathreal & Galton, 2000). From qualitative representation comes the motivation for using such *qualitative abstraction* to refine shape context computation. Corners preserve all important information required for analysis of shapes while reducing drastically the number of data points to analyse (Rao & Krishnan, 1994). Corner points of an object being landmarks on the contour; set of corner points is a good descriptor of shape.

Underlying the problem of corner detection is the problem of contour feature extraction. Contour feature extraction drew great attention in pattern recognition. The most popular ones were the curvature method by Freeman and Davis (1977) and the splitting method by Duda and Hart (1973). The curvature method requires complicated computation in measuring accuracy and localization of the corner points. The splitting method, on the other hand, is a recursive method that searches for angles on a contour and the output of this technique do not order the corner points found as they occur along the contour. The *arch height* method by Lin, Dou and Wang (1992) retains the best of both the methods. Feature set based on contour following continue to be of interest (Garg & Jindal, 2007).

The primary contribution of this paper is a robust and simple algorithm for finding correspondence between handwritten digits using a variant of shape context – a shape descriptor that describes the coarse distribution of the rest of the shape with respect to a given point on the shape. Handwritten digit recognition is explored; based on shape context computation through a reduced number of sample points. Shape context computation is based on landmarks. The corner points of the contour are the landmarks used for shape context computation.

The arch height function of computing the corner points on a given contour is exploited. The paper demonstrates the validity of the use of landmark based sampling to compute shape context. It is done by building model *content-based image retrieval* (CBIR) *system*. See (Veltkamp & Tanase, 2000) for details. To evaluate the approach, its performance is compared with the standard shape context method in terms of *precision* and *recall*. Precision and recall is defined as

$$Precision = \frac{Number\ of\ relevant\ shapes\ retrieved}{Total\ number\ of\ shapes\ retrieved}$$

$$Recall = \frac{Number\ of\ relevant\ shapes\ retrieved}{Total\ number\ of\ relevant\ shapes\ in\ database}$$

Section-II introduces the basic concepts and terminology including shape contexts and the arch height function. In section-III, we present our proposed landmark based shape context method. Section-IV presents the experimental validation of the proposed algorithm, where a

comparison of the results of the standard shape context based matching and the proposed model is presented. Results and observations are presented in section-V.

BASIC CONCEPTS AND METHODS

Shape Context Based Matching

The discussion of shape context presented here closely follows that of Belongie et al. (2002). The shape context is a descriptor to describe the coarse distribution of the rest of the shape with respect to a given point on the shape. Shapes are represented by a set of points sampled from the shape contours: internal and external; typically 100 or so pixel locations sampled from the output of an edge detector.

Consider the set of vectors originating from a point to all other sample points on a shape. These vectors express the configuration of the entire shape relative to the reference point. Obviously this set of $n - 1$ vector is a rich description, since as n gets large, the representation of the shape become exact. The full set of vectors as a shape descriptor is much too detailed since shapes and their sampled representation may vary from one instance to another in a category. Belongie et al. (2002) identify the distribution over relative positions as a more robust and compact, yet highly discriminative descriptor. For a point p_i on the shape, a histogram h_i of the relative coordinates of the remaining $n - 1$ points is computed as

$$h_i(k) = \#\{q \neq p_i : (q - p_i) \in bin(k)\}$$

where k is the number of bins used which are uniform in log-polar space as illustrated in Figure 1 (c). h_i is the shape context of p_i. Shape contexts will be different for different points on a single shape. Homologous points on similar shapes will tend to have similar shape contexts.

Prior to matching shapes, the shape correspondence is first checked. The shape context enables this by providing a basis of point correspondence checking. The correspondence to the complete shape is evaluated by estimating an aligning transformation that maps one shape onto the other. If p_i and q_j are points on first and second shapes respectively; cost of matching these two points is written as

$$C_{ij} = C(p_i, q_j) = \frac{1}{2} \sum_{k=1}^{K} \frac{[h_i(k) - h_j(k)]^2}{h_i(k) + h_j(k)}$$

where $h_i(k)$ and $h_j(k)$ denote the k-bins normalized histogram at p_i and q_j, respectively.

Figure 1. Shape context computation and matching. (a) and (b) Sampled edge points of two shapes. (c) Log-polar histogram bins used in computing the shape contexts. Five bins for log r and 12 bins for ⬜ is used. (d), (e) and (f) Example shape context for reference samples marked by of o, ◊ and ◁ in (a) and (b). Note the visual similarity of the shape contexts computed for o and ◊, which were computed for relatively similar shapes points on the two shapes. By contrast, the shape context for ◁ is different. (g) Correspondence found using bipartite matching [From (Belongie et al., 2002)]

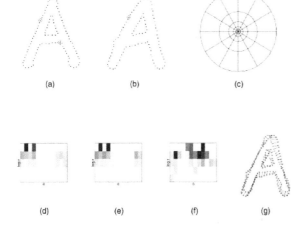

Given set of costs C_{ij} between all pairs of points: i on the first shape and j on the second shape, we want to minimize the total cost of matching, $H(\pi)$, subject to the constraint that matching be one-to-one[1].

$$H(\pi) = \sum_i C(p_i, q_{\pi(i)})$$

Finding correspondence between two shapes is equivalent to finding for each sample point on one shape, the sample point on the other shape that has the most similar shape context. Dissimilarity is computed, between the two shapes, as a sum of matching errors between corresponding points, together with a matching term measuring the magnitude of the aligning transform. The dissimilarity measure *DistMeasure* between P and Q gives the similarity of objects that are being matched. Higher the dissimilarity measure lesser is the similarity between the two shapes.

$$DistMeasure(P,Q) = SC \times D_{SC}(P,Q) + BE \times D_{be}(P,Q)$$

where $D_{sc}(P,Q)$ is the cost of matching shape contexts and $D_{be}(P,Q)$ is the *bending energy*. Bending energy is a measure of transformation necessary to closely align the stored digits with the test digit. It is, conceptually, the amount of work that is needed to transform an instance of a shape to another. The cost of aligning the shapes defines the similarity measure.

Arch Height Function to Locate Corner Points

An illustration of the Arch Height Function (AHF) method is given in Figure 2. The discussion on AHF here closely relate to the presentation by Lin et al. (1992).

For any given point on the contour, (x(l), y(l)), a chord is drawn with a specified arch length L. Let m denote the arch height i.e., the length of the straight line drawn perpendicular to the chord passing through its centre intersecting the contour. $(x(l+L), y(l+L))$ is the end point and the contour between is called the arch. Arch height m should be a function of $(x(l), y(l))$ or a function of the arc length L.

The principle of AHF is that one may locate the starting point $(x(0), y(0))$ at a distance equal to the step length, L (refer Figure 2), to the vertex of the angle. It is readily seen as the point (x,y) moves away from point $(x(0), y(0))$ along the contour clockwise, the value of function $d(l)$ increases gradually from $d(l) = 0$, reaches its maximum at $l = L/2$ and then decreases as $l > L/2$. Thus, one can perceive that the local maximum of AHF $d(l)$ corresponds to a corner point.

LANDMARK BASED SHAPE CONTEXT

Landmark shape context is a shape matching algorithm for object recognition. The essence of this algorithm is sampling of points on the contour feature of corners referred to as *landmarks* here. These points are used to compute a shape descriptor for shape based matching. Shape context is used as the descriptor. Matching is then performed to arrive at a measure of similarity. Input images are pre-processed to identify the region of interest i.e., segmenting of the object from the background. On the pre-processed image of the object a boundary tracing algorithm is run to get a set of contour

Figure 2. Illustration of arch height function method [From (Lin et al., 1992)]

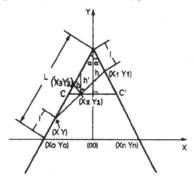

points. This set of contour points is then used to get to the shape descriptor.

Stage I is the contour feature extraction *i.e.,* *landmarks* extraction stage. If the object has holes every boundary is treated as a separate object and the result of applying stage I of the algorithm to each is concatenated to feed as the input to the second stage. The arch height is computed and recorded in an array dist[N]. Points on the contour which pass a certain threshold on the arch height distance are taken as corner points.

Stage II is the iterative shape matching stage and use shape contexts. The corner points (of stage I) are used as sample set to compute the shape contexts.

Stage I: Landmark extraction.
Input: coordinates of the boundary pixels of object *O* in an N long array $(x(i), y(i))$.
Output: coordinate of *n* corner points detected and stored at $(x(i), y(i))$
Procedure:
assign arch length L
for i = 1 to N
begin
// arch starting pixel
assign x1 = x(i) and y1 = y(i)
// arch ending pixel
assign x2 = x(i+L) and y2 = y(i+L)
draw chord of the arch and find the midpoint
if mid-point is on the arch
assign dist[i] = 0
else
find intersection point (x,y) on the arch with perpendicular from the mid-point of the cord i.e., arch height
assign dist[i] = arch height
end
for i = 1 to N
begin
if dist[i] – dist[i – 1] < L/2
dist[i] = 0;
if dist[i] = dist [i + 1]
dist[i + 1] is ignored
end

consider only those points for which distance is non zero and replace dist[N] array with the non zero distance set

for all elements in the non zero distance array

begin

if dist[i − 1] < dist[i]

or dist[i] > dist[i + 1]

label respective coordinates of the distance array as corner points.

end

Stage 2: Find similarity

Input: extracted n number of landmark of O_1 and O_2.

Output: similarity of O_1 and O_2 in terms of distance measure.

Procedure:

for i = 1 to n

begin

Compute shape contexts of the two shapes

Find point correspondence on the two shapes

Compute cost of shape contexts matching

Estimate an aligning transformation

Compute cost of estimating aligning transformation

end

Compute dissimilarity by *DistMeasure(O₁, O₂)*

In the aforementioned algorithm, n is the number of iteration. Experimentally, six iterations are affirmed to be optimum for matching. Object recognition is based on the similarity measure computed in stage II.

EXPERIMENTAL VALIDATION

The claim here is that shape context computed by sampling landmarks provides a basis for faster recognition of handwritten digits. To validate the claim a model CBIR system is built. The method is run on a dataset of 100 handwritten digits compiled from MNIST training dataset of LeCun et al. (1995). The implementation was run on a Pentium® M Processor 1.73GHz system with 768 MB of RAM. Query digits were submitted to retrieve similar shapes from the stored dataset. To find similarity, the weights SC and BE in the equation for distance (*DistMeasure*) were taken as one.

Results

Performance of Landmark based Shape Context is recorded in Table 1. Precision and recall for a number of queries is shown (in Table 1) with the time taken (in minutes) to retrieve the matched shapes. The arch height sampling used in stage I of the proposed method samples corner points on the fly. This result in the number of sample points for every query shape being different.

In order to facilitate comparison of precision and recall of Landmark based Shape Context method with the standard shape context method of Belongie et al. (2002), the same set of query shapes of Table 1 are used. Retrieval is through standard shape context but based on the number of sample points obtained using the arch height sampling (as in Stage I of Landmark based Shape Context). The corresponding results are tabulated in Table 2.

Table 1. Precision and recall of landmark based shape context method

Query	No. of samples computed	Total o. of relevant shapes in the dataset	Total no. of shapes retrieved	No. of relevant shapes retrieved	Precision	Recall	Time Taken in query (in min.)
Q1	25	11	8	5	0.625	0.454	1.06
Q2	18	9	6	6	1.000	0.677	1.05
Q3	43	6	6	4	0.667	0.677	1.10
Q4	17	8	4	4	1.000	0.500	1.02
Q5	32	10	10	4	0.400	0.400	1.05

Query shapes with landmark-based shape context computation as per Table 1 along with retrieved shapes are shown in Figure 3 below.

Standard shape context computation is based on random selection of sample points. Therefore, to observe the time taken by the standard shape context method and corresponding precision and recall, the algorithm was run for 100 number of random sample points. This is to maintain the standard number of sample points as given in (Belongie et al., 2002). Table 3 shows the observation.

Observation

Observe query Q5 in Table 1 and Table 2. In both the methods, Q5 have the lowest precision and recall. While the proposed method retrieved more similar shapes, the standard method picked up too many irrelevant shapes. This highlights the precise nature of the proposed landmark-based shape context method. Landmark-based shape context

Table 2. Precision and recall of shape context method (using same number of sample points as in Table 1)

Query	No. of sample points submitted	Total no. of relevant shapes in the dataset	No. of shapes retrieved	No. of relevant shapes retrieved	Precision	Recall	Time Taken in query (in min.)
Q1	25	11	21	9	0.429	0.818	0.42
Q2	18	9	11	7	0.636	0.778	0.33
Q3	43	6	43	5	0.116	0.833	1.27
Q4	17	8	9	5	0.556	0.625	0.31
Q5	32	10	35	4	0.114	0.400	1.07

Table 3. Precision and recall of shape context method with 100 samples (on same shapes as in Table 1 in choronology)

No. of query	Total no. of relevant shapes in the dataset	No. of shapes retrieved	No. of relevant shapes retrieved	Precision	Recall	Time Taken in query (in min.)
Q1	11	60	10	0.167	0.91	12.22
Q2	9	57	9	0.158	1.00	11.13
Q3	6	62	6	0.097	1.00	12.04
Q4	8	50	8	0.160	1.00	12.32
Q5	10	71	10	0.140	1.00	13.39

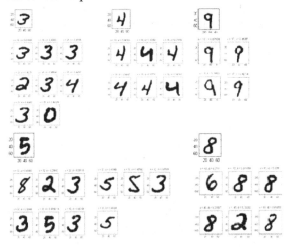

Figure 3. Query shapes and their corresponding retrieved shapes in Table 1

tends to be stricter on similarity of shapes. The shape context method of Belongie et al. (2002) has a higher recall rate but the precision drops down considerably as more number of irrelevant shapes are retrieved. Since the algorithm is iterative it takes more time if it is presented with more number of sample points.

Table 3 shows the significant drop of the precision of the standard shape context method.

The recall rate, however, is very high in this case almost all calculating up to one. The runtime is very high for the same query to retrieve the similar shapes. Runtime difference between standard shape context method (with 100 numbers of sample points) and the landmark-based shape context method (which takes the number of samples on the fly) is significant. While landmark-based shape context has its runtime in the order of 1 to 2 minutes the standard shape context method with 100 sample points takes more than 10 minutes to retrieve similar shapes.

The landmark-based shape context algorithm spends time in computing the landmark. Once the landmarks are computed, matching becomes faster on the reduced number of sample points. The landmark nature of the sample points plays an important role in the matching behaviour of the algorithm. It tends to be stricter on the similarity of the shapes. And it retrieve more of the relevant shapes i.e., the precision is higher. The recognition time is more or less uniform in the test condition but may vary as the number of samples varies according to the shape.

CONCLUSION

In this paper, an approach to recognizing hand written digits based on strict constraints on shape similarity has been presented. The algorithm uses landmark-based shape context i.e., shape context computed not through a random selection of sample points, but sampled points based on the contour feature of corners.

Standard shape context computation samples at regular interval on the contour of an object, where as here a reduced set is used. Shape context based object recognition being an iterative process; the reduction in the number of sample points provides a basis for faster recognition. Our approach is simple and easy to apply and provides a shape descriptor that greatly improves recognition; at the same time leading to appre-

ciable saving in time. This is without any loss of precision compared to shape matching using standard shape context computation with same number of sample points; based on arch height for landmark computation.

However, recall while using landmark based shape context is lower, where as recall for standard shape context with 100 sample points almost approaches one. Possibly, the use of a single contour feature for sampling points for landmark-based shape context computation may not suffice. Use of additional qualitative shape primitives and curvature extremas for sampling of points could improve recall (without loss of precision). This requires further investigation and is part of ongoing research. The two methods – standard shape context and landmark based shape context based matching were compared in recognizing hand written digits. The arch height for computation of corners is well suited for shapes of normal objects (cross-section area is of the same order as the other significant dimensions). Therefore, sampling in case of such objects would be far better than for the slender hand written digits. As such the approach presented here could be better suited for recognition of shapes of normal objects. This requires further investigation.

REFERENCES

Aradhya, V. N. M., Kumar, G. H., & Noushath, S. (2007). Robust Unconstrained Handwritten Digit Recognition using Radon Transform. In *Proceedings of IEEE-ICSCN 2007* (pp. 626-629).

Belongie, S., Malik, J., & Puzicha, J. (2002). Shape Matching and Object Recognition Using Shape Contexts. *IEEE Transactions on Pattern Analysis and Machine Intelligence, 24*(24), 509-522.

DeCoste, D., & Schölkopf, B. (2002). Training invariant support vector machines. *Machine Learning, 46*, 161–190.

Duda, R. O., & Hart, P. E. (1973) *Pattern Recognition and Scene Analysis*. New York: Wiley.

Freeman, H., & Davis, L. S. (1997). A corner finding algorithm for chain code curve. *IEEE Transactions on Computing, 26,* 297-303.

Garg, N. K., & Jindal, S. (2007). An Efficient Feature Set for Handwritten Digit Recognition. In *Proceedings of 15th International Conference on Advanced Computing and Communications* (pp. 540-544).

Gorgevik, D. (2004). *Classifier Combining for Handwritten Digit Recognition*. Ph.D. dissertation, Faculty of Electrical Engineering, Skopje, Macedonia.

Hansmann, U., Merk, L., Nicklous, M. S., & Stober, T. (2001). *Pervasive Computing 2nd Edition*. Berlin: Springer-Verlag.

Hu, Y., Zhu, F., Lv, H., & Zhang, X. (2006). Handwritten digit recognition using low rank approximation based competitive neural network. *Lecture Notes in Computer Science 3972,* 287-292.

Jain, A. K., Duin, R. P. W., & Mao, J. (2000). Statistical Pattern Recognition: A Review, *IEEE. Trans. Pattern Recognition and Machine Intelligence, 22*(1), 4-36.

Jiang, W., Sun, Z., Yuan, B., Zheng, W., & Xu, W. (2006). User-Independent Online Handwritten Digit Recognition. In *Proceedings of the Fifth International Conference on Machine Learning and Cybernetics* (pp. 3359-3364).

Lauer, F., Suen, C. Y., & Bloch, G. (2007). A trainable feature extractor for handwritten digit recognition. *Pattern Recognition 40*(6), 1816-1824.

LeCun, Y., Jackel, L. D., Bottou, L., Brunot, A., Cortes, C., Denker, J. S. et al. (1995). Comparison of learning algorithms for handwritten digit recognition. In *Proceedings of International Conference on Artificial Neural Networks* (pp. 53-60).

Lin, Y., Dou, J., & Wang, H. (1992) Contour Shape Description Based on an Arch Height Function, *Pattern Recognition, 25*(1), 17 - 23.

Liu, L., Nakashima, K., Sako, H., & Fujisawa, H. (2003). Handwritten digit recognition: benchmarking of state-of-the-art techniques. *Pattern Recognition, 36*(10), 2271-2285.

Meathreal, R., & Galton, A. (2000). Qualitative Representation of Planar Outline. In *Proceeding of 14th European Conference on AI* (pp. 224-228).

Pachter, L., & Sturmfels, B. (2005). *Algebraic Statistics for Computational Biology*, Cambridge University Press.

Plamondon, R., & Srihari, S. (2000). On-line and off-line handwriting recognition: A comprehensive survey. *IEEE Transactions on Pattern Analysis and Machine Intelligence, 22*(1), 63-84.

Rao, K. K., & Krishnan, R. (1994). Shape Feature Extraction from Object Corners, Image Analysis and Interpretation. In *Proceedings of the IEEE Southwest Symposium* (pp. 160–165).

Sadri, J., Suen, C. Y., & Tien, D. B. (2007). A genetic framework using contextual knowledge for segmentation and recognition of handwritten numeral strings. *Pattern Recognition 40*(3), 898-919.

Suen, C. Y., & Tan, J. (2005). Analysis of errors of handwritten digits made by a multitude of classifiers. *Pattern Recognition Letters 26,* 369-379.

Trier, O., Jain, A. K., & Taxt, T. (1996) Feature extraction methods for character recognition - A survey, *Pattern Recognition, 29*(4), 641-662.

Veltkamp, R., & Tanase, M. (2000). *Content-Based Image Retrieval Systems: A Survey*. Technical Report UU-CS-2000-34, Dept of Information and Computing Sciences, Utrecht University.

Xiu-fang, W., Tian, T., & Xue-song, S. (2007). Handwritten Digit Recognition Based on Nonlinear Potential Function Arithmetic. In *Proceedings of Second IEEE Conference on Industrial Electronics and Applications* (pp. 2831-2833).

Wierer, J., & Boston, N. (2007a). A Handwritten Digit Recognition Algorithm Using Two-Dimensional Hidden Markov Models for Feature Extraction. In *Proceedings of 2007 International Conference on Acoustics, Speech and Signal Processing.*

Yusuf, M., & Haider, T. (2004). Recognition of Handwritten Urdu Digits using Shape Context. In *Proceedings of INMIC 2004* (pp. 569-572).

KEY TERMS

Bending Energy: Is a measure of transformation necessary to closely align the stored digits with the test digit. It is, conceptually, the amount of work that is needed to transform an instance of a shape to another.

Feature-Based Shape Matching: Shape matching can be either feature-based or brightness-based. Brightness based methods make use of pixel brightness. Feature-based shape matching involves the use of spatial arrangements of extracted features.

Handwritten Digit Recognition: Is an area of pattern recognition involved in the recognition of handwritten numerals. Handwritten digit recognition is important for automating bank cheque processing, postal mail sorting and many other applications where numeral recognition is necessary.

Landmark-Based Shape Context: Standard shape context computation samples at regular in-terval on the contour of an object. Corner points of an object being landmarks on the contour; set of corner points is a good descriptor of shape. Landmark-based shape context is computed by sampling a reduced set of points based on such landmarks.

Offline Recognition: Offline recognition, process and recognize the user input handwritten digit based on images (the scanned images of handwritten digit).

Precision: For content-based image retrieval precision is defined as the ratio of number of relevant shapes retrieved to the total number of shapes retrieved.

Recall: For content-based image retrieval recall is defined as the ratio of number of relevant shapes retrieved to the total number of relevant shapes in the database.

Shape Context: Is one of the most striking feature-based object descriptor. The shape context is a descriptor to describe the coarse distribution of the rest of the shape with respect to a given point on the shape.

ENDNOTE

[1] This is basically a square assignment (or weighted bipartite graph matching) problem which can be solved by Hungarian method (Yusuf & Haider, 2004). The input to the assignment problem is a square cost matrix with entries C_{ij}. The result is a permutation, such as $H(\pi)$ is minimized.

Chapter IV
Enhanced Information Retrieval Evaluation between Pseudo Relevance Feedback and Query Similarity Relevant Documents Methodology Applied on Arabic Text

Sameh Ghwanmeh
Yarmouk University, Jordan

Ghassan Kanaan
The Arab Academy for Banking and Financial Sciences, Jordan

Riyad Al-Shalabi
The Arab Academy for Banking and Financial Sciences, Jordan

ABSTRACT

Information retrieval systems utilize user feedback for generating optimal queries with respect to a particular information need. However, the methods that have been developed in IR for generating these queries do not memorize information gathered from previous search processes, and hence cannot use such information in new search processes. Thus, a new search process cannot profit from the results of the previous processes. Web Information Retrieval systems should be able to maintain results from previous search processes, thus learning from previous queries and improving overall retrieval quality. In this chapter, we are using the similarity of a new query to previously learned queries. We then expand the new query by extracting terms from documents, which have been judged as relevant to these previously learned queries. Thus, the new method uses global feedback information for query expansion in contrast to local feedback information, which has been widely used in previous work in query expansion methods. Experimentally, we compared a new query expansion method with two conventional information retrieval methods in local and global query expansion to enhance the traditional information system. From the results gathered it can be concluded that although the traditional IR system performance is high, but we notice that PRF method increases the average recall and decreases the fallout measure.

INTRODUCTION

Information retrieval (IR) systems utilize user feedback for generating optimal queries with respect to a particular information need. In this research, we are using the similarity of a new query to previously learned queries, and then we expand the new query by extracting terms from documents, which have been classified as relevant to these previously learned queries. In addition, we explore to use two techniques to improve traditional IR system by expand the query terms using QSD technique as global query expansion and PRF as local query expansion. Query expansion is a well-known technique that has been shown to improve average retrieval performance. This technique has not been used in many operational systems because of the fact that it can greatly degrade the performance of some individual queries (Kise, Junker, Dengel & Matsumoto, 2001). Thus, the suggested method uses global feedback information for query expansion in contrast to local feedback information.

Global relevance feedback is learned from previous queries but Local relevance feedback is produced during execution of an individual query. If documents are relevant to a query, which has been issued previously by a user, then the same documents are relevant to the same query at later time, when that query is re-issued by the same or by a different user; this is the trivial case where similarity between two different queries is the highest. In the non-trivial case, a new query is similar to previously issued query only to a certain degree. Then our assumption is those documents, which are relevant to the previously

issued query, will be relevant to the new query only to a certain degree (Hust, Klink, Junker & Dengel, 2004).

Word mismatch is a common problem in information retrieval. Most retrieval systems match documents and queries on a syntactic level, the underlying assumption is that relevant documents contain exactly those terms that a user chooses for the query. However, a relevant document might not contain the query words as given by the user. Query expansion (QE) is intended to address this issue. Other topical terms are located in the corpus or an external resource and are appended to the original query, in the hope of fending documents that do not contain any of the query terms or of re-ranking documents that contain some query terms but have not scored highly (Kise, Junker, Dengel & Matsumoto, 2001).

A disadvantage of QE is the inherent inefficiency of reformulating a query. With the exception of our earlier work, these inefficiencies have largely not been investigated. In this chapter we have proposed improvements to the efficiency of QE by keeping a brief summary of each document in the collection in memory, so that during the expansion process no time-consuming disk accesses need to be made. However, expanding queries using the best of these methods still takes significantly longer than evaluating queries without expansion. When users try to search some information via internet, many of the information retrieved are not useful for the user, which might be because the poor queries that user entered or because the structure of IR system itself that used on this search site. So we try to update query itself by adding some key terms that considered to be relevance to the query; this is what called local QE or increase the number of relevant document that retrieved depend on the history same query on the system and other relevant query this what is called global QE.

LITERATURE REVIEW

Query expansion is a well-known technique that has been shown to improve average retrieval performance. This technique has not been used in many operational systems because of the fact that it can greatly degrade the performance of some individual queries. It has been shown that the comparison between language models of the unexpanded and expanded retrieval results can be used to predict when the expanded retrieval has strayed from the original sense of the query (Townsend, Zhou & Croft, 2004). In these cases, the unexpanded results are used while the expanded results are used in the remaining cases, where such straying is not detected.

Gathering information for fulfilling the information need of a user is an expensive operation in terms of time required and resources used. Queries may have to be reformulated manually by the user or automatically by the IR system several times until the user is satisfied. The same expensive operation has to be carried out, if another user has the same information need and thus initiates the same or a similar search process. How users can improve the original query formulation by means of automatic relevance feedback is an ongoing research activity in IR (Manning & Schutze, 1999).

In retrieving medical free text (Liu & Chu, 2004), users are often interested in answers pertinent to certain scenarios that correspond to common tasks performed in medical practice, e.g., treatment or diagnosis of a disease. A major challenge in handling such queries is that scenario terms in the query (e.g. treatment) are often too general to match specialized terms in relevant documents (e.g. chemotherapy). In this chapter, it employs a knowledge-based query expansion method that exploits the UMLS knowledge source to append the original query with additional terms that are specifically relevant to the query's scenarios. They compared the proposed method with traditional statistical expansion that expands terms, which are statistically correlated, but not necessarily scenario specific. The study on two standard test beds shows that the knowledge-based method, by providing scenario-specific expansion, yields notable improvements over the statistical method in terms of average precision-recall. On the OHSUMED test bed, for example in (Hust, Klink 7 Junker, 2005), the improvement is more than 5% averaging over all scenario-specific queries studied and about 10% for queries that mention certain scenarios, such as treatment of a disease and differential diagnosis of a symptom.

In content-based retrieval (Tesic & Manjunath, 2005), to retrieve images that are similar in texture or color, usually one computes the nearest neighbors of the query feature vector in the corresponding feature space. Given a collection of image or video data, the first step in creating a database is to compute relevant feature descriptors to represent the content. While the low-level features are quite effective in similarity retrieval, they do not capture well the high-level semantics. In this context, relevance feedback was introduced to facilitate interactive learning for refining the retrieval results (Qiu & Frei, 1993). User identifies a set of retrieval examples relevant to the image, and that information is then used to compute a new set of retrievals.

The motivation for the suggested query expansion method is straightforward, especially in an environment where document collections are static (Haav &, Lubi, 2007):

1. If documents are relevant to a query, which has been issued previously by a user, then the same documents are relevant to the same query later, when that query is re-issued by

the same or by a different user. This is the trivial case, where similarities between the two different queries are the highest.

2. In the non-trivial case, a new query is similar to a previously issued query only to a certain degree. Then the assumption is that documents, which are relevant to the previously issued query, will be relevant to the new query only to a certain degree.

The proposed system deals with these two kinds of query expansion, but query expansion has many topics, that any programmer can apply with to enhance any IR system (Tesic & Manjunath, 2005). There are some ways to refinement IR systems by Relevance feedback (Salton, 1989). In the vector model, a query is a vector of term weights; hence, reformulation involves *reassigning term weights*:

- If a document is known to be relevant, the query can be improved by *increasing* its similarity to that document.
- If a document is known to be non-relevant, the query can be improved by *decreasing* its similarity to that document, so
- What if the query has to increase its similarity to two very non-similar documents, (each "pulls" the query in an entirely different direction)?
- What if the query has to be decreasing its similarity to two very non-similar documents (each "pushes" the query in an entirely different direction)?

Critical assumptions that must be made:

- Relevant documents resemble each other (are clustered).
- Non-relevant documents resemble each other (are clustered).
- Non-relevant documents differ from the relevant documents.

QUERY EXPANSION BY TERM CLUSTERING

Expand the query with terms that are *similar* to the terms mentioned in the query. For each term, create a *cluster* of similar terms; then the relevance feedback method *shifts* the query, some terms are emphasized, others de-emphasized, consequently, new documents are discovered and some old documents are abandoned. Then by using the word-clustering method the query will expanded by adding terms, as a result new documents are discovered (but none discarded); recall increases and precision decreases.

Query-specific clusters

- Clusters are inferred from the set of documents retrieved for the present query.
- Clusters must be constructed for each query.

Global clusters

- Clusters are inferred from the entire document collection.
- Clusters are constructed once (but are specific for that document collection).
- The output of global clustering is often called *statistical thesaurus*.

Semantic thesaurus

- Clusters contain terms that are similar in *meaning*.
- Produced by linguists.
- Thesaurus is independent from particular document collections.

RESEARCH METHODOLOGY

Query expansion has been widely investigated as a method for improving the performance of IR. It is the only effective automatic method for solving the problem of vocabulary mismatch. Queries are often not well formulated, but may be ambiguous, insufficiently precise, or use terminology that is specific to country. QE—also known as pseudo-relevance feedback or automatic query expansion—is based on the observation that the top-ranked documents have a reasonable probability of being relevant. It can heuristically be assumed that the first 10 matches to a query are relevant; terms from these documents can be used to form a new query. Another QE called QSD which used to improve this system by find the relevance query to the main query from the history of the system, then recalculates the relevance document depend on all queries (Montori, Wilczynski, Morgan & Havnes, 2003). The data collection contains 242 Arabic documents from the proceedings of the Saudi Arabian National Conferences, with a different data domain. The 242 Arabic documents have been indexed using database indexing, which increases the performance in retrieving and reduces the time delay.

Traditional IR System Model

The task of document retrieval is to retrieve documents relevant to a given query from a fixed set of documents. Documents as well as queries are represented in a common way using a set of index terms.

The Vector Space Model

The basic retrieval model is the vector space model (VSM) (Yates & Neto, 1999). In this model, vectors represent documents as well as queries. The relevance of a document with respect to a query is mapped to a similarity function between the query vector and all document vectors. More formally, documents as well as queries are represented by vectors ($w1$; $w2$....; wn). Each position i in the vectors corresponds to a specific term wi in the collection. Each position i in the vectors

corresponds to a specific term wi in the collection. The value wi indicates the weighted presence or absence of the respective term in the document or query. For weighting, we rely on a variant of the standard tf-idf weighting schema. In this weighting schema, a word is weighted higher in a document/query if it occurs more often in the document/query. It is also weighted higher if the word is rare in the document collection. The similarity sim between a given query q and a document d is computed by:

$$sim\ (d;\ q) = d * q/(\|d\|*\|q\|)$$

where $k \notin k$ is the Euclidean norm of a vector. For retrieving all documents to a given query, all documents D of the underlying collection are ranked according to their similarity to the query and the top-ranked documents are given to the user. This is the one of the simplest but most popular models used in IR (VSM). Documents and queries are represented as M dimensional vectors, where different term weighting schemes may be used.

The result of the execution of a query is a list of documents ranked according to their similarity to the given query. The similarity $sim(dj\ ;\ q)$ between a document dj and a query q is measured by the cosine of the angle between these two M dimensional vectors.

$$\text{Cosine} = \frac{\sum_{k=1}^{t}(d_{ik} \bullet q_k)}{\sqrt{\sum_{k=1}^{t} d_{ik}^{2} \bullet \sum_{k=1}^{t} q_k^{2}}}$$

Several methods, called query expansion methods, have been proposed to cope with the problem that short queries rank only a limited number of documents according to their similarity (Qiu & Frei, 1993). These methods fall into three categories: usage of feedback information from the user, usage of information derived locally from the set of initially retrieved documents, and usage of information derived globally from the document collection.

Pseudo Relevance Feedback Model

Pseudo Relevance Feedback (PRF) is a well-known technique in the VSM. It can improve the effectiveness of the original VSM approach we use it in two different ways. for experimental comparisons; We combine it with our query expansion approaches QSD, to new hybrid approaches. PRF Works in three stages:

1. Documents are ranked according to their similarity to the original query.
2. Then, highly ranked documents are assumed to be relevant and their terms are used for expanding the original query.
3. Then, documents are ranked again according to the similarity to the expanded query (Montori, Morgan & Haynes, 2003).

In this chapter we have employed a simple variant of PRF. Let Dq* be the set of document vectors given by:

Dq* = {d €D| sim (d, q*)/ max d'€ D {sim (d',q*)} >= Φ}

Where q* is the original query, Φ is the similarity threshold. The expanded query vector q*exp is obtained by:

q*exp = q* + α P/‖P‖, with P = ∑d € Dq* (d)

Query Similarity and Relevant Documents Model

The simple QSD approach" Query Similarity and relevant Documents" selects those former queries, which are most similar to the new one. Averaged document vectors represent the relevant documents to each of these queries. The formal description is given here. The similarity $sim(q*;q)$ between the new query $q*$ and a query q is measured by the cosine of the angle between these two M dimensional vectors.

Query Expansion Model

1. Compute the similarities between the new query and each of the existing old queries.
2. Select the old queries having a similarity to the new query which is greater than or equal to a given threshold.
3. From these selected old queries get the sets of relevant documents from the ground truth data.
4. From each set of relevant documents compute a new document vector.
5. Use these document vectors and a weighting scheme to enrich the new query.

The similarity $sim(q_k; q)$ between a query q_k and a new query q is measured by the cosine of the angle between these two M dimensional vectors (Hust, Klink, Junker & Dengel, 2004):

$sim(q_k; q) = q_k{}^T * q$

where T indicates the transpose of the vector q_k;

Let S be the set

$S = \{qk|sim(q_k, q) >= α, 1 <= k <= · L\}$

Of existing old queries q_k having a similarity greater than or equal to a threshold $α$ to the new query q and let T_k be the sets of all documents dj relevant to the queries q_k in S.

Then the sums:

$r_k = \sum_{dj∈Tk} D_j$

Of the document, vectors in each T_k are used as expansion terms for the original query.

The expanded query vector q'` is then obtained by:

q'` = q+ ∑ $λ_k$ * r_k/‖r_k‖

Note that:

1. If δ is high then **S** maybe empty then **Tk** will be empty and the documents vectors **rk** will be $(0,.....,0)T$, this mean the new query will not be expanded.
2. Even if query **qk** is in the set **S** , the corresponding set **Tk** maybe empty, then the corresponding document vector **rk** will be $(0,.....,0)T$.

EXPERIMENTAL RESULTS EVALUATION

We use standard document test collections and standard queries. By utilizing these collections, we take advantage of the ground truth data for performance evaluation. On the other hand, we do not expect to have queries having highly correlated similarities, as we would expect in a real world application. So it is a challenging task to show performance improvements for our method. Results were evaluated using the average precision over all queries. Significance tests were applied to the results.

The Methods VSM, PRF and QSD were applied. Parameters for PRF and QSD are chosen such that average recall and precision is highest, by using 10 queries as a testing set from our collection. In a system designed for providing information retrieval, other metrics, besides time and space are also of interest, like recall and precision. Since the user query request is vague, the retrieved documents are not exact answers and have to be ranked according to their relevance to the query Such relevance ranking concept is not present in data retrieval systems. The IR systems require the evaluation of how precise is the answer set. So effectiveness is a measure of the ability of the system to retrieve relevant documents while at the same time holding back non-relevant one, it can be measured by recall and precision.

Recall Measurement

Recall is the fraction of the relevant documents, which has been retrieved.

Recall = number of relevant doc retrieved / total number of relevant documents.

Precision Measurement

Precision is the fraction of the retrieved documents, which is relevant.

Precision = number of relevant doc retrieved / total numbers of doc retrieved

Fallout Measurement

Fraction of the retrieved documents, which is non-relevant.

Fallout = number of non-relevant doc retrieved / total numbers of document in collection

The recall measurement indicates how many relevant documents are retrieved from the main database and the precision measurement indicates how many documents are actually relevant from the retrieved ones. Additionally, we can calculate the fallout measure, which indicates how many are non-relevant from document retrieved.

To evaluate the system, we entered the queries in the testing set and record the recall and the precision. Then we enhance the result by using QSD and PRF methods. The testing results of each query using traditional and PRF methods under different threshold are shown in Table 1.

It can be seen from Table 1 that the results with the traditional IR is satisfactory, which indicates that the enhancement made not clear in most queries However, it can be noted that the recall measurement is enhanced when the user use PRF method. The interpolation of each method are shown in Figure 1, Figure 2 and Figure 3. Table

Table 1. Average recall and precision

	Traditional		PRF1		PRF2	
Threshold	0.4	0.4	1.7,0.35	1.7,0.35	0.6,0.75	0.6,0.75
Query-nu	Recall	Precision	Recall	Precision	Recall	Precision
1	0.6666	0.3686	0.6666	0.3686	0.666633	0.3686
2	0.4285	0.5042	0.4297	0.1637	0.42852	0.50422
3	0.4999	0.6944	0.4999	0.668	0.49995	0.668033
4	0.3	0.625	0.6	0.1752	0.6	0.1771
5	0.5311	0.2929	0.5311	0.2929	0.566294	0.292931
6	0.3105	0.1722	0.4061	0.0925	0.40625	0.09217
7	0.53	0.769	0.53	0.767	0.566406	0.07678
8	0.4531	0.2995	0.4531	0.2995	0.40625	0.3525
9	0.357	0.1556	0.5012	0.1251	0.4974	0,12502
10	0.4	0.7882	0.4	0.7882	0.43	0.7882

Figure 1. Average recall / precision interpolation for traditional IR

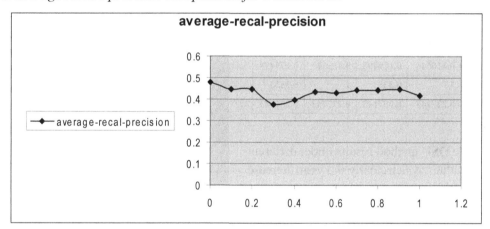

Figure 2. Average recall / precision interpolation for PRF

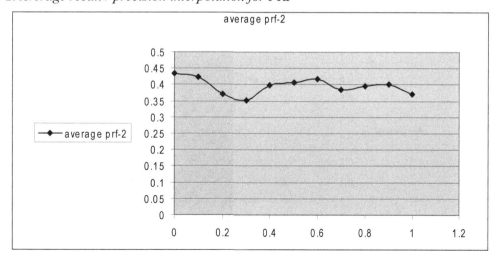

Figure 3. Average recall / precision interpolation for QSD

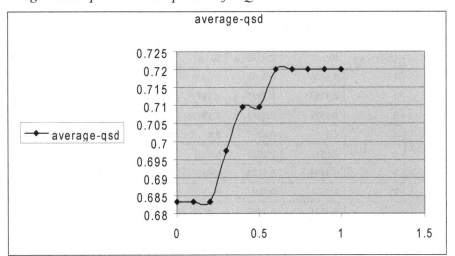

Table 2. Average recall and precision

threshold	0.4		0.5	
Q	R	P	R	P
1	0.666633	1	0.666633	1
2	0.4545	1	0.4545	1
3	0.41664	0.179498	0.41664	0.179498
4	1	0.3333	1	0.3333
5	0.227743	0.257143	0.227743	0.257143

2 shows the QSD method results under different threshold values, which clearly shows an increase in the precision measurement.

Additionally, the fallout measurement has been conducted. It can be seen (Figure 4, Figure 5 and Figure 6) that the fallout decreases in traditional / expansion methods specially in QSD method, which indicates a satisfactory result for this system and increases the effectiveness.

CONCLUSION

We have experimentally compared a new query expansion method with two conventional information retrieval methods in local and global query

Figure 4. Fallout measurement traditional IR

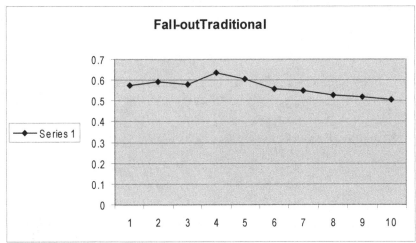

Figure 5. Fallout measurement using PRF

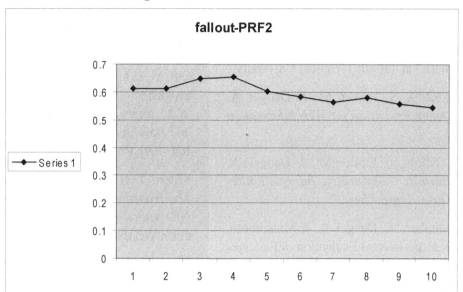

Figure 6. Fallout measure using QSD

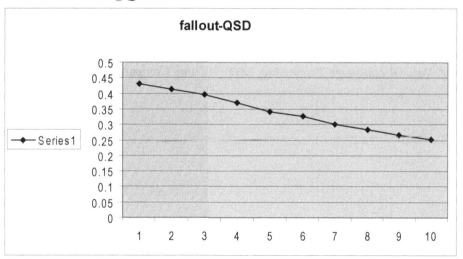

expansion to enhance the traditional IR system. From the results gathered we can conclude that although the traditional IR system performance is high, but we have noticed that the PRF method increases the average recall on the other hand and decreases the fallout measure. But it is clearly noticed that the best result was on using QSD method which increases the average recall / precision and decreases the fallout measure. The reason behind this is that the QSD depend on the history of the queries in the system, so when this history increased by the user, QSD will return more accurate relevant documents. The new method uses global feedback information for query expansion in contrast to local feedback information, which has been widely used in previous work in query expansion methods.

REFERENCES

Haav, H., &, Lubi, T. (2007). A Survey of Concept-based Information Retrieval Tools, Institute of Cybernetics at Tallinn Technical University.

Hust, A., Klink, S., Junker, M., & Dengel, A. (2004). *Query Expansion for Web Information Retrieval*.

Hust, A., Klink, S., Junker, M., & Dengel, A. (2005). *Towards Collaborative InformationRetrieval: Three Approaches*.

Kise, K., Junker, M., Dengel, A., & Matsumoto, K. (2001). Experimental Evaluation of Passage-Based Document Retrieval. In *Proceedings of the Sixth International Conference on Document Analysis and Recognition (ICDAR'01)*.

Liu, Z., & Chu, W. (2004). *Knowledge-Based Query Expansion to Support Scenario-Specific Retrieval of Medical Free Text*.

Manning, C. D., & Sch¨utze, H. (1999). *Foundations of Natural Language Processing*. MIT Press.

Montori, V., Wilczynski, N., Morgan, D., & Haynes, R. (2003). Systematic reviews: *A cross-sectional study of location and citation counts. BMC Medicine, 1*(2).

Qiu, Y., & Frei, H. (1993). Concept-based query expansion. In *Proceedings of SIGIR-93, 16th ACM International Conference on Research and Development in Information Retrieval*, (pp. 160–169), Pittsburgh, US.

Salton, J. (1989). *Automatic Text Processing: The Transformation: Analysis and Retrieval of Information by Computer*. Reading, Mass: Addison-Wesley.

Townsend, S., Zhou, Y., & Croft, B. (2004). *A Framework for Selective Query Expansion*. Whose the editors.

Te˘si´c, J., & Manjunath, B. (2005). *Nearest Neighbor Search for Relevance Feedback*.

Yates, R., & Ribeiro-Neto, B. (1999). *Modern Information Retrieval*. Addison-Wesley Publishing Company.

Chapter V
New Technique to Detect CNP Fraudulent Transactions

Adnan M. Al-Khatib
Yarmouk University, Jordan

Ezz Hattab
The Arab Academy for Banking and Financial Sciences, Jordan

ABSTRACT

Money in the e-commerce network, represents information moving at the speed of light, where fraud (digital crime) within the banking and financial services happened very fast and can cost billions of dollars each year-undetected and unreported. In this chapter we present a comprehensive framework that mines and detect fraudulent transactions of Card-Not-Present (CNP) in the e-payment systems with a high degree of accuracy.

INTRODUCTION

Fraud can be described as "a dishonest actions to make false statements in order to gain money or benefit from an individual or from an organization". Electronic systems have increased the opportunity for fraud by providing easy and fast access to the organizations networks. Fraud on the Internet includes several types such as theft of funds through illegal transfers, theft of credit card details, illegal credit card use, and others (Commonwealth of Australia Report, 2000).

Fraud detection is a process that can use data mining techniques to detect fraudulent transaction. In this paper, we propose a comprehensive framework that mines fraudulent transactions of Card-Not-Present (CNP) in the e-payment systems with high degree of accuracy. Our research used the user account profiling techniques to discover fraudulent transactions in CNP payment systems. To detect fraud using profiling technique, it is necessary to determine the normal behavior of each user account with respect to certain indicators, and to determine when that behavior has deviated significantly.

This paper presents an overview of the proposed framework in section 1. Section 2 gives an overview of fraudulent activities in financial area. Section 3 describes our methodology of the system. Section 4 presents and evaluates the results. Section 5 gives an overview of related works. Section 6 discusses the method and compares it with other techniques. Section 7 concludes the research.

FINANCIAL CRIMES

Financial Crimes consists several types of fraud such as: Credit-Card Fraud, Card-Not-Present (Internet credit-card) Fraud, Loan Default, and Bank Fraud (Jesus, 2003). *Credit-Card Fraud* can be a result of a stolen card with the PIN number, or as a result of the theft of an individual's identification (Social security number and home address) in order to create a new account under false or stolen identities. Credit-card theft will defraud the card issuer or merchant. *Card-Not-Present Fraud* like Internet and phone-order sales transactions. They are also time-sensitive crimes. In this type of fraud, thieves leave characteristic footprints. For example, fraud rates increase at certain time of the day, and order coming from certain countries exhibit a higher percentage of fraud. *Loan Default fraud* involves the manipulation and inflation of an individual credit rating prior to performing a "sting", leading to a loan default and a loss for the financial service provider. *Bank Fraud* involves the creation of fictitious bank account for the conduit of money and the siphoning of other legitimate accounts.

The critical factors for detecting all of these financial fraud crimes is to know the behavior of credit, bank accounts, and loan accounts and developing an understanding of the categories of customers. Data mining can be used to spot outliers or account usage that are normal and out of character.

RESEARCH METHODOLOGY

Problem Statement

Our research purpose is *"to present a high accuracy method or prototype to detect Card-Not-Present (CNP) Fraudulent transactions in the e-payment systems by integrating data from multiple databases (e.g., bank transactions, federal/state crime history DBs); and then using suitable and effective data mining and artificial intelligence (AI) tools to find unusual access sequences".* Accuracy means high detection rate (percentage of fraudulent transactions that are detected) and low false positive rate (percentage of normal transactions that is falsely determines to be fraudulent) (Andreas, 2000; Salvatore, 1997).

Researchers have developed two general categories of detection techniques; misuse and anomaly detections. In misuse detection, well-known fraudulent transactions are encoded into patterns, which are then used to match new transactions to identify the fraudulent ones. In anomaly detection, normal behavior of user are first summarized into normal profiles, and then used as yardsticks, so that run-time activities that result in significant deviation from the user profiles are considered as probable fraudulent transactions. In our research we are going to use the user account profiling techniques to discover fraudulent transactions in CNP payment systems. To use this technique three issues arise (Fawcett, 1997):

1. Which transaction features are important? Which features or combinations of features are useful for distinguishing legitimate behavior from fraudulent behavior?
2. How should profiles be created? Given an important feature identified in step 1, how should we characterize the behavior of a subscriber with respect to the feature?

3. When should alarms be issued? Given a set of profiling criteria identified in step 2, how should we combine them to determine when fraud has occurred?

System Framework

Based on (Fawcett, 1997) we created our system framework (*Figure 3.1*). The system consists of a warehouse, profiling module, software programs, a profiler monitor construction module, a storage component and a data mining classifiers modules such as artificial neural network (ANN), Find laws and others.

The warehouse contains transactional and historical data. Technical analysis (TA) tools (e.g., Link analysis, decision tree, etc) will analyze this data to generate the fraudulent rules as IF/THEN rules. The software programs will be used to normalize, manipulate and store the rules that are generated and selected by the analysis tools and a machine learning selection program. The

profiler monitor construction module generates a set of profilers from the discovered fraud rules and a set of profiling templates instantiated by the fraud rule conditions. In the storage component, data for different purposes will be stored such as the user profiles, training and testing data for training the detector module and so on. The training data is provided as input to the detector module, where a classifier is trained to classify the different observations of patterns into good or bad occurrences. Profiling module will be used to build user profiles according to the fraud rules conditions that selected and the set of templates provided. Each user will have a profile represent the normal profiling behaviors for that user account such as: cardholder shopping habits, frequency of purchases, average purchases, location of purchases, and other transactional factors. In the detector use step these profiles are used to match new transaction with the user profile, decide if there is a significant deviation of the transaction from the user profile, and give a numeric values

Figure 3.1. System framework

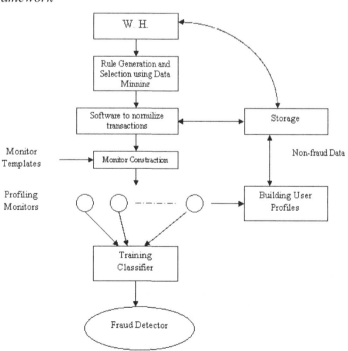

representing the fraudulent activity for each fraudulent indicator. All these numeric values then passed to the detector as input parameters, where the detector combines these evidence factors to produce an output recommendation about the new transaction.

Detector Construction

Detector construction process consists three stages: The first stage is the data mining analysis, involves combing through the transactional data searching for indicators of fraud with certainty factors above a user threshold. The transactional data are organized by account, and each transactional record is labeled as fraudulent or legitimate. When the rule learning (RL) program is applied to an account's transactions it produces a set of rules that serve to distinguish, within that account, the fraudulent transactions from the legitimate transactions. As an example, the following rule would be a relatively good indicator of fraud:

(TIME-OF-DAY = NIGHT) AND (LOCATION = far location from customer zip-code) ==➡ FRAUD, with Certainty factor = 0.85

This rule denotes that a transaction placed at night from a far location from the customer home address is likely to be fraudulent. The certainty factor = 0.85 means that, for this account, a transaction matching this rule has an 85% probability of being fraudulent.

Figure 3.2. First stage, rule generation and selection

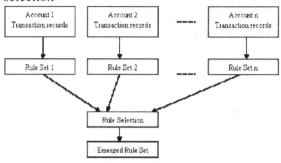

Each account generates a set of rules. After all accounts have been processed, a rule selection step is performed to derive a general covering set of rules that will serve as fraud indicators, *Figure 3.2.*

In the second stage, the profiler constructor is given a set of rules and a set of templates, *Figure 3.4*, and generates a profiler from each rule-template pair. Every profiler has a training step, *Figure 3.3*, in which it is trained on typical (non-fraud) account activity; and a Use step, *Figure 3.4*, in which it describes how far from the typical behavior a current account transaction is.

The third stage of detector construction learns how to combine evidence from the set of profilers generated by the previous stage. In training, the profilers' outputs are presented along with the desired output to the classifier. The evidence combination learns which combinations of profiler outputs indicate fraud with high confidence. A feature selection process is used to reduce the

Figure 3.3. Profiling step

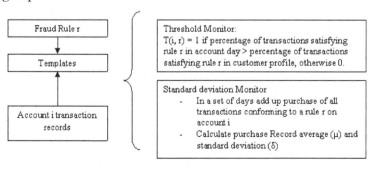

Figure 3.4. Use step

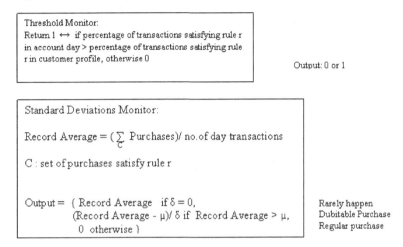

number of profilers in the final detector. This simplifies the final detector and increases its accuracy and performance. The final output of the constructor is a detector that profiles each user's behavior based on several indicators, and produces an alarm if there is sufficient evidence of fraudulent activity.

New transactions are matched first with customer profiles, checking for deviation from normal behavior, and assign numeric values for the profilers monitors. These profilers monitors output then used as input for the detector, which are combined and the detector produce an alarm if there is sufficient evidence of fraudulent activity. *Figure 3.5* is an example of evaluating a new transaction.

Figure 3.5. Detector usage

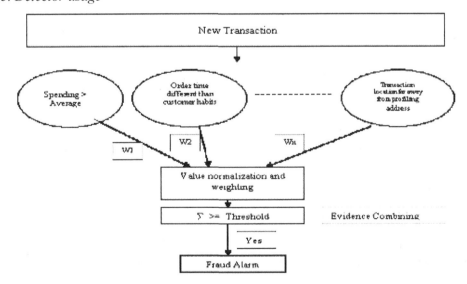

EXPERIMENT AND EVALUATION

Data

Data for our study can be collected from different available resources, but because of security considerations of this type of data from its financial resources, we used hypothetical data, which is generated by a simulation programs that generate the data randomly.

Based on reference ("Advanced Integration Method (AIM) Implementation Guide Card-Not-Present Transactions", 2005), we wrote tow simulation Visual Basic programs. First program used to create randomly customer database. The second program used to generate randomly customer transactions dataset. Customer database created with 105 customer records each record contains 26 fields contains basic information about the customer such as customer account number, customer first name, customer last name, customer address, customer email, etc. The second program generates randomly 11282 transactions, 4850 transactions of them are fraudulent transactions and the rest (6432) are legitimate transactions. Each transaction contains 53 attributes. In addition, a normalization and profiling step performed on the dataset to derive new calculated attributes with 0 or 1 value. For example "dif_cus_email" attribute hold the value 1 if customer email address in the transaction is different from the customer email address in the customer database and hold the value 0 otherwise.

Data Mining Software used (Megaputer – PolyAnalyst)

PolyAnalyst is a powerful multi-strategy data mining system that implements a broad variety of methods for the automatic data analysis ("Poly-Analyst 4 user Manual"; 2002). It contains eleven advanced knowledge discovery algorithms such as Classification, Decision Tree, Find Dependencies, Find Laws, and NN Predictor. It can perform a thorough analysis of data, automatically extracting the precious knowledge from an investigated database and presenting it in symbolic form easily understood by a human.

Learning and selection Fraud Rules

An analysis step performed on each account using the Decision tree algorithm to generate indicators of fraud in the form of classification rules. 512 rules were generated and summarized in an Excel worksheet. The following are some examples of these rules:

112 "If dif_cus_email And trans_time_of_day = Night" ➔ Fraud with CF = 86.7%"
161 "If dif_bill_ship_last_name And trans_amount >=100 And trans_time_of_day = Night" ➔ Fraud with CF = 87%"

The first rule for account 112 says that if customer email address in the transaction is different from email address in the customer profile and transaction time is night then the transaction is fraudulent with certainty factor 86.7%.

These 512 rules are normalized and sorted and a selection process performed on them to select the most general rules that covered two or more accounts, and only 46 rules were selected to build the profiling monitors.

Constructing Profiling Monitors

The monitors were used to build customer profiles; each monitor has a Profiling step and a Use step. In the profiling step, the monitor is applied to a segment of an account's typical (non-fraud) transactions in order to measure the account's normal activity. Statistics from this profiling period are saved with the account. The following are these statistics information calculated using Excel functions:

Percentage of attribute True values from the transactions (profile Threshold))

Standard Deviation for amounts for attribute True values in transactions (σ) (profile)

Record Average of amount for attribute True values in Transactions satisfy rule conditions (profile) (μ)

In the monitor's Use phase, the monitor processes a single account-day at a time. The monitor references the normally measures calculated in profiling, and generates a numeric value describing how abnormal the current account day is. The following are the statistical information calculated in the Use step by using Excel functions:

Number of attribute True values in account day

Number of Transactions in account day

Percentage of attribute True values in account day

Sum of amount for attribute True values in Transactions

Record Average of amount for attribute True values in Transactions satisfy rule

Then these information compared with the information calculated in the profiling step using two templates (Threshold and standard deviations) mentioned in the methodology section to calculate two output monitors for each rule. So 92 output monitors created for each account days. Box 1 is an example of these 92 output monitors created for account day of one account.

These output monitors were calculated for several account days for each account over a period of four months, and calculated for 48 accounts. This process produced 2083 output monitors records for the 48 accounts. These 2083 records divided into training set and testing set to be used for detector training and testing processes.

Combining Evidence from the Monitors

The training monitors set used as input to three classifier programs in order to perform Evidence combination and build classification rules and Detector. A selection process was performed on the tanning and testing monitors sets in order to reduce the number of independent attributes. This process reduced the monitors to 19 monitors only. The other monitors or rules do not perform well when used in monitors, and some monitors overlap in their fraud detection coverage. In addition, this process chooses a small set of useful

Box 1.

101 1		YES		(trans_acct_no, fraud_flag, fraud_yes_no)							
0	1	0	0	0	0	0	1	0	0	0	0
1	1	0	0	0	0	0	0	0	0	0	0
0	0	0	0	0	0	0	0	0	0	0	0
0	0	0	0	0	0	0	0	0	1		(46
Threshold monitors)											

0	424.3333333	0	0	0	0	0	2.210193235	0	
0.128199211	0	0	0.229560816	0.379616247	0	0	0	0	
0	0	0	0	0	0	0	0	0	0
0	0	0	0	0	0	0	0	0	0
0	0	0	115.9166667	(46 standard deviation monitors)					

Table 1. Testing summary statistics

(yes/no) attributes:	Values	N of 1	N of 0
fraud_yes_no	192	90 (46%)	102 (53%)
CL_PN_Liberal_Data	192	107 (55%)	85 (44%)
CL_LR_Liberal_Data	192	107 (55%)	85 (44%)
CL_FL_Liberal_Data	192	107 (55%)	85 (44%)

Table 2. Testing summary statistics

(yes/no) attributes:	Values	N of 1	N of 0
fraud_yes_no	120	53 (44%)	67 (55%)
CL_PN_L_Data_Rules	120	54 (45%)	66 (55%)
CL_FL_L_Data_Rules	120	54 (45%)	66 (55%)
MBE_L_Data_Rules	120	54 (45%)	66 (55%)
CL_LR_L_Data_Rules	120	54 (45%)	66 (55%)

monitors which simplifies the final detector and increases its accuracy and performance.

Evaluation

The three classification algorithms produce classification efficiency 100%. Summary statistics for testing the Detector rules is shown in table 1. The table shows that 192 monitors' records (90 fraud and 102 non-fraud) used for testing, and the three classifiers produced the same results with overall accuracy reached (100% - ((107-90)*100/192)) = 91.2%.

Accuracy means that the model will have high detection rate (percentage of fraudulent transactions that are detected) and low false positive rate (percentage of normal transactions that the system is falsely determines to be fraudulent) (Al-khatib dissertation, 2008).

From the information in Table 1 we can calculate the accuracy as follows:

Over all accuracy = 100% - percentage of incorrectly classified records

= 100%- (17/192)* 100 = 91.2%.

Detection Rate = percentage of fraudulent transactions that are detected = 100% (no fraudulent monitor records classified in the wrong class, which means No False negative error).

False alarm error = (17/192)*100% = 8.8% (legitimate records classified as fraudulent records)

The cost of false alarm can be estimated by the cost of a fraud analyst's time, which is very low and can be neglected comparing with the system benefits.

The training process repeated with different distribution of the training monitors set and the same testing monitors set and produced the same testing results with errors in the same accounts. This shows us that part of the error percentage (8.8%) refers to human errors in some accounts data calculations and to some transactions with very low spending amounts neglected from verification because verification cost is greater than transaction coast (according to financial institute policy). We removed these accounts from the monitor's sets and repeated the training and testing process and we get an overall accuracy results reached to 99.2%, detection rate equal 100%, and false alarm equal 0.8%. The summary statistical results for this case are shown in table 2:

From the above statistical results and testing processes we notice that all the error percentage represent False positive errors (false alarm) corresponds to wrongly deciding that an account has been frauded. While there is no False negative error corresponds to letting frauded account-day go undetected. The cost of false alarm can be estimated by the cost of a fraud analyst's time, which is very low and can be neglected comparing with the system benefits.

RELATED WORKS

In our survey (Al-Khatib, 2005), we presented an evaluation and comparisons for some detection techniques such as neural network (NN0, Rule Induction (RI), Expert systems (ES), Case-based reasoning (CBR), Genetic Algorithms (GA), Inductive logic programming (ILP) and Regression. Our study shows that the efficiency and performance of these techniques depend on there capability in dealing with several problems such as: noisy and missing in the data used, the performance measure used, scalability, different data types used, explanation capability of the technique, ease of integration with other systems, ease of operation, and skewed distribution of the data used (Al-Khatib, 2008; Salvatore, 1997; Salvatore, 1999). A comparison of these techniques with our method shows that our method outperformed all of them.

DISCUSSION

It is difficult to evaluate our method of fraud detection against existing fraud detection systems. Fraud detection departments and vendors of fraud detection systems protect details of their systems operations for trade and security purposes. We evaluated our method against known fraud techniques and against a collection of techniques as we presented them in our survey (Al-Khatib, 2005).

In our detection method, account context is important in the rule learning step: a global transaction set taken from all accounts and applying a rule learning algorithm to this set would lose information about each account's normal behavior. For example, a transaction from the east area for a customer who lives in the west area at night would be a fraud transaction, while it would be legitimate transaction for a customer who lives in or near the east area. Standard detection technique usually not consider account context in the detection process.

Applying standard classification algorithms to the account data is difficult for several reasons. For example, the description language is very detailed because many thousands of attribute values appear in the data and standard simple classifier will not perform well. In our method we performed a profiling step to change all attributes to logical (0/1) attributes which allow the classifier to perform very well.

Some fraud analysts believe that credit card fraud accompanied by large jumps in account usage or spending amount exceed normal average, and sophisticated mining of fraud is probably unnecessary. This is not true, for example in special occasion's time like Christmas, New Year and other occasion's usage of credit cards and spending amounts increased by customers. So a need for sophisticated mining system depending on combination of several variables or evidences is necessary.

Our method framework has three main components, and is more complex than other approaches, but each component has its own important contribution:

- Learning Component uncover specific indicators of fraudulent transactions.
- Our method shows the value of rule generation step, which does preserve account context.
- Our method shows the benefit of combining evidence from multiple monitors.
- Evidence combination step allows catching different and most of fraudulent transactions instead of depending only on a single or few monitors as happen in standard detection techniques.
- Composite of the three components in our system outperformed standard detector in which a significant piece of data or information is missing.

In addition our method can use different classifiers from simple linear to complex ones to combine evidence from the monitors and perform high accuracy.

CONCLUSION

In this paper, we present a comprehensive framework that mines fraudulent transactions of Card-Not-Present (CNP) in the e-payment systems with high percentage of accuracy. The framework uses data mining analysis tools to discover indicators of fraudulent behavior by analyzing a massive amount of data, and then builds modules to profile each user account's normal behavior with respect to these indicators. The profilers capture the typical behavior of a user account and, in use, describe how far an account transaction is from this typical behavior. The profilers are combined into a single detector, which learns how to detect fraud effectively based on the profiler outputs. When the detector has enough evidence of fraudulent activity on an account transaction, based on the indications of the profilers, it generates an alarm.

Our detection method present high accuracy in predicting fraudulent transactions that exceeds 91.2% and in some cases reached 99.2% as overall accuracy, with fraud detection rate equal 100%. We noticed also that part of the error percentage refer to human error in entering and calculating the data. Our method can be implemented easily to automate all its steps and to produce an automated fraud detection system that can produce a very high percentage of accuracy.

Our detection framework is not specific to credit card fraud; it can be applied to several other fraud problems in different domains.

REFERENCES

Advanced Integration Method (AIM) Implementation Guide Card-Not-Present Transactions. (2005). *Version 1.0*. Merchant Commerce and Payment Services.

Ahola, J., & Esa Rinta-Runsala. (2001). *Data mining case studies in customer profiling*. Research report TTE1-2001-29; VTT Information Technology.

Al-Khatib, A. M., & Ezz Hattab. (2007). Mining Fraudulent Transactions in e-payment Systems. *9th international conference (iiWAS2007)* (pp. 179–189).

Al-Khatib, A. M., & Hattab, E. (2005). Credit Card Fraud Detection Techniques: A survey. *7th international conference (iiWAS2005), 1*, 505–516.

Al-Khatib, A. M. (2008). *Mining Fraudulent Behavior in e-payment System*. Ph.D. Dissertation.

Commonwealth of Australia. (2000). *The changing nature of fraud in Australia*.

Dunham, M. H. (2003). *Data Mining Introductory and Advanced Topics*. Prentice Hall.

Fawcett, T., & Provost, F. (1997). *Adaptive Fraud Detection*. Data Mining and Knowledge Discovery.

Mena, J. (Ed.). (2003). Investigative Data mining for Security and Criminal Detection. B. H. pub. Company.

Phua, C. (n.d.). *Minority Report in Fraud Detection: Classification of Skewed Data*. Sigkdd Explorations, Vol. 6.

PolyAnalyst 4 user Manual. (2002). Megaputer Intelligence, Inc.

Prodromidis, A. L. (2000). *Agent-Based Distributed Learning Applied to Fraud Detection*. Columbia University.

Stolfo, S. J. (1997). *Credit Card Fraud Detection Using Meta-Learning*. Columbia University.

Stolfo, S. J., & Wei Fan. (1999). *Cost-based Modeling for Fraud and Intrusion Detection: Results from the JAM Project.* Columbia University; 0-7695-0490-6/99.

KEY TERMS

Accuracy: Means high detection rate (percentage of fraudulent transactions that are detected) and low false positive rate (percentage of normal transactions that is falsely determines to be fraudulent).

Anomaly Detection: Normal behavior of user are first summarized into normal profiles, and then used as yardsticks, so that run-time activities that result in significant deviation from the user profiles are considered as probable fraudulent

Card-Not-Present Fraud (Online Fraud): Fraud that is committed via web, phone shopping or cardholder-not-present.

Credit Card Fraud (Offline Fraud): Is committed by using a stolen physical card at storefront or call center.

Data Mining: Is a set of techniques used to extract important information from existing data and enable better decision making throughout an organization".

Detection Rate: Percentage of fraudulent transactions that are detected

False Negative Error: Error corresponds to letting fraud account-day go undetected.

False Positive Error (False Alarm): Error corresponds to wrongly deciding that an account has been fraud.

Fraud: A dishonest action to make false statements in order to gain money or benefit from an individual or from an organization.

Fraud Detection: A process that can use data mining techniques to detect fraudulent transaction.

Fraud Profiling Technique: It is a technique used to determine the normal behavior of each user account with respect to certain indicators, and to determine when that behavior has deviated significantly.

Misuse Detection: Well-known fraudulent transactions are encoded into patterns, which are then used to match new transactions to identify the fraudulent ones.

Chapter VI
Key Topics in the Ethics and Economics of Cyber Security

Sattar J. Aboud
Middle East University for Graduate Studies, Jordan-Amman

ABSTRACT

Cyber security is the significant issue for customers, sellers, and discipliners since hackers who utilize vulnerabilities can make considerable damage. In this chapter, we study key topics in a nascent literature on a cyber security. We first concentrate on how inducements influence the major topics in information security. Three significant topics pertinent for a cyber security concerns are: an exterior security, the internet consequence and information sharing which make effect in the information security. The budding literature has started to study the relationships between vulnerability revelation, patching, manufactured goods prices and profits.

INTRODUCTION

It becomes normal to receive security alerts concerning killer **viruses**. Few of them are **hoaxes**, but many of other viruses have made large damage. As the Economist magazine reported that the **Blaster worm** viruses in 2003 caused $35 billion damages. (**Weaver** and **Paxson**, 2004) reported that the worst case of state **worm** may detriment from $50 billion to $100 billion. It seems that a time from the announcement of **asset** vulnerability to the time that the **threat** is started has dropped considerably. Also, the economist magazine re-

ported that the period from revelation to **attack** for the **Slammer worm** is three months in January 2003, whilst the period from revelation to attack is just two weeks for the Blaster worm in August 2003. The **Slammer** and Blaster worms utilized vulnerabilities even if security updates removing the vulnerabilities then after that freed again by Microsoft programs. This is, despite the fact that the security updates is extensively available, fairly some entities applied them. In fact, the survey of (John Markoff, 2004) showed the following facts:

- 80% of all computers connected with the net are reported that they infected by **spy ware**.
- 20% of all computers are reported that they have **viruses**.
- 77% of those surveyed they are safe or fairly safe from online attacks.
- 67% of the computers do not have updated antivirus programs.
- 63% of the computer users without **firewall protection** software

In this chapter, we study key topics in the nascent literature of the intersection between computer science and engineering concerns, and also, the trade inducements that related with cyber security and software stipulation. The initial focus will be on the **trade** inducements that change the key concerns and topics in information security. An introduction research to the subject can be observed at (Ross Anderson, 2004)

Also, for a wealth of articles on information security see Bruce Schneiers(2005).

KEY FACTS

Three important key of fact relevant for the trade of cyber security concerns are as follows:

- The *exterior* security
- The **Internet Consequence**
- **Information Sharing**

The Exterior Security

Insecure computers are indeed very weak and can easily used by opponent to attack many other computers. There is a lack of inducement for every entity in the system to sufficiently defend versus viruses in their system, because the detriment of the spread of the virus is taken by others. Namely, information security is properties by a **confident** an *exterior* security. However, when we choose

more safety measures to protect the information in computer, this means that we improve the security of own and also the security of other entities as well. Such situations guide to a typical free difficulty. In the lack of the promotion for security, entities will select minimum security than the community most favorable. Solutions to the free difficulty are directed in many situations.

The Internet Consequence

The internet consequence appears in **software applications**. The advantages of software applications usually based on a total number of clients that buy licenses of the software applications. The direct internet consequence is present after raises in the number of clients on the internet increase the value of the trades for each entity on the internet. The most common instances are contact through internet for example chats, phones and e-mails. The internet consequence also presents if the entities use **hardware** with standard software applications. In such approach, the importance of the hardware good raises as the diversity of well-matched software applications raises. Rises the number of entities in fitting hardware will causes grows in the need for standard software applications, which gives positive motivations to software sellers to increase the supply of software application types. This will raise the advantages to all clients of the hardware, software, and the use of vitality of **network** for instance, trading goods by **roaming** the **sites** through the internet. This vitality will results in arise the e-purchasers, for example **operating systems** with applications programs and CD players with compact disks. Set the significance of interrelation in information security networks, the **business** of standardization will become the main current business. Thus (Gandal, 2002), and (Church and Gandal, 2006) they provide an introduction to internet consequences and to policy concerns.

Internet consequences are characteristically concept to benefit customers and companies that have united all over standardization. Though, internet consequences can contribute to information security difficulties. However, big networks are weaker to security infringements, because of an achievement of the internet and because of its great established base, Microsoft internet **explorer** is probably more vulnerable to attack compared with the Mosaic Firefox Browser. This is because be fruitful to hackers from using security vulnerability in internet explorer which is better than be useful to using a like vulnerability in Firefox.

Information Sharing

Information sharing is a **key factor** in developing comprehensive and workable approaches to protecting versus possible cyber and other attacks, which might threaten the public **welfare**. Information on threats, vulnerabilities, and incidents experienced via others, while hard to share and examine, can assist identify trends, improved understand the risks faced, and determine what defensive measures must be employed. As (Choucri, Madnick, Moulton, Siegel, and Zhu, 2004) stated that the effective pursuit of counterterrorism activities requests the fast and semantically important **integration** of information from different sources. For counterterrorism information sharing, just like for many other administration and military operations in the post September 11, 2001, world the customary mindset of require to know is being passed via the necessity to share amongst dynamic societies of interests (COI) (Yuan and Wenzel, 2005). Economic services is one the communities of top interest. The private sector has at all times been worried concerning sharing **data** with the government and about the problem of getting security clearances. Both congress and the government have taken steps to address information sharing issues in **law** and recent policy direction. The Homeland Security Act of 2002, which generated the Department of Homeland Security (DHS), carried together 22 varied organizations to assist prevent terrorist

attacks in the US, cut the vulnerability of the US to terrorist attacks, and reduce damage and help in recovery from attacks that do happen (Homeland security, 2003). To achieve this mission, the act established certain homeland security accountabilities for the department, which contained sharing information amongst its own individuals and with other federal authorities, state, and local governments, the private sector, and others. The GAO was asked to study DHS information sharing attempts with:

- The importance of information sharing in satisfying DHS accountabilities
- GAO related previous analyses and recommendations for improving the federal administration information sharing efforts
- Key administration issues DHS must consider in developing and applying effective information sharing processes (Homeland security, 2003).

ECONOMIC SERVICES FIRMS

Certain **economic services firms** present very economically attractive targets. Cyber attacks versus them happen with increased frequency and complexity if compared with another sector. A document from US (GAO) reported that economic services firms received an average of 1,108 attacks per firm during the six-month research period. During the same period, 46% of these firms experienced at least one attack they considered is acute. In 2004 Global Security Survey (Deloitte Global Security Survey, 2004), Deloitte and Touche indicated that 83% of economic services firms acknowledged that their systems has been compromised in the past year, compared to 39% in 2002. Of these, 40% reported that the breaches have resulted in **financial** loss. In fact the economic services trade depends greatly on public **trust**, puts it at considerable risk from all ways of cyber attacks. Each act that weakens the

confidentiality, **integrity**, and **availability** of economic information negatively impacts the influenced institution and the trade (Deloitte Global Security Survey, 2004). Increased revealing of the economic services sector is due to following properties of the trade:

- The target: 50% of cyber attacks are economic services institutions
- **Vulnerable:** Online to be there subject to software vulnerabilities of networks
- In the **trade** of **trust:** Rock layer of trade
- Highly regulated: Regularly checked for compliance
- Interconnected: To settle payment and securities transactions internationally.

During the 2007, attacks on economic services institutions have been increase. Economic services institutions are targets since they hold public money and have abundant amounts of individual information. Many global economic institutions have been subject to **phishing** attacks during the 2007 (Deloitte Global Security study, 2008). Corporate executives are relatively on standard with those of last year in that they are eager to take a direct investment in security preparedness anti physical disasters, Internet terrorism, and other possible threats (Deloitte Global Security study, 2004). A Deloitte and Touche 2005 study (Deloitte Global Security study, 2004) reported that the distribution of cyber attacks on economic institutions across the world ranges from 16% in the USA to 50% in *Canada*.

ETHICAL ATTACKS

Both (Gutman and Rieff, 1999) stress that **ethic** begins with laws. Global laws of war attempt to regulate how wars may be legally fought. The Hague Conventions between 1899 and 1907 and **Geneva Conventions** between 1949 and 1977 are the most essential. While most cyber war

attacks do not look to fall into the class of grave breaches or war crimes as per the 1949 Geneva Conventions, they can still be illegal or unethical. Article 51 of the 1977 additional **Protocols** of the Geneva Conventions prohibits attacks that use methods and means of fight whose effects can not be controlled or whose damage to civilians is disproportionate. Article 57 says "Constant care shall be taken to spare the civilian population, civilians, and civilian objects"; **cyber weapons** are difficult to target and difficult to assess in their effects.

The Hague Conventions prohibit weapons that cause unnecessary suffering; cyber attack weapons can cause mass destruction to civilian a computer that is difficult to repair. So, (Arquilla, 1999) generalizes on the laws to suggest three main criteria for an **ethical military attack**: noncombatant immunity during the attack, proportionality of the size and scope of the attack to the provocation, and that the attack does more good than harm. All are difficult to guarantee in cyberspace. Nearly all authorities agree that international law does apply to **cyber warfare** (Schmitt, 2002). We examine here the application of these concepts to cyber war attacks or cyber attacks, that is, attacks on the computer systems and computer networks of an adversary using cyber weapons built of software and data (Bayles, 2001; Lewis, 2002). A first problem is determining whether one is under cyber attack, since it may not be obvious (Molander and Siang, 1998), (Manion and Goodrum, 2000) note that legal acts of civil defiance, such as spamming oppressive governments or modifying their Web sites, can look like cyber attacks and require to be distinguished via their lack of violence. Thus, (Michael, Wingfield, and Wijiksera, 2003) suggested criteria for considered if one is under armed attack in **cyberspace** by applying the system of (Schmitt, 1998) with a weighted average of seven factors: **severity**, immediacy, **directness**, invasiveness, measurability, presumptive **legitimacy**, and responsibility. Successful cyber attacks are robust on nearness and invasiveness. However, they can vary really on cruelty, measurability and directness based on the systems. There is no assumption of legality for cyber attacks; and accountability is disreputably hard to assign in cyberspace. These make it difficult to justify counterattacks to cyber attacks.

A fascinating possibility for **ethical cyber attacks** is to design their damage to be easily repairable. For instance, damage could be in the form of an encryption of critical data or programs using a secret key known only to the attacker, so performing a decryption could repair the damage. A virus could store the code it has replaced, enabling substitution of the original code later, but this is hard to do when viruses attack many kinds of software. Repair procedures could be designed to be trigger able by the attacker at a time that they choose or could be kept in escrow by a neutral party, such as the United Nations, until the termination of hostilities

PROVISIONAL PACIFISM

An important number of international citizens consider that **military attacks** are unfair regardless of the circumstances, the concept of **pacifism** (Miller, 1991). Pacifism is a responsibility relied from the moral unacceptability of **aggression**; pragmatics relied from the find of net constructive results from attacks, or certain combination of these. Responsibility relied pacifists are most concerned about the aggression and **killing of warfare**, and **cyber attacks** may be more acceptable to them than conventional attacks, when just information is damaged. However, nonaggression can be difficult to guarantee in a cyber attack, hence for example, the no aggressive disabling of a power place can result in catastrophic accidents, looting, or health threats. To pragmatics-based pacifists, war denotes a waste of information and ingenuity that may be better spent on positive activities (Nardin, 1998), and this applies just

as to **cyber warfare**. To them, cyber attacks are just as **unethical** as other attacks since both are violent antisocial behavior.

Most psychologists can observe kinds of violence on a continuous spectrum (Leng, 1994). More popular than pure pacifism are different kinds of **conditional pacifism**, which hold that attacks are allowable under certain circumstances. The most commonly cited is counterattack in reply to attack. The United Nations Charter prohibits attacks via nations unless attacked first (Gutman and Rieff, 1999), and the wording is sufficiently general to implement to cyber attacks. Counterattacks are just permissible in international law versus nation states, not groups in countries similar to terrorists, but they can be defined. Thus, (Arquilla, 1999) reported that cyber attacks are like a tempting form of initial attack that they are likely is popular for astonish attacks.

DAMAGE IN CYBER ATTACKS

Cyber attacks use **vulnerabilities** of applications, together **operating systems** and **software applications**. Actually, the increasing standardization of software means that military **firms** often employ the same software as people use, and a lot of this software has the same vulnerabilities. Many **worms** and **viruses** that may cripple a command-and-control network can only as simply cripple a people system. The increasing interconnection of computers in networks means there are many routes via which an attack may spread from a military firm's computers to those of people innocent bystanders (Arquilla, 1999; Westwood, 1997).

Military systems attempt to isolate themselves from people **networks** but they are not very successful since access to the Internet shortens many routine jobs. In addition, data flow from people to military systems is often less limited than flow in the other direction, which actually encourages an adversary to first **attack** people sites. Disproportionate **damage** to people is a key issue in the Geneva Conventions. Incomplete knowledge of an opponent's computer systems may worsen the spread of the attack to people: What may seem a precisely targeted disabling of a **software program** on a **military system** may have profound consequences on people computers that happen, unknown to attackers, to employ that same system. Even when hackers believe they know the addresses of target military systems, the opponent may alter their addresses in a crisis state, or in the meantime have provided their old addresses to people computers.

An additional difficulty is that it is easy to generate disproportionately larger damage to people computers via a cyber attack, because there are typically more of them than military systems and their security is not as fine. Cyber attacks are more feasible for small firms, similar to terrorist type, than **conventional warfare** is (Ericsson, 1999), but like firms can lack the comprehensive intelligence essential to target their opponent accurately. In addition, it can be tempting to attack civilian systems anyhow for planned reasons.

Crippling some web sites in a state power grid, **banking system** or **telephone system** could be more destructive to its capacity to salary war than disabling some command-and-control centers, considering the back up web sites and redundancy in most **forces** command-and-control systems. Another damage difficulty is that staging a cyber attack almost invariably needs operating an important number of intermediate systems between the hackers and the victim, because such route finding has been deliberately made hard.

Actually, a route can even be not possible, since critical computers may be disconnected from all external networks. This means hackers require to significant examining intrude, perhaps unproductively, finding a way to their target. So, (Himma, 2004) reported that cyber intruding is badly justified on ethical basis. Even when it

is in chase of a criminal, which is usually not factual for cyber attacks, police do not have the right to attack each home into which a criminal may have escaped. Intruding on systems also can thieve computation time from those computers without authorization, reducing speed the legal activities.

DAMAGE ESTIMATION OF CYBER ATTACKS

Damage estimation is hard in **cyberspace**. If a computer system does not operate, it may be due to difficulties in a number of properties. For example, code destruction resulted via a virus can be scattered throughout the software. Unlike **conventional weapons**, determining how many places are damaged is hard; hence often damage is not obvious except under special tests. This encourages more **massive attacks** than necessary being sure they result sufficient damage.

The problem of damage estimation also makes repair difficult. Damage may persist for a long time and its increasing effect can be considerable even if it is subtle, so noncombatant victims of a cyber attack might continue to bear long afterwards from attacks on military computers that by mistake distribute to them, as with attacks by chemical weapons. Repair may be achieved by only reinstalling software after an attack.

However, this is usually unacceptable because it loses information. With polymorphic, or shape-changing, viruses, for example, it can be difficult to inform which software is damaged; when the infection spreads to backup copies, then reinstalling only reinfects. **Computer forensics** (Mandia and Prosise, 2003) gives tools to examine computer systems after cyber attacks, but their focus is determining the attack mechanism and constructing a legal case versus the perpetrator not repair of the system. Two factors can **mitigate damage** from **cyber attacks** which are as follows:

- Targeting precision
- Repair mechanisms

Cyber attacks often can be designed to be selective in what systems they attack and what they attack in those systems. Systems can be defined by names and Internet protocol addresses, and attacks can be limited to a few mission-critical parts of the software. So an attack might disable instant messaging, while permitting **slower email**, or insert delays into key radar defense systems; but use of denial of service, which would swamp resources with requests, would be too broad in effects to justify ethically. Naturally an adversary will make it difficult to get accurate information about their **computer systems**, their electronic order of battle. They could deliberately mislead attackers as to the addresses and natures of their sites, as with honeynets or fake computer networks (The Honeynet Project, 2004). Furthermore, (Bissett, 2004) reported that modern warfare rarely achieves its promise of precise surgical strikes for many reasons that apply to cyber attacks including:

- Political pressures to use something new whether or not it is appropriate
- The inevitable miscalculations in implementing new technology
- Lack of feeling of responsibility in the attacker due to the technological remoteness of the target
- The inevitable surprises in warfare that were not encountered during testing in controlled environments.

RESEARCH ON CYBER SECURITY

The important part of this chapter concentrates on a generation of markets regarding the **business of cyber security**. We will first briefly review this part and then study the inducements of **software sellers** concerning a providing of **cyber security**.

However, the Computer Emergency Response Team CERT Coordination Center is a center of internet security expertise and is located at the Software Engineering Institute, a federally funded research and development center operated by Carnegie Mellon University [36].

The CERT Coordination Center studies security issues and provides publications and alerts to help educate the public to the threats facing **information security**. The center also provides training and expertise in the handling of computer incidents. The CERT Coordination Center acts both as research center and outside consultant in the areas of incident response and **security practices** and programs development.

Though CERT Coordination Center is not a public agency, it acts as a mediator between entities who inform vulnerabilities to CERT Coordination Center and **sellers** who made a **software programs** and a **patches**. If reported via an entity regarding vulnerability, CERT Coordination Center guides study into the theme. When an entity has certainly exposed security vulnerability, CERT Coordination Center then reports to the software seller and gives the firm a forty five days vulnerability window.

This will let the firm to work out the software update. After this time, CERT Coordination Center is automatically revealing the vulnerability though a security update is not made obtainable. Newly, a restricted market for vulnerabilities is created where firms such as Tipping and iDefense act as mediators, automated those who informed vulnerabilities and offering the facts to software entities who are subscribed to this application. Now, there is an increasing related work on markets concerning vulnerability. So, (Camp and Wolfram, 2004) heuristically study this mater of markets for vulnerabilities. Also, (Schechter, 2004) suitably forms the market for vulnerabilities and (Ozment, 2004) describes how this market can act as a public sale market. (Kannan and Telang, 2004) introduce a model with four contributors which are as follows:

- Mediator
- Trust agent that can discover the **software vulnerability**
- Hackers
- Software purchaser

Then they ask if a market based model is different from the setting wherein a public organization works as a mediator. However, there is no role to software vendors. **Software** vendors that trade directly with **trust- agent** would likely decrease the requirement for such mediator markets.

Up to date, there are just a few empirical articles concerning with the **business of cyber security**. However, we will briefly refer to a few latest researches. Fro example, (Arora, Nandkumar, Krishman, Telang, and Yang, 2004) inspected 308 distinct vulnerabilities and reported that revelation of vulnerabilities raises the number of attacks for each **server** and setting up security updates reduces the number of attacks for each server. (Arora, Krishman, Telang, and Yang, 2005) observe that exposé deadlines are valuable. They notice that sellers react more rapidly to vulnerabilities that are handled via CERT Coordination Center compared with the others vulnerabilities that are not treated via CERT Coordination Center. In fact, in many area of researches, theoretical studies growth are faster compare with the empirical researches, because of the lack of data. There is obviously an unused latent for empirical research in the business of cyber security, because the national vulnerability database that is collected via the computer security division of the National Institute of Science and Technology and is accessible online at [52]. Top quality information is available in the level of the vulnerability and at the industry or organization level.

The information contains data regarding 70 vulnerabilities, the influence of the vulnerability, and data on the vulnerability category. This database is used by (Arora, Nandkumar, Krishman, Telang, and Yang, 2004) and (Arora, Krishman, Telang, and Yang, 2005). Proposals for empirical

study may be obtained via testing the synopsis statistics available at the national vulnerability database. They indicate that whereas the number of vulnerabilities in the national vulnerability database rose from 1,858 in 2002 to 3,753 in 2005, the number of top 70 vulnerabilities has almost resided the same throughout that period. As indicated by the national vulnerability database, acute vulnerabilities comprised around 48% of the vulnerabilities in 2002, with 33% of the vulnerabilities in 2004, and 23.5% of the vulnerabilities in 2005. These figures indicate a reduction in the proportion of top 70 vulnerabilities as a proportion of the vulnerabilities. The information also illustrate that vulnerabilities allow unauthorized access and get from input validation mistake, namely from either boundary condition fault or buffer overflow fault, explain a great and rising percentage of the top 70 vulnerabilities. Whilst they reported that about 50% of the top 70 vulnerabilities during 2001, and they reported also about 60% of the top 70 vulnerabilities in 2004. Whilst in 2005 they indicated that about 72% of the top 70 vulnerabilities.

SOFTWARE SELLERS

In this chapter, we will also introduce literature that involves **software** sellers in the system. (Arora, Telang, and Xu, 2004) hypothetically study the best plan for **software vulnerability** revelation. The software seller plan is restricted to when it will announce a patch and if yes, when to issue the patch. (August and Tunca, 2005) have a policy software seller too, although the seller policy is restricted to cost of the software. (Nizovtsev and Thursby, 2005) study the inducements of **software organizations** to reveal vulnerabilities in an open debate.

However, (Choi Fershtman, and Gandal, 2007) describe the influence of **software vulnerabilities** in the organizations that build the software program and the customers that license the **soft-**

ware program. They draw three decisions to the organization these are as follows:

- An open outlay in the quality of the software to decrease possible vulnerabilities
- A strategy decision when to publicize vulnerabilities
- A license cost for the **software application**.

They also draw two decisions of the customer these are as follows:

- Whether to license the **software program**
- Whether to use a security update.

The chapter is different from the research work since it describes the relations between vulnerability revelation, patching, creation costs and income. Whilst this approach offers a base, thus more studies are required to inspect inducements for software sellers to invest in security.

SIMPLICITY OF CYBER ATTACKS

Cyber attacks have an irregular difficulty not shared via **traditional attacks**. They can generally be extremely effective just one time (Ranum, 2004). Analysis of an attack via the victim typically discloses the software that was exploited with it. This software may be directly disabled, and then fixed patched to prevent a repeat of the attack (Lewis, 2002).

Information of the attack may be rapidly disseminated through vulnerability clearinghouse Web sites, so that other potential victims can be quickly protected, and automatic downloading of a security update for all installations can be initiated via the seller. This can be achieved these days in only some days. Thus when the hacker attempts the same attack later, it is probable to be less effective. Countermeasures also may be located, independent of attacks, via security pro-

fessionals in checking and examining software, thus a new attack can be thwarted before it may ever be employed. In contrast, cyber attacks are expensive to develop. A new attack is the most effective attack. However, new disadvantages in applications that no person has discovered are few and hard to discover. Software engineers are obtaining better at checking and examining the software for security flaws. One more difficulty is that at least part of a new attack has to be complained versus an opponent to observe when the opponent is vulnerable to it. As there are many variables such as the version of application that the opponent is running, that can prevent the achievement of an attack, such initial testing can alert the opponent of the kind of complete attack to approach. So, investigation and development of cyber attacks seems very cost ineffective and a waste of resources, and so ethically problematic.

CONFIDENTIALITY AND CYBER ATTACKS

A related difficulty in cyber attacks is the need for **confidentiality** than with traditional attacks.

With **bombs** virus do not require hiding the technology of the volatile from the opponent, since most of it is well known and better astonishes are potential with the time and location for attacks. However, knowledge regarding the nature of cyber attacks and the delivery devices usually involves ability to end them (Denning, 1999). Time and location do not give much surprise, because each person knows attacks can happen anytime at any place. So cyber attacks need confidentiality of methods for a important period of time from the detection of the attack to its employment. Hence many opponents have intelligence resources fixed to search out secrets, this confidentiality may be so hard to obtain. (Bok, 1986) reported that other weaknesses of confidentiality, containing the encouragement of choice that is out of touch in the changing requirements of the society. Confidentiality also promotes firm inadequacy, because firms easily can duplicate the same confidential investigation and development. So, cyber attack confidentiality may be said to be problematic on ethical basis.

ETHICAL CYBER ATTACKS POLICY

(Hauptman, 1996) reported that computer technology is adequately difficult that we must have a complete set of ethics, not only a set of rules. Thus **cyber warfare** must have ethics policies with related explanations. (Arquilla, 1999) suggested certain potential policies. One is a no first employ pledge for cyber attacks analogous to pledges on other types of **dangerous weapons**. One more is that cyber attacks must just be in reply to cyber attacks and must be balanced to the attack. Another one is a pledge only to never employ **cyber weapons**, because they may be weapons of group of damage. When cyber weapons are employed, other policies can need that the attacks have distinctive not reusable signatures that identify the in charge and the intended object, or that attacks are simply reversible. Policy also is required on the category of members in cyber war, thus to if they are civilians, soldiers, or otherwise (Nitzberg, 1998).

CONCLUSION

Cyber attacks raise many important ethical questions for the public, because they may result mass damage. They raise so many questions that it is difficult for a responsible country to consider them as a military option, so they are somewhat like chemical or biological arms, although not as bad. Although cyber attacks can be less lethal than other attacks and can sometimes be designed to have reversible effects, their great expense, their lack of reusability, and the problem of targeting

them precisely, usually makes them a poor option of weapon. International law must prohibit them and institute serious punishments for their use.

It will be useful for researchers to try to decide what is driving these and other trends. These simple statistics show that interdisciplinary empirical is likely to be more productive Businesses may be able to understand trends in the information, but without teamwork by computer engineers and scientists, it is not be possible to know the implications of these statistics. Expectantly this work will be available in the not as well remote future.

REFERENCES

Anderson, R. (2004). *Economics and security Resource*. Page http://www.cl.cam.ac.uk/users/rja14/econsec

Arora, A., Nandkumar, A., Krishman, R., Telang, R., & Yang, Y. (2004). *Impact of vulnerability disclosure and patch availability: An empirical enalysis*. Presented at the Third Workshop on Economics and Information Security, Minneapolis, MN.

Arora, A., Krishman, R., Telang, R., & Yang, Y. (2005). *An empirical analysis of vendor response to software vulnerability disclosure*. Mimeo.

Arora, A., Telang, R., & Xu, H. (2004). *Optimal policy for software vulnerability disclosure*. working paper, Carnegie-Mellon.

Arquilla, J. (1999). Ethics and information warfare, In Z. Khalilzad, J. White, & A. Marsall (Eds.), *Strategic appraisal: The changing role of information in warfare* (pp. 379-401). Santa Monica, CA: Rand Corporation.

August, T., & Tunca, T, (2005). *Network software security and user incentives*. Mimeo.

Bayles, W. (2001). Network attack. *Parameters, US Army War College Quarterly, 31*, 44-58.

Bissett, A. (2004). High technology war and "surgical strikes". *Computers and Society (ACM SIGCAS), 32*(7).

Bok, S. (1986). *Secret.* Oxford, UK: Oxford University Press.

Camp, L. J., & Wolfram, C. (2004). Pricing security. In L.J. Camp & S. Lewis (Eds.), *Economics of information security,* Vol. 12, *Advances in information security,* Springer-Kluwer

Choi, J., Fershtman, C., & Gandal, N. (2007). *Network Security: Vulnerabilities and Disclosure Policy.* (CEPR Working Paper #6134).

Church, J., & Gandal, N. (2006). *Platform competition in telecommunications.* In M. Cave, S. Majumdar, & I. Vogelsang (Eds.), *the handbook of telecommunications, 2,* 117-153, Elsevier.

Computer Emergency Response Team CERT Coordination Center (2000). *Results of the Security in ActiveX.* Workshop, Software Engineering Institute, Carnegie Mellon University, USA.

Deloitte Global Security Survey (2008). *Global financial services industry.*

Denning, D. (1999). *Information warfare and security.* Boston: Addison-Wesley.

Ericsson, E. (1999). Information warfare: Hype or reality? *The Nonproliferation Review, 6*(3), 57-64.

Gandal, N. (2002). *Compatibility, standardization and network effects: Some policy implications. Oxford Review of Economic Policy, 18,* 8091.

Grady and Francesco, (2006). *The Law and Economics of Cyber Security: An Introduction.* Cambridge University Press.

Gutman, R., & Rieff, D. (1999). *Crimes of War: What the public should know.* New York: Norton.

Hauptman, R. (1996). Cyberethics and social stability. *Ethics and Behavior, 6*(2), 161-163.

Himma, K. (2004). The ethics of tracing hacker attacks through the machines of innocent persons. *International Journal of Information Ethics, 2*(11), 1-13, The Honeynet Project. *know your enemy* 2nd Boston: Addison-Wesley.

Homeland security: Information sharing responsibilities, challenges, and key management issues [GAO- 03-715T]. (2003, May 8). Presented to Committee on Government Reform, House of Representatives.

*Homeland Security and Personal Safely, (*2003), *Report of the joint inquiry into the terrorist attacks of* Venice, Italy.

Kannan, K., & Telang, R. (2004). *Market for software vulnerabilities? Think again.* Working paper, Carnegie-Mellon.

Leng, R. (1994). Interstate crisis escalation and war, In M. Portegal & J. Knutson (Eds.), *the dynamics of aggression* (pp. 307-332), Hillsdale, NJ: Lawrence Erlbaum.

Lewis, J. (2002). *Assessing the risks of cyberterrorism, cyber war, and other cyber threats.* Washington, DC: Center for Strategic and International Studies.

Manion, M., & Goodrum, A. (2000). *Terrorism or civil disobedience: toward a hacktivist ethic. Computers and Society (ACM SIGCAS), 30*(2), 14-19.

Mandia, K., & Prosise, C. (2003. *Incident response and computer forensics.* New York: McGraw-Hill/ Osborne.

Markoff, J. (2004). *Home Web Security Falls Short. Survey Shows.* available at http://www. staysafeonline.info/news/safety_study_v04.pdf

Michael, J., Wingfield, T., & Wijiksera, D. (2003). *Measured responses to cyber attacks using Schmitt analysis: a case study of attack scenarios for a software- intensive system.* In *Proceedings of the 27th IEEE Computer Software and Applications Conference,* Dallas, TX.

Miller, R. (1991). *Interpretations of conflict: ethics, pacifism, and the just-war tradition.* Chicago, IL: University of Chicago Press.

Molander, R., & Siang, S. (1998).*The legitimization of strategic information warfare: Ethical considerations. AAAS Professional Ethics Report, 11*(4), Retrieved November 23, 2005, from http://www.aaas.org/spp/ sfrl/sfrl.htm

Nardin, T. (Ed.), (1998). *the ethics of war and peace.* Princeton, NJ: Princeton University Press.

Nitzberg, S. (1998). *Conflict and the computer: Information warfare and related ethical issues.* In *Proceed* Ethics of Cyber War Attack*ing of the 21st National Information Systems Security Conference*, Arlington, VA (p. D7).

Nizovtsev, D., & Thursby, M. (2005). *Economic analysis of incentives to disclose software vulnerabilities.* Mimeo,

Orwant, C. (1994). *EPER ethics.* In *Proceedings of the Conference on Ethics in the Computer Age*, Gatlinburg, TN (pp. 105 -108)

Ozment, A. (2004). *Bug auctions: Vulnerability markets reconsidered.* Mimeo.

Ranum, M. (2004). *the myth of homeland security.* Indianapolis: Wiley

Schechter, S, (2004). *Computer security, strength and risk: A quantitative approach.* Mimeo.

Schneier, B. (n.d.). At http://www.schneier.com/essays-comp

Schmitt, M. (1998). Bellum Americium: The U.S. view of twenty-first century war and its possible implications for the law of armed conflict. *Michigan Journal of International Law, 19*(4), 1051-1090.

Schmitt, M. (2002), Wired warfare: computer network attack and jus in bello. *International Review of the Red Cross, 84*(846), 365-399.

Weaver, N., & Paxson, V, (2004). *A worst case worm.* Mimeo.

Westwood, C. (1997). *The future is not what it used to be: Conflict in the information age.* Fairbairn, Australia: Air Power Studies Center.

Yuan, E., & Wenzel, G. (2005). Assured counter-terrorism information sharing using: Attribute based information security. (ABIS), In *Proceedings of IEEE Aerospace Conference* (pp. 1-12).

KEY TERMS

Cyber Attack: Is an offensive act versus networks or computer systems.

Cyber War: Is an attack to a computer networks or computer systems via software applications.

Economic Service: Is to present very economically attractive targets.

Information Sharing: Is a key factor in developing comprehensive and workable approaches to protecting versus possible cyber and other attacks, which might threaten the public welfare.

Pacifism: Is a responsibility relied from the moral unacceptability of aggression.

Patch: Is a modification of software to fix vulnerability that a cyber attack can exploit.

Trust Agent: Is an agent that can discover the software vulnerability.

Chapter VII
Using Maturity Model to Govern Information Technology

Asim El-Sheikh
The Arab Academy for Banking and Financial Sciences, Jordan

Husam A. Abu Khadra
The Arab Academy for Banking and Financial Sciences, Jordan

ABSTRACT

This chapter introduces the COBiTs' maturity model as a mean of studying the information technology (IT) governance and its affect on the perceived Security Threats. It argues that IT governance using the maturity model offers a probable influence on the level of security breaches frequency; such evidence would be extracted through a complex quantitative and qualitative approach, offers a better understanding of intricate relationships between different factors. Moreover, the authors hope that understanding the above mentioned influence using the maturity model will not only inform the researchers of a better design for IT governance and defining implementation pitfalls, but also assist in the understanding of IT governance practices trend in the Jordanian environment.

INTRODUCTION

Over the last decade, an evolution of auditing and IT security occurred as an irreversible movement toward the "electronization" of the business process. (Greenstein and Vasarhelyi, 2000). As a result many efforts herein appeared as increasing interest to evolve the audit model toward a more action-driven method of control, revision and assurance, (Timothy et al, 1998). Several profes-sional committees have undertaken this endeavor, such as the American Institute of Certified Public Accountants (AICPA). However, these initiatives were in the form of general instructions, and nothing specific can be considered as detailed guidance to the auditors in their work.

Accordingly, the responsibility has increased dramatically on the profession, to recognize and assess the threats which are associated with Control Systems (CS) in the IT environment. This partly due to the fact that technology in many cases developed faster than the advancement in CS,)Ryan & Bordoloi, 1997).

In addition, knowledge advancement in technology and related practices in the current age verify that the right practical employment is the key factor of technology and knowledge success (Oak Report, 2004). Enterprises realize that growing importance of information technology (IT) and consider it as a treasure enhancing their competitive position, adding value to their businesses. But what remains as a challenge is, which key practices that organizations should apply to get IT under control in order to deliver that desirable value? In other words what should be done to govern IT activities? (Li et. al., 2007).

To date, little experience-based studies have been conducted in Jordan and internationally to investigate security threats and what IT governance arrangement work best (Weill and Ross, A, 2004), where devising IT governance arrangements is challenging because the success of IT strategies and procedures is contingent upon a variety of internal and external factors (Bowen et. al., 2007).

This chapter aims to find the characteristics of IT governance in the Jordanian environment by using a developed model that are suitable to the domestic environment since no one size fits all (Rau, 2004), then applying this model on a sample from the Jordanian industrial companies. In addition, this study aims to investigate the security threats and control vulnerabilities that face the industrial companies.

THEORETICAL BACKGROUND

Here below the theoretical discussion is split into two main sections, IT governance and Security Threats.

First Section: IT Governance

For many organizations, IT and IT infrastructure that constitute major investments, if not managed properly, may impair and incur losses rather than enhance the organization's competitive position, on other words, organizations with effective IT governance have profits that are higher than other companies pursuing similar strategies. Moreover, the lack of effective IT governance has been shown to have adverse impacts on organizations, such as business losses, bad reputation, 'runaway projects', and inefficient operational activities (Weill and Ross,C, 2004).

The research into IT management practices at hundreds of organizations around the world has shown that most organizations are not generating optimal value from their IT investments. The most important factor distinguishing top-performing from substandard-performing is the level of leadership by business and senior managers in a handful of key IT decision. Selection from leading management literature shares the same basic idea "to be successful, the business side of an organization has to be involved and committed to what IT does". To deliver the services needs, IT has to be managed by business as a business. This is the core of IT governance (Kordel, 2004). Moreover, IT governance may be the great wall separating enterprise success from failure (Ulsch and Bamberger, 2006).

The concept of IT governance has emerged as a response to the growing pressure on all organizations to ensure that they are achieving value for money from their investment in IT and information systems, which includes ensuring that investment is aligned with organizational strategic priorities. It is based on the premise that the way in which IT is used and managed within an organization really matters, and that an institutional approach to IT needs to become embedded into central strategic planning (Coen and Kelly, 2007).

Consequently, both management and IT professionals concerned with design, implementation, and assessment of IT governance strategies to ensure that technology truly serve the needs of the business. Managers are increasingly aware that IT-related decisions and behaviors must be aligned with the organizational performance goals in order to generate value from IT, but many individuals throughout organizations make daily decisions influencing that value received. Consequently, IT governance is the process of which organizations align IT actions with their performance goals and assign accountability for those actions and their outcomes for all related parties that may affect this process (Weill and Ross, B, 2004).

The involvements of senior management in IT are positively influences on the overall effectiveness of IT governance as well as the existence of a culture of compliance in IT (Syaiful, 2006). Moreover, senior mangers awareness of IT governance is the best indicator of governance effectiveness; also managers that participate in management of IT are more progressive and advanced in their IT usage and impact (Jarvenpaa and Ives, 1991; Sohal and Fitzpatrick, 2002).

IT executives also play an important role in governing the IT activities through starting risk management by resolving factors associated with availability and access. Reducing these risks pays immediate benefits to the enterprise, and also provides a foundation for more difficult challenges of reducing accuracy and agility risks (Westerman, 2006).

Effective IT risk management requires three core disciplines. First, a well- managed, well-architected IT foundation. Second, a mature risk governance process including policies and procedures to identify, prevent and assess risky behavior. Third, risk awareness that helps everyone in the enterprise understand threats and mitigating opportunities (Schwarz and Hirschheim, 2003).

One of the most enduring problems faced by the Information Technology (IT) function is how it should organize and structure itself (Brown and Sambamurthy, 1999), where indeed implementing a sound IT governance strategy is believed to be key for having a successful IT function in organizations (Brown, 1997).

The accounting professions started to take IT governance concept as a part of the internal control system seriously since the declaration of Sarbanes-Oxley act in 2002 (Pauwels, 2006), and since the release of the Public Company Accounting Oversight Board's (PCAOB) Auditing Standard No. 2 (AS2) in 2004, even the release of Committee of Sponsoring Organization of the Treadway Commission's (COSO) Internal Control- Integrated Framework in early of the previous decade, COSO was originally formed in 1985 to sponsor the National Commission on Fraudulent Financial Reporting, an independent private sector initiative which studied the causal factors that can lead to fraudulent financial reporting and developed recommendations for public companies and their independent auditors, for the SEC and other regulators, and for educational institutions. The National Commission was jointly sponsored by five major professional associations in the United States, the American Accounting Association, the American Institute of Certified Public Accountants, Financial Executives International, The Institute of Internal Auditors, and the National Association of Accountants (now the Institute of Management Accountants). The Commission was wholly independent of each of the sponsoring organizations, and contained representatives from industry, public accounting, investment firms, and the New York Stock Exchange.

COSO framework is a highly abstract conceptual framework that does not identify control objectives at a level of specificity sufficient to design detailed audit test. Furthermore, the general nature of COSO does not address the complexity and special risk inherent in IT field (Colbert and Brown, 1996). Therefore, organizations and auditors in computerized environment start looking for a suitable framework, such as Control Objectives for Information and related Technology (COBIT) to supplement COSO framework. COBIT was initially developed as an IT benchmark consisting of best practices, then it is developed to become a framework that could be applicable as a dual use framework by which organizations can achieve efficiencies in either operation and/or IT audits through its use.

The Information System Audit and Control Foundation (ISACF) developed the COBIT, which is a framework of generally applicable information systems security and control practices of information technology control. This framework allows management to benchmark the security and control practices of IT environment. Additionally, it ensures that adequate security and controls exist (Lainhart and John, 2000).

However, control objectives under COBIT are defined in a process-oriented manner following the principle of business reengineering. This type of control is exercised at the domain and process level. The "IT control" concept is adapted by the ISACF report and defined as "A statement of the desired results or purpose to be achieved by implementing control procedures in a particular IT activity". This control is exercised at the IT activity

level (Curtis and Borthick, 1999). The COBIT IT domain consists of the following parts:

1. Planning and organization.
2. Acquisition and implementation.
3. Delivery, support and monitoring.

Thirty four IT processes are identified within each of the domains. Consequently, activities within processes are also identified activities to deal with day-to-day IT routines. The central control objective is to link IT domains, processes and activities to the entity's operational processes and activities. The basic objective of IT is to facilitate the accomplishment of business objectives. Business objectives are referred to as "Business Requirements for Information" which include the following (Hayale and Abu Khadra, 2006):

• Quality requirements (quality, cost and delivery).
• Fiduciary requirements, as defined by COSO (effectiveness and efficiency of operations, reliability of information and compliance with laws and regulations).

Figure 1. Interrelationship of COBIT components

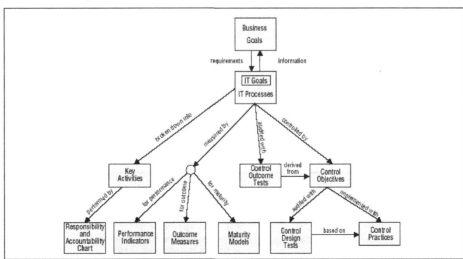

- Security requirements (confidentiality, integrity and availability).

COBIT contains other testable constructs including a comprehensive well-articulated Maturity Model for IT control. The Maturity Model enables management of a company to evaluate and determine where on the internal control spectrum their controls are currently located, especially with the increasing pressure on the senior managers to consider how well IT is being managed and what is needed to be done in future to reach an adequate level of management and control over IT function (Tuttle and Vandervelde, 2007).Maturity model enables enterprises not only to benchmark their present IT performance, but also to identify future targets for improvements. COBIT's Maturity Model is influenced by the organization's business goals, the operating environment and the industry practices.

Maturity Modeling for management and control over IT processes is based on a method of evaluating the organization, so that it can be rated from a maturity level of non-existent (0) to optimized (5). The maturity levels are designed as profiles of IT processes that an enterprise would recognize as description of possible current and future status. They are not designed as a threshold model, where one cannot move to the next level without having fulfilled all conditions of the lower level. The right level is determined by the enterprise type, environment and strategy.

COBIT's Maturity Model consists of six major attributes, awareness and communication, policies plans and procedures, tools and automation, skills and expertise, responsibility and accountability, goals and measurement. Accordingly, the authors will use the maturity model to evaluate the IT governance since this study to the best of the authors' knowledge is the first that attempts to create an overall measurement for management involvement in implementing IT governance using the six attributes of the maturity model.

Second Section: Security Threats (Control Vulnerabilities)

Reviewing the literature concerned with the security threats of Computerized Accounting Information Systems (CAIS) reveals the paucity of available studies in this particular area of research in Jordan. One reason for this is that this area is relatively new. One of the leading studies in the field of security threats was carried out by (Loch et al., 1992), who performed a survey in the United States to explore security threats in minicomputers, mainframe computers, and network environments. Loch et al. classified security threats from three dimensions (Source / Perpetrator / Intend), where the threat could be internal to the organization as the result of an employee's action or external, or the threat could be human related or non-human related. Moreover, threats

Figure 2. Graphic Representation of maturity model

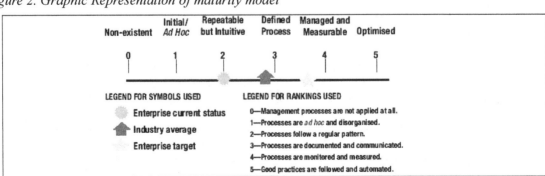

were also classified as accidental or intentional, irrespective of the source.

This model was used frequently in many later studies, because it was able to define the components of the risk that was associated with the threat. Loch et al. employed this model to develop security checklist, where the three dimensions were specified into each threat. Loch et al. didn't mention the intent in some threats figures like figure eight, because it seems that Loch considered that the intend can be realized by logic (Hackers – Intentional) and this may considered as weakness point.

Loch et al. security checklist consists of twelve security threats, as follows:

1. Accidental entry of "bad" data by the employee.
2. Intentional entry of "bad" data by the employee.
3. Accidental destruction of data by the employee.
4. Intentional destruction of data by the employee.
5. Unauthorized access to data / system by employee.
6. Inadequate control over media (Disks or tapes)
7. Poor control over manual handling on input / output.
8. Access to data / system by outsiders (hackers).
9. Access to data / system by outsiders (competitors).
10. Entry of computer viruses and worms into system.
11. Weak, ineffective, or inadequate physical control.
12. Natural disaster: fire, flood, loss of power or communication.

Loch et al. conducted an empirical survey on a sample of 657 senior MIS managers in the US. The respondents were asked to rank the top three security threats from the given list for each level of environment.

The study used three methods of data analysis; weighted votes for each security threat, 1st place votes and unit votes. The results of the study indicated that natural disasters (caused by natural factors, such as floods or earthquakes) and employees' accidental actions were ranked among the top three threats. External threats received 37% of the weighted votes while internal threats received 62.4%. These results confirmed the experts' claims in Loch's study which stated that the greatest threats came from the organization itself. The results of that study also revealed that accidental destruction of data by employees, accidental entry of bad data by employees, and inadequate control over media were perceived as the most important security threats in minicomputer environments. The most significant threats to mainframe computers were accidental entry of bad data by employees, natural disasters, and by accidental destruction of data by employees. Natural disasters, access to system by hackers, and weak controls were the main threats in the network environment.

(Davis, 1996) tried to check the status of security issues in practice. Davis used (Loch et al., 1992) list with some modifications that included adding the following security threats:

1. Poor segregation of information systems duties (e.g. Programming and operation).
2. Poor segregation of accounting duties (e.g. authorization, recoding, & custody)
3. Employee sharing passwords.
4. Interception of data transmission from remote location.
5. Technology advances faster than control practices.

Davis conducted his survey by sending the questionnaire to a random sample of the members of (AICPA) and Information Systems Audit and Control Association (ISACA). The respondents were asked to rank the top three security threats from the given list in each level of environment (Minicomputer/ Mainframe/ Network).

The results of the study indicated that accidental entry of "bad" data by employees and unauthorized Access to data and / or system by employees were ranked among the top three threats. The results of (Davis, 1996) study also revealed that unauthorized access to data and / or system by employees, accidental entry of "bad" data by employees and poor segregation of information system duties were perceived as the most important security threats in minicomputer environments. The most important threats to mainframe computers were accidental entry of "bad" data by employees, natural disaster, and unauthorized access to data and / or system by employees.

Unauthorized access to data and /or system by both outsiders (Hackers) and insiders (Employees) as well as technology advances, which are faster than control practices, were the main threats in the network environment.

(Davis, 1996) study results were similar to (Loch et al., 1992). Both studies considered the accidental threats one of the top threats in different environments, despite the fact that the sample was different in the two studies (MIS managers in Loch study/ Auditors in Davis study).

It is important to mention that (Davis, 1996) and (Loch et al., 1992) did not provide a clear differentiation between a security threat and a weak control procedure, or they assumed that a weak control procedure in a particular area could necessarily lead to a security threat in the same area.

Switching to client / server computing has recently increased because it is more flexible and offers more benefits. However, it causes additional risks; the flexibility that makes it attractive could also make it more vulnerable to security threats. (Ryan and Bordoloi, 1997) explored how companies are evaluated when they move from the mainframe to a client / server environment

and how they take security measures to protect against potential security threats.

Ryan and Bordoloi developed a fifteen point security threats list based on the information acquired from several industry consultants. Ryan and Bordoloi listed three new points of security threats while the rest of the fifteen points were a replication to the previous literature. These new security threats are:

1. Inadequate audit trial.
2. Loss due to inadequate backup or log files.
3. Single point of failure.

Ryan and Bordoloi developed a questionnaire circulated to the participants of an industrial technical conference. The conference's attendees were information system professionals.

A scale from 1 to 10 was used in Ryan and Bordoloi questionnaire to rate the seriousness of a security threat to a respondent's company in both of client / server and mainframe environments; where rating 1 meant that potential threat was not a concern to the company; and a rating of 10 meant that the threat was a high concern. In addition, the respondents were asked to rate the degree to which their companies had taken control procedures to protect against risks. Again, a scale from 10 degrees was used; where 1 meant that no procedures were taken against a potential risk; and where 10 meant that all possible measures were taken.

The Results of Ryan and Bordoloi study indicated that only seven security threats were significant. These seven threats are:

1. Accidental destruction of data by employees.
2. Accidental entry of erroneous data by employees.
3. Intentional destruction of data by employees.

4. Intentional entry of erroneous data by employees.
5. Loss due to inadequate backups or log files.
6. Single point of failure.
7. Inadequate audit trial.

In addition, the results indicated that companies were less prepared and had taken fewer measures to protect against potential security threats in a client /server environment when compared to a mainframe environment.

Again, Ryan and Bordoloi considered an inappropriate or weak control procedure as a security threat. Despite the fact that they measured the security controls separately.

Later (Davis, 1997) concluded top five security threats after performing a wider survey on 3054 members of the AICPA and Information Systems Audit and Control Association with a respond percentage of 11.6%. The Top five security threats come from seventeen potential threats which were included in the survey and for the different levels of environments (Minicomputers / Mainframe / and Network) to assist in identifying areas requiring more control emphasis. The top five security threats in microcomputer environments are:

1. Accidental destruction of data by employees.
2. Introduction of Computer viruses to the system.
3. Inadequate control over storage media.
4. Accidental entry of "bad" data by employees.
5. Weak (ineffective, inadequate) physical access controls permitting unauthorized access to systems.

Moreover, (Mccollum & Salierno, 2003) carried out a survey that covered many areas; one of which was network security threats. This survey which was performed on IS managers and auditors ranked the top four security threats as follows:

1. Viruses.
2. Unauthorized access by hackers / other external parties.
3. Internal threats.
4. Lack of security expertise in the organization.

One of the few studies in this field in the Middle East is that of (Abu Musa, 2004) who investigated the significant security threats of computerized accounting information systems (CAIS) in Saudi organizations, through conducting an empirical survey on a random sample of Saudi organizations. (Abu Musa, 2004) developed his own list of threats that contained 19 factors which represented only what were considered to be a security threat and not a control weakness. Abu Musa justified the difference between the threats by stating that "policies weakness doesn't itself create the crime", in other words weak CS don't necessary mean the occurrence of a security threat. (Abu Musa, 2004) security threat list included a new contribution that can be summarized as follows:

1. Differentiating between natural and human made disasters.
2. Focusing on the threats that relate to data output such as:
   • Suppression of the destruction of outputs.
   • Creation of fictitious / incorrect outputs.
   • Unauthorized copying of outputs.
   • Unauthorized document visibility by displaying on monitors or printing on paper.
   • Printing and distributing of information by unauthorized persons.
   • Printing and distributing information and directing it to people who are not entitled to receive it.
   • Sensitive documents handed to non security cleared personnel for shredding.

- Interception of data transmissions from remote locations.

In addition, it is important to mention that (Abu Musa, 2004) checklist contained one point not related to AIS security threats but to system effectiveness, this point is (creation of fictitious / incorrect output).

Abu Musa's methodology depended on a nineteen-figure questionnaire. The respondents were asked to scale the occurrence frequency of each security threat according to a five-grade scale (Less than once a year, once a year to monthly, once a month to weekly, once a week to daily, and daily or more frequently). Abu Musa's main concern was using frequencies that represent a proxy of threat, materiality, importance, or risks – regardless of the occurred financial losses.

Abu Musa did not ask the respondents to scale the threats in different environments like the prior studies (Minicomputer, Network...etc), to avoid excluding any observation that does not have all these environments. Abu Musa study results revealed that the most perceived security threats were accidental and intentional entry of bad data, accidental destruction of data by employees, employees' sharing passwords, introduction of computer viruses, and directing prints and distributing information to people who are not entitled to receive.

Abu Musa's results were consistent with (Ryan, 1997) and (Davis, 1997) results regarding "entry of bad data" and "data destruction", also Abu Musa's results agreed with (Mccollum & Salierno, 2003) in respect of "introduction of computer viruses".

In this article we developed a list of twenty four security threats, based primarily on the previously mentioned studies; this list also included some suggested security threats were examined in this article for the first time, these are 8, 9 and 18. The developed list explained below:

1. Sensitive documents are handed to non-Security outsiders.
2. Loss of original stored data and source documents which can not be reissued electronically.
3. Interception of data transmission from remote locations (External).
4. Accidental entry of "bad" data by employee.
5. Intentional entry of "bad" data by employee.
6. Accidental destruction of data by the employee.
7. Intentional destruction of data by the employee.
8. Accidental fault approval by seniors.
9. Intentional Fault approval by seniors.
10. CAIS output destruction by employee, such as notifications.
11. Introduction (entry) of computer viruses to the system.
12. Natural disaster such as fire, flood, loss of power.
13. Human made disaster such as fire, loss of power.
14. Employee's sharing passwords.
15. Theft of Data/ Information by hackers.
16. Unauthorized Logical Access by employees.
17. Unauthorized Logical Access by outsiders.
18. Unauthorized document visibility through displaying it monitors, etc.
19. Printing and distributing of information by unauthorized employees.
20. Unauthorized employee access server room (AIS site).
21. Unauthorized outsiders access server room (AIS site).
22. Unauthorized copying of CAIS outputs by outsiders.
23. Photocopying sensitive documents or copying system media by unauthorized persons.

24. Prints and distributed information are directed to employees who are not entitled to receive it.

RESEARCH HYPOTHESES

The current study examines the following hypotheses in null form:

H_{01}: The Jordanian Industrial companies do not have effective IT governance implementation.

This hypothesis can be divided to the following null hypotheses:

1.1 The Jordanian industrial companies do not have effective implementation of "IT awareness and communications".

1.2 The Jordanian industrial companies do not have effective implementation of "IT Tools and Automation".

1.3 The Jordanian industrial companies do not have effective implementation of "IT staff skills and expertise".

1.4 The Jordanian industrial companies do not have effective implementation of "Responsibility and Accountability".

1.5 The Jordanian industrial companies do not have effective implementation of "Goal Setting and Measurement".

1.6 The Jordanian industrial companies do not have effective implementation of "Policies, Plan and Procedures".

H_{02}: The IT governance implementation level does not affect Security Threats frequency.

METHODOLOGY

The population of the study consists of all Jordanian industrial companies that listed in Amman Stock Exchange (ASE). The number of industrial companies in Jordan is ninety. The researchers covered companies' headquarters where the targeted respondents were expected to exist. The data is collected by using a self-administered questionnaire that measures the existence of maturity model dimensions attributes using nominal scale and Security Threats frequency. The questionnaire was designed after a preliminary observation on the practice and reviewing the available literature. The researchers circulated the research questionnaire among the parties that had the ability and knowledge to answer it. Therefore, the researchers distributed the questionnaire to the internal information systems auditors (CISA holders) or Head of Computer Departments (HOCD). Researchers were not able to circulate the questionnaire to CEOs.

The aforementioned Maturity Model attributes are categorized in the first section of the questionnaire under the following dimensions according to their functions and goals, where the respondents were asked to indicate whether the point is exist or not:

- Awareness and communications (Question 1 – 3).
- Tools and automation (Question 4 – 6).
- Responsibility and accountability (Question 7 – 9).
- Skills and expertise (Question 10 –12).
- Goal setting and measurement (Question 13 –15).
- Policies, plans and procedures (Question 16 –33).

While the second section of the questionnaire listed the security threats as mentioned before.

Herein, the respondents were asked to indicate the frequency of each security threat using ordinal scale ((none, once yearly, once monthly, once weekly and daily).

Ninety questionnaires were distributed to the selected respondents; thirty three were received in a usable format, indicating a response rate of ~37%. To investigate study instrument validity, the researchers consulted thirteen experts (Professionals and Academics). The experts were asked to make sure that the research questionnaire does not miss any element that might affect the study results or create bias in the questions.

The researchers used Cronbach's Alpha to check the questionnaire stability for all of its components. Furthermore, reliability analysis allowed the researchers to study the measurement scales and the items that make them up. In the current study, the researchers did not use some of the central tendency measurements such as the mean, because it is not valid for the nominal or ordinal scale. Consequently, the researchers did not calculate the mean for respondents' answers that were measured by using nominal scale (Exist/Not exist) in the first section and by using ordinal scale in the second section. Furthermore, variance measure was not used because it is calculated by using squared distances from the mean since the researchers utilized the nominal scale. Finally, frequency distribution is a summary table in which the data is arranged into conveniently-established, numerically-ordered class grouping or categories. Due to that, frequency is a valid measurement for the nominal scale and used by the researchers in the current study.

For the first major hypothesis that measures the existence of maturity model attributes in the industrial companies, the researchers used Z-test for proportion that pertain to population proportion P Maturity Model attributes implementation percentage by calculating the sample proportion Ps, then the values of this statistic compared to the hypothesized value of the parameter P (Implantation Standards) so that the decision can be made about the hypothesis.

Herein and to apply the aforementioned statistics, the researchers convert the nominal scale qualitative responses to numerical (percentage) values through the following steps (Hyalae and Abu Khadra, 2006):

- Coding the nominal scales (Not Exist, Exist), where 0 given to not exist and 1 for exist.
- Summing up of all question values for each variable.
- Calculating the proportion by dividing the previous step result on the number of questions.

The materiality weights for the Maturity Model attributes were considered to be equal (Klapper and Love, 2002), because the materiality of each dimension is contingent upon a variety of internal and external factors related to each environment (Bowen et. al., 2007). Additionally, the researchers used the P value in order to test the sampling distribution normality using the following rule: "If the number of success (X) and the number of failures are each at least five, the sampling distribution of proportion approximately follows a standardized normal distribution"(Berenson et. al., 2002).

On the other hand, to measure the second hypothesis that measures the IT governance affect on the Security Threats frequencies, the researchers convert the ordinal scale into percentages through the following steps:

1. Data that withdrawn from the respondents' answers is coded with values ranging from one to five as follows:

None	1
Once yearly	2
Once Monthly	3
Once Weekly	4
Daily	5

2. Divide the sum of numeric values for all of the security threats on the maximum score of the security threats (24 times 5 = 120)

By doing the aforementioned steps, the independent variable and dependent variable become valid to be included in the casualty analysis. To achieve that the researchers used a measure of liner association that investigate the straight-line relationship of the type (Y= α + β X) where X (IT governance overall evaluation) is the independent variable, and Y (Security Threats Frequencies) is the dependent variable.

To check the aptness of the study regression analysis, the researchers check the following assumptions:

1. Normality of error.
2. Homoscedasticity.
3. Independence of errors.

The first assumption, normality, requires that the error around the line of regression be normally distributed at each value of X. Like the ANOVA *F*-test, regression analysis is robust against departure from the normality assumption. In other words, "The error term has a normal distribution with a mean 0". The researchers use a histogram or P-P plot of the residuals to help check the assumption of normality of the error term. To meet normality assumption, the shape of the histogram should approximately follow the shape of the normal curve, and the P-P plotted residuals should follow the 45-degree line.

The second assumption, homoscedasticity, requires that the variation around the line of regression be constant for all values of X. This means that the errors vary in the same amount when X is at low value as when X is at high value. The researchers use the plot of residuals by the predicted values. Using this procedure, the homoscedasticity assumption is violated when the plot appears to be a fanning effect in which the variability of the residuals increases as X increases.

The third assumption, independence of errors, requires that the value of the error term for a given case be independent of the values of the variables in the model and of the values of the error term for other cases. The researchers use the Durbin-Watson statistic (*D)* to measure the correlation between each residuals. When successive residuals are positively auto-correlated, the value of *D* will approach 0, if the residuals are not correlated; the value of *D* will be greater than 2 and could even approach its maximum value of 4.

RESULTS

The majority of the respondents (81%) reported that they had three or more years of experience in their current position, while only (19%) of the respondents had less than three years of experience in their current position. While almost (88%) of the respondents declared that they had three or more years of experience in the same company, while only (12%) reported that they had less than four years of experience in the observed company.

Consequently, It can be concluded that the individuals who answered the questionnaire had the minimum required level of knowledge, which may increase the credibility and reliability of their answers.

The following sections however focuses on the statistical findings related to maturity model dimensions. It consists of descriptive statistics such as frequencies and percentages.

Awareness and Communications

To explore the existence and the implementation awareness and communication procedures, the respondents were asked to indicate the existence of such procedures at their companies. The statistical findings revealed that 76% of the respondents indicated that their management created permanent communication channels with IT seniors (CIO) in order to guarantee identifying corporate strategy and goals. Furthermore, 58% of the respondents indicate that industrial companies' management receives mapping report prepared by IT seniors that illustrate the predefined current and future business needs on hand, and the probable suitable information technology solutions on the other hand. The results also showed that 85% of the respondents believed that industrial companies' management receives continuous reporting regarding IT alignment status with organization strategy, regulatory obligations and laws, prospective risks and point up the high value added from IT investments.

These results initially indicate that industrial companies' management are aware of the importance of aligning company strategy with the IT goals and making sure to have suitable and permanent communication channels.

Tools and Automation

To investigate the existence and the implementation of adequate automation tools in the industrial companies, the respondents were asked to indicate whether the related procedure existed or not. The statistical findings revealed that 39% of the respondents claimed that their companies have automation solution which is software that can detect, validate and report unauthorized changes out of policy action on the entire IT infrastructure in real time, offering immediate and effective corrections. On the other hand 76% of the respondents reported that their companies have database activity auditing tool that can automatically monitor activities and detect control exceptions. Moreover, 18% of the respondents claimed that their companies integrated software system that runs off a unified database such as Enterprise Resource Planning System (ERP), allowing departments to share information and communicate easily with each other. Such results reveal moderate to week level of using automation tools.

Responsibility and Accountability

According to 39% of the respondents their company's management has clear identification of the responsible employees for the different IT activities such as IT principles, IT architecture, IT infrastructure, business application needs and IT investment and prioritization. In addition, 76% of the respondents indicate that their management develops clearly stated policies that explicitly describe honest and dishonest behaviors. Such policies are of a written form and communicated to employees. Finally only 21% of the industrial companies' respondents revealed that the management requires material dishonest behaviors log report and the correction action for each incident. Again, we can conclude a moderate to week level of applying Responsibility and accountability aspect.

Skills and Expertise

The statistical results revealed that 73% respondents reported that their companies state high hiring standards for sensitive positioned IT employees include back ground check, educational check, confidentiality agreements. Moreover, the management requests from the IT department a continuous employee performance review where employees must confirm their understanding of and compliance with the entity security policies.

Some of the respondents indicate that management did not request from the IT department a continuous employee performance review, while (67%) of the respondents claimed that their management requested it.

Goal Setting and Measurement

Based on the results of the majority of the respondents, industrial companies' strategy clearly states the objectives of the IT department for each fiscal year while the IT department strategic plan cites the corporate business plan as the prioritization of its initiatives and projects. Management also conduct a strategic planning sessions during which all executives meet to determine the company's goals and strategies for the coming year, and where departments are urged to develop their operational plans for the year accordingly.

Significant percent of the respondents indicate that management did not measure IT department performance effectiveness and efficiency, while (61%) of the respondents claimed that their management measure it.

Policies, plans and procedures

Herein the descriptive statistics revealed some major discrepancies in this section where almost 79% of the respondents indicate that industrial companies' management did not approve employing DBMS that defines each type of data, the level of protection required for each type and to whom data is required. A close percentage was also given to both of the reporting that illustrates the required modification to internet security procedures and the simulation of a disturbance for thorough (Full) testing of the disaster recovery plan (DRP).

Moreover, 58% of the respondents claimed that the industrial companies' management does not request periodic assessment reports from

IT department on the effectiveness of control procedures concerning source data, data entry, data processing, data transmission and output controls.

Table 1 shows the statistical findings related to the hypothesis testing. To test the first major hypothesis and related minor hypotheses, Z-test for proportion was conducted.

The developed norms are used as a cut point for the minimum accepted percentages of applying maturity model, where the company is considered to apply the maturity model dimension if its own evaluation percentage exceeds this norm. The researchers then tested for significant differences between the applied percentages in the Jordanian industrial companies and these norms using Z test for proportion.

Based on the results presented in Table 1, p-value appears to be more than 0.05 for awareness all IT governance dimensions. The Z value is also less than 1.96, which means it falls in a non-rejection area. All of that lead us to not to reject all the null minor hypothesis. According to the aforementioned results, we accept the main null hypothesis that stated, (Industrial companies do not have effective IT governance implementation).

Table 2 shows the security threats that are covered in the current research ranked starting with the most frequent security threats. Accidental entry of "bad" data by employee is ranked as the

Table 1. Z-test for precent differences

Dimension	Norms	%	N	Z	Value P	S
Awareness and Communications	70%	21 %	33	(6.116)	1.0000	A
Tools and Automation.	70%	18 %	33	(6.496)	0.9999	A
Responsibility and Accountability	70%	21 %	33	(6.116)	1.0000	A
Skills and Expertise.	70%	27 %	33	(5.356)	0.9999	A
Goal Setting and Measurement.	70%	42 %	33	(1.557)	0.9403	A
Policies, Plans and Procedures.	80%	18 %	33	(6.496)	1.0000	A
Overall	70%	24 %	33	(5.736)	0.9999	A

Table 2. Ranked security threats

No	Security Threats	Total votes
1	Accidental entry of "bad" data by employee	121
2	Introduction (entry) of computer viruses to the system	64
3	Natural disaster such as fire, flood, loss of power	62
4	Employee's sharing passwords	59
5	Accidental fault approval by seniors	57
6	Prints and distributed information are directed to employee who are not entitled to receive it	50
7	Unauthorized document visibility through displaying it monitors, etc	48
8	Accidental destruction of data by the employee	44
9	CAIS output destruction by employee, such as notifications.	39
10	Loss of original stored data and source documents which can not be reissued electronically	37
11	Printing and distributing of information by unauthorized employees	37
12	Unauthorized employee access server room (AIS site).	37
13	Sensitive documents are handed to non-Security outsiders.	36
14	Intentional entry of "bad" data by employee	36
15	Unauthorized Logical Access by employees.	36
16	Theft of Data / Information by hackers.	35
17	Intentional destruction of data by the employee	34
18	Human made disaster such as fire, loss of power	34
19	Unauthorized Logical Access by outsiders.	34
20	Unauthorized outsiders access server room (AIS site).	34
21	Photocopying sensitive documents or copying system media by unauthorized persons.	34
22	Interception of data transmission from remote locations (External).	33
23	Intentional Fault approval by seniors	33
24	Unauthorized copying of CAIS outputs by outsiders	33

Table 3. Regression results

Std. Error of the Estimate	Adjusted R Square	R Square	R	Model
.04050	-.031	.001	.037(a)	1

most frequent security threats while unauthorized copying of CAIS output by outsiders is ranked as the least frequent security threat.

A measure of liner regression is used to measure the hypothesis that measure the causal relationship between IT governance implementation percentage and security threats frequencies "H0 2: The IT governance implementation level does not affect Security Threats frequency. "

The results of the regression taking into the consideration the procedure assumptions indicates that there is weak negative affect with accepted level of P (less than .05) between the IT governance and security threats, which lead to reject the null the hypothesis despite the small percent of adjusted R Square (3%)

CONCLUSION

The study showed that Jordanian industrial companies did not apply IT governance in its comprehensive methodology despite the implementation of some of its aspects. Due to the statistical findings of the current study, which indicate that major procedures of the maturity model was not applied in a proper way, we believe that industrial companies should give more attention to IT governance. Professionals industrial companies should work more to increase the IT governance strength for all of its dimensions. Also the results revealed the existence of IT governance affect over the security threats frequencies which emphasis on the importance of improving IT governance implementation in the industrial companies.

LIMITATIONS AND FURTHER RESEARCH AGENDA

As with all research, this study is subject to number of limitations and these might be explored in future research. The study adopted the quantitative

approach to test the study theoretical model, thus limiting the choice of methodology to a cross-sectional survey, which is only concerned with employing quantitative methods of data collection. Thus, a questionnaire survey was adopted in this study and the researchers were not able to question the respondents to ascertain in more details the exact nature of the responses. Therefore, extra care and caution is essential when interpreting questionnaire findings. However, the problems relating to questionnaire surveys can be minimized by undertaking a number of post-questionnaire interviews. However, a time constraint, interview accessibility, and the availability of interviewees for a significant amount of time constrains the researchers from undertaking interviews. Nevertheless, interviews to pursue issues raised by the survey results is a fruitful area for future research. In addition, the results of this study apply only to the target sample operating in Jordan. Thus, these results may not be generalizable to other sectors. Future research however needs to be extended to other industry sectors in order to generalize the results.

Despite the limitations that have been identified previously, this study has provided several important insights into issues relating to IT governance and security threats. Hopefully, this study will encourage researchers to conduct further empirical studies about the implementation of the IT governance to clarify some of the complexity and confusion that is accompanied with this approach.

REFERENCES

Abu Musa, A. (2004). *Exploring the Perceived Threats of Computerized Accounting Information Systems In Emerging Countries: An Empirical Study on Saudi Organization*. European Conference On Accounting information System, Section two.

AICPA Auditing Standards Board. (2001, April). *SAS No. 94: The Effect of Information Technology on the Auditor's Consideration of Internal Control in a Financial Statement Audit.*

Berenson et. al. (2002). *Business Statistics, Concepts and Application*, Eighth Edition. Prentice Hall.

Bowen P., Cheung M., & Rohde F. (2007). Enhancing IT governance practices: A model and case study of an organization's efforts. *International Journal of Accounting Information Systems* (pp. 191-221).

Brown, C., & Sambamurthy, V. (1999). *Repositioning the IT organization to enable business transformation.* Pinnaflex Educational Resource, Cincinnati,OH.

Brown, C. (1997). Examining the hybrid IS governance solution: evidence from a single case study. *Information System Research,* (1), 69-94.

COBiT 4.1 Executive Summary Framework. Coen, M., & Kelly, U. (2007, January). Information management and governance in UK higher education institutions: bringing IT in from the cold. *Perspectives, 11*(1).

Colbert, J. L., & Brown, P. L. (1996). A comparison of internal controls: COBIT, SAC, COSO and SAS 55/78. *IS Audit Control J, 4*, 26-35.

Curtis, M., & Borthick (1999). Evaluation of Internal Control from a Control Objective Narrative. *Journal of Information Systems, 13*(1), Spring.

Davis, E. (1996). Perceived Security Threats to Today's Accounting Information Systems: Survey of CISAs. *IS Audit & Control Journal, 3*, 38-41.

Davis, E. (1997, March). An Assessment of Accounting Information Security. *CPA Journal, 66*(3).

Greenstein, M., & Vasarhelyi, M. (2000, July). The Electronization of Business Process. *European conference on AIS, Section One.*

Hayale, T., & Abu Khadra, H. (2006). Evaluation of the Effectiveness of Control Systems in the Computerized Accounting Information Systems: An Empirical Research Applied on Jordanian Banking Sector. *Journal of Accounting – Business & Management, 13*(2006), 39-68.

Henry, L. (1997). A Study of the Nature and Security of Accounting Information Systems: The Case of Hampton Roads, Virginia. *The Mid- Atlantic Journal of Business, 33*(63), 171-189.

ITGI (IT Governance Institute) Board briefing on IT Governance 2001.

Jarvenpaa, S., & Ives, B. (1991). Executive involvement and participation in the management of information technology. *MIS Quarterly, 15*(2), 205-227.

Klapper, L., & Love, I. (2002). *Corporate Governance, Investor protection and performance in Emmerging Markets.* working paper. The World Bank.

Kordel, L. (2004). IT Governance Hands-on Using COBiT to Implement IT Governance. *Information Systems Control Journal, 2.*

Lainhart, I. V., & John, W. (2000). COBIT: A Methodology for Managing and Controlling Information and Information Technology Risks and Vulnerabilities. *Journal of Information Systems, 14*(1).

Li, C., Lim, J., & Wang Q. (2007). Internal and External influences on IT control governance. *International Journal of Accounting Information Systems,* (pp. 225-239).

Loch, D., Houston, H., & Warkentin, M. E. (1992, June). Threats to Information Systems: Today's Reality, Yesterday's Understanding. *MIS quarterly Journal,* (pp. 173–186).

Oak Vale Fund Report, www.oakvaluefund.com, p1, July 2004.

Pauwels, E. (2006, August). Change governance series- Making Sense of regulations and best practices. *Copyright ©Serena Software, Inc.*

Mccollum, T., & Salierno, D. Choosing the Right Tools. *Internal Auditor Journal*, (pp. 34-43).

Rau, K. (2004, Fall). Effective Governance of IT: Design, objectives, roles, and relationships. *Information System Management.*

Ryan, S. D., & Bordoloi, B. (1997). Evaluating Security Threats in Mainframe and Client Server Environments. *Information & Management, 32*(3), 137-142.

Schwarz, A., & Hirschheim, R. (n.d.). An extended platform logic perspective of IT governance: managing perception and activities of IT. *Journal of Strategic Information Systems, 12*(2003), 129-166.

Sohal, A., & Fitzpatrick, P. (2002). IT governance and management in large Australian organizations. *Int. J. Production Economics, 75*(2002), 97-112.

Syaiful, A. (2006 Jan-Apr). Effective information technology governance mechanisims: An Australian study. *Gadjah Mada International Journal of Business, 8*(1), 69-102.

Timothy, B., Knechel, W., Jeff, R. P. L., & Willingham, J. J. (1998). An Empirical Relationship between the Computerization of Accounting Systems and Incidence and Size of Audit Differences. *Auditing Journal, 17*(1),Spring 1998.

Tuttle, B., & Vandervelde, S. (2007). An empirical examination of COBiT as an internal control framework for information technology. *International Journal of Accounting Information Systems, 8*(2007), 240-263.

Ulsch, M., & Bamberger, J. (2006, March). *Sound IT governance needs requires breadth and depth.* Financial Executive.

Weill, P., & Ross, J. (2004a). *IT governance: how top performers manage IT decision rights for superior results.* Boston, MA: Harvard Business School Press.

Weill, P., & Ross, J. (2004b). *IT governance on one page.* MIT Sloan Management.

Weill, P., & Ross, J. (2004c). *How Top Performers Manage IT Decision Right for Superior Results.* Harvard Business School Press.

Westerman, G. (2006, December). IT risk management: From IT necessity to strategic business value. CISR WP No.366 and MIT Sloan WP No.4658-07.

Zikmond, W. (2003). *Business Research Methods,* 7th edition. Thomson publisher.

APPENDIX: QUESTIONNAIRE COMPONENTS

No	Question	Group
1	Management creates permanent communication channels with IT seniors (CIO) in order to guarantee identifying corporate strategy and goals	Awareness and Communications
2	Management receives mapping report prepared by IT seniors illustrates the predefined current and future business needs on hand and the probable suitable information technology solutions on the other hand.	Awareness and Communications
3	Management receives continuous reporting regarding IT alignment status with organization strategy, regulatory obligations and laws, prospective risks and point up the high value added from IT investments	Awareness and Communications
4	The company has automation solution which is software that can detect, validate and report unauthorized changes out of policy action on the entire IT infrastructure in real time, offering immediate and effective corrections	Tools and Automation
5	The company has database activity auditing tool that can automatically monitor activities and detect control exceptions	Tools and Automation
6	The company integrated software system that runs off a unified database such as Enterprise Resource Planning System (ERP), allowing departments to share information and communicate easily with each other	Tools and Automation
7	Management has clear identification of the responsible employees for the different IT activities such as IT principles, IT architecture, IT infrastructure, business application needs and IT investment and prioritization	Responsibility and Accountability
8	Management develops clearly stated policies that explicitly describe honest and dishonest behaviors. Such policies are of a written form and communicated to employees.	Responsibility and Accountability
9	Management requires material dishonest behaviors log report and the correction action for each incident	Responsibility and Accountability
10	Management's state high hiring standards for sensitive positioned IT employees include back ground check, educational check, confidentiality agreements.	Skills and Expertise
11	Management requests from the IT department a continuous employee performance review, where employees must confirm their understanding of and compliance with the entity security policies.	Skills and Expertise
12	Management requests implementing continuous employees training program to enhance employee's knowledge and skills and provide opportunities for individual career growth.	Skills and Expertise
13	The corporate strategy clearly states the objectives of the IT department for each fiscal year while the IT department strategic plan cites the corporate business plan as the prioritization of its initiatives and projects.	Goal Setting and Measurement
14	Management conducts strategic planning sessions during which all executives meet to determine the company's goals and strategies for the coming year, and where departments are urged to develop their operational plans for the year accordingly.	Goal Setting and Measurement
15	Management measures IT department performance effectiveness and efficiency, this is done by having integrated performance measurement system linking IT performance to business goals by global application of the IT balance scorecard.	Goal Setting and Measurement
16	Management requests that all critical personnel identified in a DRP are holding current version of the plan both onsite and offsite	Policies, Plans and Procedures
17	Management periodically requests a DRP checklist testing report from DRP team; this report goes through the DRP procedures to identify gaps bottlenecks and other weaknesses in the plan.	Policies, Plans and Procedures
18	Management assigns personnel to monitor and document variation on procedures while implementing a DRP test.	Policies, Plans and Procedures
19	Management simulates a disturbance for partial testing of the DRP.	Policies, Plans and Procedures
20	Management annually simulates a disturbance for thorough (Full) testing of the DRP.	Policies, Plans and Procedures

continued on following page

APPENDIX: CONTINUED

21	Management requests a DRP simulation test results report from DRP team, and activates required modifications and improvement to the tested plan.	Policies, Plans and Procedures
22	Management follows up and orders to correct all discrepancies that were reported by the risk-management team concerning examined security threats.	Policies, Plans and Procedures
23	Management receives a report from the IT department on updated system description to authorized users regarding sensitive data access.	Policies, Plans and Procedures
24	Management receives a report prepared by the IT department showing incident logs and potential significant security breaches in order to improve related security procedures.	Policies, Plans and Procedures
25	Management sets and emphases policies prohibiting visitors from carrying cell phones, lab tops, PDAs and other portable devices that could capture confidential information while touring the entities facilities.	Policies, Plans and Procedures
26	Due to a new implementation or acquisition, management receives a report from the IT department on modification of existing physical and logical access security procedures or the development of new access procedures.	Policies, Plans and Procedures
27	Management requests a periodic review report from the IT department regarding the appropriate use of internet resources (Trusted and un-trusted resources) within the organization.	Policies, Plans and Procedures
28	Management requests report prepared by IT department periodically illustrating the required modification to internet security procedures such as, antivirus and Firewalls.	Policies, Plans and Procedures
29	IT reports to the management frequently the audit trail record that detects material unauthorized network operations activity.	Policies, Plans and Procedures
30	Management approves employing DBMS that defines each type of data, the level of protection required for each type and to whom data is required.	Policies, Plans and Procedures
31	Automated data infrastructure management system is approved by the management to be employed, such system standardize IT operating procedures for maintaining, backups and upgrades for data libraries and directories.	Policies, Plans and Procedures
32	Management requests periodic assessment reports from IT department on the effectiveness of control procedures concerning source data, data entry, data processing, data transmission and output controls.	Policies, Plans and Procedures
33	Management emphases using strong security procedures for manual external data transmission that concerned to sensitive and confidential information	Policies, Plans and Procedures

Chapter VIII
The Critical Success Factors of Web–Based Supply Chain Collaboration Adoption:
An Empirical Study

Saad Ghaleb Yaseen
Al-Zaytoonh University of Jordan, Jordan

Khaled Saleh Al Omoush
Al-Zaytoonh University of Jordan, Jordan

ABSTRACT

This chapter aims to identify the Critical Success Factors (CSFs) and outcomes of Web-based Supply Chain Collaboration (SCC). A total of 230 questionnaires were initially distributed to sample respondents of seven manufacturing firms in Jordan that use Web systems to collaborate with supply chain members. The results showed that top management support, IT infrastructure, training and education, business processes reengineering, trust among partners, open information sharing, and performance measurement are critical factors for Web-based SCC implementation success. In addition, this study revealed that Web-based SCC implementation is positively related to supply chain relationship quality, performance effectiveness, and performance efficiency.

1. INTRODUCTION

The evolution and development of using the Internet and Web sites in business in the form of Web systems has been a major catalyst of change within and among organizations recently.

Jordan has recently embarked on an ambitious plan to make full use of the information technology capabilities. Although the Internet boom has been drastically affecting ways of doing business in Jordan, Web systems adoption by Jordan's firms is still scant, and the Web applications is relatively immature. At the same time, using Web systems is evolving, and the number of organizations involved is growing.

Raising awareness and knowledge is essential for adopting Web-based SCC concept in Jordan, at both the organizational and inter-organizational levels, especially for manufacturing firms that are at the heart of the supply chain that are insufficiently informed about Web-based SCC.

Information technology alone is an insufficient part in ensuring implementation success. **Successful deployment of Web applications requires smooth integration of a number of factors.** The challenge for organizations today is to understand the factors that play a critical role in utilizing Internet and web systems capabilities successfully, and their implications on SCC to enable them to compete in the electronic age. **Although many studies covered the role and the impact of information technology in SCM and collaboration, there are a few contributions about the CSFs that would support practitioners in their efforts to successfully achieving of Web-based SCC.**

The main objective of this research is to **identify and understand the critical factors that affect the use of the Internet and Web systems successfully in SCC, and address them effectively to ensure that the promised benefits can be realized and failures can be avoided. Therefore, the objectives of this research are to**

- Provide Jordanians supply chains members with better understanding, and a clear picture of the Web-based SCC concept and its success requirements.
- Identify the CSFs and subfactors of Web-based SCC.
- Determine the outcomes of Web-based SCC to judge whether an implementation is a success or a failure.
- Identify the relationship between the CSFs and the outcomes of Web-based SCC.

2. LITERATURE REVIEW

2.1 Supply Chain Collaboration (SCC)

The advent of SCC invents the need, at the interorganisational level, to pay special attention to the recognizing of collaboration in order to prepare the chain members to build collaborative efforts successfully (Lambert et al., 2005). Collaboration in the context of supply chain, is still relatively evolving, appeared in the mid of 1990s in the most known form of **Collaborative Planning Forecasting and Replenishment (CPER)**. The foundation of collaboration is that a single company cannot successfully compete by itself and secure higher performance by operating individually (Mason and Lefrere, 2003).

Collaboration describes the close **cooperation** among autonomous business partners connecting in common objectives and joint decision-making process. SCC characterized by sharing the information, knowledge, risk and profits, joint planning, **coordination**, process integration between supply chain members, and collective performance metrics to evaluate individual and collective performance (Simatupang and Sridharan., 2005).

There are many definitions of the term SCC present in the literature. For example, Simatupang et al, (2004) described SCC as two or more independent firms jointly working to align their supply chain process to create value to end customers and stakeholders with great success than acting alone. Bagchi and Skjoett-Larsen (2005) defined SCC as a dimension of **integration** with key suppliers and key customers that lead to involve supply chain partners in decision-making with long term relationships with key suppliers and customers. Min et al., (2005) defined SCC as **a firm's culture of working together with other firms** toward a common set of goals that bring mutual benefits to a partnering relationship.

A recent literature concluded that SCC is still far more difficult to achieve (Balasubramanian and Tewary, 2005), (Mason and Lefrere, 2003), (Kampstra et al., 2006). Based on a literature surveys on SCC, Kampstra, et al., (2006) suggested that the reasons include time span, IT infrastructure, trust, organization, competition, fear of external pressure, powerhouses within entity, financial, formal and informal business cultures, and conflicting goals and values.

2.2 Web-Based SCC

The rapid advances in technology, including the Internet and the Web, and the decrease in technological expenditures have made great increases in **Web-based systems** investments as a major trend at present's business environment. Collaboration in a Web-based supply chain environment plays a major role in achieving a sustainable competitive edge (Lefebvre et al., 2003). The Web technologies have made supply chain coordination a viable managerial and strategic choice and promote integrated SCM (Ranganathan et al., 2004). **EDI** was the first tool that was widely diffused and enabled SCC, while more recently **Internet-based applications** seem to overcome most of its original limitations (Cassivi, 2006).

There is no precise definition of Web-based SCC. There are many related terms concerning the use of the Internet and Web systems in SCM and SCC. In the context of SCM, Ngai et al. (2004) defined **Web-based SCM** system as an **Internet-enabled SCM** system that integrates networks of suppliers, factories, warehouses, distribution centers and retailers, through which the whole chain of logistic processes are managed so that faster and more flexible coordination can be achieved between a company and its customers and suppliers along the supply-chain. Williams et al. (2002) defined the **electronic supply chain** as **Supply Chain Management (SCM)** organizations that are linked within and between their trading partners by the Internet and/or EDI to buy, sell, move products, services and cash flow. Lefebvre et al. (2003) considered **electronic collaboration** as business-to-business interactions facilitated by the Internet.

For the purposes of this paper, Web-based SCC is defined as an Internet based systems that link supply chain members with sharing information and knowledge, joint decisions making and planning, integrated supply chain processes, collective performance metrics, in highly coordinated and integrated ways and on a real time basis, to improve supply chain performance and gain competitive advantages.

3. THE PROPOSED CSFS OF WEB-BASED SCC

It has been documented that SCC is facilitated by the existence of an efficient and effective information technology (IT) systems specially after transforming business operations from traditional EDI systems to Web-based systems (Ngai et al., 2004). Supply chain **IOSs** have evolved through four phases from the sharing of paper-based documents, **EDI**, **ERP** systems linked across multiple members, to the **Internet** (Defee and Stank, 2005).

Because the literature revealed that the applications of Web-based SCC are currently at the exploratory stage, an extensive literature review covered five areas: SCM and SCC, IOS and EDI, EB, ERP, and using the Internet and Web technology in SCM, to infer CSFs and subfactors of Web-based SCC. As a result, new constructs, and new multi-item measurement scales for measuring these constructs associated with the CSFs were developed. The items of research constructs had not previously been used together within a single instrument. Based on the reviewed literature, the CSFs of Web-based SCC categorized into the following seven primary categories:

Table 1. The subfactors of top management support

Authors	Subfactors	Code
(Somers and Nelson, 2001), (Ranganathan et al., 2004), (Ngai et al., 2004), (Eid et al., 2004).	Understanding of the capabilities and limitations of IT	TMS1
(Nah et al., 2003), (Loh and Koh, 2004), (Kampstra et al., 2006), (Plant and Willcocks, 2007).	Approval from top management	TMS2
(Vakola and Wilson, 2004), (Nah et al., 2003), (Loh and Koh, 2004), (Nah et al., 2001).	Identify the project as top priority	TMS3
(Ho and Pardo, 2004), (Gunasekaran and Ngai, 2004a), (Kampstra et al., 2006).	Systems alignment with business strategy	TMS4
(Vakola and Wilson, 2004), (Sherer, 2003), (Gunasekaran and Ngai, 2004b), (Eid, et al., 2004).	Allocate appropriate resources	TMS5
(Ngai et al., 2004), (Eid, et al., 2004), (Forman and Lippert, 2005), (Kampstra et al., 2006).	Establish appropriate corporate culture	TMS6

3.1 Top Management Support

Top management has been characterized as important factor for the successful implementation of any business innovation. The importance of top management support in information systems implementation has been emphasized in previous studies. Somers and Nelson (2001) stated that, no single factor is as predictive of its success as the support of top management. Obtaining senior management support is one of the most critical issues influencing Web-based SCC effectiveness. Adaptation of Web-based SCC involves deep level changes that influence core aspects of an organization, comprising mission, vision, business strategy, goals, culture, technology, training and policies. Only the top management's attention

to changes will drive the necessary adjustments toward Web-based SCC.

Based on literature review, Table 1 embraced six subfactors of Top Management Support (TMS).

3.2 IT Infrastructure

One of the challenges often cited in the literature both by the researchers and practitioners when developing an **IT-integrated SCM** is the poor **IT infrastructure** (Gunasckaran and Ngai, 2004a). A company's internal IT infrastructure and the processes they use to create and share information internally can make or break a supply chain initiative with their trading partners (Cooper and Tracey, 2005). This infrastructure must drive

Table 2. The subfactors of IT infrastructure

Authors	Subfactors	Code
(Gunasekaran and Ngai, 2004a), (Ngai et al,, 2004), (Loh and Koh, 2004).	**Software, hardware availability and reliability**	ITI1
(Soliman and Janz, 2004), (Gunasekaran and Ngai, 2004a).	**Web-based systems reliability**	ITI2
(Soliman and Janz, 2004), (Galliers and Leidner, 2003).	**Web-based Systems scalability**	ITI3
(Kim and Im, 2002), (Umble et al., 2003), (Gunasekaran and Ngai, 2004a).	Security of Web-based systems	ITI4
(Loh and Koh, 2004), (Gunasekaran and Ngai, 2004a), (Nah et al., 2001).	Integration of systems	ITI5
(Zou and Seo, 2006), (Gunasekaran and Ngai, 2004a).	IT previous experiences	ITI6

strong operational excellence and corporate competence while simultaneously promoting inter-organizational process collaboration. Due to that, the optimal deployment of IT within the company became a prerequisite to successful process integration and collaboration with chain members. Table 2 comprised the subfactors under the IT Infrastructure (ITI).

3.3 Training and Education

Training and education are the most important component of any change process in an organization, where technologies alone will not help to improve the organizational competitiveness (Gunasekaran and Ngai, 2004a). Employees are expected to be able to effectively use the new system based on training (Umble et al., 2003). Formal education and training should be provided to help users understand how the system will impact their jobs, and daily procedures (Nah et al., 2003). It is important to assess users' training requirements to reduce the knowledge gap between what they already know and what they need to know to best perform their job in the light of new IT (Peansupap and Walker, 2005). Table 3 comprised the subfactors of the Training and Education (T&E).

3.4 Business Process Reengineering (BPR)

The evolution of IT has fostered the development of powerful tools that are expected to improve supply chain performance dramatically, through higher levels of process efficiency and integration (Barratt, 2004). In most cases, the introduction of IT was an explicit objective within BPR projects (Albizu and Olazaran, 2006). BPR and IT compliment each other in their efforts to achieve dramatic improvements by radical changes (Gunasekaran and Ngai, 2004a). BPR will help process mapping in the supply chain and provide opportunities for various Web systems applications, with the aim of eliminating non-value-adding activities (Gunasekaran and Ngai, 2004b). Based on literature review, Table 4 embraced six subfactors of BRP:

3.5 Trusts among Chain Members

Trust is considered an attribute that becomes rooted in every exchange relation and leads to the commitment of interorganizational relationships. The success of collaboration depends upon the ability and willingness of supply chain members to build meaningful relationships and create trust. Trust has been viewed as the crucial

Table 3. The subfactors of training and education

Authors	Subfactors	Code
(Ngai et al., 2004), (Eid et al., 2004), (Umble et al., 2003), (Dowlatshahi, 2005).	Training and learning how to operate new IT tools	T&E1
(Yang et al., 2006), (Somers and Nelson, 2001), (Nah et al., 2001), (Loh and Koh, 2004).	Understand how the system will change business processes	T&E2
(Gunasekaran and Ngai, 2004a), (Zou and Seo, 2006). (Dowlatshahi, 2005).	Investment in knowledge capital	T&E3
(Zou and Seo, 2006), (Peansupap and Walker, 2005), (Yang et al., 2006).	Supportive environment	T&E4
(Ramamurthy et al., 1999), (Ngai et al., 2004), (Zou and Seo, 2006).	Developing own in-house training	T&E5
(Zou and Seo, 2006), (Somers and Nelson, 2001), (Eid et al., 2004).	Continuous learning and training	T&E6

Table 4. The Subfactors of BRP

Authors	Subfactors	Code
(Ramamurthy et al., 1999), (Trkman and Groznik, 2006), (Plant and Willcocks, 2007).	Diagnostic and analysis of the processes	BPR1
(Somers and Nelson, 2001), (Ranganathan et al., 2004), (Trkman and Groznik, 2006).	**Redesign of business processes**	BPR2
(Paper and Chang, 2005), (King, 2001), (Galliers and Leidner, 2003).	Contributions of IS managers	BPR3
(Simatupang and Sridharan., 2005), (Auramo et al., 2005), (Defee and Stank, 2005).	Integrated supply chain processes	BPR4
(Simatupang and Sridharan, 2005), (Skjoett-Larsen et al., 2003), (Tummala et al., 2006).	**Collaborative process improvement**	BPR5
(Trkman and Groznik, 2006), (Defee and Stank, 2005), (Tummala et al., 2006).	Continuous process improvement	BPR6

defining feature of a virtual collaboration where members believe in the character, ability, integrity, familiarity, and morality of each other (Ibbott and O'Keefe 2004). The increased interorganizational trust is not only desirable for successful SCM, but also for technology internalization, especially those used to support SCC (Forman and Lippert, 2006). Based on literature, Table 5 embraced six subfactors of Trust among Chain Members (TCM).

3.6 Open Information Sharing

Transparency and sharing information is the driving force of activities along the supply chain (Gunasekaran and Ngai, 2004b), and the core concept of successful SCM (Trkman and Groznik, 2006).

Accurate and timely information sharing cited as one method essential to avoiding the bullwhip effect in SCC. According to Sanders and Premus (2005) SCC is only made possible through the sharing of large amounts of information along the supply chain, including operations, logistics, and strategic planning data. Web-based SCC implies the ability to electronically share information about business activities and interact on a near real time basis across the supply chain. Based on literature, Table 6 embrace six subfactors of Open Information Sharing (OIS).

3.7 Performance Measurement

Effective management depends on the effective measurement of performance. The role of these

Table 5. The subfactors of trust among chain members

Authors	Subfactors	Code
(Sherer, 2003), (Ibrahim and Ribbers, 2006), (Forman and Lippert, 2005), (Tummala et al., 2006).	Reliability of Participants	TCM1
(Tummala et al., 2006), (Ibrahim and Ribbers, 2006), (Wong et al., 2005).	Competence and compatibility of partners	TCM2
(Lin, et al., 2005b), (Yeh, 2005), (Balasubramanian and Tewary, 2005).	Vulnerable to additional risks	TCM3
(Yeh, 2005), (Chu and Fang, 2006), (Defee and Stank, 2005).	Continuous communication	TCM4
(Skjoett-Larsen et al., 2003), (Simatupang and Sridharan, 2005), (Forman and Lippert, 2005).	Explicit procedures to monitor participant performance	TCM5
(Tummala et al., 2006), (Chu and Fang, 2006), (Wong et al., 2005).	Perceived satisfaction	TCM6

Table 6. The subfactors of open information sharing

Authors	Subfactors	Code
(Vakola and Wilson, 2004), (Min et al., 2005), (Chin et al., 2004), (Tummala et al., 2006).	Supportive cultural environment	OIS1
(Cooper and Tracey, 2005), (Simatupang et al., 2004), (Balasubramanian and Tewary, 2005).	Information accuracy	OIS2
(Simatupang et al., 2004), (Gunasekaran and Ngai, 2004b), (Balasubramanian and Tewary, 2005).	Real-time information sharing	OIS3
(Simatupang et al., 2004), (Kim and Im, 2002), (Auramo et al., 2005).	Reliability of information	OIS4
(Cooper and Tracey, 2005), (Sherer, 2003), (Bagchi and Skjoett-Larsen, 2005).	Sharing sensitive information	OIS5
(Peansupap and Walker, 2005), (Defee and Stank, 2005), (Gunasekaran and Ngai, 2004a), (Loh and Koh, 2004).	Information accessibility	OIS6

measures and metrics in the success of an organization is very critical because they affect strategic, tactical and operational planning and control. **Performance measurement** has an important communication role to play by making people aware of what is important to the organization success and the areas the organization needs to improve monitoring, control, evaluation, and correction of variations and improvements (Kanji, 2002). Under the SCM philosophy, the performance metrics are no longer organization based but supply chain wide (Chin et al., 2004). The success of collaborative efforts cannot be assured unless performance is properly monitored and measured to identify performance gaps that need to be addressed, and to take corrective actions if deviations occur against the planned outcomes.

A performance measurement must be deployed in a way that makes clear to each supply chain member how to contribute to the overall strategy. Table 7 embraced five subfactors of Performance Measurement (PM):

4. THE OUTCOMES OF WEB-BASED SCC

Based on the literature review, three outcomes of Web-based SCC have been considered in this research to capture the key benefits that can be attributed to Web-based SCC, namely, **relationships quality, performance effectiveness, and performance efficiency.** Building and maintaining relationships and the extent to which it meets

Table 7. The subfactors of performance measurement

Authors	Subfactors	Code
(Umble et al., 2003), (Soliman et al., 2001), (Simatupang and Sridharan, 2005), (Kanji, 2002).	Sharing a clear understanding of the objectives and goals	PM1
(Loh and Koh, 2004), (Nah et al., 2001), (Tummala et al., 2006).	Measure performance against the objectives and goals	PM2
(Mason and Lefrere, 2003), (Soliman et al., 2001), (Tummala et al., 2006), (Loh and Koh, 2004).	Identify measurable performance indicators	PM3
(Umble et al., 2003), (Simatupang and Sridharan, 2005), (Nah et al., 2001), (Defee and Stank, 2005)	Alignment of compensation and rewards with performance evaluation	PM4
(Chin et al., 2004), (Simatupang and Sridharan, 2005), (Loh and Koh, 2004), (Nah et al., 2001).	Guide the chain members to improve overall performance	PM5

the needs or expectations of supply chain members can have significant long-term implications, and therefore, affect the strategic and long-term planning of any supply chain activities. According to Wilding and Humphries (2006), relationship quality refers to creating a **win-win relationship** in which each side is delighted to be a part. A number of studies concluded that relationship quality with supply chain members was positively influenced by IT investments. Effectiveness and efficiency can be defined in different aspects and contexts. In general, effectiveness refers to the extent to which goals are accomplished, and efficiency related to the measure of how well expended resources are

utilized (Min et al., 2005). Table 8 provides the outcomes of Web-based SCC divided into three categories.

5. RESEARCH MODEL AND HYPOTHESES

Resulting from the previously discussed literature review, key success factors model was derived. The research model investigated in this study is displayed in (Figure 1.). The model includes a set of seven major critical factors and 41 subfactors of Web-based SCC implementation success. The

Table 8. The outcomes of Web-based SCC

Authors	Dimensions
Relationship Quality (RQ)	
(Fynes et al., 2005), (Chang, 2005), (de Burca et al., 2004,), (Goo and Nam, 2007).	**Long-term working relationship**
(Bagchi and Skjoett-Larsen, 2005), (Ibbott and O'Keefe, 2004), (Chu and Fang, 2006).	**Partners satisfaction**
(de Burca et al., 2004), (Yeh, 2005), (Goo and Nam, 2007).	**Commitment of partners**
(de Burca et al., 2004), (Cheng et al., 2000), (Chang, 2005), (Fynes et al., 2005), (Min et al., 2005).	**Joint problems solving**
(Chang, 2005), (de Burca et al., 2004), (Fynes et al., 2005)	Total quality improvement
Performance Effectiveness (PEV)	
(Wang et al., 2006), (Min et al., 2005), (Sanders and Premus, 2005).	Ability to develop new products
(Wang et al., 2006), (Mason-Jones and Towill, 2000)	Adjust production according to demands
(Min et al., 2005), (Mollenkopf and Dapiran, 2005), (Wang et al., 2006), (Nix and Lusch,2004).	Improved customer service
(Min et al., 2005), (Defee and Stank, 2005)	Increased market share
(Min et al., 2005), (Defee and Stank, 2005).	Increased sales
(Bagchi and Skjoett-Larsen, 2005), (Mollenkopf and Dapiran, 2005), (Defee and Stank, 2005).	Rate of returns
	Performance Efficiency (PEI)
(Bagchi and Skjoett-Larsen, 2005), (Lin et al., 2006*a*) (Mollenkopf and Dapiran, 2005).	Order fulfillment lead time
(Bagchi and Skjoett-Larsen, 2005), (Wang et al., 2006), (Sanders and Premus, 2005)	Reliability of delivery
(Lin et al., 2006*a*), (Wang et al., 2006), (Min et al., 2005), (Trkman and Groznik, 2006)	Reduced cycle time or lead-time to market
(Lin et al., 2006*a*), (Min et al., 2005), (Trkman and Groznik, 2006).	Reduced inventory cost
(Bagchi and Skjoett-Larsen, 2005), (Mollenkopf and Dapiran, 2005).	Total logistics cost

CSFs are classified into the following seven categories: Top management support, training and education, BPR, trust, IT infrastructure, open information sharing, and performance measurement. The model also includes three outcomes of Web-based SCC, namely: Relationships quality, and performance, including performance effectiveness, and performance efficiency. Figure1 illustrates the CSFs and outcomes model of Web-based SCC implementation. Each of these factors can be divided into a number of subfactors.

The model posits a relation between the Web-based SCC implementation success and three outcomes. The outcomes of Web-based SCC (OWSCC) have been considered in this research to capture some of the key benefits that can be attributed to Web-based SCC and to judge whether a Web-based SCC implementation (WSCCI) is a success or a failure.

The model deals with key areas where things must go right for the success of Web-based SCC **that would encourage and support practitioners in their efforts** towards more SCC with business partners using Web-based technology.

Through the review of literature, this study develops seven factors with 41 subfactors, which affect the Web-based SCC implementation success. Accordingly, it is hypothesized that

H1a: Top management support is critical for Web-based SCC implementation success.

H1b: IT infrastructure is critical for Web-based SCC implementation success.

H1c: Training and education is critical for Web-based SCC implementation success.

H1d: BPR is critical for Web-based SCC implementation success.

H1e: Trust among chain members is critical for Web-based SCC implementation success.

H1f: Open information sharing is critical for Web-based SCC implementation success.

H1g: Performance measurement is critical for Web-based SCC implementation success.

Based on the literature review, to judge whether an Web-based SCC implementation is a success or a failure, the study classified Web-based SCC outcomes into two dimensions, including supply chain relationship quality, and performance, including performance effectiveness and performance efficiency, thus it is hypothesized that:

H2a: Web-based SCC implementation is positively associated with supply chain relationship quality.

H2b: Web-based SCC implementation is positively associated with performance effectiveness.

H2c: Web-based SCC implementation is positively associated with performance efficiency.

Figure 1. The CSFs and outcomes model of Web-based SCC

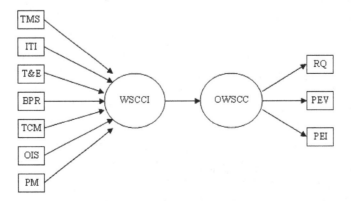

The seven independent variables are assumed as critical factors affecting Web-based SCC implementation success, which is indicated by Web-based SCC outcomes, including supply chain relationship quality, performance effectiveness, and performance efficiency. The following hypothesis examines the link between the CSFs and outcomes of Web-based SCC:

H3: There is appositive relationship between the CSFs and outcomes of Web-based SCC.

6. RESEARCH METHODOLOGY

6.1 The Population and Sampling Design

This study aims to cover a wide variety of respondents from different manufacturing industries in Jordan. Manufacturing industries were selected for to reasons:

- Manufacturing companies are at the heart of the supply chain, and the convergence point of upstream and starting point of downstream supply chain activities.
- The difficulty of access to the other members of the supply chain.

In order to examine the hypothesized CSFs that were collected from literature review, a survey of Jordanian manufacturing firms from various industries was taken. The Jordanian manufacturing companies involved in this study meet the following criteria:

- Use the Web systems to collaborate with supply chain members.
- Have strong and stable relationships with specific supply chain members.
- Familiarity with the supply SCC concept (information sharing, joint problems solving, decision making, and planning).

Based on the selection criteria; seven firms were selected to conduct this study.

6.2 Data Collection Method

Questionnaire

The questionnaire was prepared both in Arabic and English. Individuals were asked to indicate the extent of importance with the questionnaire items on a five-point Likert-type scale ranging from 1 to 5 (The rating was on a scale from 1 (unimportant) to 5 (most important) to identify the CSFs and the extent of its impact on Web-based SCC. Moreover, the questionnaire included five-point Likert scale from 1(Strongly disagree) to 5 (strongly agree) to identify the relationship between the CSFs and outcomes of Web-based SCC.

The questionnaire was divided into four major sections. The first section is devoted to identifying the sample characteristics, characteristics of surveyed organizations, and finally sample characteristics of the technology applications. The second section collects data regarding the CSFs of Web-based SCC. The third section identifies the respondents' perception of the outcomes of Web-based SCC implementation.

6.3 Response Rate and Results

Total of three hundred and twenty (320) questionnaires were initially distributed to sample respondents of seven manufacturing firms using Web-based systems in Jordanian. Two hundred and fourty-three (243) responses were received. Two hundred and twenty-four (224) were usable for analysis. Thus the gross response rate of research survey was 75.9% (243/320) of which, 224 returns, 70% (224/320) were suitable for analysis.

6.4 The Sample Characteristics

The backgrounds of respondents in successful SMEs were studied in terms of the job title, job function, and years working. Most of the respondents are employees 81.70%, while 41 or 18.30% state they are managers.

The respondents were asked to mark job functions that apply to their everyday tasks 23.21% of respondents chose sales and marketing, 17.86% chose manufacturing and production, 12.5% chose inventory and warehousing, 10.71% purchasing, 10.71% also chose IT. However, 8.48% chose distribution, 7.59% chose transportation, and 5.36% chose research and development. The rest of respondents 4.02% belong to the financial and accounting category.

Most respondents had had varied work experience. 20.98% of the respondents have been working less than 3 years. One third 33.93% of the respondents have been working between 4-10 years. Another third 33.48% have been working between 11-15 years, while 6.70% state they have worked between 16-20 years and 4.91% have worked for more than 20 years.

Among the manufacturing companies, the biggest segment in terms of the number of firms who responded were companies in the Pharmaceutical industry 28.56%, while the rest of companies were distributed equally among engineering, electronics and heavy industries, **paints** industry, aerated water, **petrochemicals industries, and** Potash **industry**.

14.29% of the manufacturing companies have fewer than 100 employees. 28.57% of the manufacturing companies have between 101-250 employees. 14.29% of the manufacturing companies also have between 251-500 employees. 14.29% of the manufacturing companies have between 501-1000 employees. Manufacturing companies with more than 1000 employees account for 28.57% of the sample.

Concerning Numbers of Years Using Web-Based Systems 13.845% of respondents engaged in using the Web systems for a year or less, 12.95% for two years, and 23.66% for three years while 17.41% engaged in using the Web systems for four years. Almost one third of respondents said

that they engaged in using the Web systems for five years or more.

More than half of the respondents 59.82% indicated that they are applying Web-based SCC with suppliers, 48.66% with customers while 46.88% of the respondents stated that they are applying Web-based SCC with logistics companies, and 27.68% with distribution channels, and 16.96% chose "other" category.

Web-Based SCC Tools

51.79% of the respondents reported that they use Web systems for online ordering while 41.52% of the respondents indicated that they use Web systems for exchanging the forecast information with supply chain members. Almost one third 31.255% for scanning the customers needs to project expected shortages. Another third 31.25% for collecting and sharing the actions that need to be taken to support the objectives and mission of the supply chain. 29.91% for determining the amount of capacity required to produce, 26.34%, 25.45%, and 21.42% of the respondents use Web systems for sharing business knowledge, developing product designs, and transfer customers orders directly to either a production line or stockrooms respectively. Less than 21% of respondents use Web systems for receiving purchasing orders from customers electronically through the Web site of the company, and delivery and tracking (See Table 9).

6.5 Descriptive Statistics and Correlation Matrix

In order to present descriptive scores such as means and standard deviation for each of the variables used in the survey, descriptive analyses and a correlation matrix to test the relationships were performed.

Table 10 shows the means and standard deviations for both the CSFs and outcomes of Web-based SCC. The majority of respondents are closed in

Table 9. Web-based SCC tools

Web-Based SCC Tools	Frequency	%
Procurement: Online ordering	116	51.79
Forecasting: Exchanges the forecast information	93	41.52
Projected shortages: Scans the customers needs to project expected shortages	70	31.25
Business strategy: Collect and share the actions that need to be taken to support the objectives and mission of the supply chain	70	31.25
Capacity planning: Determines the amount of capacity required to produce	67	29.91
Sharing business knowledge	59	26.34
Design tool: Developing product designs	57	25.45
Replenishment: Transfer customers orders directly to either a production line or stockrooms	48	21.42
Receive purchasing orders from customers electronically through the Web site of the company	45	20.09
Delivery and tracking	43	19.20

their predominantly positive attitude towards the CSFs and outcomes of Web-based SCC. Similarly, the mean and standard deviation shows that the respondents are closed in their predominantly positive attitude the outcomes of Web-based SCC, where most respondents tended to choose "Agree" regarding the three areas of Web-based SCC outcomes.

The correlations between the ten constructs of research are shown in Table 12. The analysis

Table 10. Descriptive statistics for CSFs and outcomes of Web-based SCC

Construct	Mean	Std. Deviation
CSFs of Web-Based SCC		
Top Management Support	3.93	.571
IT Infrastructure	3.99	.580
Training and Education	3.90	.699
Business Processes Reengineering	3.81	.699
Trust Among Chain Members	3.83	.704
Open Information Sharing	3.86	.682
Performance Measurement	3.88	.726
Web-Based SCC Outcomes		
Relationship Quality	3.99	.561
Performance Effectiveness	4.01	.632
Performance Efficiency	4.10	.623

of the correlation results showed that there is a significant positive relationship between all constructs at the 0.01. The closer the correlation is to +1, the stronger the correlation. If the correlation is 0 or very close to zero, there is no association between two variables. If the correlation is positive, the two variables have a positive relationship (i.e., as one increases, the other also increases). All the constructs appears to be positively associated with each other.

In the light of correlation matrix results, high correlations indicated that variables can be grouped into homogenous sets of variables, and they are thus appropriate for factor analysis.

7. FACTOR ANALYSIS

Factor analysis was conducted to analyze the scale items of the ten research constructs, and to check the construct validity of the measurement scale. To make factor analysis worthwhile, Bartlett's Test of Sphericity used to assess the suitability of data analysis and the adequacy of the sample size. Besides, Kaiser-Meyer-Olkin (KMO) used to assess the extent to which the indicators of a construct belong together (the homogeneity of variables). Kaiser recommends accepting values

Table 12. The correlations between the ten constructs of research

EF	EFV	RQ	PM	OIS	TCM	BPR	TE	ITI	TMS	Variable Pearson Correlation
									1	**TMS**
								1	.614(**)	**ITI**
									.000	
							1	.723(**)	.679(**)	**T&E**
								.000	.000	
						1	.821(**)	.660(**)	.633(**)	**BPR**
							.000	.000	.000	
					1	.805(**)	.798(**)	.639(**)	.634(**)	**TCM**
						.000	.000	.000	.000	
				1	.787(**)	.765(**)	.784(**)	.711(**)	.694(**)	**OIS**
					.000	.000	.000	.000	.000	
			1	.792(**)	.727(**)	.750(**)	.785(**)	.615(**)	.659(**)	**PM**
				.000	.000	.000	.000	.000	.000	
		1	.372(**)	.384(**)	.390(**)	.346(**)	.298(**)	.347(**)		**RQ**
			.000	.000	.000	.000	.000	.000		
	1	.441(**)	.388(**)	.448(**)	.382(**)	.386(**)	.372(**)			**EFV**
		.000	.000	.000	.000	.000	.000			
1	.538(**)	.500(**)	.463(**)	.445(**)	.436(**)	.395(**)				**EFI**
	.000	.000	.000	.000	.000	.000				

greater than 0.5 as acceptable (values below this should lead to either collect more data or rethink which variables to include) with Eigenvalues greater than one were retained in the factor loading. Varimax as the rotation method was utilized to identify the underlying subfactors of the critical factors for Web-based SCC implementation success. Factor loading below 0.5, which is the cut-off limit for loading items, should be considered low and any low items should be eliminated from the analysis for the underlying factors.

All values of factor analysis were very satisfactory. Table 13 summarizes the results of factor analysis for all constructs, including KMO, Bartlett's Test of Sphericity, Eigenvalue, and Commulative Variance %, for each construct, and factor loadings for each subfactor.

Reliability of Research Constructs Measures

Reliability refers to the extent to which the constructs are free from error and therefore yield consistent results. Cronbach's alpha was employed as the criterion to evaluate reliability of the constructs by examining their internal consistency. Estimate greater than 0.70 are generally considered to meet the criteria for reliability. Using the SPSS reliability analysis procedure, an internal consistency analysis was performed separately for each critical factor and outcome; the results are shown in Table 14.

As can be seen, the alpha values were high above the acceptable threshold 70.0 ranging from 0.789 IT infrastructure to 0.895 (BPR) and trust

Table 13. The results of factor analysis for all constructs

Constructs	KMO	Bartlett's Test Chi Square/df	Eigenvalue	Cumulative Variance%	Loadings of Subfactors
TMS	0.825	370.344/15	3.016	50.265	0.583-0.812
ITI	0.810	352.184/15	2.962	49.372	0.576-0.788
T&E	0.853	712.372/15	3.837	63.946	0.736-0.838
BPR	0.887	739.391/15	3.960	66.006	0.709-0.826
TCM	0.906	695.209/15	3.960	65.697	0.775-0.845
OIS	0.833	695.027/15	3.780	63.001	0.763-0.824
PM	0.823	677.051/10	3.519	70.357	0.748-0.891
RQ	0.811	390.874/10	2.967	59.345	0.732-0.809
PEV	0.842	614.894/15	3.665	61,086	0.736-0.815
PEI	0.828	603.431/10	3.394	67.871	0.759-0.881

Table 14. Reliability of constructs measures

Construct	No. of Items	Alpha Value
TMS	6	0.796
ITI	6	0.789
T&E	6	0.886
BPR	6	0.895
TCM	6	0.895
OIS	6	0.880
PM	5	0.890
RQ	5	0.824
PEV	6	0.870
PEI	5	0.881

among chain members, indicating that all the scales are acceptable. From the results obtained, it can be concluded that this instrument has high internal consistency, and the variables comprising each proposed research construct, and is therefore reliable.

8. STRUCTURAL MODEL TEST

Although the Pearson correlations, KMO, and factor loading are statistically significant for all hypothesized relationships, it may not be true when all the relationships are put together in a multivariate complex model due to the interactions among variables. Structural Equations Modeling (SEM) is appropriate for analyzing of the relationships between multiple dependent and independent latent constructs, specify, test, and modify the hypothesized measurement model.

Evaluation of the proposed research model was made using EQS technique, V6.1. The analysis followed the two steps. The first step involved the development of an acceptable measurement model that achieved an acceptable fit with the data through the use of factory analysis. The second step then tested the theoretical model using path analysis to demonstrate a meaningful and statistically acceptable structural model.

As recommended, multiple fit criteria are considered in order to rule out measurement biases. Table 15 presents the results of the measurement model.

A comparison of these values against those recommended in the literature suggests that the model is a good fit. All paths are statistically significant at the 0.05 level.

Table 15. Fit statistics for measurement model

Fit Statistic	Notation	Model Value	Recommended Value
Chi-square to Degrees of Freedom	X^2/df	1.49	<= 3.0
Root Mean Square Error of Approximation	RMSEA	0.058	<=0.10
Root Mean Square Residual	RMR	0.013	<=0.05
Goodness of Fit Index	GFI	0.956	>=0.90
Normed Fit Index	NFI	0.971	>=0.90
Comparative Fit Index	CFI	0.987	>=0.90
Incremental Fit Index	IFI	0.987	>=0.90

Recommended values adapted from (Gefen et al., 2000).

9. TESTING THE HYPOTHESES OF RESEARCH

The hypothesized structural causal model was tested by (SEM), which included a test of the overall model as well as individual tests of the relationships among the latent constructs. Therefore, it is concluded that the overall model fit is acceptable and the path estimates can be used for hypothesis testing. The results offered support for the relationship between CSFs and Web-based SCC outcomes at a significant level of 0.05. Figure 2 shows the path coefficient analysis resulting from the structural modeling analysis. Path analyses were conducted to provide a picture of the links between the various groups of factors.

The significance of individual paths was examined and summarized in figure 2. The Seven CSFs of Web-based SCC serve as independent variables and the three areas of outcomes serve as the dependent variable. All the coefficients are found to be significant at the $p < 0.05$ level, CSFs of Web-based SCC has a strong direct significant relationship with the outcomes (Figure 2).

The significance of the path coefficients is determined by t-statistics. The strength of hypothesized paths is evaluated by standardized path coefficient. The standardized path coefficients are tested whether the path is significant or not. It is recommended that the *t* value be < 2.0. The standardized path coefficients which explain the variance for the model constructs were positive and more than 0.75, and *t* values <13. Therefore, all constructs are significant at the $p < 0.05$. Consequently, it is conclude that the path estimates can be used for hypotheses testing.

Figure 2. The path coefficient analysis

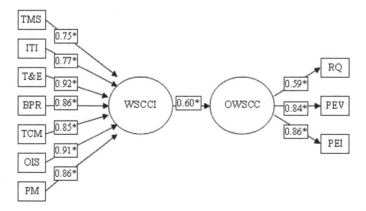

The path coefficient of an independent variable represents the direct effect of that variable on the dependent variable. Figure 5.1 show that all constructs have a strong direct significant effect on Web-based SCC success. Path coefficient analysis and the results of t value test serves as the basis of evaluation of the hypotheses. Table 16 shows the results of testing hypotheses of CSFs for Web-based SCC implementation (WSCCI) using standardized coefficient, R Squared (R^2), and t value.

As hypothesized, the result of EQS analysis showed that top management support, IT infrastructure, training and education, BPR, trust Among Chain Members, open information sharing, and performance measurement are CSFs of Web-based SCC. Therefore, all the hypotheses regarding the seven CSFs of Web-based SCC were supported as indicated by the significant path coefficient, at $p < 0.05$

In addition, Table 17 shows the result of testing hypotheses of Web-based SCC outcomes (OWSCC). The results illustrate that Web-Based SCC has a strong positive effect on the hypothesized outcomes. As a result, all the hypotheses regarding the outcomes of Web-based SCC were supported as indicated by the significant path coefficient, at $p < 0.05$.

The seven independent variables are assumed as critical factors positively related to Web-based SCC implementation success, which is indicated by Web-based SCC outcomes, including relationship quality, performance effectiveness, and efficiency. The hypothesis H3 was found to be significant. The empirical results highly support the relationship between the CSFs and outcomes of Web-based SCC. There were significant direct effects of CSFs on outcomes of Web-based SCC (standardized coefficient=0.60, R^2=0.362). Therefore, the outcomes of Web-based SCC are reasonably explained by the CSFs proposed in the research.

Table 16. Results of testing CSFs hypothesis

Path	Standardized Coefficient	R^2	t Value	Hypothesis
TMS - WSCCI	0.75*	0.563	12.169	*H1a*
ITI - WSCCI	0.77*	0.595	10.707	*H1b*
T&E - WSCCI	0.92*	0.853	16.696	*H1c*
BPR - WSCCI	0.86*	0.748	17.565	*H1d*
TAM - WSCCI	0.85*	0.730	14.159	*H1e*
OIS - WSCCI	0.91*	0.837	19.094	*H1f*
PM - WSCCI	0.86*	0.734	11.428	*H1g*
Note: Significance at p< 0.05				

Table 17. Results of testing Web-based SCC outcomes hypothesis

Path	Standardized Coefficient	R^2	t Value	Hypothesis
OWSCC - RQ	0.59*	0.698	10.546	H2a
OWSCC - PEV	0.84*	0.746	12.22	H2b
OWSCC - PEI	0.86*	0.362	8.808	H2c
Note: Significance at p< 0.05				

10. FINDINGS AND CONCLUSIONS OF RESEARCH

This study aims to identify and improve understanding of the CSFs and outcomes of Web-based SCC from the manufacturing members' perspectives in Jordan. The primary contributions of this research are the definition of new constructs associated with the CSFs and outcomes of Web-based SCC and the development of new multi-item measurement scales for measuring these constructs in a coherent model.

Based on the literature review, the research model drawn included seven CSFs for Web-based SCC, namely: Top management support, IT infrastructure, training and education, BPR, trust, open information sharing, and performance measurement. Each of these seven factors were broken down into detailed subfactors. Each subfactor is mentioned by at least two studies. To achieve the objectives of this research, the Web-based SCC model content is used to derive the hypotheses of research.

The results showed that Top Management Support, IT Infrastructure, training and education, BPR, trust among chain members, open information sharing, and performance measurement are critical factors for Web-based SCC implementation success. In addition, this research revealed that Web-based SCC implementation is positively related to supply chain relationship quality, performance effectiveness, and performance efficiency. The results are highly support the relationship between the CSFs and outcomes of Web-based SCC.

REFERENCES

Albizu, E., & Olazaran, M. (2006). BPR implementation in Europe: the adaptation of a management concept. *New Technology, Work and Employment, 21*(1), March.

Auramo, J., Kauremaa, J., & Tanskanen, K. (2005). Benefits of IT in SCM: an explorative study of progressive companies. *International Journal of Physical Distribution & Logistics Management, 35*(2).

Bagchi, P., & Skjoett-Larsen, T. (2005). Supply chain integration: a Europe survey. *International Journal of Logistics Management, 16*(2).

Balasubramanian, P., & Tewary, A. (2005). Design of supply chains: Unrealistic expectations on Collaboration. *Sadhana, 30*(2 & 3), April/June.

Barrat, M. (2004). Understanding the meaning of collaboration in the supply chain. *SCM: An International Journal, 9*(1).

Cassivi, L. (2006). Collaboration planning in a supply chain. *SCM: An International Journal, 11*(3).

Chang, K. (2006). Relationship Quality and Negotiation Interdependence: the Case Study of International Defect Claim. *Total Quality Management, 16*(7), September.

Cheng, E., Li, H., & Love, P. (2000). Establishment of Critical Success Factors for Construction Partnering. *Journal of Management in Engineering*, March/April.

Chin, K., Tummala, V., Leung, J., & Tang, X. (2004). A study on supply chain management practices. *International Journal of Physical Distribution & Logistics Management, 34*(6).

Chu, S., & Fang, W. (2006). Exploring the Relationships of Trust and Commitment in Supply Chain Management. *The Journal of America n Academy of Business, Cambridge, 9*(1), March.

Cooper, D., & Tracey, M. (2005). Supply chain integration via IT: strategic implications and future trends. *Int. J. Integrated Supply Management, 1*(3).

de Burca, S., Fynes, B., & Roche, E. (2004). Evaluating Relationship Quality in a Business-to-Business Context. *Irish Journal of Management, 25.*

Defee, C., & Stank, T. (2005). Applying the strategy-structure performance paradigm to the supply chain environment. *The International Journal of Logistics Management, 16*(1).

Dowlatshahi, S. (200515 September). Strategic success factors in enterprise resource-planning design and implementation: a case-study approach. *International Journal of Production Research, 43*(18).

Eid, R., Trueman, M., & Ahmad, A. (2004). Factors affecting the success of business-to-business international Internet marketing (B-to-BIIM): an empirical study of UK companies. *Industrial Management & Data System, 104*(1).

Forman, H., & Lippert, S. (2005). Toward the development of an integrated model of technology internalization within the supply chain context. *The International Journal of Logistics Management, 16*(1).

Fynes, B., de Burca, S., & Voss, C. (2005). Supply chain Relationship Quality: the competitive environment and performance. *International Journal of Production Research, 43*(16).

Galliers, R., & Leidner, D. (2003). *Strategic information management: challenges and strategies in managing information systems.* third Edi. Butterworth-Heinemann: UK.

Goo, J., & Nam, K. (2007). Contract as a Source of Trust-Commitment in Successful IT Outsourcing Relationship: An Empirical Study. *Proceedings of the 40th Hawaii International Conference on System Sciences – 2007 IEEE.*

Gunasekaran, A., & Ngai, E. (2004a, September). Information systems in supply chain integration and management. *Production Planning & Control, 15*(6).

Gunasekaran, A., & Ngaie, E. (2004b, September). Virtual supply-chain management. *Production Planning & Control, 15*(6).

Gefen, D., Straub, D., & Boudreau, M. (2000). Structural Equation Modeling and Regression: Guidelines of Research Practice. *Communications of the Association for Information Systems, 4*(7).

Ho, J., & Pardo, T. (2004). Toward the Success of eGovernment Initiatives: Mapping Known Success Factors to the Design of Practical Tools. Proceedings of the *37th Hawaii International Conference on System Sciences – 2004 IEEE.*

Ibrahim, M., & Ribbers, P. (2006). Trust, Dependence and Global Interorganizational Systems. the *39th Hawaii International Conference on System Sciences, 2006 IEEE.*

Kampstra, R., Ashayeri, J., & Gattorna, J. (2006). Realities of supply chain collaboration. *The International Journal of Logistics Management, 17*(3).

Kanji, G. (2002). Performance Measurement System. *Total Quality Management, 13*(5).

Kim, K., & Im, I. (2002). The Effects of Electronic Supply Chain Design (e-SCD) on Coordination and Knowledge Sharing: An Empirical Investigation. *35th Hawaii International Conference on System Sciences, IEEE 2002.*

King, L. (2001). The CSFs That Influence Organizations To Adopt Internet Technology. *Malaysian Journal of Library & Information Science, 6*(2).

Lambert, D., Knemeyer, A., & Gardner, J. (2005). Supply chain partnerships: model validation and implementation. *Journal of Business Logistics, 25*(2).

Lefebvre, E., Légerl, P., & Hadaya, P. (2003). E-collaboration within one supply chain and its impact on firms' innovativeness and performance. *Information Systems and E-Business Management, 1*(2).

Lin, F., Sung, Y., & Lo, Y. (2005). Effects of Trust Mechanisms on Supply-Chain Performance: A Multi-Agent Simulation Study. *International Journal of Electronic Commerce, 9*(4).

Loh, T., & Koh, S. (2004, September). Critical elements for a successful enterprise resource planning implementation in small- and medium-sized enterprises. *International Journal of Production Research, 42*(17).

Mason, J., & Lefrere, P. (2003, December). Trust, Collaboration, e-Learning and Organizational Transformation. *International Journal of Training and Development, 7*(4).

Mason-Jones, R., & Towill, D. (2000). Coping with Uncertainty: Reducing Bullwhip Behaviour in Global Supply Chains. *Supply Chain Forum: An International Journal, 1*.

Min, S., Roath, A., Daugherty, P., Genchev, S., Chen, H., & Arndt, A. (2005). Supply chain collaboration: what's happening? *The International Journal of Logistics Management, 16*(2).

Mollenkopf, D., & Dapiran, P. (2005, March). The importance of developing logistics competencies: a study of Australian and New Zealand firms. *International Journal of Logistics: Research and Applications, 8*(1).

Nah, F., Lau, J., & Kuang, J. (2001). Critical factors of successful implementation of enterprise systems. *Business Process Management Journal, 7*(3).

Nah, F., Zuckweiler, K., & Lau, J. (2003). ERP Implementation: Chief Information Officers' Perceptions of CSFs. *International Journal of Human-Computer Interaction, 16*(1).

Ngai, E., Cheng, T., & Ho, S. (2004). CSFs of Web-based supply-chain management systems: an exploratory study. *Production Planning & Control, 15*(6).

Paper, D., & Chang, R. (2005, January). The State of Business Process Reengineering: A Search for Success Factors. *Total Quality Management, 16*(1).

Peansupap, V., & Walker, D. (2005). Factors Enabling Information and Communication Technology Diffusion and Actual Implementation in Construction Implementation. *ITcon, 10*.

Plant, R., & Willcocks, L. (2007). Critical Success Factors in International ERP Implementations: A case Research Approach. *Journal of Computer Information Systems*, spring.

Ramamurthy, K., Premkumar, G., & Crum, G. (1999). Organizational and Interorganizational Determinants of EDI Diffusion and Organizational Performance: A Causal Model. *Journal of Organizational Computing and Electronic Commerce, 9*(4).

Ranganathan. C., Dhaliwal, J., & Teo, T. (2004). Assimilation and Diffusion of Web Technologies in Supply-Chain Management: An Examination of Key Drivers and Performance Impacts. *International Journal of Electronic Commerce, 9*(1), Fall.

Sanders, N., & Premus, R. (2005). Modeling the Relationship between Firm Capability, Collaboration, and Performance. *Journal of Business Logistics, 26*(1).

Sherer, S. (2003). CSFs for Manufacturing Networks as Perceived by Network Coordinators. *Journal of Small Business Management, 41*(4).

Simatupang, T., & Sridharan, R. (2005). An integrative framework for supply chain collaboration. *The International Journal of Logistics Management, 16*(2).

Simatrupang, T., Wright, A., & Sridharan, R. (2004). Applying the theory of constraints to supply chain collaboration. *Supply Chain Management: An International Journal, 9*(1).

Skjoett-Larsen, T., Thernoe, C., & Andresen, C. (2003). Supply chain collaboration: theoretical perspectives and empirical evidence. *International Journal of Physical Distribution & Logistics Management, 33*(6).

Soliman, F., Clegg, S., & Tantoush, T. (2001). CSFs for integration of CAD/CAM systems with ERP systems. *International Journal of Operations & Production Management, 21*(5/6).

Soliman, K., & Janz, B. (2001). *Interorganizational Information Systems: Exploring an Internet-Based Approach.* Issues in Supply Chain Management, 1.

Somers, T., & Nelson, K (2001). The Impact of Critical Success Factors across the Stages of Enterprise Resource Planning Implementations. *34th Hawaii International Conference on System Sciences - 2001 IEEE.*

Trkman P., & Groznik A. (2006). Measurement of Supply Chain Integration Benefits. *Interdisciplinary Journal of Information, Knowledge, and Management, 1.*

Tummala, V., Phillips, C., & Johnson, M. (2006). Assessing SCM success factors: a case study. *Supply Chain Management: An International Journal, 11*(2).

Vakola, M., & Wilson, I. (2004). The challenge of virtual organization: CSFs in dealing with constant change. *Team Performance Management, 10*(5/6).

Wilding, R., & Humphries, A. (2006). Understanding collaborative supply chain relationships through the application of the Williamson organizational failure framework. *International Journal of Physical Distribution & Logistics Management, 36*(4).

Williams, L., Espe, T., & Ozment, J. (2002). The Electronic Supply Chain: its impact on the current and future structure of strategic alliance, partnerships and logistics leadership. *International Journal of physical Distribution & Logistics Management, 32*(8).

Wong, P., Cheung, S., & Ho, P., (2005, October). Contractor as Trust Initiator in Construction Partnering - Prisoner's Dilemma Perspective. *Journal of Construction Engineering and Management.*

Yeh, Y. (2005). Identification of factors affecting continuity of cooperative electronic supply chain relationships: empirical case of the Taiwanese motor industry. *Supply Chain Management: An International Journal, 10*(4).

Yang, C., Ting, P., & Wei, C. (2006, March). A Study of the Factors Impacting ERP System Performance from the Users' Perspectives. *The Journal of American Academy of Business, Cambridge, 8*(2).

Zou, P., & Seo, Y. (2006). Effective applications of E-commerce technologies in construction supply chain: current practice and future improvement. *ITcon, 11.*

Umble, E., Haft, R., & Umble, M. (2003). Enterprise resource planning: Implementation procedures and critical success factors. *European Journal of Operational Research, 146.*

Wang, E., Tai, J., & Wei, H. (2006, October). A Virtual Integration Theory of Improved Supply-Chain Performance. *Journal of Management Information Systems, 23*(2).

Chapter IX
Web Engineering in Small Jordanian Web Development Firms:
An XP Based Process Model

Haroon Altarawneh
Albalqa' Applied Univesity, Jordan

Asim El-Shiekh
The Arab Academy for Banking and Financial Sciences, Jordan

ABSTRACT

Small firms do not have the managerial experience, the financial resources and the methodological know-how to manage web-based applications projects the way large firms do. Many small firms are unaware of existing software process assessment models and standards. There's often the assumption that assessments conformant to these models and standards can be expensive and time consuming, and therefore difficult to perform in small companies. This chapter proposes a theoretical model for small Web project development and its special features in the context small Web firms, which are capable of being "tailor able" to the particular stage of organizational development of small Web firms . The process model derived form Web engineering best practices, real case studies from Jordanian Web firms and agile development methodologies (extreme programming) . This chapter also contains results from tow surveys: a questionnaire to Web developers and interview with Web mangers in Jordan. The results reflect the Web industry situation in small Jordanian firms, and the major problems they face. Most of small Web projects in Jordan run over time and budget, due to the ad hoc development and the weakness of Web project management. The results showed that there is a weakness in applying Web engineering practices in small Jordanian Web development firms.

INTRODUCTION

"Web Engineering is the application of systematic, disciplined and quantifiable approaches to development, operation, and maintenance of Web-based applications"(Deshpande Y and et al 2002). It is a response to the early, chaotic development of Web sites and applications as well as recognition of a divide between Web developers and conventional software developers (Murugesan, S et al 1999, Pressman 1998). Viewed broadly, Web Engineering is both a conscious and pro-active approach and a growing collection of theoretical and empirical research. Web engineering is the process used to create high-quality Web-based systems and applications that deliver a complex array of content and functionality to a broad population of end-users (bouchaib bahli and dany di tullio 2003). Web Engineering is concerned with the establishment and use of sound scientific, engineering and management principles and disciplined and systematic approaches to the successful development, deployment and maintenance of high quality Web-based systems and applications (Web Engineering Home Page 2003).

Web-based applications are becoming so popular in our daily life in the sense that it would not go a single day without we use them. These applications range from simple to sophisticated ones, where millions of dollars in revenue are generated. Developing, testing and quality assuring these applications become a challenging task (Abdesselam Redouane 2002). Although the development of Web-based applications made many improvements, there is still a lack of an established software engineering methodology for constructing Web-based applications. Consequently, much of the development is carried out without a true understanding of analysis and design issue.

The development of Web applications (E-commerce systems, Web portals, etc.) is subject to different conditions than that of conventional software systems (Said Hadjerrouit 2001). Such

idiosyncrasies include: usability, rapid development lifecycle and short time to market. Web based systems and applications deliver a complex array of content and functionality to a broad population of end users. They require new approaches to design and development but present the same issues and challenges as traditional information systems. Therefore, the same software engineering techniques are still necessary but the process should take these differences into account.

Web-based applications differ from other applications from both the product and process point of view. As products, they differ from traditional systems in the following ways:

1. Web based applications are distributed and component based.
2. High reliability
3. High Usability
4. Security

Web applications also differ from traditional applications from the process point of view: there are more Technologies (HTML, XML, network protocols, multimedia, and Java and script languages) and thus, many Roles (authors, developers, graphic designers, legal issues etc.) that have to be managed. In addition, the shorter time to market, shorter product life cycles and continuous maintenance are much more pronounced in the case of Web applications as compared to traditional ones(D. Rodriguez et al 2002).

WEB PROJECTS DEVELOPMENT

The history of Web development is relatively short. Initially, many Web applications were small and simple with little thought given to planning or design before constructing the site, and few have been tested properly. Today, many applications are large-scale and involve sophisticated interaction with visitors and databases; such sites are often regarded as mission critical. In parallel with this evolution, a need for Web engineering has become apparent. Yet, within education, the plethora of Web courses primarily address the implementation of Web sites with very little about the analysis and design of Web applications. We believe that an early consideration of a Web engineering process suited for inexperienced users is important.

(Pressman 2003) says Web Engineering is not a perfect "Clone" of software engineering but it borrows many of software engineering's fundamental concepts and principles, emphasizing the same technical and management activities. The brief history of systems development methodologies identifies and explores eras of development and speculates on their future. Today's "post methodology" era involves methodologies that can be viewed by developers as outdated and inappropriate for rapid development, Web applications, and other current requirements. Perhaps we are in danger of returning to the bad old days of the pre methodology era and its lack of control, standards, and training (David E. Avison and Guy Fitzgerald 2002).

(Yogesh Deshpande and Martin Gaedke 2005) mentioned that "There are very few standard methods for the Web developers to use. Hence, there is a strong need to understand and undertake Web Engineering". Ad-hoc development of WBA has brought disasters to many organizations. A survey on Web based project development by the (Cutter Consortium 2000) highlighted problems for Web-based projects:

- Delivered systems didn't meet business needs 84 percent of the time.
- Schedule delays plagued the projects 79 percent of the time.
- Projects exceeded the budget 63 percent of the time.
- Delivered systems didn't have the required functionality 53 percent of the time.
- Deliverables were of poor quality 52 percent of time.

SOFTWARE PROCESS IMPROVEMENT

Software process improvement (SPI) assessments are considered by many small software development firms to be too expensive (Aileen 2004). Software process improvement (SPI) is defined as having the potential to improve competitiveness by increasing productivity; reducing costs, defect and rework; and improving time to market and customer satisfaction (M. E. Fayad et al 2000). Small software development firms recognize that software process assessments play a valuable role in improving a firm's processes and products, but most feel that SPI costs too much and takes up resources needed to deliver products. SPI is very important now days, where in the last 15 years, interest in SPI has increased as evidenced by the growing number of journal articles which include the phrase 'process improvement' in their title or abstract (L. Pringle 2001) .

Most of the empirical studies on SPI relate to large well-resourced organizations. It has been noted that very little is known about the experience of small software development firms in regard to SPI. The growth of the software industry has produced many small companies that do not do contract software, but rather compete in other areas. This gives rise to at least four significant development issues that have not been adequately addressed in software engineering literature: company size, development mode, development size, and development speed. . Definitions of "small" businesses vary by industry and by government agency from 100 to 500 employees or more. These bounds are somewhat broad for our purposes. Based on census data, we define companies of 50 or fewer employees as small (Mohamed E. Fayad et al 2000).

First step toward process improvement is identifying the strengths and weaknesses of an organization's software processes to determine effective improvement actions. An assessment can help an organization examine its processes against a reference model to determine the processes' capability or the organization's maturity, to meet quality, cost, and schedule goals (Christiane Gresse et al 2006).

A study by (Sebastian Stein 2006) showed that software process improvements are required to increase the productivity of software companies. Generally, it is the aim to increase the quality of the produced software and to keep budget and time. Quality models for software process improvements were developed in context of large organizations and multi-national companies.

AGILE DEVELOPMENT METHODS AND WEB ENGINEERING PRACTICES

The field of software development is not shy of introducing new methodologies. Indeed, in the last 25 years, a large number of different approaches to software development have been introduced, of which only few have survived to be used today. The term agile has recently been used to categories a number of lightweight approaches to building software. These include: Extreme Programming (XP), Adaptive Software Development and Dynamic Systems Development Methodology (DSDM). Seventeen advocates and methodologists of the aforementioned and other agile processes convened in February 2001. The result of this meeting was the formation of the Agile Alliance (Beck K. et al 2001)and the production of The Manifesto for Agile Software Development (Fowler M. & Highsmith J 2001).

The following quote from The Manifesto for Agile Software Development1 gives a summary of it's purpose:

"We are uncovering better ways of developing software by doing it and helping others do it. Through this work we have come to value:

i.   Individuals and interactions over processes and tools.

ii.   Working software over comprehensive documentation.

iii. Customer collaboration over contract negotiation.

iv.   Responding to change over following a plan.

That is, while we value the items on the right, we value the items on the left more."(Constantine L 2001).

Ultimately we believe that the developers and organizations involved in Web engineering projects are the primary factor in the success or failure of Web application development. Given the diversity of disciplines required to develop Web-based applications, we are of the opinion that the AWE Process, or any other process or methodology, can only hope to have a second order effect on project success. Thus, we hold the belief that the agile route with its focus on people.

Our belief that people are the most important factor in project success is the fundamental reason why we have not tried to develop a monumental process to tackle the problems associated with Web application development. Many monumental processes attempt to codify good practice and experience in too much detail and for developers who do not understand the importance of what they are doing! This often results in development projects using monumental processes as cookbook recipes, where developers are lulled into a false sense of security by following the recipe in detail rather than using the ingredients selectively to help them build software deliverables that solve their problem space.

AWE is an iterative and incremental process; we believe this will allow for: early and continuous delivery of valuable software; the ability to harness changing requirements, even late in development; and the delivery of working software frequently. The AWE Process supports multidisciplinary development treating business experts, domain experts, and creative designers as developers along side software engineers (Miller, G 2001)

The following are the characteristics of agile software processes from the fast delivery point of view, which allow shortening the life-cycle of projects:

1. Modularity on development process level
2. Iterative with short cycles enabling fast verifications and corrections
3. Time-bound with iteration cycles from one to six weeks
4. Parsimony in development process removes all unnecessary activities
5. Adaptive with possible emergent new risks
6. Incremental process approach that allows functioning application building in small steps
7. Convergent (and incremental) approach minimizes the risks
8. People-oriented, i.e. agile processes favor people over processes and technology
9. Collaborative and communicative working style (Miller, G 2001).

Surveys of Web engineering practice by (Andrew McDonald and Ray Welland 2002) have identified seven characteristics of Web engineering that must be addressed by a Web engineering processes. These are support for:

1. Short development life-cycle times
2. Different business models (Business Process Re-engineering)
3. Multidisciplinary development teams
4. Small development teams working in parallel on similar tasks
5. Business Analysis and Evaluation with End-Users
6. Explicit Requirements and rigorous Testing against requirements
7. Maintenance

Since agility is desired, the principles of Agile Modeling should be followed.

Most of today's Web application development processes are extensions of standard software engineering processes. The usual iterated waterfall model is too rigid an approach to developing Web Applications. The waterfall model process was perfect for developing a file maintenance program for mainframes, but far too restrictive a process for building a Web application. Web application development needs to be an iterative process and most agree that a spiral approach is best. But, the exact steps at each cycle of the spiral are debated, as is the metric to be used to determine the completion of a cycle.

A few of today's Web application development processes have been derived from a business-oriented approach to applications development (Standing Craig 2002). Most of these processes develop a business plan for the e-business associated with the Web application, sometimes re-engineering the business along the way, and use things like Return on Investment (ROI) as a metric for the Web application development process

Extreme Programming

Extreme Programming (XP) has evolved from the problems caused by the long development cycles of traditional development models.

It first started as "simply an opportunity to get the job done" (Beck, K 1999) with practices that had been found effective in software development processes during the preceding decades (Beck, K 1999). After a number of successful trials in practice, the XP methodology was "theorized" on the key principles and practices used. Even though the individual practices of XP are not new as such, in XP they have been collected and lined up to function with each other in a novel way thus forming a new methodology for software development. The term 'extreme' comes from taking these commonsense principles and practices to extreme levels.

XP consists of 12 related practices and works best for small teams of 5 to 15 developers. Rather than focus on paper-based requirements and design documentation, XP concentrates on producing executable code and automated test drivers. This focus on source code makes XP controversial, leading some to compare it to hacking. We believe this comparison is unjustified because XP highly values simple design, and counters hacking claims by emphasizing refactoring, strong regression testing, and continuous code inspections through pair programming (J. Zettel et al 2001).

Small Firms and Standards

Many small firms are unaware of existing software process assessment models and standards. There's often the assumption that assessments conformant to these models and standards can be expensive and time consuming, and therefore difficult to perform in small companies. Small organizations also perceive assessment models and standards—including documentation and process-formalization practices—as targeting large organizations (M.C. Paulk 1998).

Small firms do not have the managerial experience, the financial resources and the methodological know-how to manage Web-based applications projects the way large firms do. Yet despite this, some small firms are satisfying their software development needs offshore (Brian Nicholson and Erran Carme 2002) There are two battles over process that every small software company must win to be successful. The first is the battle to convince the company to adopt reasonable development processes. Discussion of what makes up a good process may be an interesting meditation, but is entirely moot until the company commits to a policy of process improvement. The second battle is never over. It is to change existing processes to match changing circumstance (Robert P et al 2001).

A first step toward process improvement is identifying the strengths and weaknesses of an organization's software processes to determine effective improvement actions. An assessment can help an organization examine its processes against a reference model to determine the processes' capability or the organization's maturity, to meet quality, cost, and schedule goals. Several software process assessment models have been developed, such as CMM/CMMI, ISO 9001 Quality Management (including 9000-3), and ISO/IEC 15504—sometimes called SPICE. However, small companies (1–49 employees) find it difficult to run assessments (T. Mäkinen 2000).

SURVEY METHODOLOGY

The units of analysis for the survey were Jordanian small Web firms undertaking Web development. The target population included all small firms in Jordan which develop Web applications for sale as well as in-house software development groups within firms. The SEI [10] questionnaire was used as the survey instrument. Prior to the data collection, the survey instrument was pre-tested to enable clarification of constructs; to provide the means of operationalising selected constructs; and because pre-tests can be useful in qualitatively establishing the reliability, construct validity, and content validity of measure. In order to locate and correct weaknesses in the questionnaire, the questionnaire was pre-tested using face-to-face interviews with 10 random developers. The selection of interviewees for these pre-tests was designed to obtain maximum feedback from Web developers in various roles.

Prior to the pre-test, the following checklist was used to review the questionnaire instrument:

- Will the words be uniformly understood?
- Do the questions contain abbreviations or unconventional phrases?
- Are the questions too vague?
- Is the question too precise, biased or objectionable?

- Is it a double-barrel question?
- Does it have a double negative?
- Are the answer choices mutually exclusive?
- Has too much knowledge been assumed?
- Is the question technically accurate?
- Are the questions too cryptic?

During the pre-test, concerns were raised about the section headings and question groupings of the SEI questionnaire (such as metrics, standards and procedures, control of development Process). During the pre-test, the respondents completed the questionnaire in the presence of the researcher, and identified any difficulties with interpretation of words or questions. As well as testing the reliability and construct validity, the pre-tests served as 'dry runs' for the final administration of the instrument. The feedback was not adequate. So, some parts of the questionnaire were translated into Arabic Language (the mother tongue of respondents), and the pre-test was carried a second time. The sample used consisted of twenty small Web development firms in Jordan. Firms were eligible for inclusion in the survey when they (1) have had developed Web applications during the last 12 months and (2) did not have more than 50 employees.

The questionnaire is organized into two sections. The first section collects information on the respondent's background.

This includes current position, past experience, roles played among others. The second section, entitled Web engineering best practices, concentrates on the adoption of best practices by the respondent's organization. These include organizational Issues, standards and procedures, Web metrics, control of the development process, and tools and technology.

RESULTS

The statistical analysis showed that the majority of respondents have 5 years or less of experience in their present organizations, and the same number of years of overall software experience. The majority of them are in software engineering process group positions. The highest percentage of the study participants is involved in design activities. The majority of the participants were never involved in software process improvement activities. The analysis showed a significant weakness in the levels of adoption of Web engineering practices by small Jordanian Web development firms. The ratios of adoption levels were as follow: organizational issues (19%), standards and procedures (18%), Web metrics (9%), control of the development process (18%), and tools and technology (63%). The statistical analysis shows that Web metrics got the lowest ratio; which implies that the majority of respondents are not familiar with this practice. Tools and technology got the highest ratio; which implies that this practice is the most applied practice in these firms, and this reflects the widespread use of these tools in the development process worldwide. Organizational issues, standards and procedures and control of the development process got similar ratios. But, for the organizational issues, and standards and procedures, the majority of respondents answered with "No". This implies that the majority of respondents are not familiar with these two practices. For the control of development process practice the majority of respondents answered with "Does not apply". This implies that the respondents are familiar with this practice, but they don't apply it, and this leads one to say that the development process models used by these firms are ad hoc. The analysis also showed that there are significant differences in the levels of adoption of Web engineering best practices between European firms and small Jordanian Web development firms. The overall average of adoption levels of best practices in European countries is 51%, while the overall average of adoption levels in small Web development firms in Jordan is 25% see (Figure 1). The big difference in average between them implies that there is a big gap between the adoption levels of best practices in European countries and

Figure 1. Overall best practices adoption in small Jordanian firms

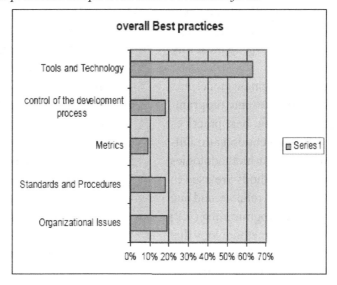

small Web development firms in Jordan. The final conclusion is that small Web development firms in Jordan have a lot to do in order to succeed in a very competitive market.

The Model

According to (Abdesselam Redouane 2002) Web-based firms have very stiff and stringent conditions. They have limited resources. This will hinder the quality of the product and ultimately the success of these companies. It is usually the case that the few people, who carried out the development, will also perform the testing of the end product. This is a poor practice, as it does not allow the test to be carried out rigorously and it will be certainly biased.

According to the results we got from the surveys that we have done, we found that small Jordanian firms have many problems:

Web projects are always, in most cases (firms) run over budget and time , have limited resources, number of developers is very small, quality assurance activities are done by the people who carried out the development, add hoc development approaches used , poor Web project management, and Web engineering practices is not implemented .

Based on results of survey and literature analysis we proposed the following model (Figure 2):

1. Start with simple Web projects or implement sub contracts projects: The surveys and literature stated that most of Web development projects in small firms are small or medium size projects (1-2 months or 3-6 months). In small Web projects it is highly desirable to plan all phases at the start of the project. This means that the phase sections of the Web project management plan, Web configuration management plan and Web verification and validation plans are combined. The plans may be generated when writing the proposal. Typically, qualified developers are involved in large or medium-size projects whereas small Web projects are carried out by under-qualified or inexperienced Web developers. The reactionary development scenario and the lack of clear guidelines to face the process, push developers to follow an ad-hoc development process.

    The heavyweight software methodologies are limited to support such scenario. This is because they involve several stages and roles that require an important amount of communication and coordination in order to get a final product. On the other hand, there are the lightweight or agile methodologies that could have an interesting applicability to the described scenario.

2. Implement an agile development model, and we recommended using extreme programming that identify specific best practices within the Web development domain: Different software development methodologies and quality assurance methods are used in order to attain high quality, reliable, and bug free software. Extreme Programming (XP) is a software development methodology that integrates many of the known ideas (that we all were familiar with) in order to achieve such software systems. Specifically, XP emphasizes code-unit testing (preferably before its writing), and thorough testing of software functionality. The contribution of XP to software development is expressed, among other ways, in the quality improvement of both the entire process of software development and of the software quality itself. Currently, XP is used mainly in small-medium size software projects [19].

3. Developers must apply the lower limit of Web engineering best practices: Many practitioners in the field of Web engineering and software engineering have commented on the lack of suitable software engineering processes that can be used to build Web applications. We investigated the way industrial Web engineering is being carried out by making a survey consists of questions relating to the development process being used to develop Web applications and Web engineering practices. If a Web engineering process is to be successful then it must address the following:

1. Short development life-cycle times.
2. Delivery of bespoke solutions.
3. Multidisciplinary development teams.
4. Small development teams working in parallel on similar tasks.
5. Analysis and Evaluation.
6. Requirements and Testing.
7. Maintenance.

4. Testing and quality assurance (QA) activities must be carried out by another qualified firm, until an internal qualified quality assurance department is established

5. Web project management issues specific to Web development; must be carried out.

In order to organize and manage a Web development project successfully, one must combine specific knowledge, skills, efforts, experience, capabilities, and even intuition.

6. Training and education: Good Web engineering practice requires expertise in a complex set of activities that involve the intellectual skills of planning, designing, evaluating, and revising. A Web engineering process must take into account the different types of developer required to build a successful solution.

In order to this framework to be successful, all of the people involved in Web development (developers, mangers,) must have a good knowledge in Web engineering development and they must be trained.

The best way to learn modified XP is in an experiential-learning training course. Your entire development team (including the testers, the customer, and the manager) Should attend a one-week immersion course on XP. While many programming teams are learning XP based solely on books and information on the Web, it is important to actually do the practices with guidance.

7. Review the current situation; evolve slowly, until development method is clear.

Figure 2 shows the model and explains the model elements.

CONCLUSION

The results showed that there is a weakness in applying Web engineering practices in small Jordanian Web development firms. The results of the study lead to the following recommendations to improve Web development practice in small Web development firms in Jordan:

1. Development teams should be multidisciplinary: A Web engineering process must take into account the different types of developer required to build a successful solution. The process
   Should ensure that all involved understand their roles and responsibilities, and where overlap occurs understand how to resolve conflict in the best interests of the project in question.
2. Firms should apply project management best practices to improve organizational issues.

3. Firms should pay attention to the quality management and standards.
4. Firms should apply software engineering best practices to improve the execution of their Web engineering projects.
5. Software process improvement initiatives should be considered.
6. Education and training: A proper and regular training of employees especially on newer aspects in Web engineering will lead to an increase of acceptance and usage.

Small firms need to adopt a suitable Web development model and must apply Web engineering best practices in order to survive. Web project management and education is also important for the development process. Testing is the main key for quality, so small firms should outsource their testing activities at the initial phases when apply the model. The model may be helpful for small Web firms in improving their way in development, where small Web firms have very stiff and stringent conditions. They have limited resources.

The model may be considered useful for Web project development in small firms, where it based on agile development methods, a set of Web engineering practices, and Web project management.

Figure 2. The model

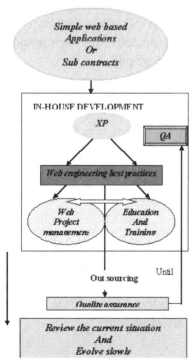

REFERENCES

Avison, D. E., & Fitzgerald, G. (2003, January). Where Now for Development methodologies. *Communications of the ACM, 46*(1), 79-82.

Bahli, B., & Di Tullio, D. (2003). Web Engineering: An Assessment of Empirical Research. *Communications of the Associations for Information Systems, 12*, 203-222.

Beck, K. (1999). Embracing Change with Extreme Programming. *IEEE Computer, 32*(10): 70–77.

Beck, K. et al., (2001, February). Manifesto for Agile Software Development. *The Agile Alliance,* http://www.agilealliance.org/

Cater-Steel, A. P. (2004). Low-rigour, Rapid Software Process Assessments for Small Software Development Firms. *Proceedings of the 2004 Australian Software Engineering Conference (ASWEC'04).*

Constantine, L. (2001, April). Lightweights, Heavyweights and Usable Processes for Usable Software. *Keynote at Software Development 2001.*

Cuitter Consortium Research Briefs (2000). http://www.cutter.com

Deshpande, Y., & Gaedke, M. (2005). Web Engineering: Developing Successful Web Applications In A Systematic Way. *14th International World Wide Web Conference,* 10-14 May, 2005, Chiba, Jap.

Deshpande, Y., Murugesan, S., Ginige, A., Hansen, S., Schwbe, D., Gaedke, M., & White, B. (2002). Web Engineering. *Journal of Web Engineering, 1*(1), 3-17. Santa Barbara, CA.

Fayad, M. E., Laitinen, M., & Ward, R. P. (2000). Software Engineering in the Small. *Communications of the ACM, 43,* 115-118.

Fayad, M. E., Laitinen, M., & Ward, R. P. (2000, March). Software Engineering in the Small. Communications of the ACM, *43*(3).

Fowler, M., & Highsmith J. (2001, August). The Agile Manifesto. *Software Development Magazine.* http://www.sdmagazine.com/documents/s=844/sdm0108a/0108a.htm

Gresse von Wangenheim, C., Anacleto, A., & Salviano, C. F. (2006). *Helping Small Companies Assess Software Processes, IEEE Software,* (pp. 91-98).

Mäkinen, T., Varkoi, T., & Lepasaar, M. (2000). A Detailed Process Assessment Method for Software

SMEs. *Proc. 7th European Software Process Improvement Conf. (EuroSPI).* www.iscn.at/select_newspaper/assessments/tampere.html.

McDonald, A., & Welland, R. (2002).. Available at http://www.dcs.gla.ac.uk/ accessed *Evaluation of Commercial Web Engineering Processes* 20/5/2006.

Miller, G. G. (2001). *The Characteristics of Agile Software Processes.*

Murugesan, S., Deshpande, Y., Hansen, S., & Ginige, A. (1999, May). Web Engineering: A New Discipline for Development of Web-based Systems. *Proceedings of the First ICSE Workshop on Web Engineering, International Conference on Software Engineering,* Los Angeles, http://aeims.uws.edu.au/WebEhome/ICSE99-WebE-Proc/San.do

Nicholson, B., & Carme, E. (2002). Offshore Software Sourcing by Small Firms. *An Analysis of Risk, Trust and Control.*

Paulk, M. C., (1998). Using the Software CMM in Small Organizations. *Joint 1998 Proc. PacificNorthwest Software Quality Conf. and 8th Int'l Conf. Software Quality, PNSQC/Pacific Agenda,* (pp. 350–361). www.pnsqc.org/proceedings/pnsqc98.pdf

Pressman, R. S. (1998, September/October). Can Internet-Based Applications Be Engineered? *IEEE Software.*

Pressman, R. S. (2003). Software Engineering: a Practitioner's Approach (4th ed.). McGraw-Hill Publishing Company.

Pringle, L. (2001). Size does matter: improvement for SMEs. *Software (SEA National),* (pp. 4-7).

Ray, K C. (2002, August). Adopting xp The path to—and pitfalls of—implementing Extreme Programming. *STQE* (pp. 34-40). www.stqemagazine.com

Redouane, A. (2002). Guidelines for Improving the Development of Web-Based Applications. *Proceedings of the Fourth International Workshop on Web Site Evolution (WSE'02)* 0-7695-1804-4/02 2002 IEEE.

Rodriguez, D., Harrison, R., & Satpathy, M. (2002). A Generic Model and Tool Support for Assessing and Improving Web Processes. *Proceedings of the Eighth IEEE Symposium on Software Metrics* (METRICS.02) 0-7695-1339-5/02 © 2002 IEEE.

Standing, C. (2002, March). Methodologies for developing Web applications. *Information and Software Technology, 44*(3), 151-159.

Stein, S. (2006). *Software Process Improvements in a Small Organization*. Master Thesis, Software Engineering Thesis no: MSE-2006:01 January 2006. Available at: http://quality.hpfsc.de/master-sstein.pdf accessed 4/6/2006.

Stein, S. (2006). Software Process Improvements in a Small Organization. Master Thesis, Software Engineering Thesis no: MSE-2006:01 January 2006. Available at: http://quality.hpfsc.de/master-sstein.pdf accessed 4/6/2006.

Stein, S. (2006). Software Process Improvements in a Small Organization. Master Thesis. Software Engineering Thesis no: MSE-2006:01 January 2006. Available at: http://quality.hpfsc.de/master-sstein.pdf accessed 4/6/2006

Ward, R. P., Fayad, M. E., & Laitinen, M. (2001, April). Software Process Improvement in the Small. *Communications of the ACM, 44*(4).

Web Engineering Home Page [http://fistserv.macarthur.uws.edu.au/san/WebEhome/]

Zettel, J., et al. (2001). LIPE: A Lightweight Process for E-Business Startup Companies Based on Extreme Programming. *Proc. Third Int'l Conf. Product-Focused Software Process Improvement (PROFES 2001)*. Berlin: Springer Verlag.

KEY TERMS

Agile Development: Refers to a group of software development methodologies that are based on similar principles.

CMMI: A process improvement approach that provides organizations with the essential elements of effective processes.

Extreme Programming: Is a software engineering methodology, the most prominent of several agile software development methodologies.

Small Firms: Small firms are companies which employ a relatively low number of workers.

Software Process: The total set of software engineering activities necessary to develop and maintain software products.

Web-Based Applications: Is an application that is accessed via Web browser over a network such as the Internet or an intranet.

Web Project Management: Project management is a methodical approach to planning and guiding project processes from start to finish.

Chapter X
A Proposed Theoretical Framework for Assessing Quality of E–Commerce Systems

Sattam Alamro
Albalqa' Applied Univesity, Jordan

Asim El-Sheikh
The Arab Academy for Banking and Financial Sciences, Jordan

ABSTRACT

Companies and institutions in the light of globalization and competitiveness are seeking to improve their services, particularly electronic access to excellence. With the tremendous growth in the global digital transactions, the entry of electronic commerce strongly in global business dealings under acceleration, heated competition in the provision of electronic services, the companies are keen on achieving the principle of comprehensive quality and special electronic sites and services on the Internet. Thus, those sites become electronic firms, so it must give good impression about the company from the outset. The significance of the study is that it addresses one of the vital issues of our time, which is the current enormous revolution in information technology and communications, it provides a framework to evaluate the quality of sites and electronic services are comprehensive, objective and flexible to reach the ideal site. The proposed framework can be used to compare the quality of E-Commerce systems, or to improve the image and performance of a particular E-Commerce systems or to provide reference guide for designers of the sites where their determination to new sites. This chapter examined and analyzed previous research studies that interrelated with the quality of sites and electronic services, and then developed an inclusive theoretical framework. This framework consisted of new indicators that are clear, measurable, and flexible to the possibility of its application on all sites and services, regardless of the nature of the company or institution. Consequently, the proposed framework can be applied easily to evaluate the quality of any system.

INTRODUCTION

Past years have seen widespread of the Internet, huge number of Websites and attendant dissemination of vast quantities of information, so we are suffering from new phenomenon inflation information, and many sites without attention to quality and their services (*Sean Quan Lau, 2006*). The number of sites has grown since the start of first electronic trading mid-nineties of the last century. This explosion of knowledge of the number of sites led to the need for standards to ensure the quality of E-Commerce systems and the services they offer. The main objective behind this number of sites is the continuous improvement of the performance of companies and the level of services they provide to the customers in the world of knowledge and the digital economy. The company's electronic site on the Internet, has a major impact on the company's performance, it has become in the world of e-business the core of the work of the companies and institutions that adopt the principle of electronic services. Therefore, firms and institutions are eager to make their best picture of the highest quality, with the aim of improving service, which contributes to the rosy picture given by the company will be reflected positively on its Performance.

E-Commerce is considered an excellent alternative for companies to reach new customers. However, many E-Commerce Websites have a short life because they don't meet the minimal software quality requirements (*Albuquerque et al. 2002*). The tendency of major companies towards electronic commerce over the last decade, and the tremendous growth in the volume of electronic commerce based on the principle of electronic services, has led to concern in recent years the quality of E-Commerce systems and the services they offer.

Ensuring the quality of E-Commerce systems is not easy, standards which can determine that vary according to location and the nature of services provided. On this basis, we find many of the studies of the quality improvement Websites on the service provided. Some researchers have gone to evaluate the quality of Web sites for business and commercial companies, while others went to evaluate the quality of Web sites for e-government sites (*Ma and Zaphiris, 2003; Choudrie et al, 2004*), while the others evaluated quality of banks and financial companies, as a number of researchers evaluated the quality of universities and educational institutions sites *(singh and Sook, 2002)*. In addition, Other Websites provide other types of services, such as Web sites for auction, or e-shopping, and so on (*Barnes and Vidgen*, 2001). We have a variety of studies and researches based upon the diversity of Web sites, the nature of services provided and the differences in the criteria used in the evaluation process, but what characterizes most of these studies is the use of descriptive style inalienable measure, and not to rely on quantitative style. In addition to previous studies that characterized most valuable improvement, particular type of E-Commerce systems have provided a unified and comprehensive standards for all E-Commerce systems and the services they offer.

Based on the foregoing, this study aims to analysis previous research studies, which dealt with evaluating the quality of E-Commerce systems, and reaching a framework for evaluating the quality of E-Commerce systems, regardless of the nature of the service provided by the electronic site, the framework contains all the key elements of inclusiveness, clarity and objectivity by the possibility of using the numerical values of the indicators for measuring process, and flexibility through the possibility of its application to all E-Commerce systems, regardless of the nature of the service provided .

WHY WE NEED A THEORETICAL FRAMEWORK

With the direction of major companies to online transactions and the growth of electronic commerce accelerating growth and entering the world economy, as one of the most important features of the modern digital economy, it has become incumbent upon companies and businesses and should pay more attention to the electronic services they provide. In spite of the continued growth of sites and the attendant electronic dissemination of vast quantities of information, whether high or low quality, it does not have very comprehensive standards serve as a basis for ensuring the quality of E-Commerce systems and the services they offer. The quality of the E-Commerce systems of the company and the services they offer over the Internet will reflect on their performance and help content of the information to give rosy picture for the company.

In the past few years, a large number of E-Commerce systems have been developed. To ensure the production of high quality of E-Commerce systems, it is important for developers to be able to assess the quality of such systems. The latter is inevitably linked with the receivers' perception of quality. It must be noted that E-Commerce systems differ from other Web applications in that a basic condition of their success is the total involvement of the end-user at almost every stage of the purchasing process (*Henfridsson and Holmstrom, 2003*), which is not the case with other Web applications. The growth that business to Consumer (B2C) E-Commerce systems have experienced in the past few years has given rise to the problem of identification of those factors that determine end-user acceptance of such systems (*Chen et al., 2004*).

A number of approaches towards assessing the quality attributes of E-Commerce systems focus on the technological aspects of such systems, thus providing a technology-oriented view of quality (*Zwass, 1996; Elfriede and Rashka, 2001*). Other approaches assess the quality of E-Commerce systems as perceived by the end-user, but focusing mainly on the usability of such systems. Such approaches use software evaluation methods such as inspection (*Nielsen, 2000*) and inquiry meth-

ods (*Shaw and DeLone, 2002*) in order to record end users' perception of usability. Studies on E-Commerce systems quality also focus on more specific quality characteristics such as issues that warrant successful transactions (*Bidgoli, 2002*), maximize the perceived trustworthiness (*Egger, 2001; Slyke et al., 2004*), or ensure E-Commerce systems reliability (*Elfriede and Rashka, 2001*). Although, all the aforementioned factors are affecting the quality of E-Commerce systems and are prerequisites for their success, they are not the only ones that relate to E-Commerce systems quality. In order to model E-Commerce systems quality, a global approach is required combining all factors affecting quality. Some related works are using questionnaires to detect users' opinions, the data from which are statistically analyzed in order to lead in values measuring quality characteristics such as usability (*Sauro & Kindlund, 2005*). This is a common practice, since users' opinion is very important for the assessment of E-Commerce systems (*Julian & Standing, 2003*), as well as the active involvement of users into the evaluation process (*Henfridsson and Holmstrom, 2003; Chen et al., 2004*). Therefore, it has become necessary to develop a framework to evaluate the quality of E-Commerce systems; to measure the efficiency and effectiveness of the E-Commerce systems to provide electronic services to the company.

LITRATURE REVIEW

The widespread of the Internet and its entering the world economy, finance and trade, and the adoption of various companies and institutions in its electronic services at the international level, led to the emergence of electronic commerce as one of the most important characteristics of the modern economy in recent years. With the heavy dependence on Websites on the Internet to manage global trade, there has been a need to evaluate the quality of sites and electronic services it provides.

There have been many studies in the area of quality Websites and E-Commerce systems as one of the most important branches of electronic commerce in recent times, and a variety of building on the diversity of electronic services provided; owner differences in the criteria used for evaluation. As a result, the existence of quality standards to evaluate Websites vary according to the nature of the site, in addition to, most of these studies focus on a particular element of evaluating the site without a comprehensive evaluation of all dimensions. In addition, most of these studies use descriptive style inalienable measure, and do not rely on quantitative criteria clear and measurable indicators. Previous studies related to the quality of Websites have been classified based upon the nature of the service offered by the site, such as: business sites, and e-government, universities, educational institutions, banks and financial institutions.

Many of the studies have addressed the quality of sites from several points of view, some dealt with in terms of quality characteristics of the site, which is sensitive and influential to the success of e-business, and it has been called "the critical success factors." Others considered quality in terms of strategies management to be followed to satisfy customers and to achieve their needs upon the use of electronic services, and the third group has addressed the quality of the sites from the perspective of the designers of sites, and a fourth team opined in their studies for the design of a general framework for measuring the quality of these systems.

Antonia Stefanil,et al (2007) in their study introduced to the reader a quality assessment model based on Bayesian Networks and presented in detail the practical application of this model, highlighting practical issues related to the involvement of human subjects, conflict resolution, and calibration of the measurement instruments. Furthermore, their paper presented the application process of the model for the quality assessment of various ecommerce systems; it also discussed in detail how particular features (data) of the assessed E-Commerce systems can be identified and, using the described automated assessment process, lead to higher abstraction information (desire data) regarding the quality of the assessed E-Commerce systems.

*Antonia Stefani et a*l (2003) proposed a model based on the ISO 9126 quality standard specifically, it relies on the set of those quality characteristics and sub-characteristics that are directly related to quality as perceived by the end-users. These quality characteristics are: functionality, usability, reliability and efficiency. The importance of each of the aforementioned quality characteristics depends on each E-Commerce system's specificities as well as the user requirements and developer priorities for the specific system.

Zaphiris et a l(2006) presented and discussed the importance of usability and accessibility in the design and evaluation of portal systems. They presented an incremental framework for taking this issues into consideration during the design of such systems.

Youngsu Lee and Jinwoo Ki(2000) suggested a comprehensive framework that covers from concrete design features to financial performance for online stock trading, which is one of the most important domains of e-business. The proposed model for online stock trading sites consists of three design principles: functional convenience, representational delight, and structural firmness. they found that the convenience, delight and firmness principles were closely related to the level of customer satisfaction, and, consequently, to the level of customer loyalty to the sites. they also identified important design features such as presentation of stock quotes in the homepage for each of the three design principles.

Turban and Gherke, (2000) suggested additional variables such as 24-hour availability, stability of software and hardware, page loading speed, the system architecture, visual appearance and accessibility as part of the E-Commerce system quality. The model highlights that such attributes of E-Commerce sites are likely to influence the Use and Customer Satisfaction of E-Commerce systems.

Zhang and Dran (2003) have built a conceptual framework to assess the quality of university sites from the point of view of achieving the desire of the user, which used five criteria as the most important criteria for this purpose, namely: ease of navigation, provide a tool for research, information accuracy and completeness of information, the presentation of information and clarity.

Luis Olsina Santos (1999), presented a methodology for the quantitative evaluation and comparison of Web site quality called Web-site Quality Evaluation Method (QEM). The core models and procedures for artifact evaluation are supported by the Logic Scoring of Preference (LSP) model and continuous preference logic as mathematical background. he discussed the process steps that the evaluators should follow by applying the Web-site QEM, namely: (a) Selecting a site or a set of competitive sites specific to a domain, (b) Specifying goals and the user view, (c) Specifying in a standard-compliant way, Web-site quality characteristics and attributes, (d) Defining the evaluation criterion for each attribute, and applying attribute measurement, (f) Aggregating elementary attributes to yield the global quality preference, and (g) Analyzing, assessing, and comparing partial and global outcomes. In order to illustrate the methodology he focuses on a case study on typical museum sites where more than ninety components were involved regarding the general visitor view. The process results may be useful to understand, control, and improve the Web artifacts quality in small, medium and large-scale projects.

The 2QCV3Q, also called 7-loci, is a conceptual model proposed by Mich li and et al (2003) to evaluate Web site quality based on seven dimensions: who-what-why-when-where-how, and feasibility (with what means and devices). It is interested and very flexible approach to evaluate a *generic Web site* takes its name from the initials of the Ciceronian *loci* on which it is based, namely: *Quis* (Identity), *Quid* (Content), *Cur* (Services), *Ubi* (Location), *Quando* (Management), *Quomodo* (Usability), *Quibus Auxiliis* (Feasibility).

A more analytic Web site quality model was proposed by Etnoteam (2000) it is based on six attributes (communication, content, functionality, usability, management, accessibility). The model can be personalized: the sub-attributes are weighted depending on the site category.

APROPOSED THEORETICAL FRAMEWORK

The literature analysis of Standards and Quality Evaluation of E-Commerce systems showed that Quality evaluation approaches suffer from several limitations, as follow:

- They often define very general criteria, do not address its specific Websites (e-government, large public sites) or page (informative, directory, service specific, etc.). These differences must be taken into account when measuring the characteristics of the sites.

- The perception of the quality changes from different user perspectives: the final user is interested in external quality related to the usability and functionality of the site, while the developer is more interested to the internal quality related to backward and forward compatibility, openness to evolution, maintainability, portability, interoperability, etc.

- Customers' quality expectations change over time, and thus no single quality checklist will be good for very long.

- Customers in a Web domain do not regard all quality factors as equally important.

- Many evaluation criteria are essentially *accessibility or usability biased*. Even if the two areas have some overlap, stressing one of them can be misleading. It occurs that a perfectly usable site is really not accessible, or that a technically accessible site may be scarcely usable.

Therefore, in this chapter we are going to propose a theoretical framework, this framework contains accurate and clear standards of objectivity, comprehensiveness and flexibility to assess the quality of E-Commerce systems. The Proposed framework consists of four main elements, these elements are: quality of content, quality of design, Quality of organizing, and Ease of use see figure (1). Each of these main elements has sub-attributes to evaluate the quality of E-Commerce systems .Moreover, The Proposed framework can be used to improve the image and performance of particular E-Commerce systems or to provide reference guide for designers of the sites.

COMPONENT OF THEORETICAL FRAMEWORK

In this context we are trying to integrate between the available studies on the quality of E-Commerce systems and the theoretical and practical experience to the researchers. Moreover, it tries

to get access to accurate and clear standards, comprehensiveness and flexibility to assess the quality of electronic services for Internet sites. The proposed framework consists of four main components: content, design, organization and ease of use, as shown in Figure (1). Each one of them contains set of indicators used to evaluate the quality of E-Commerce systems. The proposed framework can be used for comparison between the quality of E-Commerce systems, or to improve the image and performance of particular systems, or to provide a reference guide for designers of E-Commerce systems.

Quality of Content

Inflation in the huge volume of information on the Internet makes quality content the most important elements .As such , quality of content must be taken into account when conducting the evaluation of E-Commerce systems and electronic services provided. Since the content is the basic pillar in the direction of business and trade via electronic dimension to electronic commerce, Singh and Sook,(2002)deemed it as the most important element in the process of evaluation, they named it "king element." The quality of content has been addressed by many researchers in differ-

Figure 1. A proposed theoretical framework

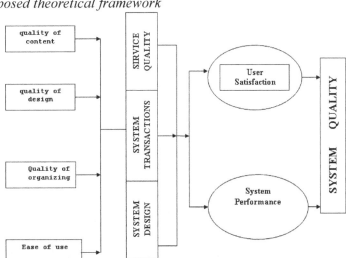

ent ways. On the first hand , Some researchers went to use it as a basic element in evaluating the quality of content sites and services provided without taking into account any another element of quality. Granath, (2006; Heimlich, 1999), on the other hand, other researchers considered it as one of the elements during the evaluation of E-Commerce systems (Barnes and Vidgen, 2002; Delone and Mclean, 2003; Lin and Joyce, 2004; Signore, 2005; Singh and Sook, 2002; Tan and Tung, 2003). The content of quality indicators including the following:

A: Update: modern information on the system.
B: The relevance of the system details: the relevance of the system the company or institution in terms of content, comprehensiveness and detail in the information.
C: Multilingualism and Culture: Browsing provide more than one language, and culture into account the different clients regardless of the state to which they belong.
D: The diversity of style of presentation: the presentation of information in different forms.
E: Accuracy: The accuracy of the information. And this indicator can be measured using a list of inspection following: The accuracy of information on the system. There are no mistakes rules or linguistic phenomenon on the system. Sources of information on the system documented.
F: Responsibility: the confidence of the user information contained on the E-Commerce system.

Quality of Design

Institutions and companies keen to show their Web sites best picture, so that attracts customers to visit and re-visited after use the first time, on the principle of giving the excellent impression since the first visit to the site to repeat his visit later.

The interest component of quality visual design qualities in the design of the site to attract users to visit the site beginning and then stay as long as possible within the site and, finally, repeating his times again in future. The companies and institutions keen to show the different Websites using the best techniques and innovative creative ways to attract the attention of users and roaming around through its pages. as the poor design may lead to fatigue and lack of desire used in navigation although the site contains rich information. Yoo and Jin,(2004)indicated in their studies to 12 feature must be taken into account for the quality of Web sites, Other researchers pointed that quality of design as one of the key elements in the process of evaluation (Barnes and Vidgen, 2002; Heimlich and Wang , 1999; Kokkinaki et al., 2005; Signore, 2005;).

The content of quality of design including the following elements:

A: Gravity: attractive of the system in terms of innovation in design, and beauty in the images and movements, so the user makes a happy and enthusiastic to visit the site.
B: Appropriate: appropriate design and images used by the type of service provided by the site.
C: Color: color characteristics backgrounds or colors used texts at the same design.
D: Video, voice and image: the characteristics of video files, voice and image used in the pages of the site.
E: Text: the properties of texts used in the pages of the site.

Quality of Organizing

This element is interested in site structure and mode of services provided by the division, it is conducted to provide various services. Firstly, an easy way to browse the site to help the user to access the required information quickly. Secondly, to feel ease during visiting the site. many researchers dealt with quality of organizing when evaluating the quality of E-Commerce systems, Heimlich and Wang (1999)presented a comprehensive study of this component and provided a model covers most indicators of this element explaining the importance of this element on the quality of the systems. The content of quality of organizing outlines the following elements:

A: Index: containment site index or links to Web pages of all Homes.
B: System map: Map occasion of the system, and links on each page for easy browsing.
C: Consistency: consistency and compatibility of all pages in the presentation.

Ease of Use

This element has emerged as one of the most important elements of evaluating sites in most previous studies, where one of the more elements that have been addressed in previous studies. The quality of the ease of use with the system, meant to ease the use of the site by any user, regardless of their scientific background to obtain the required information, the site also means the ability to provide steady performance for efficiency, in addition to possible adjustment as desired by the user (Gledec, 2005). The content of quality of ease of use outlines the following elements:

A: Ease: ease of use of the system, and finding information, and browse it.
B: Reliability: an appropriate title and the characteristics of the system and nature of the system.
C: Interactive features: the existence of clear instructions for the use of any portion of the system, and assistance program to help users, and tools of communication and feedback between users and the system through various means of communication.
D: Security and Privacy: to obtain the confidence of users through the safety of operations and services provided, in addition to maintaining the privacy of personal information to the user.

CONCLUSION

We have seen our current revolution in information and communications technology, coupled with the widespread of Internet, it led to the creation of new concepts in the world economy, finance, business, trade, which became the basis of electronic commerce in the global business dealings. Therefore, companies and institutions have given great attention to the quality of electronic services provided by through their Websites via the Internet. With the aim of improving the service provided, which contributes to giving rosy picture about the company, this will reflect positively on their performances. This chapter has provided a framework to evaluate the quality of E-Commerce systems regardless of the nature of the service offered by the system, the comprehensive of the framework contains all the key elements of the evaluation. As was clear and substantive through the possible use of numerical values to measure the main elements of evaluation, also through the possibility of flexibility applied to all systems, regardless of the nature of the service provided. The framework proposed by the quality improvement large segment of the Web sites regardless of the nature of electronic service provided or the nature of the company or institution. In addition, the proposed framework can be applied easily and easy to evaluate the quality of any system, whether for business or for electronic government, or to a financial institution, or others.

REFERENCES

Albuquerque, A. B., & Belchior, A. D. (2002). E-Commerce Website quality evaluation. *Euromicro Conference, 2002. Proceedings.* (pp. 294 – 300).

Antonia, S., Michalis, X. & Stavrinoudis, D. (2003, July). *VECIMS 2003 - International Symposium on Virtual Environments, Human-Computer Interfaces, and Measurement Systems*, Lugano, Switzerland.

Antonia, S., Stavrinoudis, D., & Michalis, X. (2007). In-Depth Analysis of Selected Topics related to the Quality Assessment of E-Commerce Systems. In J. Filipe, H. Coelhas, & M. Saramago (Eds.), *e-Business and Telecommunication Networks Vol II.* (pp. 39-48). ISBN: 978-3-540-75992-8.

Barnes and Vidgen (2002). An Integrative Approach to the Assessment of E-Commerce Quality. *Journal of Electronic Commerce Research, 3*(3), 114-127.

Barnes, S., & Vidgen, R. (2001). Assessing the Quality of Auction Web Sites. *In Proceedings of the 34th International Conference on System Sciences.*

Bidgoli, H, (2002). *Electronic Commerce Principles and Practice.* San Diego: Academic Press.

Chen, L., Gillenson, M., & Sherrell, D. (2004). Consumer Acceptance of Virtual Stores: A Theoretical Model and Critical Success Factors for Virtual Stores. *The DATA BASE for Advances in Information Systems, 35*(2).

Choudrie, J., Ghinea, G., & Weerakkody, V. (2004). Evaluating Global e-Government Sites: A View Using Web Diagnostic Tools. *Electronic Journal of e-Government, 2*(2), 105-114.

Delone, W., & Mclean, E. (2003). The DeLone and McLean of Information Systems Success: A Ten-Year Update. *Journal of Management Information Systems, 19*(4), 9-30.

Egger, F. (2001). Affective Design of E-Commerce User Interfaces: How to Maximise Perceived Trustworthiness. *International Conference on Affective Human Factors Design.* London: Asean Academic.

Elfriede, D., & Rashka, J. (2001). *Quality Web Systems, Performance Security, and Usability.* New York: Addison – Wesley.

Etnoteam, S. P. A. M. (2000). *Evaluating and designing the quality of Websites (a quality model for Websites).* University of Milan.

Franch, M., & Gaio, L. (2003). *Evaluating and designing the quality of Websites.* IEEE, Multi-media.

Gledec, G. (2005). Evaluating Web Site Quality. *In Proceedings of the 7th Internet Users Conference (CUC2005),* Croatia.

Heimlich, J. (1999). Evaluating the Content of Web Sites. *Environmental Education and Training Partnership Resource Library.* Ohio State University Extension, USA.

Heimlich, J., & Wang, K. (1999). Evaluating the Structure of Web Sites. *Environmental Education and Training Partnership Resource Library,* Ohio State University Extension, USA.

Henfridsson, O., & Holmstrom, H. (2003). Developing E-Commerce in Internetworked Organizations: A Case of Customer Involvement Throughout the Computer Gaming Value Chain. *The DATA BASE for the Advances in Information Systems, 33*(4).

Julian, T., & Standing, C. (2003). The value of User Participation in the E-Commerce Systems Development. *Informing and IT Education Conference,* Pori, Finland.

Kokkinaki, I. A., Mylonas, S., & Mina, S. (2005, September). e-Government Initiatives in Cyprus. *e-Government Workshop (eGOV05),* Brunel University, UK.

Lin, O., & Joyce, D. (2004). "Critical Success Factors for Online Auction Web Sites. *In the Proceedings of the 17th NACCQ.*

Ma, H., & Zaphiris, P. (2003). The Usability and Content Accessibility of the e-Government in the UK. *In Proceedings of Human Computer Interaction International Conference*, Greece.

Nielsen, J. (2000). *Designing Web Usability: The Practice of Simplicity.* New Riders Publishing. Indianapolis. Indiana.

Quan Lau, S.(n.d.). *Domain Analysis of E-Commerce Systems Using Feature-Based Model Templates, A thesis,* Waterloo, Ontario, Canada.

Santos, L. O. (1999). Web-site Quality Evaluation Method: a Case Study on Museums. ICSE 99 - 2nd Workshop on Software Engineering over the Internet.

Sauro, J., & Kindlund, E. (2005). A Method to Standardize Usability Metrics Into a Single Score. *CHI2005 Methods and Usability*, Portland, Oregon, USA.

Shaw, N., & DeLone, W. (2002). Sources of Dissatisfaction in End- User Support: An Empirical Study. *The DATA BASE for Advances in Information Systems, 33*(2).

Signore, O. (2005). A Comprehensive Model for Web Sites Quality. *In the Proceedings of the 7th IEEE International Symposium on Web Site Evolution (WSE'05).*

Singh, I., & Sook, A.(2002). An Evaluation of the Usability of South African University Web Sites. *In Proceedings of the 2002 CITTE Conference*, Durban, South Africa.

Tan, F., & Tung, L.(2003, December). Exploring Website Evaluation Criteria Using the Repertory Grid Technique: A Web Designers' Perspective. *In the Proceedings of the 2nd Annual Workshop on HCI Research in MIS*, WA.

Yoo, S., & Jin, J. (2004). Evaluation of the Home Page of the Top 100 University Web Sites. *Academy of Information and Management Sciences, 8*(2), 57-69.

Youngsu, L. J. K. (n.d.). From Design Features to Financial Performance for Online Stock Trading Sites.

Zaphiris, P., Dellaporta, A., & Mohamedally, D. (2006). User needs analysis and evolution of portals. In A. Cox (Ed.), *Portals: people, processes and technology.* London, UK: Facet Publishing.

Zhang, P., & Dran, G.(2001)."Expectations and Ranking of Website Quality Features: Results of Two Studies on User Perceptions. *In the Proceedings of the 34th Hawaii International Conference on System Sciences.*

Zwass, V. (1996). Structure and macro-level impacts of electronic commerce: from technological infrastructure to electronic marketplaces. *International Journal of Electronic Commerce, 1.*

KEY TERMS

Accessibility: Is a general term used to describe the degree to which a product (e.g., device, service, and environment) is accessible by as many people as possible.

E-Business: The transaction of business by way of electronic media, such as telephones, fax machines, computers, and video-teleconferencing equipment.

E-Commerce: Any on-line transaction of buying and selling where business is done via Electronic Data Interchange (EDI).

E-Government: Is the process of transforming government, so that the use of the Internet and electronic processes are central to the way that government operates.

E-Shopping: The action of online purchasing.

System Quality: Aggregate of the organizational activities, incentives, plans, policies, procedures, processes, resources, responsibilities, and the infrastructure required in formulating and implementing a total quality management (TQM) approach.

Usability: The ease that users experience in navigating an interface, locating information, and obtaining knowledge over the Internet.

Chapter XI
Information Technology and Aviation Industry:
Marriage of Convenience

Evon M. O. Abu-Taieh
The Arab Academy for Banking and Financial Sciences, Jordan

ABSTRACT

This chapter pinpoints the affects of information technology on the aviation industry, specifically on the Airline ticket prices. The chapter first introduces the different costs that comprise the airline ticket. Then the chapter introduces the different information technology systems that are used in the aviation industry which in turn reduces the price of the airline ticket.

INTRODUCTION

To fly from London to New York nowadays, it is customary to visit a traveling website such as http://travel.yahoo.com, in order to make the reservation. Surprisingly, there are more than 46 flights to choose from with varying prices ranging from $672 to $1,989. In fact, with an extra $3 the VIP services in coach would be granted, which infers that long gone are the days where many calls had to be made to compare prices then drive to the travel agent to pick up the ticket. The previous leads to two questions: why are the prices are varying? And how did this website come about?

Accordingly, the jest of this chapter is to discuss the elements that affect the travelers' ticket price as well as the role of information technology in affecting the prices of the airline tickets. In retrospect, the chapter will shed light on both sides of this issue: the airline side and the IT side.

TICKET PRICE ANALYSIS

To carry a passenger form origin A to destination B, an airline company takes many factors to mark the price of the ticket. Based on basic economic analysis, there are always cost and revenue, and thereby the airline must take into account all the cost incurred when pricing the airline ticket, as stipulated in Figure 1, and the justified margin of profit, where the profit is defined as Revenue minus Cost, in terms of pure mathematical calculation, noting that some costs can be recurring while other costs are nonrecurring costs.

In this context, the recurring cost in the air transport arena is comprised of: *airplane related operating costs, Payload Related operating costs* and *System related operating cost.* On the other hand the nonrecurring costs are *Spare parts costs* and *Initial crew training.* Next, all cost related factors will be discussed.

Airplane Related Operating Costs

Airplane Related Operating Costs (AROC) can be broken down into two sub categories: Cash Airplane Related Operating Costs (CAROC) and ownership Costs, where both can be segregated into sub-categories, the *CAROC* includes the cost of: *fuel, Cockpit Crew, Cabin Crew, Maintenance, Landing, Navigation, Ground handling,* whereas the *ownership costs* include: *Depreciation, Financing, operating lease costs,* and *Hull Insurance.*

The fuel according to (IATA, 2008) represents 32 percent of the Operating Costs in 2008; almost triple that in 2003, where it used to stand at 14 percent of the Operating costs. The consumption of fuel is usually affected by the weight, as seen in Figure 3 of the plane, speed, wind, rout, airplane age and maintenance, altitude, ambient temperature, wind speed and direction as can be seen in Figure 2, while it is worth noting that the price of fuel usually varies from country to

Figure 1. Different factors that affect the ticket price

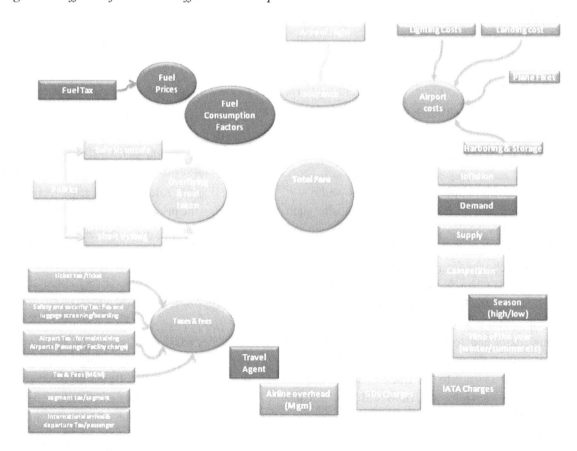

another and is affected by the political climate of the world.

The crew is a team of people, who contribute in making the flight possible, comprising from Cockpit Crew and Cabin Crew, of course, like all employees, the crew receives salaries in return for their services, in addition they squander the airline for sick leaves, vacation, insurance, etc.

According to Boeing presentation (Arvish, 2007), *Maintenance* represents 7-15 percent of AROC, albeit it is essential for safety, image, and economics as stated by (Arvish, 2007), the safety with maintenance is significant for the reliability of the equipment, in addition that it helps make the plane environment appealing and safe for the passenger, as well as maximizes the value of the equipment, while maximizing service time and therefore utilization of the plane.

Nevertheless, when tackling maintenance, many issues may rise, particularly in view of its significance; so much so that many developed "Maintenance Cost Models" just to predict the maintenance cost, in this regard, there are many types of maintenance: Pre-Flight, Transit, Daily, Weekly, cyclic (A, B, C and D Checks). Each type entails labor, labor rate labor efficiency, and down-time. In addition, there is the Total Maintenance overhead which includes: labor burden, management pay, maintenance facilities, and technical staff.

Navigation and Landing costs, while the navigation cost varies from country to another, however, the landing cost is usually determined by the airport. The navigation fees are calculated by formulas where weight, distance and countries flown over constitute the formula's variables. On the other hand, the landing costs, which are collected by airports, are mostly calculated using the maximum takeoff weight (MTOW) as the basis. Other surcharges are added, include; lighting, parking, terminal navigation aid, Noise surcharge, noting that other taxes, such as those applied in the USA, among other countries, are shown in the Table 1 with accordance to (MIT-Daniel Webster College, 2006), where it is claimed that taxes comprise more than 16 percent of the typi-

Table 1. Taxes in the USA (MIT-Daniel Webster College, 2006)

Federal ticket tax	FTT	U.S. value added tax (currently 7.5% of base fare), used to fund FAA operations and the Airport Improvement Program
Federal segment tax	FST	U.S. tax applied per segment (currently $3.30), used to fund FAA operations and the Airport Improvement Program
Passenger facility charge	PFC	U.S. "head tax" collected and used by specific airports (currently $0, $3, or $4.50), used for airport improvement projects
Federal security service fee	FSSF	U.S. security tax (currently $2.50), used for passenger and baggage screening

Table 2. Examples of airport related taxes and charges (IATA, 2006)

Country	Airports	Taxes and Charges	Estimated Cost (€m)
France	CDG / ORY	Airport Tax	319
UK	LHR / LGW	Passenger Service Charge	750
Germany	FRA	Passenger Service Charge, Security Charge	689
Italy	FCO	Embarkation Tax	124
Netherlands	AMS	Passenger Service Charge, Security Charge and Noise Charge	595
Austria	VIE	Passenger Service Charge, Security Charge	139
Portugal	LIS	Passenger Service Charge, Security Tax	81
Greece	ATH	Passenger Service Charge, Security Charge and Airport Development Tax	204

cal airfare (Boehmer, 2006), whereas, the case differs in Europe, where "the total tax burden for EU airlines is estimated to be at least €5.92 billion (US$7.3 billion) in 2004." (IATA, 2006)

Ground handling can be defined as all that is needed from equipment and machines to serve the plane on the ground of the airport including: ladder, tow trucks, etc, in addition to loading and unloading all baggage.

Payload Related Operating Costs

Payload Related Operating Costs includes two categories: *Passenger Related Costs* and *Cargo Related Costs*. The passenger related costs include: food, in flight services, handling, baggage handling, commissions, reservation and sales, advertising, security. The cargo related costs include: handling, commissions, reservations and sales, advertising, and security.

The passenger generates cost from the point of reservation until leaving the destination airport. The passenger starts the operation by picking a destination then navigating the traveling agent website, or going there in person, or over the phone, likewise, in the case of the traveling agent scenario, the operation starts when receiving the passenger's request, followed by all the process stages of searching for the appropriate airline, finding the suitable flight, date, and connections, followed by issuing the ticket (printed on paper). The operation continues to cover going to the airport and conducting the necessary security checks, which entails manpower as well as machine cost, this stage is coupled with checking with the borders control, which in turn entails manpower and computer cost. This is followed by loading and unloading the luggage and assorting the luggage to the right destination, needless to say, in case of luggage misplacement compensation is in order. The process of cost increment continues during the flight for all the food, drink, music, movies, etc, to conclude when arriving to the destination, the luggage unloading and distribution, to be followed by clearance from the border control and the customs. The foregoing demands the following: people, time, money, effort, management, machines, tools, equipment, communication etc, none of which comes cheap.

Figure 2. Fuel consumption factors

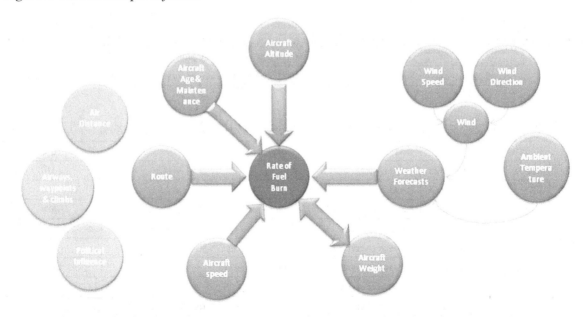

Indeed, cargo is of high significance in the aviation industry, as FedEx ranked number one in the airline with respect to the operating profitability; with a total that amounts to US\$ 1,825 million, in addition to being ranked number 22 with 8.3 percent operating profit margin according to IATA (IATA Economics, 2007). Noting, however, that according to (AIR FREIGHT MARKET OUTLOOK, 2007) "The air freight sector provides estimated total annual revenues of almost US\$ 55 billion, equivalent to 12% of the airline industry's total revenue", which concludes that the cargo cost being discussed here is the one associated with passengers rather than freight. Still, the aforementioned numbers and facts indicates the importance of this element, particularly when assuming that cargo and fuel consumption are directly correlated, whereby the more cargo is loaded on the plane the more fuel will be burnt up, as such, the Airlines take weight very seriously and penalize passengers with extra weight.

In addition the cargo handling, security, sales and reservations, and insurance (in case of loss) are considered another source of cost to the airline which seeps to the airline ticket price.

System Related Operating Cost

The system related costs include the general and administrative costs of the overall process, which comprise of the plane, passenger, and cargo. The general and administrative cost can be defined as the "General and administrative. Include all expenses incurred in performing the general and administrative functions of the airline. But not related to any specific functionality" (icao, 2008).

In this regard, it is argued that things do not just happen, as not only the manpower is required, but also the brainpower, and the necessary tools to do them, for example, the logistical procedures, legal, accounting, management, typing, etc are considered to be work that requires manpower to

conduct, albeit such work is not related to particular function like flying the plane like the Cockpit crew; nor is it related to serving the passengers like Cabin Crew. Likewise, a legal department is needed, as well as accounting department, and planning, etc.

IT AND AVIATION INDUSTRY

Information technology (IT) affected the aviation industry in many aspects, starting from the passenger, all the way through the aircraft itself. Accordingly, this section of the chapter underlines where IT affected aviation industry, namely the following: Air craft design, Airline Reservations, E-Ticketing, Self Service Kiosks (SSK), Radio Frequency Identification (RFID), Simulators and Training, Global Positioning Systems (GPS), Security Checking, Flight and Airport Management and Planning. More importantly, it is worthwhile to note that the Flight, as well as, Airport Management and Planning entail many sub-systems, *inter alia*: Aeronautical Billing, Resource Planning and Management, Airport Operational Database (AODB), Flight Information Display Systems (FIDS), Property Management, Interactive Voice Response (IVR), Incident Management, Air Traffic Control, Air Traffic Control (ATC) Billing, Airline/Handling Agents, Apron Handling, Staff Management Displays, Aeronautical Invoicing System, Ledger Systems.

Aircraft design is not an easy task; thereby many elements are taken into account when designing a commercial aircraft, albeit it is nearly impossible to take into account all the essential elements of designing the aircraft. Yet with the aim of founding an aircraft design that would be "Better Flight-control Systems, Safer, Cheaper, And Greener" as the science daily said (ScienceDaily, 2007), as such, the most significant elements can be include the following: aerodynamics & fuel consumption, capacity of the plane, noise, emission, martial used in the body of the aircraft, operating and fixed costs, etc. In this aspect, back in 1994, Boeing the aircraft manufacturer used Virtual Reality and Augmented reality "aimed at putting more information directly in front of the engineers designing aircraft and the manufacturing workers who build them" (Sims, 1994). Some of the information system applications used in the design of aircraft are Advanced Aircraft Analysis (AAA), RDS Aircraft Design Software, AirCraft SYNThesis (ACSYNT), to name a few. Another aspect is the use of software technology for Intelligent Flight control via neural networks and to utilize such "information to optimize aircraft performance" (Alfano, 1999).

On another dimension, the Information Technology played a great role in the airline reservations systems, whereby the automation and computerization of reservation systems have created an industry of its own. The five major computerized reservation systems are called Global distribution Systems: Galileo, Amadeus, world span, Sabre, and Pegasus, could not have come into existence without the IT. Simply because such systems allowed connectivity among airlines, which also gave way for price competition, although soon after, the internet provided another dimension with online reservation and E-Ticket credence, which even allowed more competition among the airlines to drive the prices of the ticket.

Indeed, using E-Ticket lead to cutting off the middle man (travel agents) in the reservation process and allowed the passenger to deal directly with the airline, such an alternative allowed cutting down the cost generated by the middle man (Abu-Taieh, 2004). More importantly, online reservation provided the passenger with a marginal freedom with respect to the purchase price of the ticket and produced an incentive for the airline to lower their prices. In a survey conducted by SITA jun-2007, almost 71 percent of ticket sales fulfilled as E-Tickets (SITA, 2007). The last straw regarding E-Ticket is that IATA, pushed such initiative to convert all paper tickets to E-Tickets starting 1 June, 2008 as publicized by (MENA News_42,

2008). Such initiative not only saves money for paper, but also has positive impact on environment. Giovanni Bisignani, IATA's Director General and CEO said "Today we say goodbye to an industry icon" also "To complete the conversion IATA has contacted 60,000 travel agents in more than 200 countries to collect the remaining unused paper tickets in the system – some 32 million worldwide" as reported by the same article.

Another form of Information Technology helping the aviation industry is the use of Self Service Kiosks (SSK), which minimizes queuing and speeds up the check-in process, not to mention reducing the number of check-in service employees

IT also affected the "lost luggage issue", in view that many passengers end up flying to one direction while their luggage land at another. The issue is of significant concern on part of the airline in terms of being a source of money spending, which will be paid for by the passenger at the end of the day, nevertheless, the airlines end up being liable for it, as the airlines paid a total of US$3.8 billion in 2007 according to SITA published report (SITA, 2008). This mishap is usually attributed to human error, in part due to extra labor and work burden, accordingly, the IT provided the solution, by placing Radio Frequency Identification (RFID) on each luggage, which in turn would save approximately US$700 million, if fully implemented. The RFID process is simple, as the transmitter announces the position of the luggage which transpires into less luggage loss cases, particularly in view that in 2007, around 2.25 billion pieces of luggage have been checked, of which 42.4 million were mishandled or delayed (SITA, 2008), even with an accuracy rate of 98 percent, nevertheless, two percent of mishandled or lost luggage result in huge number of dissatisfied passengers (SITA, 2008). Needless to pinpoint that in addition to time, money and effort saving, RFID greatly assisted in improving the image of the airline and the airport.

Figure 3. Different weight name associated with aircrafts at different stages

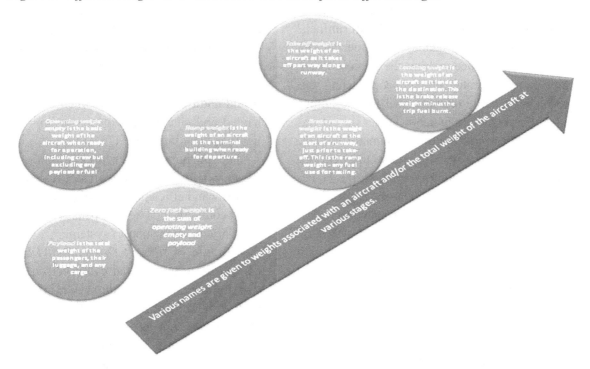

Another aspect that Information Technology helped in the aviation industry in reducing the cost is by using *simulators* to train pilot and air traffic controllers, as noted that one of the numerous uses of simulation as science is training. Real-life training of pilots and air traffic controllers can evidently be risky, to say the least, in addition to the liability in terms of money and life threatening. As such, simulators are now used to train pilots on new planes as well as old planes, whether the use of the plane would be commercial, private, military, etc, in view that simulators are usually so real that some simulators are designated for certain type and model of plane.

A different use of simulation in the aviation industry is the simulation of plane accidents (Purdue , 2002), for the purpose of accident investigations, accordingly, simulating the accident may shed some light on the causes of a certain accident, whereby such causes and conditions can be avoided in the future.

Navigation is one of the oldest sciences, thereby; the navigation with the help of satellites and information technology powers became much easier. This idea manifested itself as what is known now as Global Positioning Systems (GPS). The following quote sums up what needs to be said:

Global Positioning Systems (GPS) offers an inexpensive and reliable supplement to existing navigation techniques for aircraft. Civil aircraft typically fly from one ground beacon, or waypoint, to another. With GPS, an aircraft's computers can be programmed to fly a direct route to a destination. The savings in fuel and time can be significant.

GPS can simplify and improve the method of guiding planes to a safe landing, especially in poor weather. With advanced GPS systems, airplanes can be guided to touchdown even when visibility is poor. For the private pilot, inexpensive GPS systems provide position information in a practical, simple, and useful form. (nasm, 2008)

Another form of IT helping aviation industry is processing passengers faster at the border check points. Accessing terrorists' and criminals' records by using the database built specially for this purpose, hence making the process faster, and more accurate. Saving people using this technology is the ultimate goal for the human race. Terrorism cost money whether the act was executed (cost of destruction and human life) or the terrorism act prevented (cost of security checks, machines, etc). Within this context, the IT has another mode in terms of s-Travel. "S-Travel will include digital authentication to enable secure access to airport facilities for frequent air travelers" (KELEMEN, 2003).

In the aviation industry, two equally important dimensions are mandated in order to fly an airplane from origin to destination; the planning and man-hours invested in this aspect, not to mention calculating risk factors. As such, the IT developed many flight management systems, rout planning and airport management systems. Such systems encompass many sub-systems: Aeronautical Billing, Resource Planning and Management, Airport Operational Database (AODB), Flight Information Display Systems (FIDS), Property Management, Interactive Voice Response (IVR), Incident Management, Air Traffic Control, Air Traffic Control (ATC) Billing, Airline/Handling Agents, Apron Handling, Staff Management Displays, *Aeronautical Invoicing System*, Ledger Systems.

The foregoing systems reduced error factors and the manpower needed to conduct these jobs, while adding up to safety factors and the accuracy of the whole operation, in addition to saving the money and effort needed. In a nutshell the systems increased the efficiency of the whole operation of transporting a passenger from origin to destination, subsequently; each system will be discussed verbosely.

Aeronautical Billing System is a system that handles all the revenues for airports and civil aviation organizations. All the overfly charges are collected from many airlines that crosses the countries' land. The idea of appointing many people to collect the money from so many different airlines seems now preposterous, but pre-IT era that is what really happened. Now, however, the billing follows each plane when entering the country border until leaving it, whereby the system would additionally calculate whether the plane landed and charges the airline for any needed lighting or maintenance.

The purpose of *Resource Planning and Management* is managing airport resources effectively and efficiently, including gates, stands, ticket counters and baggage belts. The system is basically decision support system.

The aim of *Airport Operational Database (AODB)* is to ensure that every person who is working at the airport has the needed information at the time they need it. Moreover, the use of a single database by all functions ensures optimal data input and use in addition to prompt and efficient *information* distribution.

The goal of *Flight Information Display Systems (FIDS)* is to quickly and accurately display flight-related information to all members of the airport community including travelers, airline staff, retailers, ground handlers and transportation operators. In fact, FIDS provides flight-related information throughout the airport including at the check-in desks, baggage belts, gates and arrival / departure screens.

Property Management (PM), in view that some non-aeronautical related albeit income generating have become increasingly important to the airport. As such, PM system helps airports manage their rental, lease, license and concession related interests.

Interactive Voice Response (IVR) system is an automated and centralized approach to dealing with customer service requirements and enquiries via telephone. As IVR automates furnish routine enquiries with needed information, staff can focus on handling more complex issues offering the customer prompt and efficient operational benefits.

Incident Management System tracks all incident related activities within the airport, from lost and found through to security alerts. The system is designed to track activity, assign essential tasks to the correct people and provide tools for appropriate resolution.

Air Traffic Control, noting that in any air traffic environment, the data in and out flow is normally done via the AFTN, which encompasses flight plans and flights information that the unit is handling, such as slot time requests, delays etc. Typically, the required information can contain the following information: Aircraft Registration, Runway Used, Actual Time of Landing and Departure, Number of Circuits, Number and Type of Approaches, New Estimates of Arrival and Departure, New Flight Information. Such information is need by the airline, airline agents, and governmental bodies as well as the aeronautical billing system and Air Traffic Control (ATC) Billing.

Air Traffic Control (ATC) Billing, which typically includes the following information: Aircraft Registration, Point of Entry into Air Space, Point of Departure of Air Space, Airport Point of Departure and/or Landing, Times at the Different Points of Entry or Departure, Whereby the aircraft registration is entered, in order to use the aircraft type and weight in fee calculation. Airport of origin/destination or point of entry and exit are used in the calculation of the fee. Times are entered if entry and exit time in the FIR forms part of the billing calculation.

Airline/Handling Agents: Information entered can consist of the following: Block On/Off Times, Passenger and Freight Information, Check-In Desk Opening and Closing, Departure Gate Opening and Closing, New Flight Details (If not entered by ATC), New Estimates of Arrival and Departure Times (If not entered by ATC), Seasonal Schedule Information. The *Block on and off times* can be used by the aeronautical billing system to calculate parking time. Another use is for statistical purposes on the time it takes certain

aircraft types to taxi onto stand from landing and off stand to departure. Furthermore, *Passenger and freight information* can be used to calculate aeronautical charges and produce statistical information for load factor analysis. Additionally, *Check-In opening and closing* can be used for triggering the flight information display system status remarks and by the aeronautical billing system. *Departure gate opening and closing* can be used for triggering the flight information display system and by the aeronautical billing system. *Seasonal schedule information* can be entered and produces the daily mayfly information, which in turn is the basis of the daily flight information display information.

Apron Handling: the information entered includes the following: Stand Allocation, Block On/Off (If not entered by the airline/handling agent), First Bag Last Bag Times, Ground Services Supplied to the Aircraft. Allocation of stands by aircraft type can be displayed to ATC, who in turn can direct the aircraft to the correct stand/airbridge without having to contact ATC by radio or telephone. First and last bag times can be entered so that statistical information can be obtained against the published IATA unloading times, as this would assist in the apron equipment and man power planning. In addition, ground services can be entered so that these items can be calculated and invoiced by the aeronautical billing system. An interface can be provided to a specialist stand allocation system which assists in working out stand allocation. This can be a two-way interface; both entering and importing back updated stand allocation information.

Staff Management Displays: Displaying information to the staff is a vital part of any management system. With the advent of PCs and LAN/WAN networks, it is a simple task to display and update information to airport staff in real-time, in whichever format they wish. Information can also be displayed via the airport web site, thereby allowing many additional people access to information such as Customs and Excise, Immigration etc. As such, there is no longer a need for the old fashioned small monitor staff displays located at strategic locations within the airport, more importantly such useful information will cut down the amount of radio time and/or telephone calls required by staff to keep colleagues abreast of changing events.

Aeronautical Invoicing System: Invoicing is the lifeblood of any company and airports are no different. Most modern systems utilize a special billing engine specifically designed for the airport market place. The aeronautical invoicing system has to incorporate the following: Cash Invoicing, Credit Invoicing. However, it is worthwhile to note that cash invoicing should cater for aircraft size, moreover, credit invoicing should allow for multi-currency invoicing such as the Euro versus other worldwide used foreign currency.

Ledger Systems: ledger systems should contain all financial information within the following: Sales Ledger (Accounts Receivable), Purchase Ledger (Accounts Payable), and Nominal Ledger (General Ledger). In addition many systems can be supplied with the following additional modules: Bank Reconciliation, Purchase Order Processing, Sales Order Processing, Stock Control, Payroll, Fixed Asset Register, Human Resources.

CONCLUSION

IT has an undeniable cost reduction impact on airline ticket prices. Accordingly, this paper underpinned *what* and *how* did the IT resonate such impact. The paper first detailed the various costs incurred to fly a passenger. Then the paper pinpointed the different Information technology systems and the way they were used to reduce the different costs.

Costs incurred in the aviation operation are classified into two categories recurring and nonrecurring, where the recurring cost in the air transport arena is comprised of: Airplane Related Operating Costs, Payload Related Operating Costs

and System Related Operating Cost. While the nonrecurring costs encompass Spare Parts Costs and Initial Crew Training.

Airplane Related Operating Costs (AROC) can be segregated into two sub categories: Cash Airplane Related Operating Costs (CAROC) and Ownership Costs, both of which are further sub-categorized as follows; CAROC includes the cost of the fuel, Cockpit Crew, Cabin Crew, Maintenance, Landing, Navigation, and Ground handling. While the Ownership Costs include the Depreciation, Financing, operating lease costs, and Hull insurance.

Payload Related Operating Costs include two categories, the Passenger Related Costs and Cargo Related Costs. While the System Related Costs include the general and administrative costs of the: plane, passenger, and cargo.

As such, the IT affected aviation industry significantly, yet to name a few, in respect to the following: Air craft design, airline reservations, E-Ticketing, Self Service Kiosks (SSK), Radio Frequency Identification (RFID), simulators and training, Global Positioning Systems (GPS), security checking, Flight and airport Management & planning. In this context, the flight and airport management and planning entailed many subsystems: Aeronautical Billing, Resource Planning and Management, Airport Operational Database (AODB), Flight Information Display Systems (FIDS), Property Management, Interactive Voice Response (IVR), Incident Management, Air Traffic Control, Air Traffic Control (ATC) Billing, Airline/Handling Agents, Apron Handling, Staff Management Displays, Aeronautical Invoicing System, Ledger Systems.

REFERENCES

Abu-Taieh. (2004). Computer Reservations System Auditing Headache of the Airline Industry – computerized Auditing and Accounting. *Innovations through information technology* (p. 477). Idea Group Inc (IGI).

Air Freight Market Outlook. (2007). Retrieved 5 2008, from IATA ECONOMICS BRIEFING: http://www.iata.org/NR/rdonlyres/CE373AB8-1093-4192-A892-9C559F57CA29/0/Cargo_Market_Outlook_Sep07.pdf

Arvish, A. (2007). *Airplane Economics: Operating and Maintennace Cost.*

Boehmer, J. (2006). *DWC and MIT Study: Taxes Comprise 16% Of Typical Airfare.* Retrieved 5 12, 2008, from Business Travel News: http://www.dwc.edu/news/2006-2007/DWCMITstudyBTN.shtml

IATA Economics. (2007). *Airline Profitability - 2006.* Retrieved 5 2008, from IATA Economic Briefing: http://www.iata.org/NR/rdonlyres/5B3D0818-D9D0-43CB-AA65-C5548639FA85/0/Airline_2006_Profits.pdf

IATA. (2008, 3 1). *Fuel.* Retrieved 5 17, 2008, from IATA: http://www.iata.org/pressroom/facts_figures/fact_sheets/fuel.htm

IATA. (2006, 6). *IATA Economic Briefing European Aviation Taxes.* Retrieved 2008, from IATA: http://www.iata.org/NR/rdonlyres/71ABA881-5E98-411A-825A-C97A12A92164/0/EU_Taxation_June_06.pdf

icao. (2008). Retrieved 2008, from http://www.icao.int/icao/en/atb/Ead/Fep/forms/english/cost_en.pdf

MENA News_42. (2008, Jun). Industry Bids Farewell to Paper Ticket Meets deadline for 100% ET. *IATA MENA News* , (p. 3).

MIT-Daniel Webster College. (2006, 1 30). *The Ticket Tax Project.* Retrieved 5 17, 2008, from MIT Global Airline Industry Program: http://web.mit.edu/TicketTax/

nasm. (2008). *Navigation in the Air.* Retrieved 2008, from National Air and Space Museum : http://www.nasm.si.edu/gps/airnav.html

Purdue (2002, September 10). *New simulation shows 9/11 plane crash with scientific detail.* Retrieved May 1, 2008, from Purdue News : www.purdue.edu/UNS/html4ever/020910.Sozen.Pentagon.html

ScienceDaily. (2007, September). *Airplane Design: Better Flight-control Systems, Safer, Cheaper, And Greener.* Retrieved 2008, from http://www.sciencedaily.com/releases/2007/09/070915122014.htm

Sims, D. (1994). New realities in aircraft design and manufacture. *Computer Graphics and Applications, IEEE , 14*(12), 91 .

SITA. (2008). Baggage mistakes cost billions. *Middle East AirPort , 1*(1), 12.

KEY TERMS

Cash Airplane Related Operating Costs (CAROC): Includes the cost of: *fuel, Cockpit Crew, Cabin Crew, Maintenance, Landing, Navigation, Ground handling*, whereas the *ownership costs* include: *Depreciation, Financing, operating lease costs*, and *Hull Insurance.*

Maintenance Cost Models: Model to calculate the maintenance cost of an airplane.

Payload Related Operating Costs Includes two Categories: *Passenger Related Costs* and *Cargo Related Costs.*

General and Administrative: Include all expenses incurred in performing the general and administrative functions of the airline. But not related to any specific functionality.

Global Distribution Systems: Major computerized reservation systems.

Simulators: Computer hardware and software developed to train the pilot on flying an airplane.

Global Positioning Systems (GPS): a supplement to existing navigation techniques for aircraft.

Aeronautical Billing System: Is a system that handles all the revenues for airports and civil aviation organizations.

Flight Information Display Systems (FIDS): Is to quickly and accurately display flight-related information to all members of the airport community including travelers, airline staff, retailers, ground handlers and transportation operators.

Chapter XII
Dynamic Channel Allocation in Cellular Communications Networks

Hussein Al-Bahadili
The Arab Academy for Banking & Financial Sciences, Jordan

Arafat Abu Mallouh
The Hashemite University, Jordan

ABSTRACT

This chapter presents a description and performance evaluation of an efficient Distributed Artificial Intelligence (DAI) Dynamic Channels Allocation (DCA) scheme. Therefore, it is referred to as DAI-DCA scheme. It can be used for channel allocation in high traffic cellular communication networks (CCNs), such as the global system for mobile communication (GSM). The scheme utilizes a well-known DAI algorithm, namely, the asynchronous weak-commitment (AWC) algorithm, in which a complete solution is established by extensive communication among a group of neighboring collaborative cells forming a pattern, where each cell in the pattern uses a unique set of channels. To minimize communication overhead among cells, a token-based mechanism was introduced. The scheme achieved excellent average allocation efficiencies of over 85% for a number of realistic operation scenarios.

INTRODUCTION

The use of Cellular Communications Networks (CCNs) is experiencing revolutionary growth throughout the world, the growth is fuelled by: expansion of CCN, progress in data communica- tions, spectacular development of the Internet, diversity of applications and offered services, etc. CCNs offer a number of advantages over alterna- tive solutions, such as: increased capacity, reduced power usage, better coverage area, increased local availability, low cost, and ease of maintainability (Abeysundara 2005, Salmenkaita 2001).

One of the main challenges that faces and limiting further expansion in CCNs uses is scarcity of channels in CCNs. This comes from: finite spectrum, low channel capacity, and electromagnetic interferences and multi-path fading. Furthermore, in CCNs, a channel c can be used by a cell i without any interference (co-channel) if it is not concurrently used by any other cell at a limited distance from cell i (called minimum reuse distance). Also, for better Quality-of-Service (QoS) and to minimize adjacent channels interference, channels adjacent to c should not be used within cell i or any of its first-hop neighbors. Therefore, it is essential to devise suitable solutions for allocating channels to cells so as to efficiently utilize the scarce resources, to eliminate channel interferences, and to satisfy any other network operation environment and demand. In addition, solutions should meet the main design objectives, such as: minimum channel acquisition time, minimum number of denied or failed calls, minimum control message complexity, minimum communication overheads, and minimum network interruption (Stallings 2005).

A number of techniques have been developed to combat impairments in rapidly varying radio channels and to obtain high spectral efficiencies in CCNs (Kostic 2002, Kostic 2001). Some of those are channel coding and interleaving, adaptive modulation, transmitter/receiver antenna diversity, spectrum spreading, and channel allocation. In general, channel allocation techniques in CCNs can be static, dynamic, or hybrid. Dynamic Channel Allocation (DCA) techniques provide better utilization of the channels at higher traffic loads albeit at the cost of higher acquisition time and some additional control messages. There are mainly two types of DCA schemes, these are: Centralized DCA (CDCA) and Distributed DCA (DDCA). However, these techniques also have their own drawbacks and limitations, such as: slow convergence, infinite loop, high communication overheads, etc (Modi 2001).

It is believed that more efficient and reliable techniques for DCA in CCNs can be developed based on Distributed Artificial Intelligence (DAI) techniques. In this chapter, we introduce, develop, and evaluate the performance of a DCA technique that convenes all requirements and constraints imposed by the user, service providers, and technology of CCNs. The technique is based on a well-know DAI algorithm, namely, the Asynchronous Weak-Commitment (AWC) algorithm. The AWC algorithm is, in turn, based on a formalism that is widely used for various application problems in DAI, called Distributed Constraint Satisfaction Problem (DCSP) (Yokoo 2000, Yokoo 1998).

In order to minimize the data communication overheads of the AWC algorithm, a token-based mechanism is introduced, in which a token is circulating between a group of collaborative cells passing information about the channels that are allocated or in operation within each cell. In addition, the token controls the channels allocation process by only allowing the cell that hold the token to update its channels. The algorithm is characterized by its minimum channel acquisition time, minimum number of denied or failed calls, minimum control message complexity, minimum communication overheads, and minimum network interruption.

CELLULAR COMMUNICATIONS NETWORKS (CCNS)

CCNs are considered as one of the most popular and spreading applications for wireless networks; and during the last two decades CCNs have shown a huge revolutionary growth and a rapid development. The essence of a CCN is the use of multiple low-power transceivers, and because of the limited-range of such transceivers, the network area is divided into small areas (cells). Thus, a CCN is a radio network made up of a number of radio cells each served by a stationary transceiver (transmitter/receiver) that is connected to a single antenna and controlled by a local control unit. The transceiver, antenna, and the control unit forms what is known as a cell site or Base Station (BS) (Stallings 2005).

The bandwidth allocated for the network is divided, using Frequency Division Multiple Access (FDMA) scheme, into a number of channels (frequencies). Each cell is allocated a set (group) of frequencies. Adjacent cells are assigned different frequencies to avoid interference or crosstalk. However, cells sufficiently distant from each other can use the same frequency set.

CCNs offer a number of advantages, such as: increase network capacity due to spectral reuse, reduce power usage due to smaller transceivers distances, better coverage area, increase local availability, low cost, ease of maintainability, more robust as a problem in any BS only affects the immediate cell, and more predictable propagation environment due to shorter distances.

On the other hand, CCNs suffer from a number of disadvantages, examples of such disadvantages may include: need for more infrastructure, need for fixed network to connect BSs, some residual interference from co-channel cells, handover procedure required, and bandwidth limitations (Ahmad 2006, Yang 2005).

Features of CCNs

The main features of CCNs can be summarized as follows (Stallings 2005):

- The total coverage area of the network is divided into a number of limited-size cells. The size of the cells depends on the transmission power (coverage area) of the cell transceivers.
- All the available channels in the system are partitioned into sets; one set is assigned to each cell, and two cells could only be assigned the same set of channels if the two cells are separated by a sufficient geographical distance (minimum reuse distance), so that interference is minimized or eliminated.
- Each cell should be equipped with at least one active transceiver (transmitter/receiver), one control unit, and one active antenna per cell.
- Neighbouring cells interfere with each other.
- A mobile phone communicates with one antenna at a time.

Cell Shape

Determining the shape of the cell in a CCN is an important matter, that's because the cell shape will determine the area to be covered, the number of adjacent neighbours for the cell, the distance of each neighbour from the cell, and if there are gaps or overlaps areas.

If the shape of the cells that's cover an area is circular then there will be gaps that are not covered by any cell, and also there will be some area that may be covered by more than one cell which will lead to an overlapped area between two cells or more, this has unwanted consequences such as frequency interference and more than one BS that controls the overlapped area.

The shape of the cell also determines the distance of each neighbour from the cell; in this case there could be a cell that has neighbours at different distances from that cell. This could lead to a case that a mobile user within a cell moving toward the cell's boundaries is at different distances from the antennas of adjacent cells. However, it is best if all of the antennas of adjacent cells are at equal distance from the antenna of the mobile user cell; this simplifies the task of determining when to switch the user to an adjacent antenna and which antenna to choose. Figure 1 illustrates three types of cell shapes, namely, a square cell, a hexagonal cell, and a circular cell.

Figure 1. Cell shapes

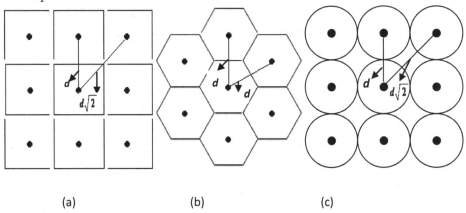

(a)　　　　　　　(b)　　　　　　　(c)

In Figure 1a, the cell shape is square; therefore, if the width of the square is d, then the cell has four neighbours at distance d and four neighbours at distance $d\sqrt{2}$. Figure 1b shows a hexagonal uniform cell shape, in which each opposite side in the hexagonal cell is separated by a distance d, thus each cell has six neighbours at distance d. A circular cell shape of a diameter d is shown in Figure 1c. In this figure it can be seen that each cell has 8 neighbours, four of them at distance d and four at distance $d\sqrt{2}$. In other words, it is similar to the square cell shape, but also there are areas that are not covered by a transmission from any cell (Stallings 2005).

Characteristics of a Hexagonal Cell

A hexagonal cell shape has many advantages that motivated its usage in CCNs, hexagonal cells cover an area without gaps or overlaps, that's because hexagonal cell is closest to a circle without having gaps or overlaps, about the hexagon radius r, it is defined to be the radius of the circle that circumscribes it, which equals the distance from the hexagon center to each vertex, which also equals the length of a side of a hexagon. As shown in Figure 2, for a cell of radius r, the distance between two adjacent cells' centers is d, which is given by:

$$d = \sqrt{3} \times r \qquad (1)$$

As a result the hexagon center (where the antenna should be placed) is at equal distance from each adjacent hexagon center, so a mobile user at the boundaries of some cell area will have a little calculations to decide to which adjacent cell he should moved to.

Frequency Reuse

In a CCN, each cell has a base transceiver. The transmission power of the transceiver is carefully controlled to allow communication within the cell using a given frequency band while limiting the power at the frequency that escapes the cell into adjacent cells. Nevertheless, it is not practical to attempt to use the same frequency set in

Figure 2. Hexagonal cell

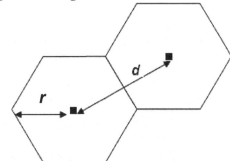

two adjacent cells. Instead, the objective is to use the same frequency set in multiple cells at some distance from one another. This allows the same frequency set to be used for multiple simultaneous conversations in different cells.

There are many reasons for the need of frequency reuse, such as:

- An increase in demand and the poor quality of existing service led to research into ways to improve the QoS and support more users in systems.
- Frequency spectrum available for mobile cellular use was limited; therefore efficient use of these frequencies was necessary, so the radio channels must be reused to carry more than one conversation at a time.

Frequency reuse could be done by using patterns (clusters), the pattern consists of a number of cells, and each cell in the pattern uses a unique set of frequencies. If each cell in the pattern assigned the same number of frequencies, then the number of frequencies that can be allotted for each cell in the pattern can be calculated by:

$$f = \frac{K}{N} \tag{2}$$

Where f is the number of frequencies allotted for each cell, K is the total number of frequencies available for the network, and N is the number of cells in a repetitious pattern.

After that this pattern is repetitious, which means the other cells in the system will be organized into another patterns of N cells that can provide sufficient isolation between two uses of the same frequency, and the repetition of the pattern depends on the number of cells in the system, the pattern will be repeated to contain all the cells in the system.

In characterizing frequency reuse, the following parameters are commonly used:

D is the minimum distance between centers of cells that use the same frequency band.

r is the radius of a cell.

d is the distance between centers of adjacent cells ($d = \sqrt{3} \times r$).

N is the number of cells in a repetitious pattern (each cell in the pattern uses a unique set of frequency bands), termed the reuse factor.

A key design issue in CCNs is to determine the minimum separation between two cells using the same frequency band, so that the two cells do not interfere with each other. There are different patterns of frequency reuse are possible, in a hexagonal cell pattern, it has been found that only the following values for N are possible:

$$N = I^2 + J^2 + (I \times J) \quad \text{where } I, J = 0, 1, 2, 3 \ldots \tag{3}$$

So possible values for N are 1, 3, 4, 7, 9, 12, 13, 16, 19, 21, and so on. Figure 3 shows some examples. It can be easily proved that the smallest pattern that can provide sufficient isolation between two uses of the same frequency is 7, i.e., $N=7$. In addition, the following equation holds the relationship between D and r:

$$\frac{D}{r} = \sqrt{3N} \tag{4}$$

Substituting Eqn. (1) into Eqn. (4) yields:

$$\frac{D}{d} = \sqrt{N} \tag{5}$$

Increasing CCN Capacity

As time move on, more customers use the network, therefore, traffic may build up and there are not enough frequencies assigned to a cell to handle

Figure 3. Patterns of frequency reuse (Stallings 2005)

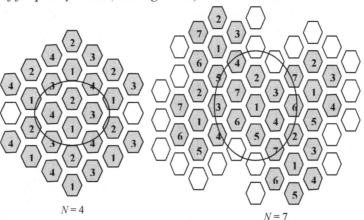

all arrived calls, and consequently some calls have to be dropped or denied services. A number of approaches have been used to cope with this evolving situation, such as:

- Adding new channels: Typically, when a CCN is set up in a region, not all of the channels are used; growth and expansion can be managed in an orderly fashion by adding new channels if available.
- Frequency borrowing: In the simplest case, frequencies are taken from adjacent cells by congested cells. The frequencies can also be assigned to cells dynamically.
- Cell splitting: In practice, the distribution of traffic and topographic features is not uniform, and this presents opportunities for capacity increase. Cells in areas of high usage can be split into smaller cells. To use a smaller cell, the power level used must be reduced to keep the original signal within the cell. Also, as the mobile unit move, they pass from cell to cell, which requires transferring the call from one BS to another.
- Cell sectoring: With cell sectoring, a cell is divided into a number of wedge-shaped sectors, each with its own set of channels, typically 3 to 6 sectors per cell. Each sector is assigned a separate subset of the cell's

Table 1. Typical parameters for macrocells and microcells

Parameter	Macrocell	Microcell
Cell radius	1 to 20 Km	0.1 to 1 Km
Transmission power	1 to 10 Watt	0.1 to 1 Watt
Average delay spread	0.1 to 10 μs	10 to 100 ns
Maximum bit rate	0.3 Mbps	1 Mbps

channels, and directional antennas at the BS are used to focus on each sector.
- Microcells: In this approach cells become smaller in size forming microcells, which are accomplished by a reduction in the radiated power levels from the BS antenna. Microcells are useful in city streets in congested areas, along highways, and inside large buildings.

Table 1 summarizes typical radius and transmission power parameters for traditional cells, called macrocells and microcells with current technology (Mahdavi 2007, Stalling 2005)

Minimum Interference Constraints in CCNs

Radio signal interference depends on various parameters, such as cell shape, size, layout, defined protection ratio, applied modulation, etc. In general there are two types of interference in mobile CCNs, these are (Stallings 2005):

- Co-channel interference: occurs when two sufficiently close cells use the same channel simultaneously. To reduce this type of interference, channels should be reused simultaneously in cells which are sufficiently far apart so that an acceptable level of carrier-to-interferer ratio is maintained.
- Adjacent-channel interference: appears when a signal is deteriorated by interference caused by signal(s) in other radio channel(s) used in the same cell or in one or more other cells. The term "adjacent" originates from interference caused by usage of two channels adjacent in radio-spectrum in FDMA.

For classification purposes and depending on the type of interference which may occur between two cells, we distinguish two types of radio neighbours as shown in Figure 4, these are:

- The first-order neighbours: are cells in the first-tier around cell A.
- The second-order neighbours: are cells in the second-tier around cell A.

The group of cells that forms first and second tiers around a central cell, which are shown in Figure 4, is called frequency reuse pattern. Depending on the previous definitions, the usage of channel

Figure 4. First and second tier cells

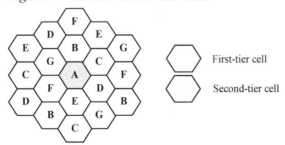

First-tier cell

Second-tier cell

k in cell A imposes the following constraints on the channel allocation algorithm:

- Channel k cannot be allocated to other wireless terminals in cell A or in the first and second tiers of cells.
- The two adjacent channels of k cannot be allocated to other wireless terminals in cell A or in the first-tier of cells.

However, considering the second constraint, that the adjacent channels of k are not allowed to be used in the first-tier of cells, reduces the total number of channels that can be allotted for each cell (f) in Eqn. (2) to be calculated as:

$$f = \frac{K}{N+2} \qquad (6)$$

Where K is the total number of channels allotted for the system, N is the reused factor (or number of cells within the pattern).

Thus, for a GSM CCN, since $K = 124$ and $N = 7$, then f is approximated to either 17 or 13 according to Eqns. (2) and (6), respectively. The first one means neglecting the adjacent channels interferences with the first tier neighbours, while the second one means taken it into consideration.

CHANNELS ALLOCATION

The use of CCNs is experiencing a revolutionary growth throughout the world. The growth is fuelled by the expansion in data communications, and the spectacular development of the Internet. This rapid growth in the size of CCNs, and the complexity of applications and offered services induce numerous challenges in the design and development of CCNs. Optimal channel allocation is considered as the most critical and effective challenge that plays an ever-increasing role in the future expansion of CCNs. This is because of scarcity of channels, demand for better QoS, low capacity channels, and interference among users. Thus, practical methods must be found for allocating the scarce channels that satisfy users' needs adequately and efficiently Yang 2007, Zhang 1989).

Desirable Characteristics of Channel Allocation Techniques

Channel allocation techniques deal with the allocation of channels (frequencies) to cells in a CCN. Once the channels are allocated, cells may then allow users within the cell to communicate via the available channels.

A number of desirable characteristics are identified that any satisfactory channel allocation techniques should have, such as (Lee 2007, Boumerdassi 2000):

- Minimum connection set-up time.
- Adaptable to changing load distribution.
- Fault tolerance.
- Scalability.
- Low computation and communication overheads.
- Minimum handoffs.
- Maximum number of calls that can be accepted concurrently.

Channel Allocation Techniques

Many channel allocation techniques have been proposed during the last two decades for infrastructure CCNs to avoid channel interference, efficiently utilize the limited bandwidth available, provide an adequate QoS for the mobile users, reduced the rate of dropped calls, etc.

These techniques can be classified into three different categories; these are:

- Static Channel Allocation (SCA) techniques (Tokekar 2006)
- Dynamic Channel Allocation (DCA) techniques (Salmenkaita 2001, Priscoli 1997)
- Hybrid Channel Allocation (HCA) techniques (Ahmad 2006)

In what follows a brief description is given for each of the aforementioned techniques.

Static Channel Allocation (SCA) Techniques

SCA techniques, alternatively referred to as Fixed Channel Allocation (FCA) techniques, allocate specific channels to specific cells. In SCA techniques the allocated channels can not be changed. However, for efficient operation, SCA systems typically allocate channels in a manner that maximizes frequency reuse. Thus, in a SCA technique, the distance between cells using the same channel is the minimum reuse distance for that CCN.

The problem with SCA techniques is occurring whenever the offered traffic to a CCN is not uniform. Considering a case in which two adjacent cells are allocated f channels each. There clearly can be situations in which one cell has a need for $f+k$ channels while the adjacent cell only requires $f-l$ channels (where both k and l are positive integers). In such a case, k users in the first cell would be blocked from making calls while l channels in the second cell would go unused. Clearly in this situation of non-uniform spatial offered traffic, the available channels are not being used efficiently. Despite this fact, SCA has been implemented on a widespread level to date.

Dynamic Channel Allocation (DCA) Technique

DCA techniques attempt to alleviate the problem mentioned for SCA techniques when offered traffic is non-uniform. In DCA techniques, no set relationship exists between channels and cells. Instead, channels are part of a pool of resources. Whenever a channel is needed by a cell, the channel is allocated under the constraint that frequency reuse requirements can not be violated.

Two problems that typically occur with DCA techniques, these are (An 2007, Wang 2005):

- DCA techniques typically have a degree of randomness associated with them, and this leads to the fact that frequency reuse is often not maximized, unlike the case for SCA systems in which cells using the same channel are separated by the minimum reuse distance.
- DCA techniques often involve complex algorithms for deciding which available channel is most efficient. These algorithms can be very computationally intensive and may require large computing resources in order to be real-time. However, this problem has been overcome with high increase of the speed of processing systems.

There are mainly two types of DCA techniques (Lee 2007):

- Centralized DCA (CDCA) techniques. CDCA techniques involve a single controller selecting a channel for each cell. CDCA techniques can theoretically provide the best performance. However, the enormous amount of computation and communication among BSs leads to excessive system latencies and renders CDCA techniques impractical.
- Distributed DCA (DDCA) techniques. DDCA techniques involve a number of controllers scattered across the network.

In DDCA techniques, a BS communicates with each other without any central control to find the channel that does not interfere with the neighboring cells.

The main features of the SCA and the DCA are compared in Table 2.

Hybrid Channel Allocation (HCA) Techniques

In HCA techniques, each cell has a static channel set permanently allocated to it and a reserved pool of channels that can be borrowed. This scheme is a trade off between SCA and DCA techniques and so are their merits and demerits.

REVIEWING CURRENT DCA TECHNIQUES

There are a number of techniques that have been developed throughout the years to solve the channel allocation problem in CCNs. These techniques aim to:

- Make the system highly adaptive to traffic changes.
- Utilize the available spectrum efficiently.
- Allocate channels optimally to all cells within the network.

Table 2. A comparison between the static and the dynamic channel allocation techniques

DCA	SCA
Performs better under light or moderate traffic	Performs better under heavy traffic
Not always maximum channel reusability	Maximum channel reusability
Insensitive to time and time spatial changes	Sensitive to time and spatial changes
Suitable in micro cellular environment	Suitable for large cell environment
High flexibility	Low flexibility
High computational effort	Low computational effort
Moderate to high implementation complexity	Low implementation complexity
Centralized and distributed control	Centralized control

In this section, a review is given for some of the most recent and related work.

Abeysundara (2005) proposed a DCA technique using intelligent agents. Under his implementation, agents only interact with the environment and the network cells. An aspect of self-organization is the reliance on multiple interactions, and the ability of agents to make use of the results of their own actions and the actions of others. In fact, the use of the action of other cells is not very apparent in this technique; and more precisely agents are only made very little use of the actions of other cells.

Yang et. al. (2005) proposed an efficient fault-tolerant channel allocation algorithm which can achieve high channel utilization. In their proposed algorithm, a cell may borrow a channel even based on some partial channel usage information it receives from some of its neighbours. Moreover, a cell can lend a channel to multiple borrowers (at most three) as long as any two of them are not neighbours.

Zhang et. al. (2005) formalized the distributed scheduling problems in distributed sensor networks as DCSPs and modeled them as distributed graph coloring. They found that to cope with limited resources and restricted real-time requirement, it is imperative to use distributed algorithms that have low overhead on resource consumption and high performance. In order to meet these requirements, they studied two existing DCSP algorithms, distributed stochastic search algorithm (DSA) and distributed breakout algorithm (DBA), for solving the distributed scheduling problems. Their results showed that DSA is superior to DBA when controlled properly, having better or competitive solution quality and significantly lower communication cost than DBA.

Bejar et. al. (2005) reported an experimental study of the average-case computational complexity of two early algorithms, ABT and AWC search on an application in distributed sensor networks. They also showed that random effects, both intentional such as random value selection and unintentional such as random delays, have a significant effect on the performance of the algorithms. Finally, they pointed-out that there are big performance differences between solvable and unsolvable instances.

Kostic et. al. (2001) examined techniques for increasing spectral efficiency of CCNs by using slow frequency hopping (FH) with dynamic frequency-hop (DFH) pattern adaptation. Their analysis and simulations considered the effects of path loss, shadowing, Rayleigh fading, co-channel interference, coherence bandwidth, voice activity, and occupancy. The results indicated that systems using DFH can support substantially more users than systems using RFH.

Salmenkaita et. al. (2001) presented a practical DCA scheme for cellular GSM networks that is called a dynamic frequency and channel assignment (DFCA) scheme. They showed that the behaviour of DFCA was satisfactory in very high load situations where the gain remains stable or is even increasing as happened with 50 km/hr mobile speed. In their model, a base station (BS) is capable of base band frequency hopping, and can only utilize part of the DFCA frequency band, therefore, limiting the freedom of radio channel selection. Their DFCA scheme can be used to provide radio channel differentiation based on connection type, and this can be utilized to maximize the network performance. Their results showed that in a typical case the gain of DFCA was reduced in a linear manner as the share of base band hopping BSs increases.

Al-Agha (2000) proposed a multi-agent solution for intelligent BSs in wireless networks to verify its feasibility as a main target. He found that agents are able to combine knowledge and experience with neighbouring agents to make the best decisions; also he demonstrated that, the intelligent agent approach to introduce the self-adaptive resource allocation feature in mobile networks remains an attractive and formal way of integrating intelligence in BSs.

Yubin et. al. (2000) discussed the problem of DCA in CCNs. They developed a simple but useful method to calculate the lower limit of call blocking probability of DCA, this method could be used to compare the performance of SCA with any kinds of DCA schemes easily and clearly. They found that the lower limit of blocking probability of DCA is related to the cluster size N, the lower limit of blocking probability of DCA will decrease if N increases. They proved that in GSM system the application of DCA strategy would greatly improve the overall system capacity, while in CDMA systems in which N is less than 3 the improvement by DCA is not so obvious.

Prakash et. al. (1999) presented an efficient DDCA algorithm, which distributes the responsibility for channel allocation among the mobile service stations of the network, and it keeps the involvement of mobile hosts in channel selection to a minimum, thereby conserving the limited energy at their disposal. The algorithm keeps the number of handoffs to a minimum as it does not induce any intra cell handoffs. The algorithm is dynamic and can be easily adjusted to meet changes in the network load distribution by transferring allocated channels from lightly loaded cells to highly loaded cells. The distributed nature of the algorithm and the symmetry of the channel allocation procedure across the entire network make the system scalable. The simplicity of the algorithm makes it easy to implement on a real-life network. The algorithm withstands failures of mobile hosts and mobile service stations without significant degradation in performance. In addition, even when the channel demand is high, a very small fraction of channel requests are dropped.

DISTRIBUTED ARTIFICIAL INTELLIGENCE (DAI)

Definition

DAI is a sub field of Artificial Intelligence (AI) (Russell 2003) that is concerned with interaction, especially coordination among artificial automated agents. Since distributed computing environments are spreading very rapidly due to the advances in hardware, software, and networking technologies, there are pressing needs for DAI techniques. DAI is dedicated to the development of distributed solutions for complex problems regarded as requiring intelligence.

DAI techniques are extremely useful and widely used in solving and studying Multi-Agent Systems (MASs). Today, MASs are a very active area of research and are beginning to be extensively used in many commercial and industrial applications. Also, the exponential growth of the Internet and its ability to connect people and machines from all over the world is making the arrival of MASs an inescapable consequence of such high degree of interconnectivity.

DAI is an extension of ideas derived from AI that applies to MASs. Instead of one centralized and usually very large application that encodes the complete intelligence of the system, a number of relatively small systems, or agents, are involved in a cooperative effort to resolve a problem. This does not imply that the large system is merely divided into smaller pieces, but there are several centralized applications, each capable of addressing a certain aspect of a problem, can be tied together by a communication system. It would allow for exchange of their viewpoints and coming up with strategies to make progress or to combine the results into a solution. This kind of problem solving is called distributed problem solving (DPS) (Yokoo 2000).

DAI aims to construct systems composed of multiple problem solving entities, which interact with one another to enhance their performance. With this "divide and conquer" approach the scope of each component is limited; meaning the complexity of the computation is lower, thus enabling the processing elements to be simpler and more reliable. This increased demand on software systems has also coincided with important advances in hardware technology, meaning it is now economically feasible and technically viable to connect together large numbers of powerful, yet inexpensive, processing units that execute asynchronously.

Most DAI research has concentrated on developing communities in which both control and data are distributed. Distributed control means that individuals have a degree of autonomy in generating new actions and in deciding which tasks to do next. When designing such systems it is important to ensure that agents spend the bulk of their time engaged on solving the domain level problems for which they were built, rather than in communication and coordination activities.

The main reason to deal with DAI is that MASs have the capacity to play a key role in current and future computer science and its application. Modern computing platforms and information environments are distributed, large, open, and heterogeneous. Computers are no longer stand-alone systems, but have become tightly connected both with each other and their users. The increasing complexity of computer and information systems goes together with an increasing complexity of their applications.

These often exceed the level of conventional, centralized computing because they require, for instance, the processing of huge amounts of data, or of data that arises at geographically distinct locations.

Applications of DAI

Many existing and potential industrial and commercial applications for DAI and MASs are described in the literature, examples of such applications are:

- Real-time monitoring and management of telecommunications networks, where agents are responsible, for example, for call forwarding and signal switching and transmission.
- Electronic commerce and electronic markets, where "buyer" and "seller" agents purchase and sell goods on behalf of their users.
- Modeling and optimization of in-house, in-town, national or world-wide transportation systems, where agents represent, for example, the transportation vehicles, the goods, or the customers to be transported.
- Information handling in information environments, like the Internet, where multiple agents are responsible for information filtering and gathering.
- Improving the flow of urban or air traffic, where agents are responsible for appropriately interpreting data arising at different sensor stations.
- Automated meeting scheduling, where agents act on behalf of their users to fix meeting details like location, time, and agenda.
- Optimization of industrial manufacturing and production processes like shop-floor scheduling or supply chain management, where agents represent, different work cells or whole enterprises.
- Analysis of business processes within or between enterprises, where agents represent the people or the distinct departments involved in these processes in different stages and at different levels.
- Electronic entertainment and interactive virtual reality-based computer games, where animated agents equipped with different characters play against each other or against humans.
- Design and re-engineering of information- and control-flow patterns in large-scale natural, technical, and hybrid organizations, where agents represent the entities responsible for these patterns.
- Investigation of social aspects of intelligence and simulation of complex social phenomena, such as: the evolution of roles, norms, and organizational structures, where agents take on the role of the members of the natural societies under consideration.

What these applications have in common is that they show one or several of the following features (Yokoo 2000):

- Inherent distribution: they are inherently distributed in the sense that the data and information to be processed.
- Arise at geographically different locations and different times.
- Structured into clusters whose access and use requires familiarity with different ontology's and languages (semantic distribution) and/or are structured into clusters whose access and use requires different perceptual, effectual, and cognitive capabilities (functional distribution).
- Inherent complexity: they are inherently complex in the sense that they are too large to be solved by a single, centralized system because of limitations available at a given level of hardware or software technology.

Constraint Satisfaction Problem (CSP)

CSP is one of the most successful problem solving paradigms in AI. It has found numerous applications in almost all areas of AI. The most common applications of CSP are in configuration, planning, scheduling and resource allocation. In addition, it forms a basis for significant software industries (Faltings 2004, Silaghi 2004).

The main strength of CSP derives from its ability to flexibly combine a set of constraints with its own specific solution sets. A constraint satisfaction achieves this combination through the use of consistency and search techniques. Consistency is used to eliminate many possibilities for each local constraint, and search is used to find a consistent solution within the space of possibilities and still preserves consistency.

CSPs have been defined for a centralized architecture. A constraint network is defined by a triple (X, D, C) where $X=\{X_1 \ldots X_N\}$ is a set of N variables, $D=\{D(X_1), \ldots, D(X_N)\}$ is the set of their respective finite domains, and C is a set of constraints specifying the acceptable value combinations for variables. The CSP involves finding values that satisfy all the constraints.

The constraints here involve two variables only, namely binary constraints. General CPSs may involve constraints of any arity, but since network communication is only pairwise, the focus in this work will be on this subclass of problems which is binary. A constraint between X_i and X_j is denoted by C_{ij}. Any two variables are said to be constrained if and only if there is a conflict between their values.

For example, in the well known 8-queens problem, it is obvious that only one queen can be placed in each row. Therefore, we can formalize this problem as a CSP, in which there are 8 variables $X_1, X_2, \ldots, X_8$, each of which corresponds to a position of a queen in each row. The domain of a variable is {1, 2, ..., 8}. A constraint between any 2 variables is that they must not be in the same row, column or in the same diagonal. A solution is a combination of values of these variables.

Another typical example problem is a graph coloring problem. The objective of a graph-coloring problem is to paint nodes in a graph so that any two nodes connected by a link do not have the same color. Each node has a finite number of possible colors. This problem can be formalized as a CSP by representing the color of each node as a variable, and the possible colors of the node as a domain of the variable. If all constraints are binary (i.e., between two variables), a CSP can be represented as a graph, in which a node represents a variable, and a link between nodes represents a constraint between the corresponding variables.

If the variables of CSP are distributed among agents, then solving a CSP in which multiple agents are distributed is called a DCSP, and can be considered as achieving coherence among the agents. Many application problems in DAI can be formalized as DCSPs, such as: interpretation problems, assignment problems, multiagent truth maintenance tasks, and resource allocation in communication systems.

Distributed Constraint Satisfaction Problem (DCSP)

Cellular wireless systems, computer networks, and Internet pose themselves in a multi-agent setting where variables and/or constraints of the problem are controlled by different centralized or distributed agents.

Distributed, collaborative agents play an important role in large-scale multiagent applications such as cellular networks. Collaborative agents in such applications must coordinate their plans, resolving conflicts, if any, among their resource choices. DCSP is a major technique in multiagent coordination and conflict resolution in collaborative settings. DCSP provides rich foundation for the representation of multiagent coordination and conflict resolution, and there exist highly efficient baseline algorithms.

The combined problem is simply the aggregation of variables and constraints from different agents into a single problem. Each variable and constraint in the resulting DCSP is owned by one particular agent who ensures that the variable is assigned a value and constraint is satisfied. The actual search for solving the DCSP can be carried out by a central agent, but most work has focused on distributed search through message exchange among the agents. If all knowledge about the problem can be gathered into one agent, this agent could solve the problem alone using traditional centralized constraint satisfaction algorithms. However, such a centralized solution is often inadequate or even impossible.

The advantage of DCSP is that an agent only need to know about agents that own a variable it has a constraint with, but not about the entire problem. It is particularly applicable to problems of coordination between agents. Constraints are a good notion to express dependencies between

agents' actions, and DCSP algorithms exploit this structure to localize communication among agents. Such coordination problems occur, for example, in military or transportation planning, and there are numerous application opportunities in electronic commerce. Another application area of DCSP is in networks of simple, identical agents such as sensor networks.

In DCSP, each agent is assigned one or more variables along with the constraints on their variables. The goal of each agent, from a local perspective, is to ensure that each of the constraints on its variables is satisfied. Clearly, each agent's goal is not independent of the goals of the other agents in the system, but the goals of the agents are strongly interrelated. For example, in order for one agent to satisfy its local constraints, another agent, potentially not directly related through a constraint, may have to change the value of its variable.

The DCSP Methodology

In a distributed resource allocation problem in a CCN, each agent has its own tasks, and there are several ways (plans) to perform each task. Since resources are shared among agents, there exists constraints/contention between plans. The goal is to find the combination of plans that enables all the tasks to be executed simultaneously. This problem can be formalized as a DCSP by representing each task as a variable, and possible plans as variable values. Since a variety of DAI application problems can be formalized as DCSPs, therefore, distributed algorithms for solving DCSPs are considered as an important infrastructure in DAI.

In a DCSP, the following communication model is assumed:

- Agents communicate by sending messages. An agent can send messages to other agents if the agent knows the addresses of the agents.

- The delay in delivering a message is finite, though random. For any pair of agents, messages are received in the order in which they were sent.

It must be noted that this model does not necessarily mean that the physical communication network must be fully connected (i.e., a complete graph). Unlike most parallel/distributed algorithm studies, in which the topology of the physical communication network plays an important role, the existence of a reliable underlying communication structure among the agents is assumed; and do not care about the implementation of the physical communication network. This is because the primary concern in this research is cooperation among intelligent agents, rather than solving DCSPs by certain multiprocessor architectures.

There are problems that could be solved using traditional centralized constraint satisfaction algorithms. However, such a centralized solution is often inadequate or even impossible. Here are some reasons why distributed methods may be desirable.

- **Cost of creating a central authority:** A constraint satisfaction problem may be naturally distributed among a set of peer agents. In such cases, a central authority for solving the problem would require adding an additional element that was not present in the architecture. Examples of such systems are sensor networks, or meeting scheduling.
- **Knowledge transfer costs:** In many cases, constraints arise from complex decision processes that are internal to an agent and cannot be articulated to a central authority. Examples of this range from simple meeting scheduling, where each participant has complex preferences that are hard to articulate, to coordination decisions in virtual enterprises that results from complex internal planning. A centralized solver would require such constraints to be completely articulated for all possible situations. This would entail prohibitive costs.
- **Privacy/Security concerns:** Agents constraints may be strategic information that should not be revealed to competitors, or even to a central authority. This situation often arises in e-commerce and virtual enterprises. Privacy is easier to maintain in distributed solvers.
- **Robustness against failure:** The failure of the centralized server can be fatal. In a distributed method, a failure of one agent can be less critical and other agents might be able to find a solution without the failed agent. Such concerns arise for example in sensor networks, but also in web-based applications where participants may leave while a constraint solving process is ongoing.

These reasons mainly have motivated significant research activities in DCSP. The field has reached a certain maturity and has developed a range of different techniques. All of the characteristics of DAI and DCSP methodologies, made an inescapable motivation to try to use them to achieve efficient and reliable DCA in CCNs.

TECHNIQUES FOR SOLVING DCSPS

There are many algorithms that have been developed to solve DCSPs. The most widely used algorithms are (Yokoo 1998, Yokoo 2000, Bessiere 2004, Saenchai 2005, Silaghi 2006):

- The asynchronous backtracking (ABT) algorithm.
- The asynchronous weak-commitment (AWC) algorithm.

In what follows, a detail description, main features, and implementation of the AWC algorithm is given as it is going to be utilized for developing an efficient DCA technique for DCA in CCNs.

The Asynchronous Weak-Commitment (AWC) Algorithm

The AWC algorithm was proposed and developed by Makoto Yokoo et. al. in 1995 (Yokoo 1995) for solving DCSP. It is based upon the asynchronous backtracking (ABT) algorithm and inspired by the weak-commitment (WC) algorithm. Two main keys represent the strength of this algorithm; it uses the min-conflict heuristic as a value ordering heuristic to reduce the risk of making bad decisions, and it abandons the partial solution and restarts the search process if there is no consistent value with the partial solution, which means AWC weakly commits to a partial solution that constructed from bad decisions.

In the AWC algorithm, agents asynchronously assign values to their variables and communicate the values to neighbouring agents with shared binary constraints; the priority order is dynamically changed using the communicated priority values. If the current value is not consistent because some constraint with variables of higher priority agents is not satisfied, the agent changes its value so that the value is consistent, and also the value minimizes the number of constraint violations with variables of lower priority agents. But when it cannot find a consistent value, it sends *nogood* messages to other agents, and increments its priority value. If it has already sent an identical *nogood*, it will not change its priority value but will wait for the next message.

In the AWC algorithm, all variables have temporal initial values. A consistent partial solution is constructed for a subset of variables, and this partial solution is extended by adding variables one by one until a complete solution is found. When a variable is added to the partial solution, its tentative initial value is revised so that the new value satisfies all the constraints between the variables included in the partial solution, and

satisfies as many constraints as possible between variables that are not included in the partial solution, this value ordering heuristic is called the min-conflict heuristic which has a great effect on finding a solution with small number of cycles as possible.

When there exists no value for one variable that satisfies all the constraints between the variables included in the partial solution, this algorithm abandons the whole partial solution, and starts constructing a new partial solution from scratch, using the current value assignment as new tentative initial values. This algorithm records the abandoned partial solutions as new constraints, and avoids creating the same partial solution that has been created and abandoned before. Therefore, the completeness of the algorithm is guaranteed.

The main two features of the AWC algorithm can be described as follows (Yokoo 2000):

- **Min-conflict:** When selecting a variable value, if there are multiple values consistent with the *agent_view*, the agent prefers the value that minimizes the number of constraint violations with variables of lower priority agents.

- **Weak-commitment:** When an agent cannot find a value consistent with the current *agent_view*, it increases its priority value to be the maximum of neighbours. The mechanism of dynamically changing priority whenever a new *nogood* created; enables agents weakly commit to the partial solution, which means It abandons the partial solution and restarts the search process if there exists no consistent value with the partial solution. By increasing a priority value in this way, a wrong variable value of a high priority agent can be revised without performing exhaustive search by lower priority agents, which is the main characteristic of the AWC algorithm.

Since agents act concurrently and asynchronously, and no agent has exact information about the partial solution, furthermore, multiple agents may try to restart the search process simultaneously, so for establishing the priority order and changing the priority values, the following rules will control the process:

- For each agent, a nonnegative integer value representing the priority order of the agent is defined; this value is called the priority value.
- The order is defined such that any agent with a larger priority value has higher priority.
- If the priority values of multiple agents are the same, the order is determined by the alphabetical order of the identifiers.
- For each agent, the initial priority value is 0.
- If there exists no consistent value for agent X_i, the priority value of X_i is changed to k +1, where k is the largest priority value of the related agents.

The AWC algorithm works as follows:

- There exist N agents.
- Each agent has to know only the identifiers of an agent with which it must establish a constraint in order to direct the constraint.
- The priority value is initially zero for all agents, but it is dynamically changed during the execution, if two agents have the same priority value the alphabetical order of identifiers will determine who is greater (i.e., X_1 priority is higher than X_2).
- Each agent must establish a link from itself to lower priority agents if it has a constraint with.
- Each agent has a set of values from the agents that are connected by incoming links. These values constitute the agent's *agent_view* which has the same definition as in the ABT algorithm.

- Agents communicate their location values and priority values with constrained agents, by sending ok messages for both lower and higher priority agents, the lower and higher priority agents are called neighbours.
- After that, the agents wait for and respond to messages.
- If an ok message is received by some agent by an incoming link, the evaluating agent adds the message sending agent index, priority, and value to his neighbours, and if the agent who sent the message has a higher priority, then it will be added to the evaluating agent *agent_view*, and then checks whether its own value assignment is consistent with its *agent_view*.
- The agent's own assignment is consistent with the *agent_view*, if all constraints the agent evaluates are true under the value assignments described in the *agent_view*.
- If an agent's own assignment is not consistent with the *agent_view*, the agent will try to change the current value so that it will be consistent with its *agent_view* and also the value minimizes the constraint violations with lower priority agents, and then send ok message to his neighbours.
- If an agent's own assignment is not consistent with the *agent_view* and the agent is unable to find any consistent value, then a subset of the *agent_view*, which caused the problem is defined and is called a *nogood*, after that the agent will check if it has already sent an identical *nogood* message to this subset, if yes it will not change its priority nor send *nogood* message but will wait for another messages.
- If the agent has not sent an identical *nogood* message to the same subset, then the agent will increase it priority value to be the maximum priority value of all agents connected to it by constraints plus one, then it will change the current value to another

value that minimizes the constraint violations with lower priority agents, and then send ok message to his neighbours.

- If a *nogood* message is received by some agent by an outgoing link, the agent will check if its current value is consistent with

Figure 5. AWC procedures and functions

Receiving *ok* procedure

when received (ok?, $(x_j, d_j, priority)$)
{
    add $(x_j, d_j, priority)$ to *agent_view*;
    check_*agent_view*;
}

Receiving *nogood* procedure

when received ($nogood$, x_j, $nogood$)
{
    add *nogood* to *nogood_list*;
    when $(x_k, d_k, priority)$ where x_k is not in neighbors is contained in *nogood*
    {
        add x_k to neighbors, add $(x_k, d_k, priority)$ to *agent_view*;
    }
    check_*agent_view*;
}

Check_*agent_view* function

when *agent_view* and current_value are not consistent
{
    if (no value in D is consistent with *agent_view*) **then**
    {
        backtrack;
    }
    else
    {
        select d_i belongs D where *agent_view* and d_i are consistent and d_i minimizes the number
            of constraint violations with lower priority agents;
        current_value = d_i;
        send (ok?, $(x_i, d_i,$ current_priority)) to neighbors;
    }
}

Backtrack procedure

when an empty set is an element of *nogoods*
{
    broadcast to other agents that there is no solution, terminate this algorithm;
}
when no element of *nogoods* is included in *nogood*_sent
{
    for each V belongs *nogoods*
    {
        add V to *nogood*_sent;
        for each (x_j, d_j, p_j) in V
        {
            send ($nogood$, x_i, V) to x_j;
        }
        $P_{max} = max(x_j, d_j, p_j)$ belongs *agent_view* (p_j);
        current_priority = $1 + P_{max}$;
        select d_i belongs D where d_i minimizes the number of constraint violations with lower
            priority agents;
        current_value = d_i;
        send (ok?, $(x_i, d_i,$ current_priority)) to neighbors;
    }
}

its *agent_view*, depending on the result the agent will respond as described before.

- The algorithm will terminates when a solution is found or when there is an empty *nogood* element set is found, so there is no solution.

Figure 5 summarizes the AWC procedures when agents receive *ok* and *nogood* messages, and other related functions.

THE DAI-DCA SCHEME

The AWC algorithm discussed in the previous section is used to develop a new DCA scheme. Since this new scheme is based on a DAI algorithm, namely the AWC algorithm, it is referred to as a DAI-DCA scheme to distinguish it from other non-intelligence DCA techniques (e.g., CDCA and DDCA techniques).

However, in order to use the AWC algorithm to solve the channel allocation problem in CCNs, first, the problem should be formulated as a DCSP. Therefore, to do so, assume the following:

- An agent stands for a BS (cell), which is responsible for controlling all mobile users within the cell.
- Variables stand for the channels allocated for each cell.
- Constraints stand for the legal usage of the available channels and the legal channel reuse to eliminate any radio interferences.

There are two mechanisms that can used in implementing the AWC algorithm for DCA, these are:

- On-demand mechanism. In this mechanism, each cell collaboratively updates its resources (allocate new channels as needed and as available). Cells instantly and si-

multaneously exchange information on the allocated frequencies as depicted by the algorithm. It is clear from the description of the AWC algorithm; it involves a huge data communications between cells and may cause a lot of interruption during the network operation.

- Token-base mechanism. In this mechanism, each pattern (a group of collaborative cells) has a token circulating between these cells and carrying information about the channels that are currently allocated for each cell. In this mechanism, only a cell that holds the token is allowed to update its resources. So that data communication is minimized and the process of resource update does not interrupt the network operation. Since, the token is continuously circulating between collaborative cells; if possible, a cell updates its resources if it is equal to or less than a certain threshold value. Thus, each cell can update its resources independently and as long as resources are available. However, in this mechanism, a cell needs to have a mechanism to initiate resources update, such as when the cell resources below a certain threshold value, otherwise it just bypasses the token to the next cell to minimize delay.

In order to practically implement the AWC algorithm or any other algorithm efficiently for DCA in CCNs with minimum communication overheads, minimum system interruption, and not affecting the system operation, a token-based mechanism can be used.

PERFORMANCE MEASURES

There are a number of parameters that can be used for evaluating the performance of the allocation techniques, such as:

- Number of successfully allocated channels ($C_{a,i}$). It is defined as the number of channels that are successfully allocated for the ith cell during network operation, to satisfy specific values and distributions of initial and traffic loads.

- Number of failed channels ($C_{f,i}$). It is defined as the number of channels that are failed to allocate (i.e., calls are dropped) for the ith cell during network operation, to satisfy specific values and distributions of initial and traffic loads.

- Allocation efficiency (E_i). It is defined as the number of channels that are successfully allocated ($C_{a,i}$) divided by the total number of channels ($C_{t,i}$) that are requested during the simulation period, where $C_{t,i} = C_{a,i} + C_{f,i}$. Thus, E_i can be calculated by:

$$E_i = \frac{C_{a,i}}{C_{t,i}} = \frac{C_{a,i}}{C_{a,i} + C_{f,i}} \qquad (7)$$

Since, these parameters can be computed for a number of neighbouring cells; it has been found that it is more indicative to evaluate the performance in terms of the average values of the aforementioned parameters over a network of k cells, for a certain period of operation and network environment. The average values of the channels allocated, failed, and the allocation efficiency are referred to as $\overline{C_a}$, $\overline{C_f}$, and $\overline{E}$, respectively.

Evaluating the performance of channel allocation techniques in terms of the computed average values is very useful. This is because a technique may perform well and allocate all channels required by a certain cell, but it may fail to allocate enough channels for another demanding cell. Furthermore, the effects of a number of networks parameters need to be investigated, such as:

- Cell traffic load (α) which represents the number of calls arrives to a cell (calls/sec).
- Cell initial load (β) which represents the

number of channels that are initially allocated to a cell (channel/cell)

SIMULATIONS AND RESULTS

The DCCA technique is coded using Borland Java Builder9 Enterprise edition, since Java has many advantages and programming abilities that could be used to implement distributed and constrained environments, such as the multithreading technique, which will be used to represent agents that may work concurrently and asynchronously, each agent will be represented by a single thread that works independently from other threads, each thread will process its own data and data from the thread environment, and then respond without waiting other threads to finish.

A number of simulations are carried-out to evaluate and analyze the performance of the DAI-DCA technique, and consequently the AWC algorithm, in providing a DDCA solution in GSM systems that satisfies all constraints within a reasonable processing time and minimum data exchange. These simulations are grouped into two different scenarios. These two scenarios can be summarized as follows:

- Scenario #1. It simulates and investigates the performance of the DAI-DCA technique in a uniform initial and traffic loads. In particular, it simulates a GSM network in suburban or rural areas, where the traffic load is low and uniformally distributed.
- Scenario #2. It simulates and investigates the performance of the DAI-DCA technique in a uniform initial and nonuniform traffic loads. In particular, it simulates a GSM network in an urban downtown area, where the traffic load is centralized in shopping or business districts.

In these two scenarios, first, similar infrastructure network topology of CCN is used, as shown in Figure 6. Second, the initial load is always uniform regardless of its initial value (number of channels per cell). However, the only thing that is varied in these two scenarios is the traffic requirements.

The total number of cells that are considered is 37 cells, with one central cell encircled by three tiers. The duration of calls is modelled as a random variable that varies between 20 and 360 sec with an average value of 180 sec approximately. The arrivals of calls in each cell are modelled as independent and distributed processes with various arrival rates assigned for the neighbouring cells. The total simulation time is taken to be 1000 cycles, and each cycle is equivalent to 1 sec. For simplicity, at this stage, the hand-offs is not considered.

In all simulations, the DAI-DCA technique begins with a certain initial load (β), where a specified number of channels are considered as busy channels. Thus, after initialization, if the number of incoming calls is more than the normally concluded calls, a new channels need to be allocated. In other words, each cell requests channels for the new coming calls depending on the traffic load. It is important to realize that each channel can accommodate 8 calls, because a GSM system under consideration utilizes a time division multiple access (TDMA) technique, and each channel is divided into 8 time slots.

Scenario #1. Uniform Initial and Traffic Loads

This scenario simulates a network with a uniform traffic load (α=0.2 calls/sec) in each cell, and uniform initial loads of β=8 and β=10 channels/cell. This scenario represents a GSM in a suburban or a rural area, which is usually characterized by a uniform initial load, and relatively low and uniform traffic load.

The results computed by using the DAI-DCA technique for the average values of $\overline{C_a}$, $\overline{C_f}$, and $\overline{E}$, and their associated standard deviations σ_a, σ_f, and σ_e, respectively, are listed in Table 3. It demonstrates that the technique has an excellent performance in a suburban and rural area as it responses positively to almost all arrived calls. It provides an efficiency of 100% (i.e., the number of dropped calls is 0) for all cells when α=0.2 and β=8. However, when β increases to 10 channels/cell, the number of free channels are reduced, which causes channel allocation failure and in some cells some calls are dropped.

For Scenario #1, when β=8 channels/cell, the technique succeeds to allocate resources to all incoming calls, and the number of calls that are denied services is zero for all cells. Thus, the technique achieves an average allocation efficiency of 100% as all arrived calls granted services. When β=10 channels/cell, the technique still offers an excellent performance as it provides an average allocation efficiency of 96%. The results obtained also show that, when β=10 channels/cell, all cells

Figure 6. Topology of a CCN

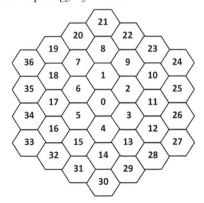

Table 3. Results for scenario #1

Values of $\overline{C_a}$, $\overline{C_f}$, and $\overline{E}$ and their respective standard deviations σ_a, σ_f, and σ_e for a uniform traffic load (α = 0.2 calls/sec) and for a uniform initial load (β = 8 and 10 channels/cell).						
β	$\overline{C_a}$	σ_a	$\overline{C_f}$	σ_f	$\overline{E}$(%)	σ_e
8	3.16	0.93	0.00	0.00	100	0.00
10	2.43	0.65	0.14	0.42	96	0.13

are allocated the required channels, except cells number 0, 5, 14, and 31.

Scenario #2: Uniform Initial and Non-Uniform Traffic Loads

This scenario represents a GSM network with a nonuniform traffic load. It simulates a "hot-spot" in cell 8, in which the traffic load (α) is varied from 0.4 to 1.0 calls/sec in step of 0.2. Each cell around cell 8 (cells 1, 7, 9, 20, 21, and 22) has traffic load of 0.4 calls/sec. The traffic load of all other cells is 0.2 calls/sec. This scenario represents a GSM in an urban downtown area, where the traffic load is centralized in shopping or business districts. Results obtained for $\overline{C_a}$, $\overline{C_f}$, $\overline{E}$ are presented in Figures 7 to 10, respectively.

Figure 7 shows that as β increases, the average numbers of channels that are successfully allocated are decreased for all values of α. This is because a limited number of channels that can be allocated for the demanding cells and the traffic load is very high. Figure 8 demonstrates that the average number of channels failed increases as α is increasing regardless of the value of β. Thus, the average allocation efficiency decreases as α is increasing for all values of β, as shown in Figure 9.

Finally, in Figure 10, the values of E_i for the hot-spot cell (cell number 8) are summarized. The results clearly show that the efficiency reaches a very low value when α=1.0 calls/sec (high traffic load) and β=10 channels/cell. This is because of the following reasons:

- High traffic load.
- Limited number of channels available.
- Constraints imposed by the network to avoid all forms of interferences.
- Constraints imposed on the algorithm for not changing any of the allocated channels during operation, and the algorithm should only manipulate the currently available channels in the best way to achieve the optimum performance.

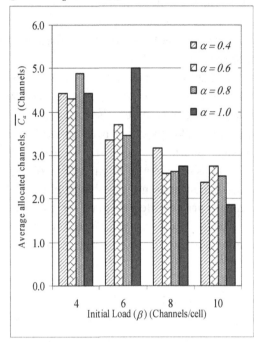

Figure 7. $\overline{C_a}$ versus β for scenario #2.

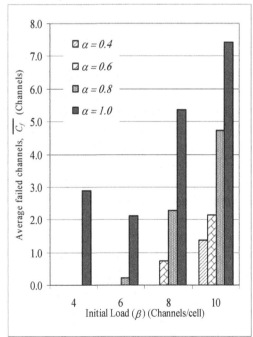

Figure 8. $\overline{C_f}$ versus β for Scenario #2.

Figure 9. $\overline{E}$ versus β for Scenario #2.

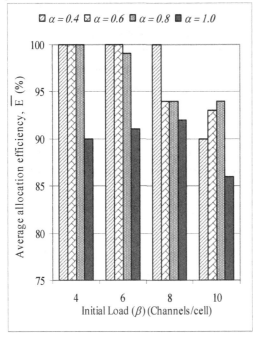

Figure 10. E_i versus β for cell 8 for Scenario #2

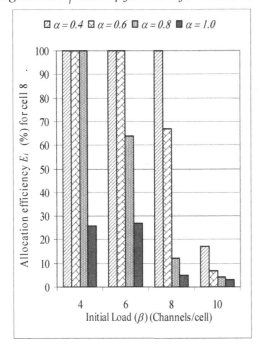

CONCLUSIONS

The DAI-DCA technique presented an excellent performance for allocating and reusing channels efficiently under different network operation environments without violating the co-channel and adjacent channel interference constraints. This is mainly because the AWC algorithm could satisfy cells needs by intelligently allocating and reusing channels. The results obtained showed that an average allocation efficiency of 100% was achieved when the initial and the traffic loads are low and uniform as in suburban or rural areas, and the average allocation efficiency was reduced to 96% when the initial load is increased by 25% from 8 channels/cell to 10 channels/cell, while the traffic load remains unchanged at 0.2 calls/sec throughout the network.

Furthermore, the DAI-DCA technique offered an excellent performance at a heavily loaded network operation environment in an urban down-town area, where the traffic load is centralized as in shopping or business districts. The minimum average allocation efficiency achieved was 86%, when the initial load at the hot-spot cell reaches 10 channels/cell and the traffic load is 1.0 calls/sec. The results obtained also showed that the performance of the DAI-DCA scheme was highly affected by the number of unused (free) channels remained after initialization, and the performance decreases as the number of free channels after initialization is decreased.

The following scheme do not consider hand-off that may occur due to nodes movement between cells, therefore, it is important to modify the DAI-DCA technique to consider hand-offs. It is important to modify the DAI-DCA technique to consider total channels re-distribution if there are many cells asking for more channels and they can not served, due to interference constraints, while there are many unused channels in neighbouring cells. It is believed that the DAI-DCA technique could solve this situation by redistribute both the allocated and unused channels in a way that satisfies all cells needs in the system.

REFERENCES

Abeysundara, G. (2005). *Dynamic cellular channel allocation using intelligent agents.* School of Computer Science, University of Catleton.

Ahmad, R. (2006). *A hybrid channel allocation algorithm using hot-spot notification for wireless cellular networks.* IEEE CCECE/CCGEI, 891-894.

Al-Agha, k. (2000). Resource management in wireless networks using intelligent agents. *International Journal of Network Management, 10*(1), 29-39.

An, J., Hines, E. L., Leeson, M. S., Sun, L., Iliescu, D. D., & Wang, K. Y. (2007). Genetic algorithms and fuzzy logic for dynamic channel allocation in cellular radio networks. *IEEE Radio and Wireless Symposium,* Long Beach, California, USA.

Bejar, R., Domshlak, C., Fernandez, C., Gomes, C., Krishnamachari, B., Selman, B., & Valls, M. (2005). Sensor networks and distributed CSP: Communication, computation and complexity. *Journal of Artificial Intelligence, 161,* 117–147.

Boumerdassi, B. (2000). An efficient reservation-based Dynamic channel assignment strategy. *IEEE 3G Mobile Communication Technologies, 1ˢᵗ International Conference, 471,* 352-355.

Bessiere, C., Maestre, A., Brito I., & Meseguer P. (2004). Asynchronous backtracking without adding links: a new member in the ABT family. *Artificial Intelligence Journal, 161,* 7-24.

Faltings, B., & Yokoo, M. (2004). Introduction: Special issue on distributed constraint satisfaction. *Journal of Artificial Intelligence, 161*(1-2), 1-5.

Kostic, Z., Maric, I., & Wang, X. (2001). Fundamentals of dynamic frequency hopping in cellular systems. *IEEE Journal on Selected Areas in Communications, 19*(11), 2254-2266.

Kostic, Z., & Sollenberger, N. (2002). Performance and implementation of dynamic frequency hopping in limited-bandwidth cellular systems. *IEEE Transactions on Wireless Communications, 1*(1), 28-36.

Lee N. H., & Bahk S. (2007). Dynamic channel allocation using the interference range in multi-cell downlink systems. *IEEE Wireless Communication and Networking Conference,* (pp. 1716-1721).

Mahdavi, M., Edwards, R. M., & Ladas, C. V. (2007). On the effect of a random access protocol on the performance of the session-based data subsystem in GSM/GPRS. *IEEE Transactions on Vehicular Technology, 56*(4), 1781-1796.

Mishra, A. R. (2006). *Advanced Cellular Network Planning and Optimisation: 2G/2.5G/3G... Evolution to 4G.* John-Wiley.

Modi, P. J., Jung, H., Tambe, M., Shen, W. M., & Kulkarni, S. (2001). Dynamic distributed resource allocation: Distributed constraint satisfaction approach. *Proceedings of the 8ᵗʰ International Workshop on Intelligent Agents,* (pp. 264-276).

Prakash, R., Shivaratri, N. G., & Singhal, M. (1999). Distributed dynamic fault-tolerant channel allocation for cellular networks. *IEEE Transactions on Vehicular Technology, 48*(6), 1874-1888.

Priscoli, F. D., Magnani, N. P., Palestini, V., & Sestini, F. (1997). Application of dynamic channel allocation strategies to the GSM cellular network. *IEEE Selected Areas in Communications, 15*(8), 1558-1567.

Russell, S., & Norvig, P. (2003). *Artificial Intelligence: A Modern Approach.* Prentice-Hall, 2ⁿᵈ Edition.

Saenchai, K., Benedicenti, L., & Paranjape, R. (2005). A dynamic extension of the asynchronous weak commitment search algorithm. *IEEE Canadian Conference on Electrical and Computer Engineering*, (pp. 1112-1115).

Salmenkaita, M., Gimenez, J., & Tapia, P. (2001). A practical DCA implementation for GSM networks: Dynamic frequency and channel assignment. *IEEE Vehicular Technology Conference, 4*, 2529-2533.

Silaghi, M. C. (2006). Framework for modeling reordering heuristics for asynchronous backtracking. *IEEE International Conference on Intelligent Agent Technology*, (pp. 529-536).

Silaghi, M. C., & Faltings B. (2004). Asynchronous aggregation and consistency in distributed constraint satisfaction. *Journal of Artificial Intelligence, 161*, 25-53.

Stallings, W. (2005). *Wireless Communications and Networks*. Prentice-Hall, 2nd Edition.

Wang, Z., & Mathiopoulos, P. T. (2005). On the performance analysis of dynamic channel allocation with FIFO handover queuing in LEO-MSS. *IEEE Transactions on Communications, 53*(9), 1443-1446.

Yang, J., & Manivannan, D. (2007). Performance comparison of two channel allocation approaches: Channel pre-allocation vs. non pre-allocation. *IEEE Proceedings of the 3rd International Conference on Wireless and Mobile Communications*, (pp. 61-61).

Yang, J., Jiang, Q., Manivannan, D., & Singhal, M. (2005). A Fault-Tolerant Distributed Channel Allocation Scheme for Cellular Networks. *IEEE Transactions on Computers, 54*(5), 616-629.

Yokoo, M., & Hirayama, K. (2000). Algorithms for distributed constraint satisfaction: A review. *Journal of Autonomous Agents and Multi-Agent Systems, 3*(2), 198-212.

Yokoo, M., Durfee, E. H., Ishida, T., & Kuwabara, K. (1998). The distributed constraint satisfaction problem: Formalization and algorithms. *IEEE Transactions on Knowledge and Data Engineering, 10*(5), 673-685.

Yokoo, M. (1995). Asynchronous weak-commitment search for solving distributed constraint satisfaction problems. *Proceedings of the 1st International Conference on Principles and Practice of Constraint Programming*, (pp. 88–102).

Yubin, S., Huan, H., Hua, L., & Shaowen, Y. (2000). Performance analysis of the minimum call blocking probability for dynamic channel allocation in mobile cellular networks. *Proceedings of the IEEE International Conference on Communication Technology, 1*, 269-273.

Zhang, M., & Yum, T. S. P. (1989). Comparisons of channel assignment strategies in cellular mobile telephone systems. *IEEE Transactions on Vehicular Technology, 38*(4), 211-215.

Zhang, W., Wang, G., Xing, Z., & Wittenburg, L. (2005). Distributed stochastic search and distributed breakout: Properties, comparison and applications to constraint optimization problems in sensor networks. *Journal of Artificial Intelligent, 161*(1-2), 55-87.

Chapter XIII
Discovering Knowledge Channels in Learning Organization:
Case Study of Jordan

Maha T. El-Mahied
The Arab Academy for Banking and Financial Sciences, Jordan

Firas Alkhaldi
The Arab Academy for Banking and Financial Sciences, Jordan

Evon M. O. Abu-Taieh
The Arab Academy for Banking and Financial Sciences, Jordan

ABSTRACT

The aim of this research is to discover the knowledge channels in the learning organization in Jordan. The research studied three aspects of the trusted knowledge channels: first studied the worker perspective and understanding of the TRUST issue. Second the research studied the worker perspectives of the knowledge channels, finding that the worker consider boss, colleague, and assistant as the most important sources of knowledge in the organization. Third the research studied how the organization by providing the right environment will encourage knowledge sharing. For the organization to foster the proper channels, the organization must know that "it takes two to tango". In other words the organization must take the initiative to set the proper channels. Finally this chapter proposes a model that represents the knowledge channels in the learning organization.

INTRODUCTION

In the learning organization, the value of the organization stems from the people that work in it. The purpose of this paper is to build a model that shows the channels that employees acquire such knowledge and experience. Usually an employee has many channels to acquire the knowledge: Documents, colleagues, subordinates, superiors. Yet the previously mentioned channels are not the only channels, there are other sources of knowledge such as family, friends, etc.

In the life cycle of knowledge management there are many phases, benefits and many challenges. One of the challenges is culture. By studying the channels of knowledge dissemination one can designate the resources, whereby, one can utilize such finding to better improve the value of the organization via building knowledge repository.

Learning Organizations in Jordan may or may not be different. In this empirical study, the student is trying to study these organizations through a questionnaire study of the AABFS students. AABFS students are representative sample of Jordanian workers. So the main question of this paper is: What are the main knowledge channels of learning organizations in Jordan?

LITERATURE REVIEW KM AND ORGANIZATION LEARNING

There are two types of learning associated with Organization Learning (OL): adaptive learning and proactive learning[1]. The adaptive learning is usually in reaction to changes in the environmental conditions of the organization. Proactive learning is made on willful basis.

Several models have been proposed that facilitate understanding of organizational learning: March and Olsen model published in 1975, Argyris and Schon model published 1978, Peter Senge *The Fifth Discipline* published in 1990, Kim model published in 1993, Nonaka and Takeuchi model published in 1995, Flood model published in1999, Nick Bontis model published in 2002.

The first model (March and Olsen model)[2]. In the model the authors attempted to link the individual to OL. In the model

- Individual beliefs lead to individual action
- Individual action may lead to an organizational action and a response from the environment
- Which may induce improved individual beliefs

The second model is related to Gregory Bateson's concepts of first and second order learning. Argyris and Schon[3] (1978) distinguish between *single-loop and double-loop* learning. "In *single-loop learning*, individuals, groups, or organizations modify their actions according to the difference between expected and obtained outcomes. *In double-loop learning*, the entities (individuals, groups or organization) question the values, assumptions and policies that led to the actions in the first place; if they are able to view and modify those, then second-order or double-loop learning has taken place."

The third model is Peter Senge *The Fifth Discipline*[4] published in 1990. The model focused on group problem solving using the systems thinking method in order to convert companies into learning organizations. In the book published specially for this model there are 5 disciplines:

1. Building shared vision
2. Mental models
3. Team learning
4. Personal mastery
5. Systems thinking- The Fifth Discipline that integrates the other 4

In the book Senge discuss the learning hurdles and the laws of the fifth Discipline. The fourth model was introduced by Kim, D.H. in 1993[5] by a research titled 'The link between individual and organizational learning' published in the Sloan Management Review. The model integrated Argyris, March and Olsen and another model by Kofman. The paper was not available to the student but the idea of the model is to analyze all possible breakdowns in the flow of the information that may lead to the failure of the organization learning.

In 1995 Nonaka and Takeuchi introduced a spiral model based on Polanyi's[6] concept of differentiating tacit from explicit knowledge (the original idea is based on philosophical point of view). In an interview with Nonaka[7] explained the famous model taught in text books as follows:

In the West, there is a long history of philosophical inquiry into knowledge or epistemology from Plato to Descartes to Michael Polanyi. Drawing especially on Polanyi, I conceptualized knowledge in terms of two types, tacit knowledge and explicit knowledge. Tacit knowledge is personal, context-specific, and therefore hard to formalize and communicate. Explicit knowledge, on the other hand, is transmittable in formal and systematic language.

Tacit knowledge and explicit knowledge are not totally separate but mutually complementary entities. Without experience, we cannot truly understand. But unless we try to convert tacit knowledge to explicit knowledge, we cannot reflect upon and share it organizationally. Through this dynamic interaction between the two types of knowledge, personal knowledge becomes organizational knowledge. And the organizational knowledge or intellectual infrastructure of an organization encourages its individual members to develop new knowledge through new experiences.

This dynamic process is the key to organizational knowledge creation. This interaction between the two types of knowledge brings about what we call four modes of knowledge conversion – that

is, socialization (from individual tacit knowledge to group tacit knowledge), externalization (from tacit knowledge to explicit knowledge), combination (from separate explicit knowledge to systemic explicit knowledge), and internalization (from explicit knowledge to tacit knowledge)

Socialization *is a process of creating common tacit knowledge through shared experiences. For socialization, we need to build a "field" of interaction, where individuals share experiences and space at the same time, thereby creating common unarticulated beliefs or embodied skills.*

Externalization *is a process of articulating tacit knowledge into such explicit knowledge as concepts and/or diagrams, often using metaphors, analogies, and/or sketches. This mode is triggered by a dialogue intended to create concepts from tacit knowledge. Creating a new product concept is a good example.*

Combination *is a process of assembling new and existing explicit knowledge into a systemic knowledge, such as a set of specifications for a prototype of a new product. Often, a newly created concept should be combined with existing knowledge to materialize it into something tangible.*

Internalization *is a process of embodying explicit knowledge into tacit, operational knowledge such as know-how. This mode is triggered by "learning by doing or using." Explicit knowledge documented into text, sound, or a video format facilitates the internalization process. Therefore, manuals, a quintessential example of explicit knowledge, are widely used for internalization.*

In conclusion *explicit knowledge* (sometimes referred to as *formal knowledge*) and *tacit knowledge* (also, *informal knowledge*), personal knowledge rooted in individual experience and involving personal belief, perspective, and values.

Another model was introduced in 1999 published by Flood. The major idea is rethinking

Figure 1. Nonaka and Takeuchi model according to Nonaka's interview and explanation

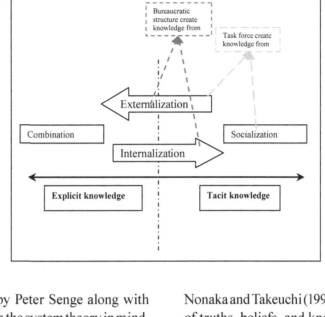

The Fifth Discipline by Peter Senge along with Argyris and Schon with the system theory in mind. The system theory looks at the organization with components linked by links.

The last model was introduced in 2002 by Nick Bontis[8]. The model thinks of the organization with eye of stock and flow of knowledge. The knowledge crosses 3 levels of analysis: Individual, Team, and Organization.

One cannot discuss knowledge without mentioning **Plato**[9] point of view on knowledge. Plato showed that knowledge as subset of the intersection between truths and beliefs as seen in Figure 3.

This leads us to suggested a more comprehensive view of knowledge by super imposing

Figure 2. Plato's view of knowledge

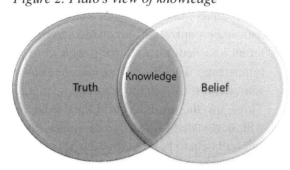

Nonaka and Takeuchi (1995) model on Plato model of truths, beliefs, and knowledge

PROBLEM DEFINITION

In learning organizations there are many channels that are utilized to facilitate knowledge transfer. Once such channels are established and learned by the researcher one can utilize such finding in the progress of the organization hence increase the value of the organization itself.

Also, such finding will help in capturing knowledge, organizing knowledge, refining and then transferring knowledge. Such life cycle of knowledge management is defined by (Eliase, et al., 2004). While (Turban et al, 2001) define knowledge management life cycle as: Create knowledge, Capture knowledge, Refine knowledge, Store knowledge, Manage knowledge, Disseminate knowledge.

Furthermore, one of the challenges in building Knowledge management systems is "Culture" (Eliase et al., 2004), which what is intended to be partially studied in this research. Other challenges may exist such as: knowledge evaluation,

Figure 3. Super imposing Nonaka and Takeuchi (1995) model on Plato model of truths, beliefs, and knowledge

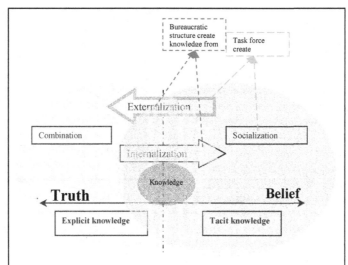

knowledge processing, knowledge implementation suggested by (Eliase et al., 2004) are outside the scope of this research. Culture generally affect the way people share, disseminate, and create knowledge.

THE IMPORTANCE OF THE RESEARCH

The importance of the research stems from the importance of knowledge management in learning organization; hence knowledge is the commodity of such organizations. Where 'innovation is core competency' (Eliase et al., 2004). Sharing knowledge creates exponential benefits, rather than recreating the wheel.

To create knowledge a great deal of time, effort and money is used. On the other hand, easily such knowledge is drained when the brain carrying such knowledge is recruited or transferred. Knowledge management will allow the business to react to business opportunity. Also, knowledge management shortens the learning curve.

Hence, the paper will study the channels that propagate knowledge then designate the knowl-

edge resources. In a later stage, one can use such results to build knowledge repository. Which solves the culture challenge mentioned previously by (Eliase, et al., 2004)

OBJECTIVE OF THE RESEARCH

Knowledge management benefits stated best by (Eliase, et al., 2004) as:

1. Sharing knowledge creates exponential benefits.
2. Stopping the 'brain drain'
3. Reacting to business opportunity
4. Shorten learning curve.

The objectives of this paper are to first study the channels that propagate knowledge in the learning organization. Second, compare the different knowledge channels, in regards to which is most used. Therefore, designate the knowledge sources most used in the learning organizations. Third, use the result to build knowledge model with designated knowledge resources. Such result will help to build knowledge repository in a later stage.

METHODOLOGY

The research was be implemented in the Arab Academy for Banking and Finance (AABFS). The sample included the bachelors, master and Ph.D. students because they will be in the age reflecting the answers to the questions. Only Jordanian students were questioned since none-Jordanians will not work in the Jordanian organization which is the emphasis of this research.

Collection Mythology

The data was be collected in two ways: questionnaire and observation. The primary collection methodology is questionnaire since it will cover greater number of people; the questionnaire is included in appendix 1. The secondary methodology will be observation, which will reflect the idea of the researcher.

The questionnaire had 4 bases: The first base contains questions 1-6 which studies the demography of the sample. The second base contains one question (question #7) which reflect what the sample consider a trusted source of knowledge regarding work and the measures the comprehension of the sample to the appropriate source of knowledge. The third base contains 8 questions which reflect the view of the worker towards knowledge channel in the organization. The fourth base contains 12 questions which reflect the role of the organization in developing the proper channels of knowledge. Which really reflect what the organizations perceived as channels of knowledge.

DEMOGRAPHY SAMPLE ANALYSIS

The sample chosen was all of the AABFS students. The research distributed 250 questionnaire and 203 were returned. In this section the demography of the sample will be analyzed regarding age, experience, gender, level of educations (BSC, Master, PHD), specialty (MIS, CIS, Banking, Business) and sector of work (private, public, international).

Age

The age of the sample ranged from less than 30 years old to above 50 years old. As Table 1 shows that 137 or 67% of the sample was below 30 years old this can be explained since the AABFS is a university. The second majority is the 30-39 years old representing 24% .

As Table 1, although the majority of the questionnaire sample is in the range "below 30" still the range "30-39" has 24% and the range "40-50" is 7%. The above 50 range is only 1%. These results are reflection to the fact that the questionnaire was carried in a university.

Experience

The sample of the research reflected in experience as follows: 36% had less than 5 years of experience. While 48% of the sample had 5 - 9 years of experience. As for the sample of 10 to 15 years of experience there was 13 %. For the categories "more than 15 years" the sample reflected 2%.

The majority of the sample 63% had more than 5 years of experience (Table 2) which really indicates that the sample is well experienced and had enough knowledge about what they are answering.

Table 1. Age distribution of the sample

Age	Count	Percentage
less than 30 years	137	67%
30-39 years	48	24%
40-50 years	15	7%
more than 50 years	2	1%
Unanswered	1	0%
Total	203	100%

Levels of Education

Level of education was an important factor in this research. Since education level reflects the maturity of the answers given. The sample reflected 73% to be master students. As for the PhD students the where 9% of the sample. In regards to the B.Sc. and high diploma they were 8% and 4% respectively.

One can notice that 92% of the sample (see Table 3) is of higher education category. This gives more confidence in the answers of the sample. Also this indicates the importance of such highly educated sample and their answers.

Specialty

The specialty demography factor is also a significant factor for the research. The computer information systems (CIS) where 37% of the sample of the research. On the other hand 29% of the sample was Management information systems (MIS). As for the Business major they were 11% of the sample. Banking major reflected 5% of the sample.

The sample is representative as can be seen in Table 4. Different specialties and majors answered the questionnaire. Therefore the sample is representative from this angle of the study.

Gender

The gender of the sample was biased since 25% of the sample was of female students; on the other hand 75% of the sample was male students as seen in Table 5 which is also can be used for future research indicator..

Sector

The sector is where the students work the researcher devised this factor in three categories. Public sector, private sector and international organizations sector. Surprisingly the 56% of the sample came from private sector. While 35% came from public/governmental sector. While 5% came from international sector.

As can be seen in Table 6 the distribution of the different sectors reflected in this sample gives a good indicator that such results are not only in one sector or other. Rather it is dispersed in many types of sectors.

Table 2. Experience distribution of the sample

Experience	Count	Percentage
less than 5 years	73	36%
5-9 years	97	48%
10 -15 years	26	13%
more than 15 years	5	2%
Unanswered	2	1%
Total	**203**	**100%**

Table 3. Education-levels distribution of the sample

Education	Count	Percentage
B.Sc.	16	8%
High Diploma	9	4%
Masters	157	77%
PhD	18	9%
Unanswered	3	1%
Total	**203**	**100%**

Table 4. Specialty distribution of the sample.

Specialty	Count	Percentage
CIS	75	37%
MIS	58	29%
Business	22	11%
Banking	11	5%
Others	33	16%
Unanswered	4	2%
Total	**203**	**100%**

Table 5. Gender distribution of the sample

Gender	Count	Percentage
Male	151	75%
Female	51	25%
Total	**202**	**100%**

THE COMPREHENSION OF THE TRUSTED SOURCE OF KNOWLEDGE

The trust as a factor in knowledge sharing a transfer is an essential one. The trust factor affects the source of knowledge as well as the recipient in trusting the knowledge. In both cases the knowledge source when divulging the knowledge that s/he owns believes that her/his leverage stems from the tacit knowledge that s/he owns. Once this knowledge is accessed by others the organizations may relinquish her/his services. On the other hand the recipient party must trust the source of the knowledge else s/he will not use the knowledge.

In the next section, the research studies how the Jordanian employee view sources of knowledge and what channel of knowledge is most trusted to the worker. Some of the results were as predicted yet some came as surprise

The Trust Issue

In regards to the trust issue the sample was asked to rank the sources of information in work environment in Table 7 from 1 (the most trusted) to 8 (the least trusted). The results as shown in Figure 4 were as expected.

Documents were ranked as number 1 since 111 out of 203 choose *documents* as number 1 source. Followed by *family* as number 1 (22 out of 203), and rank *family* as number 2 with (42 out of 203) while *boss* ranked number 2 with (53 out of 203). Another interesting result friend was ranked as level 6 of trust (43 out of 203). *Distant family* was ranked the least trusted source of information with (89 out of 203).

The answers were proper and expected, yet do workers practice what they preach. The following section of the questionnaire results will show that

Table 6. Working sector distribution of the sample

Working Sector	Count	Percentage
Public	71	35%
Private	114	56%
International	11	5%
Unanswered	7	3%
Total	**203**	**100%**

Table 7. Levels of trust vs. sources of information

Source of information / Level of trust	Documents	Family	Distant Family	Friend	Colleagues	Assistant	Boss	Internet
1	**111**	42	1	9	4	4	24	19
2	22	34	9	27	16	12	**53**	38
3	20	19	14	32	29	**42**	34	24
4	9	15	17	23	**54**	40	23	18
5	17	15	15	25	35	**38**	17	31
6	6	25	12	**43**	31	35	13	14
7	8	**37**	34	25	18	16	18	21
8	3	7	**89**	8	5	4	11	27
Unanswered	7	9	12	11	11	12	10	11

although workers believe in documentation yet they do not practice this approach.

The Worker View of Knowledge Channels in the Learning Organization

In this section the researcher lays the results of the first section of the questions. The goal of this section of the question is to investigate the worker view of the knowledge channels. In other words the major goal is to find out if the worker practices what they preach.

1. If you have a question regarding your social security who do ask?

This question is essential in every worker's life; it is their financial security of the future the results are shown in Figure 5. When asked the question 36% of the sample answer they will consult *Documents*. 18% said they will consult the *Boss*. 12% said they will ask a *colleague*. While 9% (respectively) will ask *friend* or the *internet*. Which really brings the question how come a *boss*, *friend*, *colleague* will know about the rules and regulations of the social security?

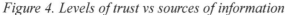

Figure 4. Levels of trust vs sources of information

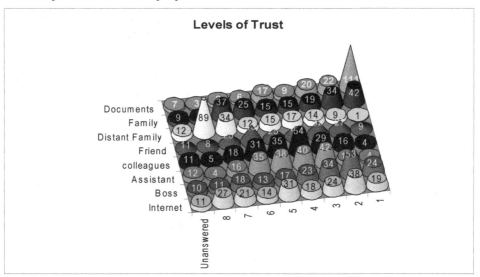

Figure 5. Social security question

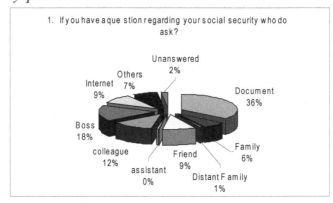

2. If you have a question regarding taxes discounted from your salary, who do you ask?

Paying taxes is also an essential part of every worker. Usually in Jordan it is discounted from salary automatically. When asking the question regarding taxes discounted from a worker's salary and who does s/he asks 34% answered *documents*, yet a large percentage 20% answered *Boss*. Another interesting result 13% will ask a *colleague* and 10% will turn to the *internet*. The results are best reflected in Figure 6.

Notice both question 1 and 2 reflect almost same result both initially answered documents yet the answer of Boss collect 18% and 20% respectively. Having in mind the sample of the workers are educated people mainly master students as seen in Table 3.in the demography analysis in the previous section

3. If you have a question regarding work procedures (same organization-same department) who do you ask?

When asked who do ask regarding work procedure inside the department 55% said they will ask the *Boss* and 23% will ask *colleague* while only 14% will consult *documentation*, see Figure 7. Which is exactly the opposite of the trust issue question where 111 out of 203 (almost 55%) said they trust documents, seen the previous section.

4. If you have a question regarding work procedures (same organization-different department) who do you ask?

Figure 6. Taxes question

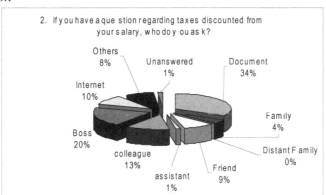

Figure 7. Work procedure (same organization-same department)

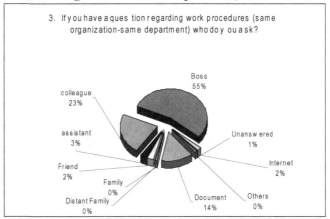

The fourth question was if you have a question about work procedure in the same organization but different department. The answers reflected similar results as question 3. 39% will ask the *boss* 23% will ask *colleague* only 12% said that they will consult *documents*. The interesting answer was that 12% will ask a friend as seen in Figure 8.

5.   If you have a question regarding work procedures (outside the organization-concerning work) who do you ask?

When asked if you have a question regarding work procedure that is outside the organization but concerns work. Amazing answers resulted in Figure 9. 31% will consult the *Boss* and 23%

will consult a *colleague* 12% will consult *internet* 12% will consult a *friend* only 10% will consult *documents*. Therefore *documents* ranked 5th place after the *boss, colleague, internet* and *friend*.

This question completely disagrees in results with the following question (question # 6). Where almost 74% claimed they will do the proper thing.

6.   If you go to an organization (you don't know anyone in it)- who do you ask to get to the right office?

Question 6 was a trick question to see if a worker will follow the right procedure when conducting business in an organization that s/he knows nobody in. The Figure 10 shows the results

Figure 8. Work procedure (same organization- different department)

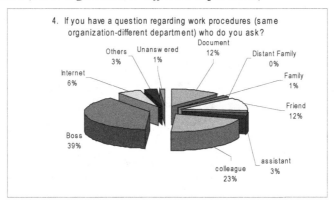

Figure 9. Work procedure (outside org-concerning work)

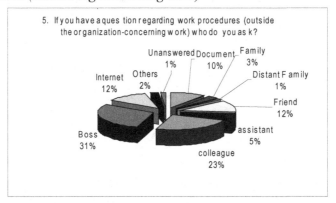

of the answer. The answers reflect that a worker will seek the reception office to give her/him directions regarding finding unknown office. Still 6% answered the will seek the help of a colleague and 9% will seek the help of a friend. A small percentage 2% will consult a document.

7.   If you need a legal consultation concerning work who do you ask?

Question 7 is regarding legal consultation concerning work. Many answer the will consult a *lawyer* 57% (see Figure 11) still 15% will ask the *boss* and 9% will consult *documents*. The interest answers that 7% and 6% will ask *colleague* and *friend* respectively. In this regards *documents*

ranked 3[ed] place. This total change in the next question where they lawyer get 0%.

8.   If you get into dispute with a colleague, who do you seek?

This question was designed to reflect and complement question 7. The question asks if a works has a dispute with a colleague who s/he turns to. The *boss* got 40% while *colleague* 24% a *friend* got 19% while the *lawyer* got 0%. The interesting fact here that document received only 3% after boss, colleague, friend, others and family to be ranked 6th place

Figure 10. Reception question

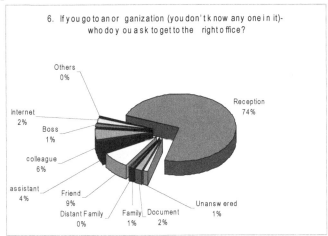

Figure 11. Lawyer question

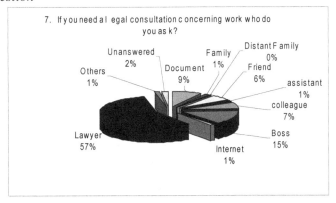

Figure 12. Disputes question

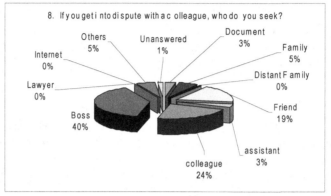

THE ORGANIZATION ROLE IN PROVIDING THE RIGHT ENVIRONMENT OF KNOWLEDGE SHARING

This section reflects how the organization by providing the right environment that will encourage knowledge sharing. For the organization to foster the proper channels, the organization must know that "it takes two to tango". In other words the organization must take the initiative to set the proper channels.

9. When you were appointed, were you given formal documented instruction regarding work procedures?

This question measures if the organization started the worker on the right path. Did the worker

receive any documentation that describes for her/him the work procedure. Astonishingly 34% answered negatively as seen in Figure 13.

10. When you were appointed, did you get "New employee workshop"

The second question asks if the worker was given the proper training before starting the job. As seen in Figure 14 from the sample 52% answered negative to such a question.

11. Were you given a job description to your job?

When asking if the worker did get a job description 38% said no, as seen in Figure 15. When a worker does not know the job description how

Figure 13. Organization gives formal documented instruction regarding work procedures.

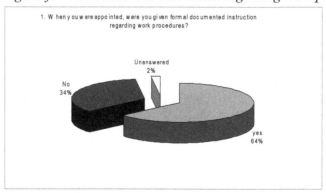

Figure 14. did you get "New employee workshop"

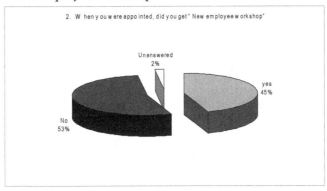

would the worker carry out the job? Fernandez (2004) places "people" at the beginning of the chain that affects "Organizational performance". Surely, if the worker does not know what to do the performance is bound to suffer. Therefore, the organization in this sample are not doing step 1 which informing the worker of the most essential part of the job which is "job description"

12. If you want to suggest an improvement for work procedures, to whom do you submit the suggestion?

This question really reflects how much we trust the proper channels. If a worker has a suggestion s/he will submit to the *Boss* (72%) as seen in Figure 16. On the other hand only 13% would

Figure 15. Were you given a job description to your job?

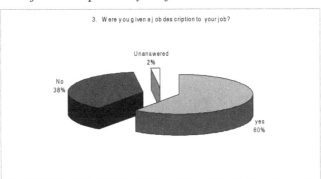

Figure 16. To whom do you submit suggestions?

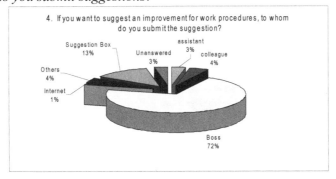

put the suggestion in the *suggestion box* which the more proper channel than the *boss*.

13. When you hear about new legislation regarding your job, who informs you?

When a new legislation, rules, regulation is pertaining to the worker's job is passed 36% said the *boss* will inform them while the documented source (*newspaper*) only got 25%. The interesting answer was that *colleagues* got 15% as seen in Figure 17.

14. Do you follow the news about your organization in the official news papers & TV?

When asking do follow *up* about your organization in news paper or TV 33% answer negative, which only reflect the cordiality of answers in the previous question see Figure 18.

15. From whom do get the latest news about your organization?

When asking regarding how the worker gets the latest news about the organization 31% said the boss, while 22% said colleagues 16 % answered documents while 8% answered Internet as seen in Figure 19. The interesting part here is that documents ranked 3ed and that 5% relied on rumors which ranked 5th.

16. To whom do you refer to in your work?

In the daily work who do refer to? 44% answered the *Boss* while 23% answered *colleagues* the *documents* ranked 3ed with 15%. The interesting answers here are 4% relied on *assistants*, 4% relied on a *friend* and 3% relied on the *internet* see Figure 20.

Figure 17. When you hear about new legislation regarding your job, who informs you?

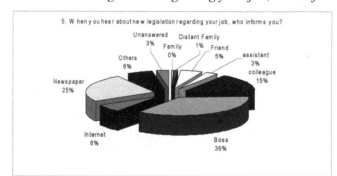

Figure 18. Do you follow the news about your organization in the official news papers & TV?

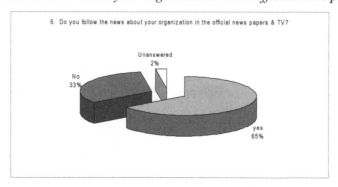

Figure 19. From whom do you get the latest news about your organization?

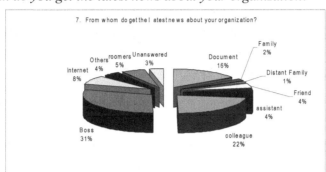

17. How did you know about your current job?

The question was to measure where workers got the current job. As seen in Figure 21 newspapers which a form of document measured 25% while friend is 23% of the answers along with family 14% and "wasta" 13%. Colleagues and internet were 10% and 8% respectively. In other words to hear about a job newspaper and internet only represented 33% almost the third of the answers.

18. From where do you learn regarding promotion?

Figure 20. To whom do you refer to at your work?

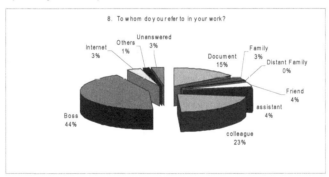

Figure 21. How did you know about your current job?

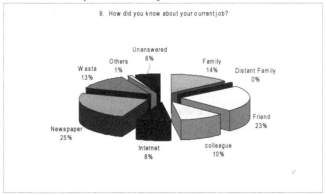

This question should reflect how aware is the worker about how to climb the career ladder, again documents failed and word of mouth and other channels prevailed as seen in Figure 22. The organization is not transparent and does not tell the worker how to get promoted.

19. Who taught you, how to write your first vacation request?

Basic operations like make a request for vacation time and how to get the first salary is not cleared in the organization. Mainly workers relied on the boss or colleague for that as seen in Figure 23 and Figure 24. While documents got only 12% in the first, it got 9% in the second.

20. Who taught you how to get your first salary?

This question is really reflect the previous question but also is an indicator that the organization is not setting standards and procedure and precedence for the worker that such organization is an organization plays by the rules. When 38% of the sample answers that a colleague is telling them how to get (see Figure 24) paid then the organization is really sending a hint to the worker indicating that there are no procedures to neither follow nor rule.

RESULTS AND FINDINGS

The worker trust the documents the most yet when working the worker really relies on the word of mouth more (boss, colleague etc). Therefore the document is not a primary source of information/knowledge in these organizations. As a matter of fact this reminds the research of the

Figure 22. From where do you learn regarding promotion?

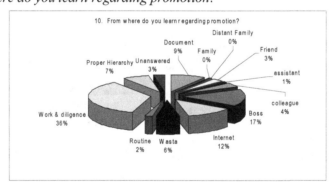

Figure 23. Who taught you, how to write your first vacation request?

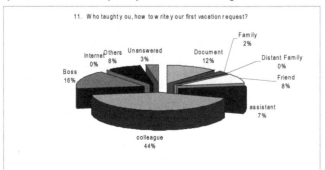

Figure 24. Who taught you how to get your first salary?

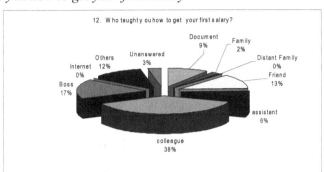

taxonomy of (Fernandez et al., 2004) knowledge application two parts: Direction and Routines. Obviously the Jordanian worker in the sample prefers Direction rather than routines. "Direction refers to the process through which individuals possessing knowledge directs the action of another individual without transferring to that person the knowledge underlying the direction "(Fernandez et al., 2004). On the other hand "routines involve the utilization of knowledge embedded in the procedures, rules, and norms that guide future behavior" "(Fernandez et al., 2004).

The organization does not set the path for knowledge sharing not does set precedence for the worker to follow rules and regulation in documented manner. From the previous there is a raising interest and affect for the internet in setting things in the right direction.

THE PROPOSED MODEL OF KNOWLEDGE SHARING

As seen in the graph (Figure 25) the worker learning which is really the organization learning is affected the most by Boss, colleague, assistant, document and internet which are in the macro

Figure 25. Proposed model

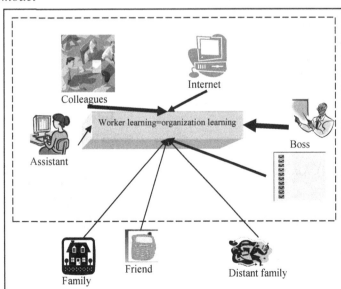

environment of the organization (organization can control these factors). On the other hand family, friends, distant family are factors in the macro environment. Therefore the organization does not and cannot control those factors.

The author suggests using the internet/intranet technology to affect the micro environment by influencing the boss, colleague and assistant, and documenting everything on the intranet.

As seen, in Figure 25, the thickness of the arrow represent the amount of affect of the boss, assistant, colleague etc on the learning worker. For example the arrow extended from the Boss to the worker has the most thickness which means that the boss has the most affect on the worker. While assistant, family, friend, distant family all have less affect therefore the arrows extended are thinner. While colleague has more affect than internet which also represented in the thickness of the arrows.

FUTURE RESEARCH

Due to lack of time and fund this research stopped on the edge of the results. Yet many aspects can be studied from the sample collected. First the affect of the gender factor on the answers of the sample. Second the affect of types of sector (public, private, international) and the affect of such factor on the answers. Another aspect that can be researched is the affect of years of experience on the answers of the sample.

REFERENCES

Elias, A. G. M. (2004). *Knowledge management*. Prentice-Hall, Inc.

Fernandez, I., Gonzalez, A., & Sabherwal, R. (2004). *Knowledge Management, solutions, technology*. Prentice-Hall, Inc.

Luftman, J. (2004). *Managing the Information Technology Resource*. Pearson.

McBride, J., McNurlin, A., & Sprague, R. (2005). *Information Systems Management In Practice*. 6th Edition, Prentice-Hall.

Turban, E., & Aronson, J. (2001). *Decision Support Systems and Intelligent Systems*. 6th edition, Prentice Hall, Upper Saddle River, NJ.

Turban, E., Aronson, J., & Liang, T. (2005). *Decision Support Systems And intelligent Systems* Seventh Edition. Prentice Hall.

KEY TERMS

Combination: Is a process of assembling new and existing explicit knowledge into a systemic knowledge.

Double-Loop Learning: *In double-loop learning*, the entities (individuals, groups or organization) question the values, assumptions and policies that led to the actions in the first place; if they are able to view and modify those, then second-order or double-loop learning has taken place."

Explicit Knowledge: On the other hand, is transmittable in formal and systematic language.

Externalization: Is a process of articulating tacit knowledge into such explicit knowledge.

Internalization: Is a process of embodying explicit knowledge into tacit, operational knowledge such as know-how.

Single-Loop Learning: "In *single-loop learning*, individuals, groups, or organizations modify their actions according to the difference between expected and obtained outcomes.

Tacit Knowledge: is personal, context-specific, and therefore hard to formalize and communicate.

ENDNOTES

[1]   http://www.sfb504.uni-mannheim.de/glossary/orglearn.htm

[2]   March, J.G. & Olsen, J.P. (1975): The Uncertainty of the Past: Organizational Learning under Ambiguity. *European Journal of Political Research*, 3, 147-171.

[3]   Argyris, C. & Schön, D. (1978): *Organizational Learning*. Reading, MA: Addison-Wesley.

[4]   http://en.wikipedia.org/wiki/The_Fifth_Discipline

[5]   Kim, D.H. 1993 'The link between individual and organizational learning'. Sloan Management Review 35/1: 37-50.

[6]   http://www.compilerpress.atfreeweb.com/Anno%20Polanyi%20Structure%20of%20Consciousness%20Brain%201965.htm

[7]   Knowledge Has to Do with Truth, Goodness, and Beauty, Conversation with Professor Ikujiro Nonaka Tokyo, Japan February 23, 1996 Claus Otto Scharmer, (http://www.dialogonleadership.org/Nonaka-1996.html#three)

[8]   http://en.wikipedia.org/wiki/

[9]   http://en.wikipedia.org/wiki/

Chapter XIV
Performance Optimization of DWT–Based Image Watermarking Using Genetic Algorithms

Ali Al-Haj
Princess Sumaya University for Technology, Jordan

Aymen Abu-Errub
The Arab Academy for Financial and Banking Sciences, Jordan

ABSTRACT

The excellent spatial localization, frequency spread, and multi-resolution characteristics of the discrete wavelets transform (DWT), which are similar to the theoretical models of the human visual system, facilitated the development of many imperceptible and robust DWT-based watermarking algorithms. However, there has been extremely few proposed algorithms on optimized DWT-based image watermarking that can simultaneously provide perceptual transparency and robustness Since these two watermarking requirements are conflicting, in this paper we treat the DWT-based image watermarking problem as an optimization problem, and solve it using genetic algorithms. We demonstrate through the experimental results we obtained that optimal DWT-based image watermarking can be achieved only if watermarking has been applied at specific wavelet sub-bands and by using specific watermark-amplification values.

INTRODUCTION

The widespread of the Internet and the continuous advancements in computer technology have facilitated the unauthorized manipulation and reproduction of original digital multimedia products. The audio-visual industry has been the main victim of such illegal reproduction, and consequently, the design and development of effective digital multimedia copyright protection methods have become necessary more than ever. Encryption and authentication have always been the traditional methods of providing multimedia security (Furht & Kirovski, 2006), however, they fell short in providing the required copyright protection. Instead, digital watermarking technology has been recently advocated as the best solution to the multimedia copyright protection problem (Cox et al., 2002; Langelaar et al., 2000; Katzenbeisser & Petitcolas, 2000; Potdar et al., 2005). Its expected that digital watermarking will have a wide-span of practical applications in digital cameras, digital libraries, medical imaging, image databases, surveillance imaging, and video-on-demand systems, among many others (Arnold et al., 2003).

The watermark itself is usually a random number sequence, a copyright message, an ownership identifier, or a control signal carrying ownership information. In order for a digital watermark to be effective, it should be robust to common image manipulations like compression, filtering, rotation, scaling cropping, collusion attacks, among many other digital signal processing operations. The watermark should also be imperceptible, which means that the addition of the watermark should not degrade the perceptual quality of the host image. In general, it is not difficult to achieve imperceptibility. Indeed, its robustness that is usually the kernel that decides the success of watermarking algorithms.

Current digital image watermarking techniques can be grouped into two major classes: spatial-domain watermarking techniques and watermarking frequency-domain techniques (Cox et al., 2002). Spatial-domain techniques embed a watermarks in a host image by directly modifying its pixels (Sebe et al, 2000; Chan & Cheng, 2004) . These techniques are easy to implement and reacquire few computational resources, however, they are sensitive to alternations and are not robust against common digital signal processing operations such compression. On the other hand, transform-domain watermarking techniques modify the coefficients of the transformed image according to a predetermined embedding scheme. The scheme disperses the watermark in the spatial domain of the image, hence making it very difficult to remove the embedded watermark. Compared to spatial domain techniques, frequency-domain watermarking techniques proved to be more effective with respect to achieving the imperceptibility and robustness requirements of digital watermarking algorithms (Cox et al., 2002). Commonly used frequency-domain transforms include the DWT: Discrete Wavelet Transform (Mallat, 1989), the DCT: Discrete Cosine Transform (Rao & Yip, 1990), and the DFT: Discrete Fourier Transform (Mitra, 1998).

DWT has been used in digital watermarking more frequently than other transforms. This is due to its excellent spatial localization, frequency spread, and multi-resolution characteristics, which are similar to the theoretical models of the human visual system (Vetterli & Kovačević, 1995). By virtue of these properties, an efficient relationship between the transform and coefficients and visual masking properties of the human visual system has been constructed (Wolfang et al., 1999). Effective utilization of this relationship facilitated the development of many imperceptible and robust DWT-based watermarking algorithms. Although there has been an active research on the application of the discrete wavelets transform (DWT) in image watermarking systems by virtue of its attractive features mentioned before, as afore mentioned, there has been also extremely little literature on optimized DWT-based image watermarking that can simultaneously provide perceptual transparency and robustness . Since these two requirements are conflicting, we applied genetic algorithms (GA) in order to reach the optimal performance .

The rest of the paper is organized as follows. In section 2, we give a brief review on the current status of DWT-based watermarking research. In section 3, we describe our DWT-based image watermarking algorithm, including the watermarking embedding and watermark extraction procedures. In sections 4, we define the genetic parameters for optimizing the proposed DWT-based algorithm. In section 5, we describe execution of the GA-based optimization process. Performance of the proposed algorithm is evaluated in section 6, and concluding remarks are given in section 7.

2. DWT-BASED WATERMARKING RESEARCH

Wavelets are special functions which, in a form analogous to sines and cosines in Fourier analysis, are used as basal functions for representing signals (Strang & Nguyen, 1996). For 2-D images, applying DWT corresponds to processing the image by 2-D filters in each dimension. The filters divide the input image into four non-overlapping multi-resolution sub-bands LL_1, LH_1, HL_1, and HH_1. The LL_1 sub-band represents the coarse-scale DWT coefficients while the LH_1, HL_1, and HH_1 sub-bands represent the fine-scale DWT coefficients. To obtain the next coarser scale of wavelet coefficients, the LL_1 sub-band is further processed until some final scale N is reached. When N is reached, we will have $3N+1$ sub-bands

Figure 1. Three-level DWT decomposition.

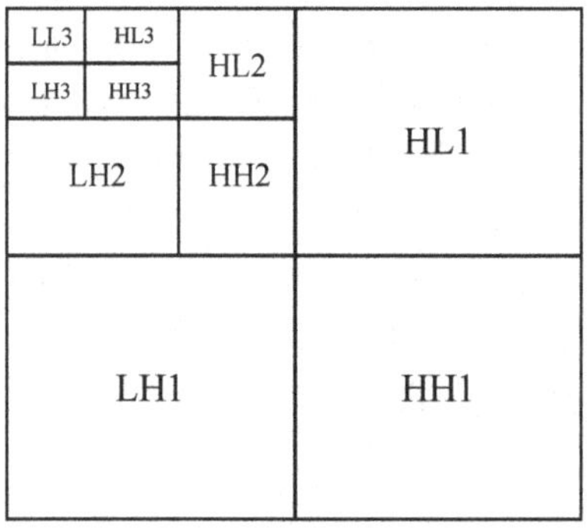

LL3	HL3	HL2	HL1
LH3	HH3		
LH2		HH2	
LH1		HH1	

consisting of the multi-resolution sub-bands LL_N and LH_x, HL_x and HH_x where x ranges from 1 until N. Figure 1 shows the wavelet decomposition when the scale N equals to 3.

Due to its excellent spatial-frequency localization properties, the DWT is very suitable to identify areas in the host image where a watermark can be embedded effectively. In particular, this property allows the exploitation of the masking effect of the human visual system such that if a DWT coefficient is modified, only the region corresponding to that coefficient will be modified. In general, most of the image energy is concentrated at the lower frequency sub-bands LL_x, and therefore embedding watermarks in these sub-bands may degrade the image significantly. Embedding in the low frequency sub-bands, however, could increase robustness significantly. On the other hand, the high frequency sub-bands HH_x include the edges and textures of the image, for which the human eye is not generally sensitive to changes in such sub-bands. This allows the watermark to be embedded without being perceived by the human eye. The compromise adopted by many DWT-based watermarking algorithm, is to embed the watermark in the middle frequency sub-bands LH_x and HL_x where acceptable performance of imperceptibility and robustness could be, at least theoretically, achieved.

Active research based on the aforementioned reasoning has been done (Wang et al., 2002; Reddy & Chatterji, 2005; Tay & Havlicek, 2002; Huang & Yang, 2004; Guzman et al., 2004; Jung et al., 2003; Guo & Georganas, 2002; Safabakhsh et al., 2004; Niu et al., 2000; Hsu and Wu, 1998). However, there has been also extremely little literature on optimized DWT-based image watermarking that can simultaneously provide perceptual transparency and robustness (Kumswat, et al., 2005; Huwang & Wu, 2000; Shieh, et al., 2004).

3. THE PROPOSED DWT-BASED WATERMARKING ALGORITHM

We describe in this section our proposed DWT-based watermarking algorithm. The algorithm consists of two procedures; watermark embedding and watermark extraction procedures.

3.1 Watermark Embedding Procedure

The watermark embedding procedure is depicted in Figure 2, and described in details in the following steps.

- **Step 1.** Apply DWT to the original host image repeatedly up to the third level. This operation produces 64 non-overlapping multi-resolution sub-bands

- **Step 2.** Select one sub-band for embedding the watermark.

- **Step 3.** Re-formulate the grey-scale watermark image into a vector of zeros and ones.

- **Step 4.** Generate a uniformly distributed, highly uncorrelated, zero-mean, two-dimensional pseudorandom sequence (*PN*)

using a secret seed value. The *PN* sequence is used to embed the zero watermark bit in the host image.

- **Step 5.** Embed the pseudorandom sequence *PN* in the selected DWT sub-band with a gain factor *α*. Number of elements in the selected sub-band and the pseudorandom sequence *PN* must be equal for embedding to take place. If we donate *X* as coefficients matrix of the selected sub-band, then embedding is done according to Equations 1 and 2:

If the watermark bit is *0* then

$$X' = X + \alpha * PN \qquad (1)$$

otherwise,
if the watermark bit is *1* then,

$$X' = X \qquad (2)$$

- **Step 6.** Apply the inverse DWT (IDWT) on the DWT transformed image, including the modified sub-band, to produce the watermarked host image.

Figure 2. DWT-based watermark embedding procedure

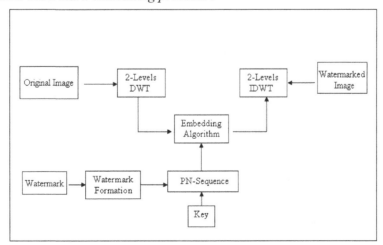

Figure 3. DWT-based watermark extraction procedure

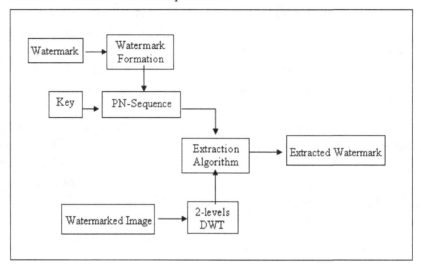

3.2 Watermark Extraction Procedure

The watermark extraction procedure is depicted in Figure 3, and described in details in the following steps. Since the proposed DWT-based algorithm is a blind watermarking algorithm, the original host image is not required in the watermark extraction procedure.

- **Step 1.** Apply DWT to the watermarked image repeatedly up to the third level. This operation produces 64 non-overlapping multi-resolution sub-bands.
- **Step 2.** Select the sub-band into which the watermark was embedded.
- **Step 3.** Regenerate the pseudorandom sequence (PN sequence) using the same seed used in the watermark embedding procedure described before.
- **Step 4.** Calculate the correlation between the watermarked sub-band and the generated pseudorandom sequence (PN sequence). This step is repeated m times, where m is number of bit elements in the watermark vector.

- **Step 5.** Compare each correlation value with the mean correlation value. If the calculated value is greater than the mean, then the extracted watermark bit will be taken as a 0, otherwise its taken as a 1. A mean correlation value of 0.75 is used.
- **Step 6.** Reconstruct the watermark image using the extracted watermark bits, and compute the similarity between the original and extracted watermarks.

4. OPTIMIZATION PROBLEM FORMULATION

Genetic algorithms (GAs) are adaptive heuristic search algorithms that were developed based on the evolutionary ideas of natural selection and genetics.They have been widely used in real-world applications to find optimal parameters which were difficult to find using traditional optimization methods. Applying GAs to watermarking has been based on the fact that effective watermarking has two conflicting requirements; perceptual transparency and robustness. These two requirements are related to each other, and therefore the watermarking algorithm described in the previous section must be optimized. In this section we define the optimization search space and the relevant GA operators.

4.1. Search Space

The appropriate DWT sub-band and the value of the watermark amplification factor are the two key elements that, if chosen properly, will result in optimal simultaneous imperceptible and robust watermarking. It's the role of the GA to find such elements, where the GA's search space is all possible combinations of the DWT sub-bands and watermark amplification factor. The two elements are described as follows.

DWT Sub-band. The discrete wavelet transform decomposes the host image into four sub-bands of different resolutions. Decomposition can be done at different DWT levels; 1st, 2nd 3rd, 4th and higher, however, in this paper we decided to decompose up to the 3rd DWT level and apply genetic algorithms to find the optimal sub-band from a total number of 64 sub-bands produced as follows. The 1st level produces 4 sub-bands, the 2nd level takes each sub-band of the 1st level

and decomposes it further into four sub-bands. This results in 16 sub-bands. Similarly, the 3rd DWT-level decomposes each 2nd level sub-band into 4 sub-bands, giving a total of 64 sub-bands, as shown in Figure 4. The genetic algorithm procedure will attempt to find the specific sub-band that will provide simultaneous perceptual transparency and robustness.

Watermark Amplification Factor α. The value of watermark amplification factor, α, should be used in a way to provide balanced imperceptibility and robustness. Since these requirements are conflicting, then the value of α should be an optimization parameter to be determined using genetic algorithms. The value of α can be varied depending as different sub-bands may require different values of α.

4.2 GA Operators

The GA is an iterative procedure that achieves optimization in a give search space using three operators and a fitness function. It starts with some randomly selected population made of individuals, each corresponding to a solution to the problem. The fitness function is used to evaluate the quality of each solution so that individuals with

Figure 4. Sixty-four non-overlapping, multi-resolution sub-bands

0 A1A2A3	1 A1A2H3	2 A1H2A3	3 A1H2H3	4 H1A2A3	5 H1A2H3	6 H1H2A3	7 H1H2H3
8 A1A2V3	9 A1A2D3	10 A1H2V3	11 A1H2D3	12 H1A2V3	13 H1A2D3	14 H1H2V3	15 H1H2D3
16 A1V2A3	17 A1V2H3	18 A1D2A3	19 A1D2H3	20 H1V2A3	21 H1V2H3	22 H1D2A3	23 H1D2H3
24 A1V2V3	25 A1V2D3	26 A1D2V3	27 A1D2D3	28 H1V2V3	29 H1V2D3	30 H1D2V3	31 H1D2D3
32 V1A2A3	33 V1A2H3	34 V1H2A3	35 V1H2H3	36 D1A2A3	37 D1A2H3	38 D1H2A3	39 D1H2H3
40 V1A2V3	41 V1A2D3	42 V1H2V3	43 V1H2D3	44 D1A2V3	45 D1A2D3	46 D1H2V3	47 D1H2D3
48 V1V2A3	49 V1V2H3	50 V1D2A3	51 V1D2H3	52 D1V2A3	53 D1V2H3	54 D1D2A3	55 D1D2H3
56 V1V2V3	57 V1V2D3	58 V1D2V3	59 V1D2D3	60 D1V2V3	61 D1V2D3	62 D1D2V3	63 D1D2D3

high quality will survive and form a population for the next generation. GA recombines a new generation to the find the best optimal solution using three operators: reproduction, crossover, and mutation. The GA procedure is repeated until a predefined number of iterations is reached. The fitness function and the three genetic operators are described as follows.

The Fitness Function. Two common performance evaluation metrics are combined to form the fitness function; the peak signal to noise ratio (PSNR) and the correlation factor ρ. The fitness function is formed by combining the two metrics as given is Equation 3. The correlation value has been multiplied by 100 since its normal values fall in the range 0 ~ 1, whereas PSNR values may reach the value of 100.

$$\text{Fitness Function} = \text{PSN}R + 100 * \rho \qquad (3)$$

Where PSNR in decibels (dB) is represented as shown in Equation:

$$PSNR_{dB} = 10 \cdot \log_{10}\left(\frac{MAX^2{}_I}{MSE}\right) = 20 \cdot \log_{10}\left(\frac{MAX_I}{\sqrt{MSE}}\right) \qquad (4)$$

where *MSE* is the mean square error between the original image and the watermarked image, and MAX_I is the maximum pixel value of the image which is equal to 255 in our implementations since pixels were represented using 8 bits per sample. The correlation factor ρ measures the similarity between the original watermark and the watermark extracted from the attacked watermarked image (robustness). The correlation factor ρ is computed using Equation 5:

$$\rho(w, \hat{w}) = \frac{\sum_{i=1}^{N} w_i \hat{w}_i}{\sqrt{\sum_{i=1}^{N} w_i^2} \sqrt{\sum_{i=1}^{N} \hat{w}_i^2}} \qquad (5)$$

where N is the number of pixels in watermark, w and $w^\wedge$ are the original and extracted water-

marks respectively. The correlation factor ρ may take values between 0 (random relationship) to 1 (perfect linear relationship).

Reproduction. Individuals with low fitness values are discarded through this genetic operator. The discarded individuals will be replaced by new offsprings after executing the crossover and mutation genetic operators.

Crossover. This operator is responsible for producing better offsprings by inheriting high-quality genes from their parents (Goldberg, 1989). In this paper we used a crossover rate of 0.6.

Mutation. Refers to the occasional random alteration of the value in some positions of some chromosomes (Goldberg, 1989). The mutation is usually selected with a probability between 0 and 1, so that only a small portion of the genes in the chromosomes will be selected to be muted. We selected the mutation rate to be 0.05.

5. GA-BASED OPTIMIZATION PROCEDURE

The GA-Training operates on the optimization problem formulated in the previous section. Two optimization parameters were described; the DWT sub-band and the optimal watermarking amplification factor α. The standard GA-based optimization procedure is depicted in Figure 5 and described as follows

- **Step 1.** Initialize the GA-training parameters:
  - Select a value for α between 0 and 1.
  - Define initial population size, crossover rate, mutation rate, number of iterations.
- **Step 2.** Generate the first generation of GA individuals based on the parameters specified by performing the watermark embedding procedure described in sub-section 3.1. A different watermarked image is generated for each individual.

Figure 5. GA-based optimization procedure

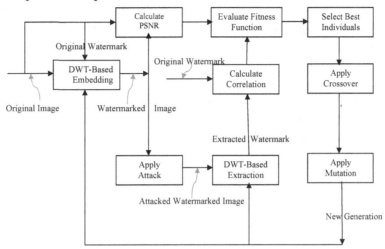

- **Step 3.** Evaluate the perceptual transparency of each watermarked image by computing the corresponding PSNR value, using Equation 4.

- **Step 4.** Apply a common attack on the watermarked image. Common attacks include Gaussian noise, image compression and image cropping. The three attacks are a few, however, they are good representatives of the more general attacks.

- **Step 5.** Perform the watermark extraction procedure described in sub-section 3.2 on each attacked watermark image.

- **Step 6.** Evaluate robustness by computing the correlation between the original and extracted watermarks, according to Equation 5.

- **Step 7.** Evaluate the fitness function for the PSNR and ρ values using Equation 3.

- **Step 8.** Select the individuals with the best fitness values.

- **Step 9.** Generate new population by performing the crossover and mutation functions on the selected individuals.

- **Step 10.** Repeat steps (2-9) until a predefined iteration count has been reached.

- **Step 11.** According the obtained results, select the optimal level of decomposition,

the optimal sub-band and optimal value of α.

6. EXPERIMENTAL RESULTS AND PERFORMANCE EVALUATION

We evaluated the performance of the optimized DWT-based algorithm using a 512 x 512 'Lena' as the original host image, and a 256 x 256 grey-scale image of the expression '**Copyright**' as the

Figure 6. The 'Lina' host image

Figure 7. Original watermark

Copyright

watermark image. The two images are shown in Figures 6 and 7, respectively.

We executed the GA-based training procedure described in the previous function using 14 individuals (chromosomes), crossover rate of 0.6, a mutation rate of 0.05, and a pre-set maximum iteration number of 1000. The GA procedure was repeated for three attacks that have been commonly used to benchmark watermarking algorithms; JPEG compression and Gaussian noise addition, which are classified as watermark removal and

degrading attacks, and image rotation, which is classified as a geometrical attack. The results are described in the following paragraphs.

Image Compression

The watermarked image was compressed with different quality factors. As shown in Figure 8, the result of the GA optimization for a JPEG quality factor of 50 % indicates that the fitness function was maximum (141.3629) for the D1H2A3 sub-

Figure 8. GA-based optimization procedure under the image JPEG attack

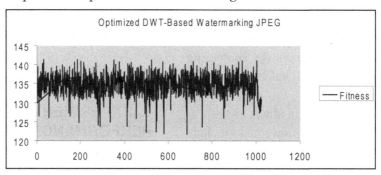

Figure 9. (a) Watermarked image, and (b) extracted watermark from the image

(a).   (b)

Figure 10. GA-based optimization procedure under the image rotation attack

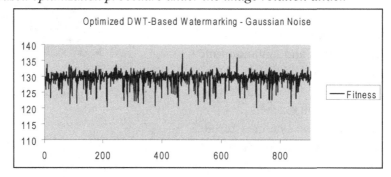

band, with a watermark amplification value α of 0.1739. This result was obtained at the 185th iteration of the GA optimization process.

The watermarked image and extracted watermark for the optimal D1H2A3 sub-band are shown in Figure 9.

Gaussian Noise

A Gaussian noise was added to the watermarked image. As shown in Figure 10, the result of the

GA optimization indicates that the fitness function was maximum (137.1884) for the V1A2H3 sub-band, with a watermark amplification value α of 0.1162. This result was obtained at the 147th iteration of the GA optimization process.

The watermarked image and extracted watermark for the optimal V1A2H3 sub-band are shown in Figure 11.

Image Rotation

The watermarked image was rotated with different angles. As shown in Figure 12, the result of the

Figure 11. (a) Watermarked image and (b) extracted watermark from the image

(a).   (b)

Figure 12. GA-based optimization procedure under the image rotation attack

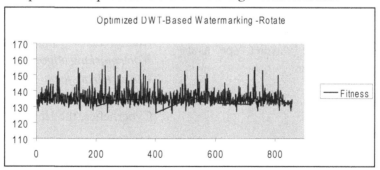

Figure 13. (a) Watermarked image and (b) extracted watermark from the image.

(a).   (b)

GA optimization process indicates that the fitness function was maximum (157.95) for the V1H2H3 sub-band, with a watermark amplification value *α* of 0.2257. This result was obtained at the 350th iteration of the GA optimization process.

The watermarked image and extracted watermark for the optimal D1H2A3 sub-band are shown in Figure 13.

7. CONCLUSION

Digital image watermarking algorithms based on the discrete wavelet transform (DWT) have been widely recognized to be more prevalent than the others. This is due to the wavelets' excellent spatial localization, frequency spread, and multi-resolution characteristics, which are similar to the theoretical models of the human visual system. However, improvement in their performance can still be obtained by viewing the DWT-based image watermarking problem as an optimization problem. In this paper we applied genetic algorithms to locate the optimal DWT sub-band and the corresponding watermark amplification factor that will lead to maximum imperceptible and robustness. Ongoing and future research is concentrating on enlarging the GA-based the search space by adding the 'wavelet type' as a vital optimization parameter.

REFERENCES

Arnold, M., Schumucker, M., & Wolthusen, S. (2003). *Techniques and Applications of Digital Watermarking and Content Protection*. Boston, MA: Artech House.

Chan, C., & Cheng, L. (2004). Hiding Data in Images by Simple LSB Substitution. *Pattern Recognition, 37*(3), 469-474.

Cox, I., Miller, M., & Bloom, J. (2002). *Digital Watermarking*. CA, USA: Academic Press.

Furht, B., & Kirovski, D. (2006). *Encryption and Authentications: Techniques and Applications*. USA: Auerbach Publications.

Goldberg, D. (1989). *Genetic Algorithms in Search, Optimization, and Machine Learning*. USA: Addison-Wseley Professional.

Guo, H., & Georganas, N. (2002). *Multi-resolution Image Watermarking Scheme in the Spectrum Domain*. Presented at the IEEE Canadian Conference on Electrical and Computer. Engineering, Canada.

Guzman, V., Miyatake, M., & Meana, H. (2004). *Analysis of Wavelet –Based Watermarking Algorithm*. Paper presented at the 14th International IEEE

Conference on Electronics, Communications and Computers, Veracruz, Mexico.

Hsu, C., & Wu, J. (1998). Multiresolution Watermarking for Digital Images. *IEEE Transactions on Circuits and Systems- II, 45*(8),1097-1101.

Huang, C. & Wu, J. (2000). *A Watermark Optimization Technique Based on Genetic Algorithms*. Presented at the 2000 SPIE – Visual Communications Image Processing, Perth, Australia.

Huang, J., & Yang, C. (2004). *Image Digital Watermarking Algorithm Using Multiresolution Wavelet Transform*. Paper presented at the International IEEE Conference on Systems, Man, and Cybernetics, the Hague, the Netherlands.

Jung, H., Cho, S., Shik, S., Koh, Chung, Y., Lee, K., Lee, S., & Kim, C. (2003). *Image Watermarking Based on Wavelet Transform Using Threshold Selection*. Paper presented at the International IEEE SICE Conference.

Katzenbeisser, S., & Petitcolas, F. (2000). *Information Hiding: Techniques for steganography and digital watermarking*. Boston, MA: Artech House.

Kumswat, P., Attakitmongcol, K., and Striaew, A. (2005). A New Approach for Optimization in Image Watermarking by Using Genetic Algorithms. *IEEE Transactions on Signal Processing, 53*(12),4707-4719.

Langelaar, G., Setyawan, I., & and Lagendijk, R. (2000). Watermarking Digital Image and Video Data: A State-of-Art Overview. *IEEE Signal Processing Magazine, 17*(5), 20-46.

Mallat,S. (1989). A theory for multi-resolution signal decomposition: The wavelet Representation. *IEEE Transactions on Pattern Analysis And Machine Intelligence, 11*(7), 674-693.

Mitra, S. (1998). *Digital Signal Processing.* Columbus, OH: McGraw –Hill.

Niu, X., Lu, Z., & Sun, S. (2000). Digital Image Watermarking based on multi-resolution Decomposition. *IEEE Electronics Letters, 36*(13), 1108-1110.

Potdar, V., Han, S., & Chang, E. (2005). *A Survey of Digital Image Watermarking Techniques.* Paper presented at the 3rd International IEEE Conference on Industrial Informatics, Perth, Australia.

Rao, K., & Yip, P. (1990). *Discrete Cosine Transform: algorithms, advantages, applications.* USA: Academic Press.

Reddy, A., & Chatterji, B. (2005). A New Wavelet Based Logo-watermarking Scheme. *Pattern Recognition Letters, 26*(7), 1019-1027.

Safabakhsh, R., Zaboli, S., & Tabibiazar, A. (2004). *Digital Watermarking on Still Images Using Wavelet Transform.* Presented at the International IEEE Conference on Information Technology: Coding and Computing, Las Vegas, Nevada.

Sebe, F., Domingo-Ferrer, J., & Herrera, J. (2000). *Spatial Domain Image Watermarking Robust Against Compression, Filtering, Cropping, and Scaling.* Paper presented at the 3rd International Workshop on Information Security, Wollongong, Australia.

Shieh,C., Huang, H., Wang, F., & Pan, J. (2004). Genetic Watermarking Based on Transform Domain Techniques. *Pattern Recognition, 37*(3), 555-565.

Strang, G. & Nguyen, T. (1996). *Wavelets and Filter Banks.* Wellesley, MA: Wellesley-Cambridge Press.

Tay, P., & Havlicek, J. (2002). *Image Watermarking Using Wavelets.* Presented at the IEEE Midwest Symposium on Circuits and Systems, Tulsa, Oklahoma.

Vetterli, M., & Kovačević, J. (1995). *Wavelets and Subband Coding.* USA: Prentice Hall.

Wang, C., Doherty, J., & Van Dyke, R. (2002). A Wavelet-Based Watermarking Algorithm for Ownership Verification of Digital Images. *IEEE Transactions on Image Processing, 11*(2), 77-78.

Wolfgang, R., Podilchuk, C., & Delp, E. (1999). Perceptual Watermarks for Digital Images and Video. *Proceedings of the IEEE, 87*(7), 1108-1126.

Yang, S. (2003). Filter evaluation for DWT-domain image watermarking. *Electronics Letters, 39*(24), 1723 – 1725.

Chapter XV
Internet Banking System in South Asian Countries:
Preliminary Findings

Farrukh Amin
Institute of Business Management, Pakistan

ABSTRACT

The Banking Sector in Pakistan is in its developing state of employing Internet Technology for conducting transactions, interactivity and customer relationship management. Government of Pakistan has brought in efforts to improve the situation. In this regard many of the Public sector banks have been privatized in the last decade. The State Bank of Pakistan (Central Bank in Pakistan) has adopted effective measures and introduced reforms for application of Information Technology for using Internet Banking services. This chapter identifies the implementation of the Internet Technology in Pakistan in particular and in South Asian countries in general. The chapter replicates the Diniz (1998) model using the case of Pakistan and other South Asian countries as an example of an emerging banking sector using Internet.

LITERATURE REVIEW

Over the past two decades banks have invested heavily in the Information Technology sector. The banking sector, in both developed and emerging markets, is clearly recognizing the importance of information technology to their continued success. For example, Pollalis (1994), linked the success of banks surveyed to the use of integrating technology in the strategic plan, while Van Aswegen (1993) found that investments in technology increased shareholder value. Eze (1999) reported that the management of 58% of Nigerian commercial banks believed that investing in information technologies will improve their competitive advantages, such as, customer retention, cost reduction, and in forming alliances or mergers. By the end of 1997, a survey of United States banks with more than $1 billion in deposits by Martin (1998) found that 45% offered direct banking while another 38 percent planned to offer the service. While not all banks offered Internet banking services, 53% have such service menus under development. In addition, Martin found that almost all small and money center banks maintain their Websites where clients can view the services offered.

One of the main incentives that encourages banks to adopt new technologies of operations is not only maintaining operational efficiency but also achieving competitive advantages. Banks that exploit new technologies can gain competitive advantages through market share, customer satisfaction, and overall business performance. Peffers (1991) argues that banks which were early adopters of the Automated Teller Machines (ATM) gained significantly more edge than later adoptee. He claims that the use of even a single information technology application can affect a wide range of performance variables. Information Technology also impact organization in other ways, such as, changing the decision pattern of banks to deal better with competition (Clarke, 1989).

It is becoming evident that companies as well as individuals are becoming more likely to manage their accounts and do their banking operations through the internet. Web based banking can, for example, allow a relatively small company to structure and issue basic financial tools such as letters of credit. Other companies are attracted to online banking because it enables them to monitor accounts on a 24-hours basis. As online banking evolves, it is giving some corporations more than just an account-monitoring tool. Several banks for instance provide corporate online banking and allow their clients to invest overnight funds. This can generate substantial profits for a company that has significant, but temporarily, ideal cash funds (Martin, 1998). Companies will also be able to do some sophisticated bargaining and comparison shopping for banking services, since the size and location of the client becomes less important. Other banks have developed online banking products specifically tailored to their smaller business clients.

From an individual perspective Web based banking is a very attractive option. It is proven to be fast, economical, and flexible. Chatzky (1998) focuses on four major Web based banking services. First; direct deposit, where a customer can manage deposits, reimbursements, mutual fund distribution, and tax refunds. Second; electronic bill payment, where lenders and borrowers are authorized to withdraw the amount from a customer's account. Third; automatic investing plans, which debit the customers account monthly and finally, electronic budgeting, where some financial packages offer advice to manage income and make key financial decisions.

In Pakistan, the 'dot com' culture is emerging at a very fast pace and there has been a significant growth of Pakistani commercial Web sites and information portals. Electronic commerce in Pakistan is growing at a slow pace, which has prompted the government to take a number of e-commerce development initiatives.

INTRODUCTION

Internet and Internet Based Banking

It is global network of using and sharing data and information form one computer systems to another computer system using internet accessibility, browsing software and communication network with acceptable protocols. This phenomenon is not new and spread over the globe very rapidly in few years. In the beginning, Internet was considered to be fairly means of exchange of data and information, but with the passage of time, it has proved its utility and effectiveness in every department of our lives. It is useful at homes and beneficent in the offices. Similarly commercial organizations use Internet services for recording their sales, accounting transactions and monitoring employees' performance. Banks adopted this technology a little late and started their business operation using Internet technology for various purposes. There are no geographical boundaries and restrictions to do internet based banking unless the laws and regulations of that country permits to do so. The major course of action by a bank Website can perform

Internet based banking is in its developing phase and has not been improved yet in Pakistan and other south Asian countries at its full pace as compared to developed countries. A couple of Internet Service Providers started this business in Pakistan in early 1994. Initially the purpose of using Internet was only to avail e-mail facility and surf on the World Wide Web for data acquiring purposes but later on the usage and application of Internet and its related services have proved as a valuable and swift source for successful business operations. Presently Internet has been employed by various industries in Pakistan. Banking sector has also started using it for their business operations such as Opening of accounts, Funds transfer facility, Bill payment, Personal loan acquisition and Stock trading.

Pakistani Banking sector is in its developing phase for Internet based banking operations. The Internet market has grown rapidly since 1995 in Pakistan, and therefore, the investors are ready to invest in online banking. There has been a significant improvement in the past few years but still lot has to be done in this regard. Furthermore, a well-suited legal system governing data transmission is still required to be implemented. The Pakistani banking sector makes a significant contribution to the Pakistan's economy. The capability of banks to get benefited from the Internet will not only increase their contribution to country's economic growth but will also help in making financial services cost effective and competitive to customers. It is globally considered that Internet based banking improves their customers relationship.

Presently, almost all the banks provide their Web site to advertise their products and services. The main benefit of using Internet based banking is derived from reduction of walk-in customers,

which ultimately helps in reducing number of branches and so its operation cost. According to Shuman (1998), the Federal Reserve documented that over 63 billion consumer and commercial paper cheques were written in 1996 in the United States alone. Assuming there were 1.5 additional back office transactions per cheque, a total of more than 157 billion non-cash paper-based transactions took place in 1996. This clearly shows that the Web based banking persuades because of potential and feasibility. Churbuck (1998), for example, found that in the beginning of 1997, only 30,000 accounts of top international investments companies were conducted on-line. One year later the number crossed over one million. To conclude, as the number of Internet users are extending, the banks are also enhancing their internet based banking as a practicable choice.

BENEFITS OF USING INTERNET BASED BANKING

There are number of factors which further motivate banks to develop on-line services, for example:

Low Cost

The average cost of direct banking transaction via Web is $0.010. In comparison an ATM transaction cost $0.27, phone transaction $0.54, and physical transaction $1.07 (Kurtas, 2000).

Increased use of the Web

There is an increasing trend in the use of the internet. In France, for example, the growth in the use of the Web based banking is about 75% annually (Kurtas, 2000).

Ease of Access to the Internet

Nowadays, most of the computer users have Internet connection either at home or in the business offices. Every day they read and send e-mail messages to friends, family members and for commercial purpose. Presently, the wireless technology has become so popular that most of the people in the country use GSM technology as well as many other emerging technologies through which they have access to Internet easily.

Convenience

Many customers now prefer to do their financial operations from home and offices. Such as balance inquiry, bill payments and fund transfers etc.

Efficiency and Profitability

Online Banking surely reduces the operating cost that will eventually improve their level of profitability.

Accessibility and Availability

The chief benefit of using banking over internet is to make available banking services and consumber products 24/7 and 365. There would be no geographical boundaries which will restrict to do banking from one particular location to another location in the world. Since Internet facility is usually available globally by millions and millions end-users, therefore, doing banking over Internet would bring ease in the lives of consumers.

Mobility and Portability

Another advantage of doing banking using Interent is that it may not be resticted to only wired communication networking enviornment. People now use mobile phones for Funds Transfer, Bill Payments and receive altert messages from the bank whenever they make any banking related transaction using phone banking option or Internet based banking. It is easier to carry a hand set for this purpose. GPRS has made accessibility of using Internet over mobile phone and added more convenience to this business.

The main purpose of this study is to assess the application of the Web based banking in Pakistan. A secondary issue is to examine the extent to which Pakistani banks or the foreign banks operating in Pakistan are applying evolving technology to achieve efficiency in their operations. In general, the objectives of this research are threefold. A) Examine the extent to which Web based banking is practiced in Pakistan. B) Identify barrier to Internet banking and C) Offer future directions for both practice and research. The paper would also try to investigate the reasons whey Internet based banking has been flourished yet in the developing countries, particularly in South Asian countries.

METHODOLOGY

I designed a questionnaire for data collection. The data collected in the month of March 2008 by using banks' Website operating in Pakistan (47), India (43), Bangladesh (33) and Sri Lanka (5). I evaluated the results of collected data by using Diniz Model (Diniz, 1998). The model focuses on three dimensions of a bank's activities using internet Website. These dimensions are Interactivity, Conducting Transaction on net and Customers Relationship through Website. Each of the dimension is further decomposed into three levels; Basic, Intermediate and Advanced.

The Interactivity Dimension describes the bank's Website features related to preliminary information about the organization data, promotional features, News and Publications by the bank, search Engine and downloading facility, recruitment and information links, economic and financial information, online customers' input and advertising space on the Web site. Conducting Transaction focuses on the features such as account opening facility, financial payments/receipt tools, exchange rate feature, bill payments and funds transfer facility, stock trading option and e-banking features. While the Customer Relationship deals with e-mail facility and provides comments and suggestions by the customers to the bank using surfing. It also helps to know if Website provides any financial decision making tools.

The sample size turns out to be 47, 43, 33 and 5 for Pakistan, India, Bangladesh and Sri Lanka respectively. For this study almost all the commercial banks, few non-banking financial institutions, such as Agriculture Development Bank of Pakistan, and few Islamic banks were selected. Details are presented in the Appendix: A.

RESULTS

The major findings of this preliminary study of the paper are presented in Tables 1-1, 1-2, and 1-3. These tables present summary information using the dimensions of the Diniz Matrix. There are graphs; Graph 1-1, Graph 1-2, Graph 1-3, which exhibit banks performance according to the analyzed data. These graphs and Table 1-1 relate the utilization of internet based banking in Pakistan, India, Bangladesh and Sri Lanka as Information Vehicle. Banks use their Web sites to conduct transaction is depicted in Graph 2-1, Graph 2-2, Graph 2-3 and Table 1-2, while Graph 3-1, Graph 3-2, Graph 3-3 and Table 1-3 provide information to build relationships with customers. The finding demonstrates that banks in Pakistan are utilizing the concepts and applications of internet banking in certain areas. In contrast to developed international market, it is fair to say that this sector is largely under developing phase.

Internet Website as Vehicle for Information (Interactive Level & Dimension)

The results show that most of the banks in this region provide information about bank and its history over internet. The respondents banks in Pakistan, India, Bangladesh and Srilanka exhibit

80%, 92%, 93% and 80% respectively. Banks do provide information about their product promotion mostly in India and Banglades which is 96% and 93% respectively. However, the situation in Pakistan is only 63% banks offer their product promotino and 80% of Srilankan banks do so. Almost every bank does provide contact information about itself on their Website. It is 89% in Pakistan, 100% in India, 93% in Bangladesh and 80% in Srilanka. There are few banks in Pakistan that provide information about special event (say 46%) whereas most of the bank in India, Bangladesh and Srilanka have adopted this option (say 92%, 93% and 80% respectively). 100% banks in India and Srilanka exhibit their branches information over internet but in Pakistan and Bangladesh there are only 83% and 80% . Not all the banks in any of the countries included in the sample provide data of Board of Directors and other administrative structure over Website. The worst situation is lying with the part of sending welcome letters to their clients by any of these countries in the sample. It is 43%, 21%, 7% and 20% in Pakistan, India, Bangladesh and Srilanka respectively. Overall 65% of the banks have adopted Basic Level of this dimension, whereas, the situation in the neighboring countries is healthy and quite satisfactory as compared to Pakistan. 79% of the banks' site use internet as source for Interactivity in India, 78% in Bangladesh and 68% in Sri Lanka. Pakistan is quite behind in this area.

At the intermediate level of the dimension, 38% to 66% banks have features of downloading facility of Economic data. Pakistan excels better as compared to neighboring countries. i.e. 66% of the banks provide this facility. 40% to 66% banks provide search engine facility, stock data and Web links. Lastly, 37% to 69% banks' sites feature on employment recruitment offer and online job offer facility. Overall 51% of the bank's site follows the Intermediate level of this dimension in all the selected countries except Sri Lanka. Majority of the banks (70% or more) provide product promotion but other options are poorly used at the Advanced level of the dimension. Over all 16% to 26% banks' responses are in favor of Advanced Level of this dimension.

Table 1-2 shows that majority of the Pakistani banks do not conduct transactions using internet banking facility. There is only 1 bank in Pakistan which offers Check Book Facility option and no bank in other countries offer this option. There are 51% of the bank that provide Account Opening Application in Pakistan while 33% bank in Bangladesh, 13% in India and no bank in Sri Lank has this facility on their Web site. 40% banks offer Credit Card Request, 34% provide Loan Application and 31% offer Investment applications facilities. 40% of the bank offer Exchange rate facility. Overall 33% banks follow the Basic Level of this dimension in Pakistan but situation is better in India, Bangladesh and Sri Lanka.

This looks as most of the banks have some reservation in this level because other countries are also weak in conducting transaction at Intermediate level of the dimension except India (48%). One of the reasons may be of NRI (non-Indian Residents) accounts facility.

Overall 35% of the banks provide options related to Transaction Conducting via Web sites. Similarly Bill Payment, Fund Transfer, Balance of Account and History facilities are provided at 34%, 37%, 37% and 43% respectively. Only 14% of the banks deal with e-Cash and e-cheques etc. Overall 33% of the banks have adopted Conducting Transaction facility over internet.

Customer Relationship Dimension

Table 1-3 clearly shows that services of this type are highly concentrated in the basic level. For example, the use of E-mail facilities, suggestions & complaints forms are available on most of the Website of the bank say (81%). At the intermediary level, only 17% bank choose to provide financial advising tools in Pakistan however it is 71%, 47% and 40% in India, Bangladesh and Sri Lanka respectively. However, at the advanced

level, there is no provision for services such as videoconferencing but 63% banks offer to promote their products and services.

At the intermediary level, only 17% bank choose to provide financial advising tools in Pakistan however it is 71%, 47% and 40% in India, Bangladesh and Sri Lanka respectively. However, at the advanced level, there is no provision for services such as videoconferencing but 63% banks offer to promote their products and services.

However, at the advanced level, there is no provision for services such as videoconferencing but 83% banks offer to promote their products and services through Web sites and provide comprehensive information. In India 87% banks, in Bangladesh 100%, and in Sri Lanka 100% bank follow this option.

Overall usage of customer relationship using Websites by the banks is satisfactory. In Pakistan 53% of the banks' population follow this dimension. But in India it is 68%, in Bangladesh it is 61% and 56% is in Sri Lanka.

DISCUSSION

Study shows that there is wide gap between South Asian and the developed countries' banks for employing internet for their business operations. In a more common framework we can generalize this summary to the gap between internet usage in developing and developed countries. Kurtas (2000) found that developed countries banks use their Web sites not only to provide classical operations such as fund transfer or account details, but also to provide stock trading in the world markets, financial calculators, investment advice and bill payments. American banks are now using very high technology in encryption in order to provide safety and privacy. They have reached a stage where a number of banks are operating completely via internet without any need for physical location. On the other hand not much evidences of Web usage at this level were found among the Pakistani and other south Asian banks. The Pakistani banking sector has improved some of its weaknesses of early age of using Internet technology in the advanced levels of all Web opportunities, particularly with regard to Customer Relationship, however a lot has to be done for conducting the transaction and interactivity dimension using internet.

Developing nations, such as Pakistan has a number of inherited difficulties in working with Internet based banking culture. Generally saying that the rate of literacy is not as good as in the other neighbouring countreis in South Asia. Similarly the technological skill level is corelated with basic education and literacy leve. Most of the population still live and work in remote areas where at some places it is difficult to get electricity to run their daily course of lives, how could be expect that telcommunication facilities would be effective which ultimately invites other entities to get benefit of the infrastrurcture. Internet based banks live in the domain of an electronic business environment and E-commerce. This requies a swift telecommunication system, skilled and trained human resources, software and related hardware beside other factors. The key element of success in this environment is the development of telecommunication infrastructure. The major challenges being faced for further development of Web banking in Pakistan is high inflation rate and unavailability of highly skilled and trained human resource poor computer literacy rate, lack of awareness of technical and regular education, limited access to internet in most of the cities in Pakistan except few developed cities like Karachi, Lahore, Islamabad etc. Other elements may include the non-availability of information technologies, packages and solutions, which facilitates optimum use of technology. Mainteneance of Law and Order situation has been acute in the recent years but still there is very clear development has been observed with respect to banking network and its transaction over Internet or Website. A lot of people have started using ATM Cards at ATM machine to settle their bill payments, using funds tranafer facility over internet from one bank to another bank or one location to another one. Number of Government agencies started asking people to deposit the governemtn fee and taxes online using Online banking features.

In a more general framework Kurtas (2000) articulated a set of factors that hinder Web-banking applications. These included computer piracy and general security issues, telecommunication infrastructure, and possible social implications, such as, downsizing and lay offs.

CONCLUSION

Internet banking is increasingly used by banks and other financial institutions to gain competitive advantages, operational efficiencies and direct marketing opportunities. It is important to reaffirm that Electronic banking is a rapidly growing trend. We have observed a major change from metal and paper money, to plastic cards, to smart cards, to online payments and fund transfers.

Our preliminary results indicate that Pakistani banks have been successful in the introductory phase of Web based banking. Now it is required for Pakistani Web based banking to move forward with a view of conducting real financial transactions and improving electronic customer relationship. These objectives can be generalized to banks in developing economies, which can no longer ignore the internet as a strategic weapon and distribution channel for their services.

Future research should focus on methods of advancing the interactivity levels towards the higher end of the matrix. Specifically, the factors that influence the internet based banking activities in Pakistan. It will also be needed to find out how linkages between investments in Web based banking and organizational performance need to be given importance. These linkages are crucial to provide feedback to decision-makers in both banks and concerned governmental and nongovernmental bodies.

ACKNOWLEDGMENT

I am grateful to Dr. Javed A Ansari, Dr. Ejaz Ahmed and Mr.Sagheer Muhammad for reviewing and guiding me for presentation of this research paper. I also like to extend my gratitude to the MBA class of E-Commerce (Spring 2008) for data collection process.

REFERENCES

Awamleh, R., Evans, J., & Mahate, A. (2000). *Internet Banking in Emergency Markets: The case of Jordon – A Note*. University of Wollongong, Dubai Campus.

Chatzky, J. S. (1998). Taking time to automate. *Money Magazine, 27*(12), 196

Churbuck, D. (1998). What are you waiting for? *Forbes, 161*(12)261.

Clark, R. (1989). *Congruence between strategy, IT, and decision making at the unit level: A comparison of U.S.A and Canadian retail banks*. Unpublished dissertation, University of Massachusetts.

Diniz, E. (1998). *Web Banking in USA. Journal of Internet Banking and Commerce*. www.arraydev.com/commerce/jibc/9806-06.htm

Eze, E. (1999). *The potential use of IT for competitive advantage: An empirical examination of Nigerian commercial banks*. Unpublished dissertation, Walden University.

Jarrah, F. (1999a). *Internet shoppers in the Arab world spend US$ 95 million.* www.dit.net/itnews/newsjune99/newsjune22.html

Jarrah, F. (1999b). *Internet users in the Arab world close to one million.* www.dit.net/itnews/newsmay99/newsmay77.html

Web site of State Bank of Pakistan www.sbp.org.pk

Web site of the Banks Directory. www.bankdirectory.ws

APPENDIX: A

Sample Size Calculation

Since there are three dimensions have been identified and each of these dimension is further decomposed into three levels, therefore we can describe it as 3 x 4 matrix as:

Interactivity	Basic	Intermediate	Advanced
Conducting Transactions	Basic	Intermediate	Advanced
Customers Relationships	Basic	Intermediate	Advanced

Sample

The sample size computed on the following formula:

$$f = p \times (1-p) * Z_{\alpha/2}^2 / d^2$$
$$n = f / [1 + (f / Population)]$$

Where **p** is Expected Frequency Value i.e. 50%
    Z is 1.96 with Confidence Interval of 95%
    d is Worst Acceptable Frequency say 5%
    f is Sample Size Factor value
    Population is the total number of objects available for a particular study
    n is Sample size

A bank performs number of activities related to its business operations for example, opening of customers account, providing accounts statements, funds transfer, Letter of Credit opening facility, encashment of Notes, leasing, providing guarantee against a business, pledging documents and releasing funds and other activities. If we assume that 50% of these activities are being used by these banks via their Websites, the sample size turns out to be 50, 43, 33 and 14 for Pakistan, India, Bangladesh and Sri Lanka respectively. For this study almost all the commercial banks, few non-banking financial institutions and few Islamic banks were selected.

Table 1. Showing population and sample size of South Asian countries

Countries	Pakistan	India	Bangladesh	Sri Lanka
Population Size	53	48	36	5
Sample Size	47	43	33	5

QUESTIONNAIRE

Name of the Bank:_____

If a bank has its Web site   Yes_____   No _____

If Yes, then its Website URL:_____ _____

Q. No	Interactive Level & Dimension	Yes	No
	Basic Level		
1	Does Your Website provide Institutional Information?		
2	Does it provide Promotional information?		
3	Does it provide how to contact information?		
4	Is there any special event information?		
5	Does it provide addresses and Branch Information?		
6	Does it have Board of Directors' Information?		
7	Does it have any News Letter there?		
8	Are letters welcomed on the site?		
	Intermediate Level		
9	Is there any Search Engines facility available?		
10	Is there any report download facility available?		
11	Does it provide stock trading Information?		
12	Does it provide a recruitment Form?		
13	Does it offer any Job facilities?		
14	Does it provide Information Links?		
15	Does if provide Economic Information?		
16	Does it provide Financial Market Information?		
17	Does it provide detailed articles?		
	Advanced Level		
18	Does it have ability to customize the interface?		
19	Is there any Stock Subscription Option?		
20	Is there Online Chat with Customer services?		
21	Is there any Discussion group available on the site?		
22	Is there any Advertisement and Promotion facility?		

	Conducting Transactions			
	Basic Level			
23	Is there any Account Opening Facility?			
24	Is there any Card Request facilities?			
25	Is there any Loan Application Facility?			
26	Is there any Investment Applications Facility?			
27	Is there any Exchange Rate Inquiry Facility?			
28	Can Customer Request for Cheque Book?			
	Intermediate Level			
29	Is there any Bill Payment Facility?			
30	Is there any Fund Transfer Facility?			
31	Is there Balance Inquiry Facility?			
32	Is there History of Accounts available?			
33	Is there Stock Trading Facility available?			
	Advanced Level			
34	Is there Virtual Bank facility with solutions, such as e-cash, e-signature, and e-Cheque, available?			
	Customers Relationship			
	Basic Level			
35	Is there any E-mail facility to customer available?			
36	Can Customer post Suggestions and Complaint through Website?			
	Intermediate Level			
37	Does it Provide tools to make financial decisions, such as what if Calculator?			
	Advanced Level			
38	Is there any Video Conferencing facility available on its site?			
39	Is there Information Gathering on products and services available?			

List of Banks in Pakistan

1. Askari Bank Limited
2. Faysal Bank Limited
3. Citi Bank Inc.
4. Bubai Islamic Bank
5. Hongkong Shehangai Bank Corporation
6. Oman International Bank
7. Bank of Khayber
8. Orix Investment Bank
9. Deutsche Bank Limited

10. Bnak Al-Habib Ltd
11. Soneri Bank Limited
12. Bank AlFalah Limited
13. Doha Bank Limited
14. Platinum Commercial Bank
15. Allied Bank Limited
16. Industrial Development Bank of Pakistan
17. First Women Bank Limited
18. Meezan Bank Limited
19. NIB Bank Limited
20. Emirates Bank Limited
21. National Bank of Pakistan
22. ABN Amro Bank
23. Muslim Commercial Bank Ltd
24. Jehangir Siddique Investment Bank Ltd
25. Habib Bank Limited
26. Indus Bank Limited
27. Standard Chartered Bank
28. Trust Investment Bank Limited
29. Bank Islami Pakistan
30. United Bank Limited
31. Saudi Pak Commercial Bank
32. KASB Bank Limited
33. Habib Metropolitain Bank Ltd
34. Cresent Commercial Bank Ltd
35. Atlas Bank Limited
36. Zarai Taraqiati Bank Limited
37. SMEs Bank Limited
38. The Bank of Panjab
39. Khushhali Bank
40. Pak Microfinance Bank Limited
41. Arif Habib Bank Limited
42. My Bank Limited
43. Dawood Islami Bank
44. Al-Barakah Islami Bank
45. Arif Habib Rupali Bank Limited
46. Habib Metropolitan Bank Limited
47. Habib Bank A.G. Zurich

List of Banks in India

1. ABN AMRO India
2. Abu Dhabi Commercial Bank
3. Allahabad Bank

4.   Andhra Bank
5.   Bank of Baroda
6.   Bank of India
7.   Bank of Madura
8.   Bank of Punjab
9.   Birla Global Finance
10. Canara Bank
11. Citibank
12. City Union Bank
13. Corporation Bank
14. Cosmos Bank
15. Dena Bank
16. Development Credit Bank Limited
17. Export-Import Bank of India
18. Federal Bank
19. Financial institutions in India
20. First Leasing Company Of India Ltd.
21. Global Trust Bank
22. HSBC in India
23. ICICI Bank
24. India
25. Indian Bank
26. Indian Overseas Bank
27. IndusInd Bank Limited
28. Industrial Development Bank of India (IDBI)
29. Mandvi Co-operative Bank Ltd.
30. National Bank for Agriculture and Rural Development
31. Nedungadi Bank Ltd
32. Punjab & Sind Bank
33. Reserve Bank of India
34. SBI
35. SREI Industrial Finance
36. Standard Chartered
37. State Bank of
38. State Bank of Travancore
39. Syndicate Bank
40. TimesBank
41. UCO Bank
42. Union Bank of India (UBI)

List of Banks in Bangladesh

1.   Agrani Bank
2.   Al-Baraka Bank Limited

3. Arab Bangladesh Bank Limited
4. Bangladesh Bank
5. BAnk Asia Limited
6. Basicbank
7. Dutch Bangla Bank
8. Eastern Bank Limited
9. Grameen Bank
10. HSBC in Bangladesh
11. I.D.L.C. of Bangladesh
12. International Finance Investment Commerce Bank (IFIC) Limited
13. Islami Bank Bangladesh Limited
14. Islami Bank Bangladesh Limited
15. Jamuna Bank
16. Janata Bank
17. Krishi Bank
18. Mercantile Bank Limited
19. National Bank Limited
20. NCC Bank Limited
21. ONE Bank Limited
22. Premier Bank Ltd
23. Prime Bank Ltd
24. Pubali Bank Limited
25. Pubali Bank Ltd
26. Rupali Bank
27. Shahjalal Bank
28. Social Investment Bank Ltd
29. Sonali Bank
30. Southeastbank Bangladesh Bank
31. Standard Chartered
32. The City Bank Limited
33. United Commercial Bank Limited

List of Banks in Sri Lanka

1. Hatton National Bank
2. HSBC in Sri Lanka
3. National Development Bank of Sri Lanka
4. Sampath Bank
5. Standard Chartered

Tables

Table 1-1. Showing YES Percentage of Responses for Interactivity Dimension via Bank Web sites

Q.#	Countries / Description	Pak	India	BD	SL
		N = 47	N = 43	N = 33	N = 5
		%age of YES	%age of YES	%age of YES	%age of YES
	Interactive Level & Dimension				
	Basic Level				
1	Does Your website provide Institutional Information	80	92	93	80
2	Does it provide Promotional information	63	96	93	80
3	Does it provide how to contact information	89	100	93	80
4	Is there any special event information there	46	92	93	80
5	Does it provide addresses and Branches Information	83	100	80	100
6	Does it have Board of Directors' Information	69	67	80	40
7	Does it have any News Letter there	49	63	87	60
8	Are letters welcomed on the site?	43	21	7	20
	Total Response for Basic Level	**65**	**79**	**78**	**68**
	Intermediate Level				
9	Search Engines available	40	58	47	80
10	Is there any report download facility available	66	38	40	40
11	Does it provide stock Information	49	17	20	0
12	Does it provide a recruitment Form	37	54	40	60
13	Does it offer Job facilities	69	54	47	60
14	Does it provide Hot Links	46	88	87	80
15	Does if provide Economic Information	66	83	80	60
16	Does it provide Financial Market Information	57	58	47	40
17	Does it provide detailed articles	31	13	53	0
	Total Response for Intermediate Level	**51**	**51**	**51**	**47**
	Advanced Level				
18	Does it have ability to customize the interface	9	8	0	0
19	Is there any Stock Subscription Option	31	8	7	0
20	Is there Online Chart with Customer services	14	8	0	0
21	Is there any discussion group on the site?	0	8	0	0
22	Is there any Advertisement and Promotion	71	96	87	80
	Total Response for Advanced Level	25	26	19	16
	Overall Response for Interactive Level	50	55	54	47

Table 1-2. Showing percentage of YES responses for conducting transactions by the Bank Web site

Q. No	Countries	Pak	India	BD	SL
	Description	N = 47	N = 43	N = 33	N = 5
		%age of YES	%age of YES	%age of YES	%age of YES
	Conducting Transactions				
	Basic Level				
23	Is there any Account Opening Facilities	51	13	33	0
24	Is there any Card Request facilities	40	29	40	60
25	Is there any Loan Application Facility	34	92	80	100
26	Is there any Investment Applications facility	31	96	80	100
27	Is there any Exchange Rate Inquiry facility	40	50	53	40
28	Can Customer Request for Cheque Book	3	0	0	0
	Total Response for Basic Level	**33**	**47**	**48**	**50**
	Intermediate Level				
29	Bill Payment Facility	34	79	33	60
30	Fund Transfer Facilities	37	75	40	60
31	Balance Inquiry Facilities	37	46	33	20
32	History of Accounts	43	33	33	20
33	Stock Trading	26	8	7	0
	Total Response for Intermediate Level	**35**	**48**	**29**	**32**
	Advanced Level				
34	Virtual Bank with solutions, such as e-cash, e-signature, and e-chques	14	17	13	20
	Total Response for Advanced Level	**14**	**17**	**13**	**20**
	Overall Response for Conducting Transaction Dimension	**33**	**45**	**37**	**40**

Table 1-3. Showing Percentage of YES responses for Customer Relationship by the Bank Web site

Q. No	Countries	Pak	India	BD	SL
	Description	N = 47	N = 43	N = 33	N = 5
		%age of YES	%age of YES	%age of YES	%age of YES
	Customers Relationship				
	Basic Level				
35	E-mail facility	89	96	87	80
36	Suggestions and Complaint forms	74	75	87	60
	Total Response for Basic Level	**81**	**85**	**87**	**70**
	Intermediate Level				
37	Providing tools to make financial decisions, such as what if Calculator	17	71	47	40
	Total Response for Intermediate Level	**17**	**71**	**47**	**40**
	Advanced Level				

continued on following page

Table 1-3. continued

38	Does the Web site provide Video Conferencing facility?	0	0	0	0
39	Information Gathering on products and services	83	100	87	100
	Total Response for Advanced Level	**41**	**50**	**43**	**50**
	Overall Response for CRM Dimension	**53**	**68**	**61**	**56**
	Overall Internet Banking Progress	**45**	**54**	**50**	**46**

Figures

Graph 1-1. Showing % of YES response by the bank for interactivity dimension at basic level

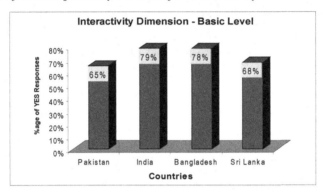

Graph 1-2. Showing % of YES response by the bank for interactivity dimension at intermediate level

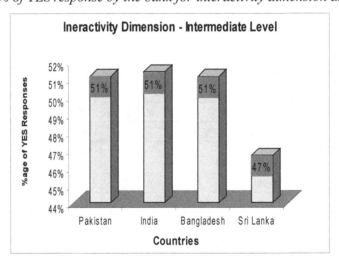

Graph 1-3. Showing % of YES response by the bank for interactivity dimension at advanced level

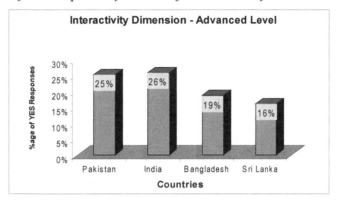

Graph 2-1. Showing % of YES response by the bank for conducting transaction dimension at basic level

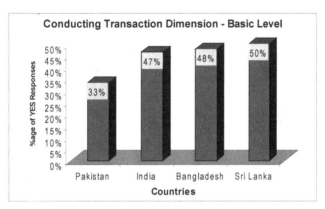

Graph 2-2. Showing % of YES response by the bank for conducting transaction dimension at intermediate level

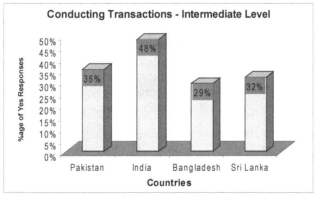

Graph 2-3. Showing % of YES response by the bank for conducting transaction dimension at advanced level

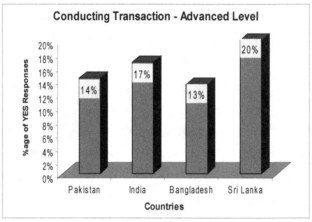

Graph 3-1. Showing % of YES response by the bank for customer relationship dimension at basic level

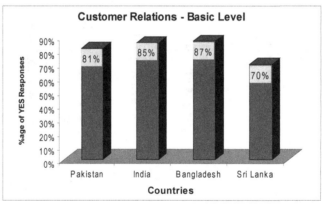

Graph 3-2. Showing % of YES response by the bank for customer relationship dimension at intermediate level

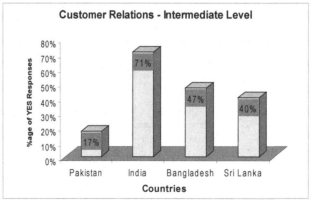

Graph 3-3. Showing % of YES response by the bank for customer relationship dimension at advanced level

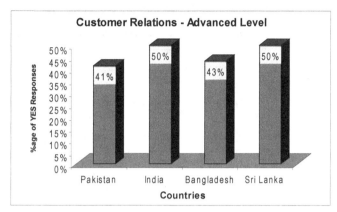

Graph 4-1. Showing % of YES Response by the Bank for Interactivity & Information Dimension

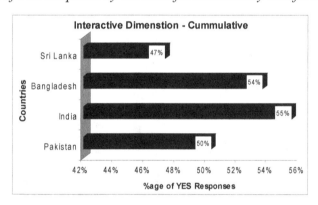

Graph 4-2. Showing % of YES response by the bank for conducting transactions dimension

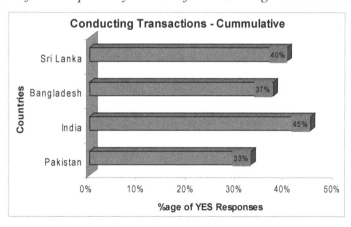

Graph 4-3. Showing % of YES response by the bank for conducting transactions dimension

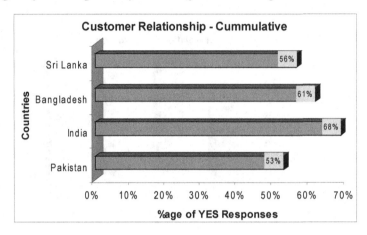

Graph 7-1. Showing % of YES response by the banks for overall usage of Internet banking

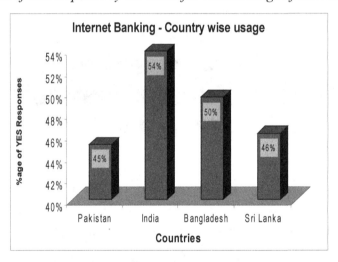

Chapter XVI
Computer Simulation of Particle Packing in Bituminous Concrete

Kasthurirangan Gopalakrishnan
Iowa State University, USA

Naga Shashidhar
Corning Inc., USA

ABSTRACT

Although computer simulation methods have been used extensively in modeling the microstructure of Portland cement concrete, their application for studying asphalt concrete is relatively new. In this chapter, the nature and distribution of inter-particle contacts in computer-simulated compacts with a wide particle size range such as those found in asphalt pavements are discussed. The aggregates were modeled as hard spheres and some typical aggregate gradations used in AC were packed using a computer program. The application of particle packing simulation concepts discussed in this chapter to the study of aggregate structure in asphalt pavements, in conjunction with the recent advances in nondestructive imaging techniques and DEM simulations have tremendous potential to help us to develop a deeper understanding of the aggregate structure in asphalt concrete, develop and optimize the various parameters that describe the aggregate structure and relate them to the performance of pavements in a scientific way.

INTRODUCTION

Asphalt concrete (AC) or bituminous concrete is a composite material consisting of mineral aggregates, asphalt binder and air in a ratio 80:10:10 (by volume), respectively. Currently, choosing the gradation to construct the pavement is based on experience and consensus. It will be of benefit to the pavement community to develop computer modeling techniques to better understand the aggregate structure and its dependence on various factors such as surface roughness, angularity, etc. of the aggregates and various properties of the binder. The ultimate goal is to model the microstructure of AC using volumetrics and particle packing concepts to predict the volumetric properties for given aggregate properties and gradation.

The modeling work can begin by simulating the packing of spherical/ellipsoid particles having a specified gradation, then add other factors such as surface roughness, presence of asphalt binder and aggregate angularity. The model is expected to calculate characteristics of the compacted asphalt mixture such as bulk density, voids content, void distribution, average coordination number of each particle, etc., and yield information useful to mixture design and particulate mechanics modeling of asphalt concrete.

Particle packing has both theoretical and practical importance in many areas of science and engineering. Computer simulation of particle packing is becoming increasingly attractive with the rapid increase in computing power. Particle packing simulations have been widely applied to mono-size particles (Visher and Bolsterli, 1972; Jullien and Meakin, 1987), particles with a slight spread in sizes (Soppe, 1990), and log-normal distributions spanning as much as 1.5 decades in sizes (Powell, 1980).

In some industries, it is necessary to deal with wide particle size distributions. For instance, the aggregates used in asphalt pavements typically have a 19 mm maximum size and about 5% of the particles (by weight) finer than 75 μm—a span of two and a half decades. In such cases, in order to have a representative number of large particles (25-mm particles), tens of millions of small particles have to be considered. Such simulations present significant challenges in terms of both computing requirements and algorithms to handle particles two orders of magnitude next to one another.

The effect of the size distributions on packing characteristics of the particle have been primarily studied through physical experiments (Sohn and Moreland, 1968; Dexter and Tanner, 1972)

and through computer simulations (Nolan and Kavanagh, 1992). In areas such as ceramics and powder metallurgy, a particle system (e.g., powder) with a spread of particle sizes is closely approximated to a known size distribution and is studied by computer simulated packing of spheres. These studies have typically used log-normal or Gaussian particle size distributions with systematic variation of the standard deviation (or range of particle sizes). In these studies, it was found that the packing fraction increased when the standard deviation of the distribution increased.

In many of these studies, a rather narrow size range was considered. Nolan and Kavanagh (1992) used a particle size range of 0-20, while Powell (1980) used sizes from 0 to 1.0, and Bierwagen and Saunders (1974) used particles of sizes from 0.1 to 10, a 2-decade range. In the systems that were of primary interest to the authors, asphalt concrete, this was not an adequate range of distribution of sizes.

The Discrete Element Method (DEM) (Cundall and Strack, 1979) has been used for modeling granular systems. In order to extend the DEM techniques to real aggregates, one major step involves using a range of particle sizes. Zhong et al. (2000) developed methods to use this technique for accommodating particles with sizes spanning two decades. The determination of the initial structure of the granular assembly is an important input to this modeling. The typical technique to obtain this starting assembly is particle packing simulations. Although computer simulation methods have been used extensively in modeling the microstructure of Portland cement concrete (Bentz, 1997), their application for studying asphalt concrete is relatively new. In this chapter, the nature and distribution of inter-particle contacts in computer-simulated compacts with a wide particle size range such as those found in asphalt pavements are discussed. First, it is important to understand how stress is transmitted in asphalt concrete under traffic loading.

STRESS DISTRIBUTION IN ASPHALT CONCRETE

The study of inter-particle contacts is especially beneficial for modeling the microstructure of asphalt concrete. It is generally recognized that in asphalt pavements, the coarse aggregates form a skeleton that primarily supports the load. Shashidhar et al. (2000) showed that the stress is transmitted from particle to particle through the aggregate skeleton in asphalt pavement, similar to granular solids. Using photoelastic methods, it was shown that the loads were transmitted from aggregate to aggregate in a two-dimensional representation of asphalt concrete (see Figure 1). The details of the experiment conducted by Shashidhar et al. (2000) are discussed as follows.

Of the methods to measure load/stress in a system, the photoelastic stress measurement is the most non-intrusive. This technique has been used extensively in the study of granular materials (Dantu, 1957). However, in order to visualize the stresses in such a system, the aggregates have to

Figure 1. Stress distribution in stone-matrix asphalt concrete made with glass disks replacing large aggregates. A static load is applied on the top and the entire apparatus imaged in polarized light. The brightness of the region is directly proportional to the stress at that region. (Shashidhar et al. (2000))

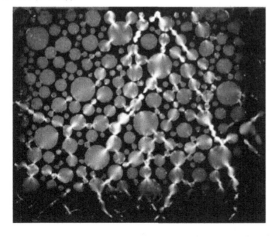

be photoelastic and transparent to light. Further, in order to conduct 3-D experiments, the granular material has to be immersed in a fluid that is transparent and has the same refractive index as the aggregates. Such a requirement is to ensure that minimum reflections occur at the interfaces between aggregate and the medium. When a greater degree of reflections take place within the system, the light is scattered more and the photoelastic observations cannot be made. Under such requirements, it is evident that real aggregates cannot be used, as they are not transparent and further, that asphalt cannot be present in a 3-D system since it is opaque. This naturally forces the preliminary photoelastic experiments to be done in 2-D (Shashidhar et al., 2000).

From among the several photoelastic materials available as surrogates to commercially used aggregates, it is beneficial to choose glass as an appropriate candidate material. Firstly, glass is resistant to high temperatures to which the sample would get heated during mixing and compaction. Secondly, the stress optic coefficient for glass is low enough, such that the intensity of transmitted light will be proportional to the stress in the system for the range of applied stresses. Having selected glass as the choice of material to model the aggregate, the next step is to obtain different sizes/shapes of the glass to simulate the aggregates in the pavement. In reality, the selected sizes /shapes should be as close as possible to those of the aggregates in the pavements. However, practical difficulties limit this selection. Different sized discs can be readily cored out of a sheet of glass without much difficulty and, hence, discs became the preferred choice of shape of the model aggregates for the experiment. It might have been preferable to use discs of complex angular shapes; however, practical ease of getting circular discs dictated the choice (Shashidhar et al., 2000).

The specimens were prepared with discs replacing all the aggregates greater in size than 4.75 mm size. Further, the number of aggregates calculated for a 3-D sample was raised to the power

2/3 in order to estimate them for a 2-D sample. The finer aggregates were mixed with the minimum asphalt needed for a complete coating.

Figure 1 shows the stress distribution when a uniform load is applied. The brightness of the light is directly proportional to the stresses in the discs. The stresses are distributed as stress chains in the system. The stresses travel from one particle to another through contacts. With time, the particles move and configuration change. These experiments show that the stresses are distributed as stress chains as it would in any granular material. In the literature, the stress distributions in unbounded granular materials have been shown to be distributed in form of chains. This experiment showed that in asphalt concrete, even with asphalt present, the material behaves as a granular material (Shashidhar et al., 2000).

This is a significant finding since this is a departure from the assumptions of traditional mechanics-based modeling. Most traditional modeling considers asphalt as a homogenous isotropic material. Such models are used to estimate layer thickness and to predict distresses in pavements. It is not known how much of a departure such models with their attendant simplifications have on the accuracy. Perhaps, with proper calibration of the model such departures can be accounted for (Shashidhar et al., 2000).

The real power of this technique is the relationship that we can develop between the aggregate structures and the mechanical performance of mixes that traditional mechanics-based methods cannot determine. The continuum models can predict the degree of performance a pavement can have. If the prediction turns out to be lower than expected, the models would not know why they are lower, and how we could improve this. By developing the relationship between aggregate structure and performance, the proposed methodology can potentially suggest ways to change the aggregate structure to improve the performance. This could be in the form of changes in gradation or changing the shape characteristics of aggre-

gates (such as adding 10 percent more crushed aggregates, etc). The other benefit will be the development of scientific methods to evaluate the affect of some of the new aggregate specifications that Superpave has developed. For this to happen, significantly more research has to be done in this area (Shashidhar et al., 2000).

MODELING GRANULAR SYSTEMS

Modeling granular systems has been accomplished by discrete element methods (DEM) since the pioneering work of Cundall and Strack (1979). In this method, the granular system is treated as being composed of distinct particles, which displace independently and interact only at contact points. Upon the application of stress, the discrete character of the medium results in complex behavior. In the discrete element method, the equilibrium contact forces and displacements of a stressed assembly of particles are found through a series of calculations tracing the movements of individual particles.

In order to use this method, an assembly of particles is required for which the precise co-ordinates of particles and the contacts between particles are known. When this assembly is stressed, the particles rearrange, and the forces are distributed such that at equilibrium, the total unbalanced forces and the total velocities of the particles approach zero. Rather than explaining the mathematical steps involved in such a modeling, the outcome of such modeling will be discussed in this paper. The mathematics of such modeling can be found in another paper (Zhong et al., 2000). DEM has been used to model circular and elliptical discs in 2-D (Rothenburg and Bathurst, 1992) and spheres and ellipsoids in 3-D (Lin and Ng, 1997). Some investigators have also used random polygons to simulate the angular particles in 2-D (Ullidtz, 1998). In order to extend these systems to real aggregates, one major step involves using a range of particle sizes that most researchers have not yet attempted. We had to develop methods to use this technique for accommodating particles with sizes spanning 2 decades. These details are again addressed in another publication (Lin and Ng, 1997).

The determination of the initial structure of the granular assembly is an important input to this modeling. This is a major issue. The typical technique to obtain this starting assembly is particle packing simulations. Simulation methods have been used extensively in modeling the microstructure of Portland cement concrete (Bentz, 1997). For asphalt concrete, it has not been established which technique (there are a variety in the literature) gives a structure close to reality. Research studies have been carried out at the U.S. Federal Highway Administration to simulate particle packing in asphalt concrete.

POTENTIAL BENEFITS OF COMPUTER SIMULATION

Computer simulations could be used to study the aggregate skeleton. For instance, Gopalakrishnan et al. (2007) have successfully developed a method to estimate the degree of compaction in HMA by studying the aggregate structure from two-dimensional image analysis of HMA specimens and from results obtained from computer simulations. A two-dimensional cross-section of HMA was simulated in computer using the mixture design information and certain statistical parameters based on nearest-neighbor distance methods were computed. The simulation results were compared with the results obtained from the image analysis of actual HMA specimens and both results compared favorably.

In computer packing simulation, the gradation is input into the computer. The computer then packs the particles into a compact. An advantage of studying computer-simulated models as opposed to physical models is that the geometrical properties of the packing structure can be ac-

curately determined, as the particle coordinates are precisely known to the machine accuracy of the computer. Since the exact locations of these particles are known, the number of contacts, the coordination number of these contacts and other characteristics of the compact can be estimated. It is possible to use mathematical descriptors for particle shape and surface texture, introduce flat and elongated particles, and thereby study their effects on HMA properties.

Also, the computer could be programmed to find the optimized gradation that would yield a mix with desired properties. In this loop, the computer would start with an initial gradation and calculate the characteristics of the compact. It could then vary the inputs and check the characteristics of the compact in a closed loop until the desired characteristics are achieved. Perhaps, the most significant benefit is that computer simulations cost less and take less effort than conducting real experiments. It is admitted that it takes effort to develop the computer code, theory and validate the code. But, once developed, several simulations can be run in short time.

For instance, if the effect of different gradations on the density of HMA were to be evaluated, the aggregates have to be sieved and batched. They have to be heated, mixed with hot asphalt, compacted, and cooled. Then the specific gravity has to be measured by say, the saturated surface dry method (AASHTO T166). The whole process could take as long as a day to test one sample. If, however, a computer simulation technique has been developed, the complete testing for a given gradation can be done in few minutes. Furthermore, the variability in measured properties would be much higher that what could be obtained through computer simulation techniques. Sometimes the real differences between properties may not be detected by physical testing since the noise level is so high. In simulation, it is possible to achieve much lower coefficient of variation. Multiple simulation runs can further reduce the coefficient of variation.

If an anomalous result is obtained by computer simulation, one can examine the resultant compact to determine if there was anything unusual in the compact. However, in a physical sample, it is extremely difficult to pinpoint the cause of such anomalies unless one has access to techniques like X-ray computed tomography.

An important benefit of modeling and simulations is that they increase our understanding of the mechanism behind certain phenomena. For instance, when the permeability of concrete was higher than it should have been, several tests were conducted. Scanning Electron Microscopy (SEM) of the concrete indicated the cement matrix to contain more air-voids adjacent to the aggregate particles. Computer modeling of diffusion (Garboczi and Bentz, 1992) was able to show that the increased air-voids could indeed increase the diffusion rate. By knowing this information, low-permeability concrete could be designed.

PARTICLE PACKING SIMULATIONS APPROACH

Aggregates with particle size distributions that follow a simple Power law (see (Eq. 1)) were considered in this paper.

$$F = \left(\frac{d}{d_{max}}\right)^k \qquad (1)$$

where d_{max} is the maximum particle size, d is the diameter of the sieve in question and F is the fraction finer than sieve.

A maximum particle size (d_{max}) of 19 mm was chosen for all the experiments since this is a popular size used in asphalt concrete. A choice of minimum size was necessary since the number of particles increase exponentially with decrease in size. The choice for the minimum particle was made by choosing values for F of 0.225, 0.25, 0.275 and 0.3. This defined the d_{min}

between 0.375 for (low k and low F) to 3.066 for high k and high F.

The span from d_{min} to d_{max} was divided into 10 logarithmically equal intervals to obtain discrete sizes for packing. The number of particles of each size was calculated and the total number was adjusted to be 80,000 particles.

PACKING ALGORITHM

Computer simulation of random packing of spheres involves using an algorithm to generate the coordinates of spheres in contact (Powell, 1980). The advantage of studying computer-simulated models as opposed to physical models is that the geometrical properties of the packing structure can be accurately determined, as the sphere coordinates are precisely known to the machine accuracy of the computer. This is especially invaluable in the study of granular materials as their properties are directly related to their packing geometry (Oger et al., 1989).

In this study, the packing algorithm used was similar to that of Vischer and Bolsterli (1972) and Jullien and Meakin (1987), in which the spheres fall under gravity sequentially and roll to their stable position. The stable position is defined as the position when the sphere rests on three contacts. The particles were dropped from random locations within the box. The algorithm included five attempts for each particle to find the lowest position, which was characterized by Vischer and Bolsterli (1972) as reproducing the effect of vibration on the settling particle. The packing fraction, defined as the volume occupied by particles per unit volume of the compact, was calculated on a smaller box that was 60% of each dimension, placed centrally. This was done to avoid edge effects on the packing results. The characteristics of the packing were estimated from these reduced boxes as well.

The first step in packing simulation is to study if the packing program yields results comparable to data reported in the literature. To study this, two different studies were conducted. In the first study, 10,000 of 10-mm diameter spheres were packed in a box of dimensions 200-mm × 200-mm box. This set-up had a box size to sphere diameter ratio of 20:1. To avoid edge effects, the outer 10-mm layer of this box was cut from all sides and only the inside core was used for further analysis. Four independent simulations gave an average packing fraction of 0.5939 and a standard deviation of 0.0011. In the second experiment, 80,000 of 3-mm spheres were packed in a 120-mm × 120-mm box to yield a box size to sphere diameter of 40:1. Four independent simulations yielded an average packing fraction of 0.5940 with a standard deviation of 0.0006. By increasing the box-size to sphere diameter ratio from 20:1 to 40:1, the mean packing fraction changed a little while halving the standard deviation. These results are comparable to the values reported in the literature, which are generally in the range of 0.58 to 0.60 for monosized spheres (Vischer and Bolsterli, 1972; Jullien and Meakin, 1987).

In random packings, the coordination number need not necessarily be an integer. In most random packing studies, the distribution of coordination numbers has been found to be effective in characterizing the packing geometry and as well as in studying the structural properties of particle packings (Powell, 1980). The value of the coordination number depends on the definition of nearest neighbors. In a packing of monosized spheres, the value of average coordination numbers can range from 6 to 13.4 depending on how the contacts are defined (Troadec et al., 1994). Since mechanical stresses are transmitted only when there is good contact between spheres, the contacts are considered when L-R1-R2 <0.001 mm where L is the distance between two spheres of radius R1 and R2.

For the both the studies, the distribution of coordination numbers of the spheres was obtained. This distribution in both the studies was found to be Guassian with a mean coordination number

of 6. The standard deviation for the Guassian distributions was 0.8707 showing that the distribution was narrow with very few spheres having a coordination number of 3 or 9. The maximum coordination number for these trials was found to be 9. This value is similar to the value obtained by Gotoh and Finney (1974) for a dense packing.

PACKING FRACTION RESULTS

As mentioned previously, there are certain difficulties in applying particle packing concepts to packing of aggregates used in asphalt concrete. To simulate the packing of aggregates in asphalt concrete, it would be necessary to pack the entire particle size distribution, which spans over 2.5 decades. This means that to represent 2 to 3 particles in coarse sizes, it is required to pack hundreds of thousands of small particles. To simplify the simulations, the particle size distributions were truncated at F = 0.30, 0.275, 0.25 and 0.275. Note that F (see Eq. 1) refers to the passing fraction as described in Eq. 1. Thus, a value of F = 0.30 means that 70% of the distribution is considered

Figure 2. Computer simulated compact with wide particle size distribution

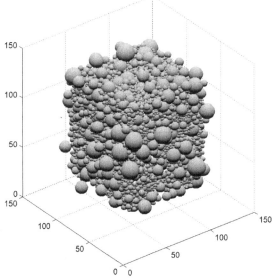

by the packing program. As F decreases, more of the particle size distribution is considered in the packing. Pictorial representation of a computer simulated packing structure obtained in this study is shown in Figure 2.

The packing fraction is plotted as a function of F in Figure 3. The packing fraction increases as F decreases. This observation corroborates the findings of other researchers who show a higher packing fraction as more particles are considered (Vischer and Bolsterli, 1972; Powell, 1980).

For any curve in Figure. 3, say k = 0.52, a decrease in passing fraction, say from 0.275 to 0.25, which is equivalent to an increase in fractional volume of 0.025, shows only a 0.00239 increase in packing fraction. The cases, F = 0.275 and F = 0.25 at k = 0.52 correspond to minimum particle sizes of 1.587 mm and 1.321 mm, respectively. It appears that the additional volume of particles that came about in transitioning from 1.587 mm to 1.321 mm does not all go in to the interstices. If every particle went into the interstices, the packing fraction would have increased from 0.6813 to 0.6813 + 0.025 = 0.7063. But, the actual increase is only to 0.6837 indicating that these additional particles actually dilate the packing. It is thus incorrect to assume that smaller particles will all go into interstitial spaces.

Since from Eq. 1, changing F is, in effect, changes the minimum particle size, d_{min}, the packing fraction was plotted as a function of

d_{min} as shown in Figure 4. Also, some additional cases were run for k = 0.38 and F = 0.230, 0.235, 0.240 and 0.245; and k = 0.52 and F = 0.20, 0.15 and 0.125. The plot shows that regardless of the exponent k, the packing fraction increases as d_{min} is decreased until d_{min} = 0.5 mm. The packing fraction then decreases fairly steeply when d_{min} decreases below 0.5 mm. Also, the data is noisier at this transition zone. This behavior can either be attributed to a failure of packing algorithm to pack particles having a large size differences or a physical phenomenon that impedes the particles from packing closely. In either case, it is safe to assume that the current packing algorithm may run into difficulty when the maximum to minimum particle size ratio becomes higher than 1: 40.

Since the particle sizes have been truncated at d_{min}, the appropriate equation to use is as follows:

$$w = \frac{d^k - d^k_{min}}{d^k_{max} - d^k_{min}} \qquad (2)$$

Zheng et al. (1990) showed that the exponent k is related to the packing fraction according to the following equation:

$$k = -\frac{\log \boxtimes}{\log R} \qquad (3)$$

where φ is the packing fraction and R is a ratio of the "coarse" and "medium" particle sizes, which is also the same as the ratio between "medium" and "fine" particle sizes.

The designation of the different sizes of particles into "coarse", "medium" and "fine" is an outcome of the Furnas (1931) model. Zheng et al. (1990) considered a continuous particle size distribution as made up of several "coarse", "medium" and "fine" sets. In the context of the current study, if d_{max} is defined as the "coarse" particle and the gradation is considered to be an

Figure 3. Packing fraction results

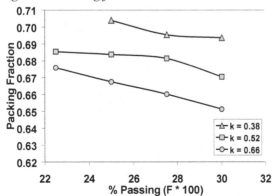

Figure 4. Packing fraction results by minimum particle size

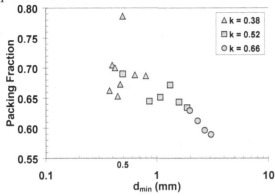

Figure 6. log (φ) versus log (1/R) for the cases considered in this study

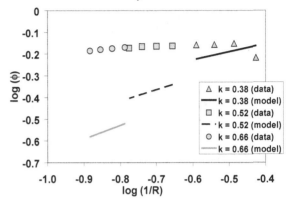

addition of several sets of coarse, medium and fine particles, the diameter of the fine particles is expected to be slightly greater than d_{min}. In Figure 5, the derivation of R is shown to be equal to $(d_{max}/d_{min})^{(1/3)}$. According to Eq. 3, a plot of log(φ) versus log(1/R) should be a straight line passing through the origin with a slope equal to k. Based on the results of the current study, Figure 6 shows that the data does not fit this model.

Although Zheng et al. (1990) derived the expression for k (see Eq. 3), examples to illustrate that the proposed methodology agrees with experimental results were not provided. Perhaps, a continuous distribution such as that considered in this study cannot be considered as a combina-

tion of several sets of coarse, medium and fine particles. This is because for a typical mixture of coarse, medium, and fine particles, the coarse particles will have large enough void spaces to accommodate some medium particles and the fine particles could fill the remaining voids. However, in a continuous distribution of particle sizes, the voids do not exist in quite the same way, as it would be if it were just coarse particles.

Other researchers have tried to extend the binary and ternary mixtures of particles to apply for continuous particle size distributions (Funk and Dinger, 1994) based on the work done by Westman and Hugill (1930). However, the equations proposed by Westman and Hugill (1930) apply only for the limiting case when the ratio of "coarse" to "medium" diameters and "medium" to "fine" diameters is infinite. In a continuous particle size distribution, the ratio between consequent sizes is hardly "infinite" and therefore the equations proposed by Westman and Hugill (1930) cannot be applied. To demonstrate this, the equations proposed by Westman and Hugill (1930) were actually applied to the cases considered in this study and they were not found to predict the packing fraction.

In this study, when k = 0.38, n = 16 and CSR=1.275, and a_n for the random close packing of monosize spheres is 1/0.5872 = 1.703. Using these values, we get V_a = 0.767 or φ = 1.304.

Figure 5. Derivation of particle size ratio, R (after Zheng et al. (1990))

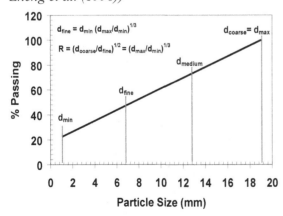

Since this packing fraction is unrealistic, it could be concluded that the equations proposed by Westman and Hugill (1930) cannot be applied to continuous particle size distributions considered in this study.

DISTRIBUTION OF CONTACTS

The particle-particle contacts are more important to evaluate the stability of the packing. The approach taken here is to measure the distribution of contacts for any given size particle. This distribution of contacts was found to be a Guassian distribution, which is similar to the distribution of contacts for random packing of monosize particles. This distribution normalized by the total number of particles of that size is plotted in Figure 7.

Several observations can be made from Figure 7. The distributions of contacts are narrow for smaller size particles and broad for larger size particles. The mean number of contacts increases as the particle size increases. In other words, the larger the particle size, the more contacts it is likely to have. The data tends to get noisier as the particle size increases. The reason for this is that there are fewer larger particles than there are smaller particles. Therefore, the smaller sizes have better statistics than larger particles. The larger particles have a wider range of number of

contacts. This is because the size of the particles in contact with a give particle dictates how many particles can be in contact. A particle can have many smaller particles contacting it or fewer larger particles touching it.

Each of these distributions were characterized using a Gaussian distribution function and the mean and standard deviations were estimated. The regression results were excellent with R^2 greater than 0.99 for smaller particles. However, as the particle size increased, the noise in the data caused poorer fits and curves with lower R^2 values were not considered for further analysis.

In figures 8 and 9, the mean and standard deviations of the Gaussian curves are plotted as a function of the particle size (d). When the mean and standard deviations were normalized by the minimum particle size (d_{min}), the individual curves collapsed into a single master curve in each case. The results are shown in Figs. 10 and 11. A quadratic equation could be fit for each of the master curves (one for mean and one for standard deviation). The following equations for mean and standard deviation represented the data well:

$$Mean = A + B\left(\frac{d}{d_{min}}\right) + C\left(\frac{d}{d_{min}}\right)^2 \qquad (7)$$

$$S\tan dard\ Deviation = D + E\left(\frac{d}{d_{min}}\right) + G\left(\frac{d}{d_{min}}\right)^2 \qquad (8)$$

The R^2 for these second-order polynomial regression equations were greater than 0.97 indicating good fits. The coefficients A-G for these fits are displayed in Table 1. This approach can be used to compare different particle size distributions, or aggregate gradations in the case of asphalt pavement mixtures, as shown in Figs. 12 and 13. These plots show that particle size gradation influences the mean number of contacts to some extent and the standard deviation of contacts to a large extent. For a given particle size diameter, the higher k-value has a lower standard deviation.

Figure 7. Distribution of contacts

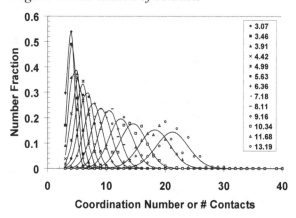

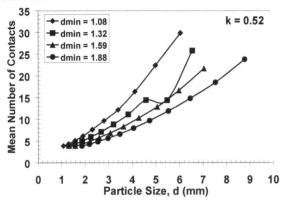

Figure 8. Mean number of contacts versus particle size

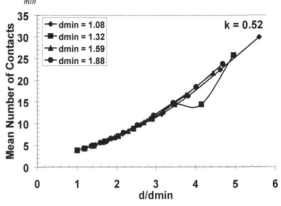

Figure 10. Mean number of contacts versus d/d_{min}

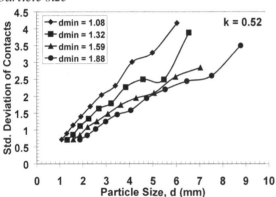

Figure 9. Standard deviation of contacts versus particle size

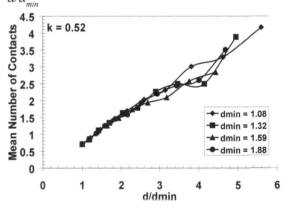

Figure 11. Standard deviation of contacts versus d/d_{min}

The mean number of particles is almost independent of k-value.

In a different experiment, particles with a lower maximum size (d_{max}) of 13.3 mm was repeated

Table 1. Regression analysis results

Regression Model Coefficients	k = 0.38	k = 0.52	k = 0.66
A	2.054853	2.002355	1.655982
B	1.075094	1.12836	1.336999
C	0.739957	0.696957	0.718803
D	-0.27737	0.019299	0.03865
E	1.019175	0.763897	0.725217
G	-0.00372	-0.01366	-0.01691

since these maximum sizes represent one of the typical particle size distributions used in asphalt pavements. The maximum size also matches the experiments for which the physical results have been obtained previously (Goode and Lufsey, 1962). The results were very similar to those shown in Figs. 7 to 11. Thus, the behavior of contact distribution is independent of the maximum particle size (d_{max}).

The distribution of contacts for a given particle size is consistent with the observation for monosize particles. Equations (7) and (8) that describe the master-curves for contacts contain lot of useful information. Due to current computational limitations, the packing program could only pack to a minimum size of 1.08 mm for k = 0.52 gradation.

Figure 12. Comparison of contact distribution statistics for different gradations (mean)

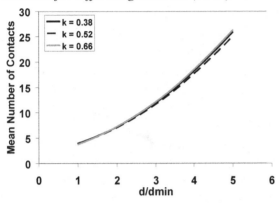

Figure 13. Comparison of contact distribution statistics for different gradations (standard deviation)

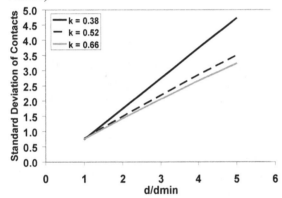

With these master-curves it would be possible to estimate what the number of contacts would be if the gradation were packed down to smaller size particles. For instance, if a powder with maximum size of 19 mm and a minimum size of 0.075 mm were packed, a 2.36 mm particle would have a mean number of contacts of 728 and a standard deviation of 10.53. This certainly is a large number of contacts. The mechanical properties of the packing are dependent on how many of these contacts actually transmit force when the packed assembly is stressed. Travers et al. (1986) showed through photo-elastic experiments on a two dimensional packing of cylinders that only

two or three contacts seemed to transmit load even though there seemed to be six contacts on an average. It is therefore necessary to come up with an additional criterion to define load-transmitting contacts.

Consider Figure 14, which is a close-up of a likely scenario in a two dimensional packing assembly. When this assembly of particles is stressed, the most likely situation is that the force will travel through a path that will bypass the small particles. In other words, the contact must be a stable part of a skeleton for the stress to pass through it. If we consider all the particles that form such a stable skeleton to be load-bearing, then there has to be some criteria to classify the load-bearing particles. Future studies will focus on deriving such a criterion to divide a particle as load-bearing or non-load bearing.

Shashidhar et al. (2000) demonstrated that asphalt concrete behaves more like a granular system and have shown the possibility of developing a relationship between the aggregate structure and asphalt pavement performance through micromechanics based modeling and image processing techniques. The knowledge of the relationship between the aggregate structure and the mechanical properties will enable one to engineer pavements

Figure 14. A schematic of 2D packing assembly of particles

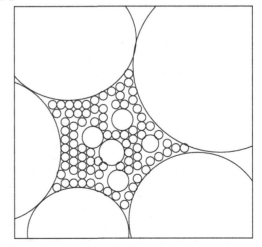

to have the appropriate aggregate structure to maximize the field performance.

The results from this current study, especially the contact distribution characteristics, together with the principles of granular mechanics, could be used in understanding the transmission of load through aggregate contacts.

ROLE OF AGGREGATE STRUCTURE IN ASPHALT CONCRETE

When a truck applies a load on the pavement, the load gets distributed and is transmitted to the layers underneath. The function of the pavement is thus to transfer and distribute the load and provide a smooth surface for a pleasant ride. This discussion will concentrate on the ability to transfer and distribute load in AC pavements.

A typical dense graded AC pavement is made of 86% by volume of aggregates bound with about 10% by volume of asphalt and incorporates 4% of air-voids. The asphalt binder is a visco-elastic material that has much lower ability to carry loads when compared to aggregates. Since the binder is viscoelastic, it will deform and flow under load. The conventional wisdom is that in AC pavements the coarse aggregates form a skeleton that primarily supports the load. As discussed previously, using photoelastic methods, Shashidhar et al. (2000) showed that the loads were transmitted from aggregate to aggregate is a two-dimensional representation of asphalt concrete. It was shown that the different gradations give different aggregate structure and therefore different stress patterns.

The asphalt also has a significant effect on the rutting performance of the AC pavement. Given the same gradation, a stiffer binder will show a higher resistance to rutting than a binder that is less stiff. The effects of the binder and the aggregate structure can be understood if the aggregate skeleton is considered to be unstable.

In the defective skeleton theory, it is argued that this coarse aggregate skeleton in AC is primarily unstable and will collapse under load. The binder present slows this collapse since the binder has to yield and give way for this collapse. The ability of the pavement to resist rutting is improved by either improving the aggregate skeleton or by using a stiffer binder. If the skeleton is kept constant (by using the same aggregate gradation) stiffer binders will yield better rut resistance. The skeleton that is not defective when application of the load will not collapse the skeleton. In that case, the binder provides little support and therefore does not affect the rutting characteristics of the pavement. Since this condition rarely exists, most aggregate skeletons are defective, with some more defective than the others.

The evaluation of the aggregate skeleton is very difficult. There are no direct methods of evaluating the aggregate skeleton. In fact there are no known ways of describing the aggregate skeleton. There are many key evidences that support the defective skeleton theory. They are as follows:

- In a manner similar to the saturation of sand, the rutting properties are very sensitive to asphalt content. If more than an optimum (design asphalt content) volume of asphalt is added to the AC, the asphalt will push aggregate apart thereby loosening the aggregate skeleton.
- The better performance of stone matrix asphalt (SMA) is attributed to better coarse aggregate skeleton in these mixes compared to the dense graded AC (Brown et al., 1998; Scherocman, 1991).
- The Bailey method of asphalt mix design (Vavrik et al., 2001) attempts to maintain the aggregate skeleton that exists in a packing of just coarse aggregate. This procedure has reportedly been used to design pavements in Illinois that have been doing well. However, whether the procedure results in a better aggregate structure is yet to be verified.

The concept, though intuitive, has several points that needs clarification. It is generally considered that coarse aggregates form the skeleton. It is unclear how these coarse aggregates are defined. Aggregates greater than 4.35 mm (No. 4) sieve or a 2.36 mm (No. 8) sieve is considered as coarse aggregates. Bailey method defines this cutoff as the nominal maximum aggregate size multiplied by 0.22. Since the origins of these cut-off limits are uncertain, it is unclear if the aggregates below this cut-off will not participate in aggregate skeleton.

It is also uncertain what effects the aggregate gradation will have on this cut-off. It is possible that this cut-off size is dependent on the aggregate gradation.

If the role of coarse aggregates is defined as skeleton forming, what would the role of fine aggregates be? Do they just fill the voids in the skeleton and make the mix less pervious. This is an important function since in this role, they increase the durability of the pavements.

Aggregate interlock can be fully characterized if all the particle-particle contacts in a compact are counted, the average contacts per particle is calculated and the stability of this structure is somehow established. If all the characteristics can be measured, one can then study the effects of various parameters on interlock such as aggregate gradation, angularity, influence of flat and elongated particles etc. The mix can then be optimized to give the most stable structure. If the aggregate characteristics can be optimized to give the most stable structure, the mix should become extremely resistant to rutting and the influence of the binder should be minimal.

In recent years, there has been significant research on qualitative or/and quantitative assessment of AC internal structure using two-dimensional (2-D) and three-dimensional (3-D) image analysis techniques (Masad et al.,1999a; Masad et al., 1999b; Tashman et al., 2001; Saadeh et al., 2002; Wang et al., 2004). These imaging methods quantify the distribution of aggregate skeleton, voids in the mineral aggregate, and air voids in AC by analyzing images of the internal structure, acquired either two-dimensionally using a microscope connected to a camera or three-dimensionally with an X-ray Computed Tomography (XCT) system (Masad and Button, 2004).

Several cross-sectional images of a single HMA specimen or core acquired using a XCT system can be put together and rendered to produce a volume image. The volumetric images permit study of various aspects of HMA such as the structure of the aggregate skeleton, the orientation of particles, any lack of homogeneity (segregation) in aggregate sizes, distribution of air-voids, presence of cracks, the distribution of asphalt, etc. Information such as the inter-connectivity of air-voids, the number and the direction of aggregate-aggregate contacts and aggregate orientation cannot be accurately determined from two-dimensional images. A 3-D rendered image from a series of 2-D image slices scanned in a XCT system is shown in Figure 15.

Ketcham and Shashidhar (2001) used a software program, BLOB3D®, to analyze 3-D images of HMA quantitatively. The BLOB3D® program implements a 3-D version of what is traditionally called a "blob analysis" for extracting objects from 2-D images. The three-dimensional rendering

Figure 15. A 3-D Rendered image from a series of 2D slices scanned in X-Ray CT system

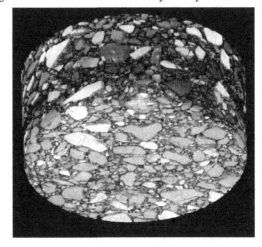

of a sub-volume for HMA quantitative analysis using BLOB3D® software is shown in Figure 16. Ketcham and Sashidhar (2001) demonstrated that it is possible to extract particle size, location, aggregate-aggregate contact vectors, and contact area using the BLOB3D® program. Other features of interest such as aggregate volume, surface area, center of mass, orientation, aggregate-aggregate contact normal vectors, and contact surface areas could be measured too.

Thus, by thorough examination of the AC internal structure, aggregate matrices that exhibit enhanced performance can be identified and steps can be taken to develop compaction techniques that can produce this structure. The variation in aggregate structure within a pavement layer can be better quantified, thus improving the accuracy of QC/QA methods. Also, by investigating the aggregate structure, the cause of premature failure of an asphalt pavement may be determined (Shashidhar, 1999).

SUMMARY AND CONCLUSIONS

In this research, particle packing simulation concepts were applied to the study of aggregate structure in Asphalt Concrete (AC) or bitumi-

Figure 16. Quantitative Analysis of 3-D Images of HMA using BLOB3D®

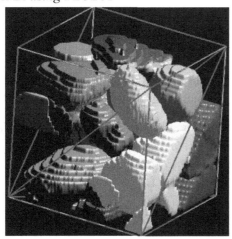

nous concrete. Previous research by the authors showed that the changes in AC aggregate structure due to compaction could be quantified through two-dimensional image analysis techniques and computer simulations. In this study, the aggregates were modeled as hard spheres and some typical aggregate gradations used in AC were packed using a computer program. The packing characteristics of the compact were studied in terms of packing fraction and distribution of contacts.

The coordination number of any size particles in the packing of particles with a continuous size distribution was found to be a Guassian distribution whose mean and standard deviation can be estimated. The mean number of contacts and the standard deviation of this distribution increased with particle size. Regression equations were developed to predict the mean and standard deviations of contacts in simulated packing structures.

The contacts can be distinguished between those that are likely to transmit load and those that are not likely to transmit load according to the coordination number of the particle it is touching. Future research efforts will focus on deriving such a criterion.

Future research should focus on deriving an appropriate criterion based on the coordination number to qualify each contact as active (or load-bearing) or passive (or space-filling) in load transmission. Future research efforts will also focus on applying suitable contact mechanics principles to introduce the asphalt binder (or mastic) at the particle-particle contacts and apply this model to virtual specimens reconstructed from non-destructive images of pavement core sections.

The application of particle packing simulation concepts discussed in this chapter to the study of aggregate structure in asphalt pavements, in conjunction with the recent advances in nondestructive imaging techniques and DEM simulations have tremendous potential to help us to develop a deeper understanding of the aggregate structure in asphalt concrete, develop and optimize the various parameters that describe the aggregate structure and relate them to the performance of pavements in a scientific way. This will provide the foundations to building more durable and long-lasting pavements.

ACKNOWLEDGMENT

The authors gratefully acknowledge the valuable contributions of Dr. Xibing Dou, Senior Research Engineer at the Turner-Fairbanks Highway Research Center towards this study. The first author would like to thank the National Highway Institute (NHI) for financial assistance in conducting this study through the Dwight D. Eisenhower Graduate Research Fellowship.

REFERENCES

Bentz, D. P. (1997). Three Dimensional Computer Simulation of Portland Cement Hydration and Microstructure Development. *J. Am. Ceram. Soc., 80*(1), 3-21.

Bernal, & Mason, G. (1960). Coordination of Randomly Packed Spheres. *Nature 188*, 910.

Bernal, J. D., Cherry, I. A., Finney, J. L., & Knight, K. R. (1970). An Optical Machine for Measuring Sphere Coordinates in Random Packings. *J. Phys., E 3*, 388-90.

Bierwagen, G. P., & Saunders, T. E. (1974). Studies of the Effects of Particle Size Distribution on the Packing Efficiency of Particles. *Powder Technology 10*, 111-19.

Brown, E. R., Haddock, J. E., Crawford, C., Hughes, C. S., & Lynn, T. A. (1998). "Designing Stone Matrix Asphalt Mixtures. Volume II(a). NCHRP Report 9-8/2, TRB, Washington, D.C.

Cundall, P. A., & Strack, O. D. L. (1979). A Discrete Numerical Model for Granular Assemblies. *Geotechnique, 29*, 47-65.

Dantu, P. (1957). Contribution à l'étude mécanique et géométrique des milieux pulvérulents. *Proc. of the 4th Int. Conf. on Soil Mech. and Found. Eng, 1*, 144-148.

Dexter, A. R., & Tanner, D. W. (1972). Packing Densities of Mixtures of Spheres with Log-Normal Size Distributions. *Nature Phy. Sci. 238*, 31-32.

Funk, J. E., & Dinger, D. R. (1994). *Predictive Process control of Crowded Particulate Suspensions*. Boston: Kluwer Academic Publishers.

Furnas, C. C. (1931). Grinding aggregates I—mathematical relations for beds of broken solids of maximum density. *Ind. Eng. Chem. 23*, 1052.

Garboczi, J. F., & Bentz, D. P. (1992). Computer Simulation of the Diffusivity of Cement-Based Materials. *Journal of Materials Science, 27*, 2083-2092.

Goode, J. F. & Lufsey, L. A. (1962). A New Graphical Chart for Evaluating Aggregate Gradations. *Assoc. Asphalt Paving Technologists, 31*, 176-207.

Gopalakrishnan, K., & Shashidhar, N. (2007). Characterising the aggregate structure variations in asphalt concrete during compaction using computer automated imaging techniques. *Int. J. Computer Applications in Technology, 28*(4), 295–303.

Gotoh, K., & Finney, J. L. (1974). Statistical Geometrical Approach to Random Packing Density of Equal Spheres. *Nature, 252*, 202-205.

Jullien, R., & Meakin, P. (1987). Simple Three-Dimensional Models for Ballistic Deposition with Restructuring. *Europhysics Lett., 4*, 1385-90.

Ketcham, R. A., & Shashidhar, N. (2001). Quantitative Analysis of 3-D Images of Asphalt Concrete. *Proceedings, 80th Annual TRB Meeting*, Washington, D.C.

Lin, X., & Ng, T. T. (1997). A Three-Dimensional Discrete Element Model Using Arrays of Ellipsoids. *Geotechnique, 47*(2), 319-29.

Masad, E., & Button, J. (2004). Implications of Experimental Measurements and Analyses of the Internal Structure of Hot-Mix Asphalt. *Transportation Research Record, 1891, TRB*, 212–220.

Masad, E., Muhunthan, B., Shashidhar, N., & Harman, T. (1999a). Internal Structure Characterization of Asphalt Concrete Using Image Analysis. *Journal of Computing in Civil Engineering, 13*(2), 88–95.

Masad, E., Muhunthan, B., Shashidhar, N., & Harman, T. (1999b). Quantifying Laboratory Compaction Effects on the Internal Structure of Asphalt Concrete. *Transportation Research Record, 1681, TRB*, 179–185.

Nolan, G. T., & Kavanagh, P. E. (1992). Computer Simulation of Random Packing of Hard Spheres, *Powder Technology, 72*, 149-55.

Oger, L., Lichtenberg, M., Gervois, A., & Guyon, E. (1989). Determination of the Coordination Number in Disordered Packings of Equal Spheres. *Journal of Microscopy 156(1)*,. 65-78.

Powell, M. J. (1980). Computer-Simulated Random Packing of Spheres. *Powder Technology, 25*, 45-52.

Rothenburg, L., & Bathurst, R. J. (1992). Micromechanical Features of Granular Assemblies with Planar Elliptical Particles. *Geotechnique, 42*(1), 79-95.

Saadeh, S., Tashman, L., Masad, E., & Mogawer, W. (2002). Spatial and Directional Distributions of Aggregates in Asphalt Mixes. *Journal of Testing and Evaluation, ASTM, 30*(6), 483–491.

Scherocman, J. A. (1991). Stone Mastic Asphalt Reduces Rutting. *Better Roads, 61*(11), 26.

Shashidhar, N. (1999). X-ray Tomography of Asphalt Concrete. *Transportation Research Record: Journal of the Transportation Research Board, 1681, TRB*, 186–192.

Shashidhar, N., Zhong, X., Shenoy, A., & Bastian, E. (2000). Investigating the role of aggregate structure in asphalt pavements. In *Proc., 8th Annual Symposium on Aggregates, Asphalt Concrete, Bases and Fines*, ICAR, Denver, Colorodo, 2000.

Sohn, H. Y., & Moreland, C. (1968). The Effect of Particle Size Distribution on Packing Density. *Canadian J. Chem. Eng. 46*, 162-67.

Soppe, W. (1990). Computer Simulation of Random Packings of Hard Spheres. *Powder Technology, 62*,. 189-96.

Tashman, L., Masad, E., Peterson, B., & Saleh, H. (2001). Internal Structure Analysis of Asphalt Mixes to Improve the Simulation of Superpave Gyratory Compaction to Field Conditions. *Journal of the Association of Asphalt Paving Technologists, 70*, 605–645.

Travers, T., Bideau, D., Troadec, J. P., & Messager, J. C. (1986). Uniaxial Compression Effects on 2D Mixtures of 'Hard' and 'Soft' cylinders. *J. Phys. A 19*, L1033-L1038.

Troadec, J. P., Gervois, A., Annic, C., & Lemaître, J. (1974). A model of binary assemblies of dises and its application to segregation study. *J. Phys. (France) I 4*, 1121-1132.

Ullidtz, P. (1998). *Modelling Flexible Pavement Response and Performance*. First Edition, Lyngby: Polyteknisk Forlag.

Vavrik, W. R., Pine, W. J., Huber, G., Carpenter, S .H., & Bailey, R. (2001). The Bailey Method of Gradation Evaluation: The Influence of Aggregate Gradation and Packing Characteristics on Voids in the Mineral Aggregate. *Journal of the Association of Asphalt Paving Technologists, 70*.

Vischer, W. M., & M. Bolsterli (1972). Random Packing of Equal and Unequal Spheres in Two and Three Dimensions. *Nature (London) 239*, 504.

Wang, L. B., Paul, H. S., Harman, T., & Angelo, J. D. (2004a). Characterization of Aggregates and Asphalt Concrete Using X-Ray Computerized Tomography: A State-of-The-Art Report. *Journal of the Association of Asphalt Paving Technologists*, 73, 467-500.

Westman, A. E. R., & H. R. Hugill (1930). The Packing of Particles. *J. Amer. Ceram. Soc. 13*, 767-79.

Zheng, J., Johnson, P. F., & Reed, J. S. (1990). *J. Amer. Ceram. Soc. 73*, 1392.

Zhong, X., Shashidhar, N., & Chang, C. S. (2000). DEM Stability for Static Analysis in Aggregate Packing. *Proceedings of 14th Engineering Mechanics Conference*, Austin, Texas.

KEY TERMS

Aggregate Structure: Aggregate Structure, also referred to as Internal Structure Internal structure refers to content and distribution of air-voids, aggregates, and asphalt. This also includes aggregate structure or skeleton, which serves as a backbone in bearing loads and in resisting pavement distresses such as rutting and cracking.

Bituminous Concrete: Bituminous Concrete, referred to as Asphalt concrete in the U.S., is a composite material commonly used for construction of pavement, highways and parking lots. It consists of asphalt binder and mineral aggregate mixed together then laid down in layers and compacted.

Image Analysis: Image analysis is the extraction of meaningful information from images; mainly from digital images by means of digital image processing techniques.

Pavement: Pavement (American English) or road surface (British English) is the durable surface material laid down on an area intended to sustain traffic (vehicular or foot traffic). Such surfaces are frequently marked to guide traffic. The most common modern paving methods are asphalt and concrete.

Simulation: A computer simulation, a computer model or a computational model is a computer program, or network of computers, that attempts to simulate an abstract model of a particular system, to gain insight into the operation of that system, or to observe its behavior.

Chapter XVII
Information Technology as a Service

Robin G. Qiu
The Pennsylvania State University, USA

ABSTRACT

In this information era, both business and living communities are truly IT driven and service oriented. As the globalization of the world economy accelerates with the fast advance of networking and computing technologies, IT plays a more and more critical role in assuring real-time collaborations for delivering needs across the world. Nowadays, world-class enterprises are eagerly embracing service-led business models aimed at creating highly profitable service-oriented businesses. They take advantage of their own years of experience and unique marketing, engineering, and application expertise and shift gears toward creating superior outcomes to best meet their customers' needs in order to stay competitive. IT has been considered as one of the high-value services areas. In this chapter, the discussion will focus on IT as a service. We present IT development, research, and outsourcing as a knowledge service; on the other hand, we argue that IT as a service helps enterprises align their business operations, workforce, and technologies to maximize their profits by continuously improving their performance. Numerous research and development aspects of service-enterprise engineering from a business perspective will be briefly explored, and then computing methodologies and technologies to enable adaptive enterprise service computing in support of service-enterprise engineering will be simply studied and analyzed. Finally, future development and research avenues in this emerging interdisciplinary field will also be highlighted.

INTRODUCTION

With the significant advances in networks, tele-communication, and computing technologies, people, organizations, systems, and heterogeneous information sources now can be linked together more efficiently and cost effectively than ever before. The quick advances of IT in general significantly transform not only science and engineering research, but also expectations of how people live, learn, and work as we witnessed during the last decade or so. Life at home, work, and leisure gets easier, better, and more enjoyable.

In the business world, because of rich information linkages, the right data and information in the right context can be delivered to the right user (e.g., people, machines, devices, software components, etc.) in the right place and at the right time, resulting in the substantial increase of the degree of business-process automation, the continual increment of production productivity and services quality, the reduction of service lead time, and the improvement of end users' satisfaction. As a variety of devices, hardware, and software become network aware, almost everything is capable of being handled over a network. Many tasks can be done on site or remotely, and in the same manner, so are a variety of services provided or even self-performed over the Internet. At the end of day, end users or consumers do not care about how and where the product was made, by whom, and how it was delivered; what the end users or consumers essentially care about is that their needs are met in a satisfactory manner.

In manufacturing, the deployment of integrated information systems is accelerating (Qiu, 2004). A typical IT-driven manufacturing business can be created by deploying enterprise-wide information systems managing the life cycle of both the business and its electronic aspects; that is, an order is taken over the Internet, and the products are made and delivered as promised. For instance, customers submit their orders via Internet browsers directly through a sales-force automation center, which automatically triggers the generation of the appropriate material releases and production requirements. It also informs all the other relevant planning systems, such as those for advance production schedule, finance, supply chain, logistics, and customer-relationship management, of the new order entry. The scheduler then assigns or configures an on-site or remote production line through the production control in the most efficient way possible, taking into

account raw material, procurement, and production capacity. A shop-floor production-execution schedule is then generated, in which problems are anticipated and appropriate adjustments are made accordingly in a corresponding manufacturing execution system. In the designated facility, the scheduled work is accomplished automatically through a computer-controlled production line in an efficient and cost-effective manner. As soon as the work is completed, the ordered product gets automatically warehoused and/or distributed. Ultimately, the customers should be provided the least cost and best quality goods, as well as the most satisfactory services (Qiu, Wysk, & Xu, 2003).

No matter what is made and how services are delivered, in reality, high living standards with a better quality of life are what we are pursuing as human beings. When the communities we are living in are deeply studied, we understand that our communities are truly IT driven and service oriented in the information era. Here are a few daily noticeable, inescapable, and more contemporary service examples that could be on demand at any time and place (Dong & Qiu, 2004; Qiu, 2005).

- A passenger traveling in a rural and unfamiliar area suddenly has to go to a hospital due to sickness, so local hospital information is immediately required at the point of need. The passenger and his or her companions wish to get local hospital information through their cellular phones. Generally speaking, when travelers are in an unfamiliar region for tourism or business, handy and accurate information on routes and traffic, weather, restaurants, hotels, hospitals, and attractions and entertainment in the destination region will be very helpful.

- A truck fully loaded with hazardous chemical materials is overturned on a suburban highway. Since the chemicals could be poisonous, people on site need critical knowledge (i.e., intelligent assistance) to quickly perform life-saving and other critical tasks after one calls 911 (in the United States). However, people on site most likely cannot perform the tasks effectively due to limited knowledge and resources. Situations could be worse if tasks are not done appropriately, which could lead to an irreversible and horrible result. Intelligent assistant services are necessary at the point of need. Obviously, the situation demands a quick response from the governmental IT-driven emergency response systems.

- Transportation plays a critical role in warranting the quality service and effectiveness of a supply chain. When a truck is fully loaded with certain goods, certain attention might be required from the driver from time to time, for instance, to the air, temperature, and/or humidity requirements. Only when the requirements are met on the road can the goods in transit be maintained with good quality. Otherwise, the provided transportation service will not be satisfactory. Due to the existence of a variety of goods, it is impossible for drivers to master all the knowledge on how the goods can be best monitored and accordingly protected on the highway as many uncertain events might occur during the transportation of the goods. On-demand services to assure warranty are the key for an enterprise to lead competitors. As manufacturing and services become global, more challenges are added into this traditional service.

- The growing elderly population draws much attention throughout the world, resulting in issues on the shortage of laborers and more importantly the lack of effective health-care delivery. Studies show that elderly patients (65 or older) are twice as likely to be harmed by a medication error because they often receive complex drug regimens and suffer from more serious ailments that make them

particularly vulnerable to harmful drug mistakes. Outpatient prescription-drug-related injuries are common in elderly patients, but many could be prevented. For instance, about 58% adverse drug events could be prevented if continuity-of-care record plans and related health-care information systems are adopted for providing prompt assistant services; over 20% of drug-related injuries could be prevented if the given medication instructions are provided at the point of need so the instructions are adhered to by the patients.

Apparently, the real-time flow of information and quick delivery of relevant information and knowledge at the point of need from an information-service provider or system is essential for providing quality services to meet the on-demand needs descried in all the above scenarios.

In a broader view, the service-oriented society is clearly evidenced by the largest labor migration in history around the world. According to Rangaswamy and Pal (2005), total-solution services (enabled performances for the customer's benefit rather than a physical good) constitute the prime marketplace battlefield of the day. For instance, in the U.S. economy, over 70% of the 2005 gross domestic product was generated from services businesses. Similar numbers dominate many other developed economies worldwide. Even in some developing countries like China and India, 35% of labor is service oriented, and the number continues to climb every year. The world-developed economy is clearly heading to one that is IT driven, technology based, and services led.

Because of the fast development of IT, the globalization of the world economy is accelerating. Under the umbrella of global virtual enterprises through collaborative partnerships, enterprises can provide best-of-breed goods and services at a more competitive price while meeting the changing needs of today's on-demand business environment. As competition in the globalizing economy unceasingly intensifies, it becomes essential for enterprises to rethink their operational and organizational structures to meet the consumers' fluctuating demand for innovation, flexibility, and shorter lead times for their provided goods and services. For example, for farsighted manufacturers in the developed economy, as their product technologies might quickly lose their competitiveness, they recognize that only their services components would distinguish themselves from their competitors. Therefore, enterprises are keen on building highly profitable service-oriented businesses by taking advantage of their own unique engineering and application expertise, aimed at shifting gears toward creating superior outcomes to best meet their customers' needs in order to stay competitive (Rangaswamy & Pal, 2005).

The value of provided goods or delivered services lies in their ability to satisfy an end user's need, which is not simply and strictly seen in the physical attributes of the provided product or the technical characteristics of the delivered service. For today's competitive enterprise, a superior outcome provided to its customer inevitably constitutes services contributing to the entire customer solution through the well-established and highly collaborated value net, including the support of solution engineering, the sale of a physical product, product sustaining, personnel training, and/or a knowledge-transformation service in a satisfactory manner. This new and emerging field is truly interdisciplinary in nature and explores new frontiers of research, attempting to build a true science and engineering base and establish the foundation for understanding future competitiveness (IBM, 2004; Rangaswamy & Pal, 2005).

As discussed above, IT plays a critical role in facilitating today's geographically dispersed manufacturing and services delivery. It is IT that enables real-time information flow. When enterprise-wide information systems are fully integrated throughout the whole customer order

fulfillment process, all of the order information, lot travelers, material consumptions, customer services, and accounting ledgers can be continuously updated. Therefore, top management can keep abreast of how efficiently the enterprises are running and thus make the optimal decisions possible with real-time information on sales, finances, resources, and capacity utilizations. As a result, enterprises are staying due to better competitive advantages as customers are totally satisfied with their on-demand needs. Total satisfaction typically drives further sales.

As the economy shifts from being manufacturing based to information-services based, better understanding of services marketing, innovation, design, engineering, operations, and management will be essential. Evidently, IT is a service from an end user's perspective. By aggregating the concepts and research from the latest literature, this chapter presents the author's point of view on this emerging interdisciplinary field, focusing on how enterprise service computing might be evolving from the current research and development. In the remainder of the chapter, numerous research and development aspects of service-enterprise engineering from the business perspective will be first discussed, and then some technologies to enable adaptive enterprise service computing in support of future service-enterprise engineering will be briefly introduced and analyzed.

ASPECTS OF SERVICES-ENTERPRISE ENGINEERING

With the push of the ongoing industrialization of information technologies, enterprises must aggregate products and services into total solutions by implementing an integrated and complete value net over all of their geographically dispersed collaborative partners to deliver services-led solutions in order to stay competitive (Figure 1). The essential goal of applying total solutions to value networks is to enable the discovery, design, deployment, execution, operation, monitoring, optimization, analysis, transformation, and creation of coordinated business processes across the value chain: a collaborating ecosystem. Ultimately, the profit across the whole value network can be maximized as it becomes the top business objective in today's global business environment (Karmarkar, 2004).

The shift from a manufacturing base to a services base makes enterprises rethink their business strategies and revamp their operational and organizational structures to meet the customers' fluctuating demands for services delivered in a satisfactory fashion. Enterprises across the board in general are eager to seek new business opportunities by streamlining their business processes; building complex, integrated, and more efficient IT-driven systems; and embracing the worldwide Internet-based marketplace. It is well recognized that business-process automation, outsourcing, customization, offshore sourcing, business-process transformation, and self-services became another business wave in today's evolving global services-led economy.

Services sectors nowadays cover commercial transportation, logistics and distribution, healthcare delivery, financial engineering, e-commerce, retailing, hospitality and entertainment, issuance, supply chains, knowledge transformation and delivery, and consulting. In the developed countries, services enterprises are the new industrial base of the economy. For instance, almost four out of five jobs are currently offered by these services

sectors in the United States. On the other hand, in the developing countries, more traditional labor-intensive manufacturing and services are still the core businesses. However, the developing countries actively participate in the global economy, mainly providing the physical attributes of goods and services through the manufacturing and delivering of labor-intensive services and business functions. The global economy in the 21st century requiring a business ecosystem for better effectiveness, efficiency, and manageability thus involves all the collaborated business-function organisms with their operational settings. The global ecosystem indeed includes participants from both the developed and developing countries.

Although this new wave seems to be repeating the trends that afflicted U.S. manufacturing in the 1970s, it gets more complicated in demanding higher efficiency and better cost effectiveness across the geographically dispersed value chains. Moreover, compared to industry's knowledge of mature manufacturing business practices, services-enterprise engineering is still substantially uncharted territory (Rangaswamy & Pal, 2005). According to IBM (2004):

Services sciences, Management and Engineering [as an emerging interdisciplinary field] hopes to bring together ongoing work in computer science, operations research, industrial engineering, business strategy, management sciences, social and cognitive sciences, and legal sciences to develop the skills [and knowledge] required in a services-led economy.

Figure 1. Service-oriented business value net

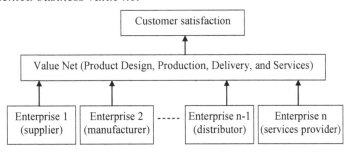

Only recently have there been some international initiatives to promote research and education in this emerging field in a comprehensive manner.

Research and education in services-enterprise engineering to cultivate and empower the ecosystem driven by services, technology, and management have been lagging behind when compared to many other areas as many scholars from leading universities and professionals from industrial bellwethers have only recently started to pay more attention to services-enterprise-engineering research. More importantly, the services and services-enterprise-engineering scope have evolved and expanded enormously as the world economy accelerates the pace of globalization due to the tremendous advances in IT (including computing, networks, software, and management science). Consequently, little is really known about how services sciences, management, and engineering can be systematically applied for the delivery of a services-led value chain from end to end.

As mentioned earlier, today's services concept evolves beyond the traditional nonagricultural and/or nonmanufacturing performance for the consumer's benefit. For example, many new and emerging high-value areas, such as IT outsourcing, postsales training, and on-demand innovations consulting (including any work helping customers improve their products, business processes, goods and services delivery, and supportive IT systems), are well recognized as services, drawing substantial attention from many industrial bellwethers (Fitzgerald, 2005; Rosmarin, 2006). On one hand, unique and satisfactory services differentiate an enterprise from its competitors; on the other hand, highly satisfactory services delivery frequently drives more product sales. As the shift from a manufacturing base to a services base becomes inescapable for both the developed countries and the developing countries, enterprises are gradually embracing defining and selling anything as a service (Rosmarin).

To ensure the prompt and cost-effective delivery of innovative and satisfactory services for customers throughout the geographically dispersed value net, enterprises nowadays have to rethink their operational and organizational structures by overcoming a variety of social and cultural barriers. Challenges appear in many aspects from business strategy, marketing, modeling, innovations, design, and engineering to operations and management. Since the general services topic is too broad and vague, the following discussions mainly focus on the needs for research and education in IT services, aimed at providing some fundamental understanding for business executives, managers, knowledge workers, and professionals in the relevant business sectors and research fields.

Business Strategy

As an enterprise is diving into building a highly profitable service-oriented business by taking advantage of its own unique engineering expertise and services knowledge, aimed at shifting gears toward creating superior outcomes to best meet customer needs, an adequate business-service strategy will be vital for the enterprise's growth in the long run. As discussed earlier, it is the mainstream for enterprises to collaborate with their worldwide partners to deliver best-of-breed services to their customers.

Despite the recognition of the importance of service-enterprise-engineering research, the shift to focus on services in the information era has created a research gap due to the overwhelming complexity of interdisciplinary issues across service-business modeling, information technologies, and workforce management. Filling the gap is essential. According to Rust (2004, p. 211):

We can move the field forward not only by understanding and serving the customer but by designing efficient systems of service delivery; training and motivating service providers; using new service technologies; and understanding how service affects the marketplace, the economy, and government policy.

The development of a business strategy meeting the long-term growth of a services enterprise should ensure that the defined business road map organically integrates corporate strategy and culture with organizational structure and functional strategy, and allows managing the interface of strategy and technology in a flexible and cost-effective fashion.

In general, the development of business strategy for enterprises adaptable to a new business environment requires great understanding of incorporations of solutions to addressing at least the following challenges in the services-led economy (Cherbakov, Galambos, Harishankar, Kalyana, & Rackham, 2005; Wright, Filatotchev, Hoskisson, & Peng, 2005).

- **Maximizing the total value across the value chain:** The outcome of the value chain nowadays is clearly manifested by customer satisfaction, which is mainly dependent upon the capability of providing on-demand, customizable, and innovative services across the value net.
- **The international transferability of staying competitive:** Enterprises reconstruct themselves by taking advantage of globalization in improving their profit margins, resulting in the fact that subcontracting and specialization prevail. Radically relying on efficient and cost-effective collaborations, a services provider essentially becomes a global ecosystem in which international transferability plays a critical role. International transferability could cover a variety of aspects from human capital, worldwide trade and finance, social structures, and natural resources to cultures and customs.
- **Organizational learning as competitive advantage:** The globalization of the services

workforce creates new and complex issues due to the differences in cultures, time, and skills.

- **Coping with the complexities, uncertainties, and changes:** Change is the only certain thing today and tomorrow. As the complexities, uncertainties, and changes are reconfiguring the business world, an enterprise should be able to quickly adapt to the change.
- **Aligning business goals and technologies to execute world-class best practices:** Business componentization cultivates value nets embracing best-of-breed components throughout collaborative partnerships. The value nets essentially are social-technical systems and operate in a network characterized by more dynamic interactions, real-time information flows, and integrated IT systems. Apparently, aligning business goals and IT is indispensable to the successful execution of applied world-class best practices in services enterprises.

Services Marketing

"[Today's] business reality is that goods are commodities; the service sells the product," says Roland Rust (2004, p. 211), a leading professor and the David Bruce Smith chair in marketing at the Robert H. Smith School of Business at the University of Maryland. It is not a secret that quality services essentially lead to high customer satisfaction. Satisfaction characterized as a superior outcome then further drives customer decisions. The services-led total solution measured by performance for the customer's final benefit rather than the functionality of physical goods become the prime competition in the global services-led marketplaces.

There are many new business opportunities in numerous newly expanded areas under the new concept of services, for example, e-commence, e-services, auctions, and IT consulting (Menor,

Tatikonda, & Sampson, 2002). Although these emerging services have gained much popularity with consumers, many new issues solicit more exploration for a better understanding of marketing to ensure that business goals can be met in the long run. Rust and Lemon (2001) discuss that Internet-based e-services can better serve consumers and exceed their expectations through real-time interactive, customizable, and personalized services. Effective e-service strategy and marketing play a significant role in growing the overall value of the services provider. A set of research questions in many customer-centric areas is proposed, aimed at leading to a stronger understanding of e-service and consumer behavior. Cao, Gruca, and Klenz (2003) model the relationships between e-retailer pricing, price satisfaction, and customer satisfaction so a more competitive business can be operated.

According to Rangaswamy and Pal (2005), service marketing as a fundamental service-value driver is much less understood compared to product marketing. Typically, a service outcome is freshly "manufactured" or "remanufactured" at the customer's site when it is delivered; it depends heavily on a well-defined and consistent process applied by trained personnel time after time, and leads to winning future competition through future innovations. It is hardly an easy transition from traditional business or consumer-product marketing techniques.

Services Design and Engineering

There have been many publications in the literature illustrating a variety of approaches to services design and engineering across industries. Although some of them present their scientific methodologies to realize the targeted goals specified by customers, the majority of them simply show their empirical and heuristic methods to deliver services design and engineering processes. In the emerging high-value IT-services area, there

is a great need for methodologies for the design and engineering of long-term, high-quality, and sustaining services in order to meet the defined business strategy of a services provider.

Zhang and Prybutok (2005) study the design and engineering factors impacting service quality in the e-commerce services sector. Introducing new products and services indeed would certainly help new revenue generation. However, retaining customers' high satisfaction and alluring them for purchasing further products and services are highly dependent upon other numerous critical factors, for instance, system reliability, ease of use, localization and cultural affinity, personalization, and security. As the levels of price satisfaction might not be increased simply by lowering prices, competing on price hence is not a viable long-term strategy for online retailers. Cao et al. (2003) model the relationships between e-retailer pricing, price satisfaction, and customer satisfaction through analyzing the whole services process. They find that the design and engineering of a satisfactory ordering process generates higher overall ratings for fulfillment satisfaction, which better retains loyal customers and accordingly helps a services provider to stay competitive.

As discussed earlier, services sectors cover both traditional services (e.g., commercial transportation, logistics and distribution, health-care delivery, retailing, hospitality and entertainment, issuance, and product after-sale services) and contemporary services (e.g., supply chains, knowledge transformation and delivery, financial engineering, e-commerce, and consulting). The competitiveness of today's services substantially depends on efficient and effective services delivery networks that are constructed using talent and comprehensive knowledge with a combination of business, management, and technology. The services processes should be flexibly engineered by effectively bridging the science of modeling and algorithms on one hand, and business processes, people skills, and cultures on the other hand.

Services Modeling and Innovation Framework

Services innovations are the key to stay a step or two ahead of competitors. James Spohrer, director of IBM Services Research, has an insightful view of the need for the investigation of service innovations and modeling. He states:

Increasingly over the past ten years, the new frontier of service research and teaching has shifted more and more towards business-to-business process transformation models. Process reengineering, IT productivity paradox, and other case studies highlight the need to constantly redesign work to improve productivity through multiple types of innovation in demand, business value, process, and organization.

A well-defined services model and innovation framework will effectively guide services enterprises to best design, develop, and execute their well-defined strategic plan for long-term growth.

New service-delivery models are essentially derived by working closely with customers to cocreate innovative and unique solutions best meeting customers' inevitably changing needs. According to Rangaswamy and Pal (2005), a competitive service business model for an enterprise should be clearly described using a service innovation framework (Figure 2):

The framework can guide the creation of customer value and demand, and the processes and organi-

zations that deliver services successfully—all of it catalyzed by emerging technologies.

Although detailed panel views of customer value, demand, process, and organization have been given in the white paper by Rangaswamy and Pal (2005), there is still the lack of a systematic approach to address how such a model and innovation framework can be enabled in practice. Given the tremendous complexity and variance from service to service, vertical service-domain knowledge of modeling and frameworks should be first investigated. Only when a better understanding of a variety of services domains is accomplished can an integrated and comprehensive methodology to address the services model and innovation framework across industries be explored and acquired.

Services Operations and Management

Operations research and management with focus on business-internal efficiency has made significant progress and developed a huge body of knowledge during the last 65 years or so. The relevant research and algorithm development has been mainly conducted in the areas of optimization, statistics, stochastic processes, and queuing theory. Current applications cover areas from vehicle routing and staffing, supply-chain modeling and optimization, transportation modeling, revenue management, risk management, services-industry resource planning and scheduling to airline optimization and forecasting. In general,

Figure 2. Services innovations framework and modeling

operations research has unceasingly improved living standards as it has been widely applied in practice for the improvement of production management and applications productivity.

Operations research and management originated from practice and has been growing as a more quantitative, mathematical, and technical field. Larson (2005) argues that practice makes perfect operations research. As new problems are identified and framed, formulated, and solved by applying operations-research approaches, tremendous impact will be provided and accordingly a new theory might be created. Sociotechnical services systems show a more practical nature and are extremely complex, and they are typically modeled and formulated using qualitative approaches. An understanding of such a complex problem involves deep and thoughtful discussion and analysis using common sense, basic principles, and modeling. Through new initiatives, the operations-research body of knowledge can be perfectly applied to these practical problems. Services operations and management are essentially operations research and management applied to services settings.

As discussed earlier, on one hand, the research and development of IT is a service. On the other hand, when IT helps enterprises streamline their business processes to deliver quality and competitive goods and services, it essentially functions as a knowledge service. However, efficient IT-service delivery to meet the needs of adaptive enterprises requires talent and comprehensive knowledge with a combination of business, management, and IT. Therefore, service-based operations research and management is in demand as it matches the emerging realization of the importance of the customer and a more customer-oriented view of operations. Services operations and management fits well with the growing economic trend of globalization, which requires operations research in services practice.

According to Bell (2005), operations research applied to services has much to offer that could improve the lives of everyone. He presents seven useful operations research frameworks that can be effectively used in addressing practical and complex problems like services delivery networks. Moreover, services operations are closely synchronized with the business operations of other collaborative partners as well as customers, aimed at cocreating value for customers in a satisfactory manner while meeting the business objectives across the value net. Given the industrialization of services and the economy of globalization, reorganizing, realigning, redesigning, and restructuring enterprises' strategies, processes, IT systems, and people for the challenges ahead are essential for ensuring that services providers are agile and adaptive, and stay competitive (Karmarkar, 2004).

In summary, given the increasing complexity of building sociotechnical services systems for improving living standards by applying operation research and management science in practice, services operations and management should cover more initiatives for the rooted practical aspects of research, linking operational performance to business drivers, performance measurement and operations improvement, service design, service technology, human capital, the design of internal networks, and the management of service capacity (Johnston, 1999). The study should also take into consideration high performance, distributed computing, humans' and systems' behavioral and cognitive aspects (which emerges as the new look of the interface to systems engineering), and highly collaborative interaction natures.

ADAPTIVE ENTERPRISE SERVICE COMPUTING

Enterprises are eagerly embracing building highly profitable service-oriented businesses through properly aligning business and technology and cost effectively collaborating with their worldwide partners so that the best-of-breed services will be generated to meet the changing needs of customers. To be competitive in the long run, it is critical for enterprises to be adaptive given the extreme dynamics and complexity of conducting businesses in today's global economy. In an adaptive enterprise, people, processes, and technology should be organically integrated across the enterprise in an agile, flexible, and responsive fashion. As such, the enterprise can quickly turn changes and challenges into new opportunities in this on-demand business environment.

IT service is a high-value services area that plays a pivotal role in support of business operations, logistics, health-care delivery, and so forth. IT service in general requires people who are knowledgeable about the business, IT, and organization structures, as well as human behavior and cognition that go deep into successful services operations (IBM, 2004). For IT systems to better serve the service-oriented enterprise, service-oriented business components based on business-domain functions are necessary (Cherbakov et al., 2005). The question is what systematic approach and adequate computing technologies will be suitable for IT development leading to the success of building an adaptive enterprise.

Computing technologies (e.g., software development) unceasingly increase in their complexities and dependencies. Aiming to find a better approach to managing complexities and dependencies within a software system, the practice of software development has gone through several methods (e.g., conventional structural programming, object-oriented methods, interface-based models, and component-based constructs). The emergence of developing coarse-grained granularity constructs as a computing service allows components to be defined at a more abstract and business-semantic level. That is, a group of lower level and finer grained object functions, information, and implementation software objects and components can be choreographically composed as coarse-grained computing components, supporting and aligning business services.

The componentization of the business is the key to the construction of best-of-breed components for delivering superior services to the customers. Successful operations of a componentized business require seamless enterprise integration. Thus, service-oriented IT systems should be able to deal with more amounts of interaction among heterogeneous and interconnected components, and be more flexible and adaptive. Obviously, adaptive and semantic computing services representing business functions meet the needs of the service-oriented IT systems. When computing components manifest business services at the semantics level, an IT system is a component network, fundamentally illustrating a logic assembly of interconnecting computing components:

The need for flexibility across the value net requires that the component network be flexible; that is, the enterprise can "in-source" an outsourced component and vice versa; replace, on demand, a

Figure 3. Service-oriented component-network architectural model

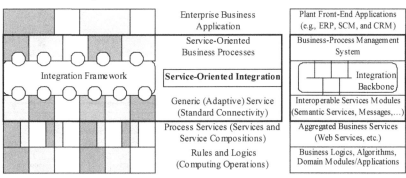

(a) The enterprise service computing architectural model   *(b) An implementation*

current partner with a different partner; change the terms of the contract between the two components, and so on. (Cherbakov et al., 2005)

A generic service-oriented IT computing architecture for the development of a component network is illustrated in Figure 3. The top two layers represent services operations from the business-process perspective while the bottom three layers show the value-adding services processes from the computing perspective. Apparently, how to optimally align enterprise-level business strategies with value-adding operations and activities is the key to the success of the deployment of an agile enterprise service-oriented IT system (Qiu, in press).

However, the exploitation, establishment, control, and management of dynamic, interenterprise, and cross-enterprise resource-sharing relationships and the realization of agility in a service-oriented IT system require new methodologies and technologies. The remaining discussions focus on the following four emerging synergic IT research and development areas aimed at providing some basic understanding of the emerging methodologies and technologies in support of the future deployment of IT services that enable adaptive enterprise service computing.

• **Service-oriented architecture (SOA):** SOA is considered the design principle and mechanism for defining business services

and computing models, thus effectively aligning business and IT.

• **Component-process model (CPM):** A component business-process model facilitates the construction of the business of an enterprise as an organized collection of business components (Cherbakov et al., 2005).

• **Business-process management (BPM):** BPM essentially provides mechanisms to transform the behaviors of disparate and heterogeneous systems into standard and interoperable business processes, aimed at effectively facilitating the conduct of IT-system integration at the semantics level (Smith & Fingar, 2003).

• **Web services:** Web services are simply a suite of software-development technologies based on Internet protocols, which provide the best interoperability between IT systems over the network.

Service-Oriented Architecture

According to Datz (2004), "SOA is higher level of [computing] application development (also referred to as coarse granularity) that, by focusing on business processes and using standard interfaces, helps mask the underlying complexity of the IT environment." Simply put, SOA is considered the design principle and mechanism for defining business services and computing models, thus

Figure 4. Aligning business and information technology

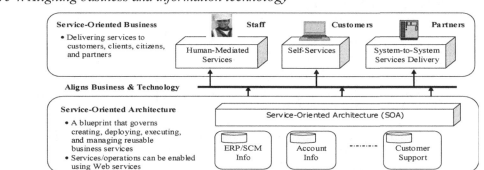

effectively aligning business and IT (Figure 4; Newcomer & Lomow, 2005).

Based on the concept of SOA, a deployed service-oriented IT system can provide a common way of cost effectively and efficiently managing and executing distributed heterogeneous services across enterprises. To properly implement service-oriented IT systems complying with SOA, three major levels of abstraction throughout collaborated IT systems are necessary (Zimmermann, Krogdahl, & Gee, 2004).

- **Business processes:** A business process typically consists of a set of actions or activities executed with specifically defined long-term business goals. A business process usually requires multiple computing services. Service invocations frequently involve business components across the network. Examples of business processes are the initiation of a new employee, the selling of products or services, a project's status, and order-fulfillment information.
- **Services:** A service represents a logical group of low-level computing operations. For example, if customer profiling is defined as a service, then looking up customers from data sources by telephone number, listing customers by name and postal code on the Web, and updating data for new requests represent the associated operations.
- **Operations:** A computing operation represents a single logical unit of computation. In general, the execution of an operation will cause one or more data sets to be read, written, or modified. In a well-defined SOA implementation, operations have a specific, structured interface and return structured responses. An SOA operation can also be composed of other SOA operations for better structures and maintainability.

SOA as a design principle essentially is concerned with designing and developing integrated systems using heterogeneous network-addressable and standard interface-based computing services. Over the last few years, SOA and service computing technology have gained tremendous momentum with the introduction of Web services (a series of standard languages and tools for the implementation, registration, and invocation of services). Enterprise-wide integrated IT systems based on SOA ensure the interconnections among integrated applications in a loosely coupled, asynchronous, and interoperable fashion. It is believed that BPM (as transformation technologies) and SOA enable the best platform for integrating existing assets and future deployments (Bieberstein, Bose, Walker, & Lynch, 2005).

Component-Process Model

Given the increasing complexity and dynamics of the global business environment, the success of a business highly relies on its underlying IT-supportive systems to support the changing best practices. In adaptive enterprise service computing, the appropriate design of IT-driven business operations mainly depends on well-defined constructs of business processes, services, and operations. Hence, to make this promising SOA-based component-network architectural model able to be implemented, it is essential to have a well-defined, process-driven analytical and computing model that can help analysts and engineers understand and optimally construct the business model of an enterprise for IT implementation.

A business process typically consists of a series of services. As a business process acts in response to business events, the process should be dynamically supported by a group of services invoked in a legitimate sequence. To ascertain the dynamic and optimal behavior of a process, the group of underlying computing services should be selected, sequenced, and executed in a choreographed rather than predefined manner according to a set of business rules. A service is made of an ordered sequence of operations. CPM

Figure 5. Component business-process schematic view

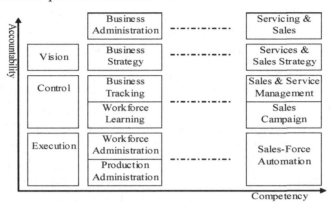

basically is a design and analytical method and platform to ensure that well-designed operation, service, and process abstractions can be characterized and constructed systematically for adaptive enterprise service computing (Cherbakov et al., 2005; Kano, Koide, Liu, & Ramachandran, 2005; Zimmermann et al., 2004).

CPM essentially provides a framework for organizing and grouping business functions as a collection of business components in a well-structured manner so that the components based on business processes can be modeled as logical business-service building blocks representing corresponding business functions. Figure 5 schematically illustrates a simplified components-process model for a service provider (Cherbakov et al., 2005). Just like many business-analysis diagrams, CPM can also be refined into a hierarchy. In other words, a process can be composed of a number of refined processes in a recursive fashion.

As CPM can accurately model business operations using well-defined services in SOA terms, CPM helps analyze a business and develop its componentized view of the business. Furthermore, the developed model for the business will define components concentrating on the interfaces and service-level agreements between the services. As a result, each business component will be supported by a set of IT-enabled services, while meeting the requirements of the deployment of

adaptive enterprise service computing. Most importantly, as the business evolves, CPM can help analyze the hot spot of the business operations. When business-performance transformation is required as the business settings change, CPM and the underlying IT systems can be quickly transformed to meet the needs of on-demand businesses (Cherbakov et al., 2005).

Business-Process Management

BPM emerges as a promising guiding principle and technology for integrating existing assets and future deployments. BPM is new in the sense that it describes existing disparate and heterogeneous systems as business-process services when conducting IT-system integration for better business agility rather than simply integrating those systems using EAIs (enterprise application integrations), APIs (application programming interfaces), Web-services orchestration, and the like. By providing mechanisms to transform the behaviors of disparate and heterogeneous systems into standard and interoperable business processes, BPM essentially aims at enabling a platform to effectively facilitate the conduct of IT-system integration at the semantics level (Smith & Fingar, 2003). Since an SOA computing service at the system level essentially is the business function provided by a group of components that

Figure 6. BPM merging with SOA services

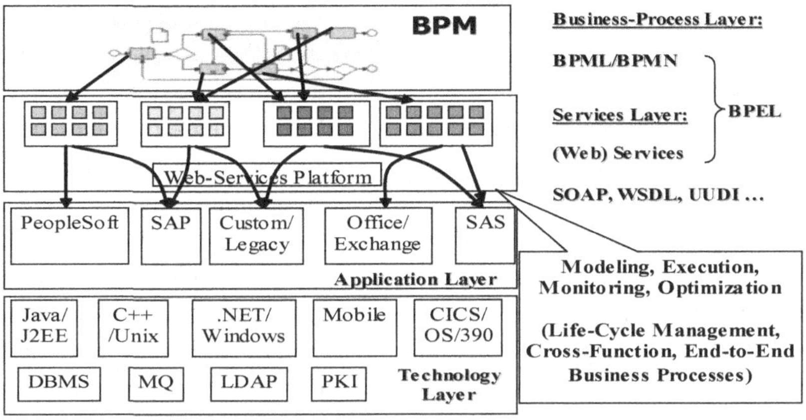

are network addressable and interoperable, and might be dynamically discovered and used, BPM and SOA computing services can be organically while flexibly and choreographically integrated, which is schematically illustrated in Figure 6 (Newcomer & Lomow, 2005).

In essence, BPM takes a holistic approach to enterprise service computing from the business-process execution perspective, substantially leveraging the power of standardization, virtualization, and management. BPM initiatives include a suite of protocols and specifications, including the business process modeling language (BPML), business process modeling notation (BPMN), and business process execution language (BPEL). By treating the business-process executions as real-time data flows, BPM provides the capability of addressing a range of choreographic business challenges and improving business operations in nearly real time.

BPML is defined for modeling complex business processes. Using the BPML specification to describe the business model of an enterprise provides the abstract model of the enterprise. The abstracted model is programmatically structured and represented using extensible markup language (XML) syntax to express the defined executable business processes and supporting entities for the enterprise. BPMN provides the capability of defining and understanding internal and external business operations for the enterprise through a business-process diagram. Through visualization, it gives the enterprise the ability to communicate these modeling and development procedures in a standard manner. BPEL for Web services then defines a standard way of representing executable flow models, which essentially extends the reach of business-process models from analysis to implementation through leveraging the power of Web-service technologies.

The emergence of BPM introduces an innovative platform for conducting IT-system integration. BPM enables service-oriented IT systems over the network to be able to dynamically and promptly coordinate the behaviors of disparate and heterogeneous computing services across enterprises. It is through BPM that business agility is retained while the return of IT investment is maximized.

Web Services

Apart from traditional software technologies, Web technology in general is nonproprietary and platform independent. Using standard Internet protocols, a Web service is a self-contained, self-describing, and network computing component. A Web service can be conveniently deployed, published, located, and invoked across the network. As Web services can be assembled and reassembled as needed across the network, the needs of adaptive enterprise computing of a business can be cost effectively supported.

Web-services technology essentially consists of a stack of protocols and specifications for defining, creating, deploying, publishing, locating, and invoking black network components. The stack mainly includes the simple object access protocol (SOAP), XML and XML namespaces, Web service description language (WSDL), and universal description, discovery, and integration (UDDI).

A computing service deployed as a Web service has to strictly comply with the stack of protocols and specifications. SOAP is the underlying communication protocol between the service provider and consumer, and explicitly defines how the service provider and consumer interact and what the enabled computation results in. WSDL is the language for defining the computing service, and basically specifies the location of the computing service and the operations the service exposes. UDDI then provides the formal interface contract and the global base for the registration and discovery of the deployed computing service.

Web services are standard run-time technologies over the Internet, providing best-ever mechanisms for addressing heterogeneous computing issues. By converging SOA and Web technology, Web services represent the evolution of Web technology to support high performance, scalability, reliability, interoperability, and availability of distributed service-oriented IT systems across enterprises around the whole world.

CONCLUSION

This chapter aimed at providing a basic understanding of the IT-driven, service-led economy. By discussing the challenges of services marketing, innovations, design, engineering, operations, and management from an IT perspective, this chapter gave the author's point of view on how service-enterprise engineering should be evolving from the current research and development. For an enterprise to be adaptive and able to quickly turn changes and challenges into opportunities so that the needs of the on-demand business can be optimally met, the workforce, processes, and technologies have to be organically aligned and integrated across the enterprise in an agile, flexible, and responsive fashion.

The following four design and computing methodologies and technologies are currently proposed as the necessities of enabling adaptive enterprise service computing. SOA is the design methodology to ensure the best aligning of the business and IT-driven system. CPM is a structured view of a business, which helps analysts and designers to optimally construct the long-term architectural and functional models for IT implementation. BPM is a rigorous method to embody the design and development of CPM, which essentially provides mechanisms to transform the behaviors of disparate and heterogeneous systems into standard and interoperable business processes so that the conduct of IT-system integration can be accomplished at the semantics level. BPEL and Web services are the run-time technologies suited for this need of BPM materialization.

Grid computing is emerging as a new and powerful computing technology to enable resource sharing for complex problem solving across businesses, institutions, research labs, and universities. Well-informed operational, tactical, and strategic decisions can only be made when nearly perfect and real-time visibility of the fulfillment of products and services can be provided in the on-demand e-business environments. It is envisioned that grid computing will join services science, management, and engineering in support of IT-driven system deployment for enabling real-time adaptive enterprise service computing in the near future.

REFERENCES

Bell, P. (2005). Operations research for everyone (including poets). *OR/MS Today, 32*(4), 22-27.

Bieberstein, N., Bose, S., Walker, L., & Lynch, A. (2005). Impact of service-oriented architecture on enterprise systems, organizational structures, and individuals. *IBM Systems Journal, 44*(4), 691-708.

Cao, Y., Gruca, T., & Klemz, B. (2003). Internet pricing, price satisfaction, and customer satisfaction. *International Journal of Electronic Commerce, 8*(2), 31-50.

Cherbakov, L., Galambos, G., Harishankar, R., Kalyana, S., & Rackham, G. (2005). Impact of service orientation at the business level. *IBM Systems Journal, 44*(4), 653-668.

Datz, T. (2004). What you need to know about service-oriented architecture. *CIO Magazine*, 78-85.

Dong, M., & Qiu, R. (2004). An approach to the design and development of an intelligent highway point-of-need service system. *The 7th International IEEE Conference on Intelligent Transport Systems*, 673-678.

Fitzgerald, M. (2005). Research in development. *MIT Technology Review*. Retrieved February 4, 2006, from http://www.technologyreview.com/articles/05/05/issue/brief_ibm.asp

IBM. (2004). *Service science: A new academic discipline?* Retrieved February 4, 2006, from http://www.research.ibm.com/ssme

Johnston, R. (1999). Service operations management: Return to roots. *International Journal of Operations & Production Management, 19*(2), 104-124.

Kano, M., Koide, A., Liu, T., & Ramachandran, B. (2005). Analysis and simulation of business solutions in a service-oriented architecture. *IBM Systems Journal, 44*(4), 669-690.

Karmarkar, U. (2004). Will you survive the services revolution? *Harvard Business Review, 82*(6), 100-107.

Larson, R. (2005). Practice makes perfect O.R. *OR/MS Today, 32*(2), 6-7.

Menor, L., Tatikonda, M., & Sampson, S. (2002). New service development: Areas for exploitation and exploration. *Journal of Operations Management, 20*(2), 135-157.

Newcomer, E., & Lomow, G. (2005). *Understanding SOA with Web services*. Addison-Wesley Professional.

Qiu, R. (2004). Manufacturing grid: A next generation manufacturing model. *2004 IEEE International Conference on Systems, Man and Cybernetics*, 4667-4672.

Qiu, R. (2005). An Internet computing model for ensuring continuity of healthcare. *2005 IEEE International Conference on Systems, Man and Cybernetics*, 2813-2818.

Qiu, R. (in press). A service-oriented integration framework for semiconductor manufacturing systems. *International Journal of Manufacturing Technology and Management*.

Qiu, R., Wysk, R., & Xu, Q. (2003). An extended structured adaptive supervisory control model of shop floor controls for an e-manufacturing system. *International Journal of Production Research, 41*(8), 1605-1620.

Rangaswamy, A., & Pal, N. (2005). Service innovation and new service business models: Harnessing e-technology for value co-creation (eBRC white paper). *2005 Workshop on Service Innovation and New Service Business Models*. Retrieved September 10, 2005, from http://www.smeal.psu.edu/ebrc/

Rosmarin, R. (2006). *Sun's serviceman*. Retrieved February 6, 2006, from http://www.forbes.com/2006/01/13/sun-microsystems-berg_cx_rr_0113sunqa_print.html

Rust, R. (2004). A call for a wider range of service research. *Journal of Service Research, 6*, 211.

Rust, R., & Lemon, K. (2001). E-service and the consumer. *International Journal of Electronic Commerce, 5*(3), 85-101.

Services Science Global (SSG). (2006). *Services Science Global: A non-profit research consortium.* Retrieved February 6, 2006, from http://www.ssglobal.org

Smith, H., & Fingar, P. (2003). *Business process management: The third wave.* Tampa, FL: Meghan-Kiffer Press.

Wright, M., Filatotchev, I., Hoskisson, R., & Peng, M. (2005). Strategy research in emerging economies: Challenging the conventional wisdom. *Journal of Management Studies, 42*(1), 1-33.

Zhang, X., & Prybutok, V. (2005). A consumer perspective of e-service quality. *IEEE Transactions on Engineering Management, 52*(4), 461-477.

Zimmermann, O., Krogdahl, O., & Gee, C. (2004). *Elements of service-oriented analysis and design.* Retrieved February 5, 2006, from http://www-128.ibm.com/developerworks/library/ws-soad1/

This work was previously published in An Overview of Knowledge Management, edited by R. Qiu, pp. 1-24, copyright 2007 by IGI Publishing (an imprint of IGI Global).

Chapter XVIII

The Impact of Sociocultural Factors in Multicultural Communication Environments:
A Case Example from an Australian University's Provision of Distance Education in the Global Classroom

Angela T. Ragusa
Charles Sturt University, Australia

ABSTRACT

Changes in the availability and quality of communication technology have revolutionized, and fundamentally altered, learning environments. As citizens of the "Information Age," the breadth and impact of global communication are triggering unprecedented transformation of social structures and institutions. This chapter explores the impact of commodification on education when institutions of higher education sell knowledge as a commercial good. The contemporary phenomenon of distance education is increasingly offered and purchased by an international market which experiences heightened pressure for standardization from the global citizens it serves. It is argued here that technological changes necessitate reevaluation of communication processes, discursive practices, and organizational policies. To stay competitive and produce quality products for increasingly international audiences, institutions must create well-articulated policies. By providing insight on the impact multiple sociocultural and communicative norms have on virtual communication, this research uses qualitative discursive analysis of case examples to examine how variance in the structure and delivery of virtual communication environments at a leading distance education university in Australia affects student satisfaction, perception, and learning outcomes. Whereas previous research fails to include a theoretical or conceptual framework, this work draws upon interdisciplinary work from the fields of sociology, education, and science and technology studies. How "cyberspace" changes interaction rituals, masks cultural norms, and alters entrenched social expectations by creating new sensitivities is discussed, along with the ramifications of variation in technological availability, competence, and expectations in global classrooms. In sum, ideas for informing change in policy, administration, and the delivery of distance education and virtual communication in global environments are discussed to equip leaders and participants with skills to foster effective communicative and interaction strategies.

INTRODUCTION

Analyzing the "Australian experience" with distance education[1] (DE), this chapter uses qualitative data to show how the type and design of virtual learning environments influence both the process and purpose of communication outcomes in global learning environments. DE is a global phenomenon with "over 130 countries developing or offering distance courses, many of them based on new information and communication technologies (ICTs)" (Shields, Gil-Egui, & Stewart, 2004, p. 120). However, the "global marketplace for e-learning products and services" varies widely among and within countries, courses offered, and technologies (Bowles, 2004). As multiple sectors (education, corporate, government) are involved in its development and delivery, inclusion of culture as a primary foci of analysis remains limited (Bowles, 2004; Monolescu, Schifter, & Greenwood, 2004; Palloff & Pratt, 2001; Brooks, Nolan, & Gallagher, 2001). Failing to prioritize cultural analysis may be costly and ineffective in communicative environments with multinational participants. Applying secondary data analysis techniques using a sociological and science and technology studies (STS) lens, this chapter informs existing literature not only by prioritizing culture, but moreover overcomes the methodological challenge facing international studies (Au-Yeung, Ha, & Au, 2004; Hawkey, 2004) of isolating "pure e-learning" (Bowles, 2004) environments in higher education to study virtual interaction without the added presence of face-to-face interaction. Ac-

cording to situated learning theory, knowledge cannot be removed from learning context and environment. Hence, not only are local norms set within a larger, global community, but a host of interaction-based, communicative norms are called into question as participants negotiate the boundaries of electronic communication dynamics.

Critical analysis of such dynamics provides insight into the symbiotic relationship between culture and technology in affecting communication. As such, the principal objective of this chapter is to enable better-informed decision making and the refinement of virtual communication (VC), in learning and other environments, by offering in-depth examples of how cultural norms and interactions can, and do, impact VC. By exploring how structure impacts virtual dialogue, the chapter asks how normative assumptions affect the negotiation of communication rituals based on situational meanings. Anticipated to be of particular interest to academic researchers, teachers, managers, and administrators of cross-cultural online learning environments, as well as business leaders working in international VC environments, this chapter uses case examples to demonstrate the strategic value of effective management; offers pragmatic steps that managers, teachers, and participants can take to maximize the virtual communicative experience; and asks all to reflect upon how sociocultural experiences interact with technologies to affect successful VC delivery.

BACKGROUND

Education as a Setting for Virtual Communication

Education, as an institution, is a field complete with theories, methodologies, and practices which can lead to the dichotomization of knowledge production into either positivism or social constructivism. Classical educational theorists such as Dewey (1938) and Piaget (1927) have argued that learning can be understood as a process of *praxis,* or doing. *Praxis* stands in contrast with the ancient *tabula rasa/* "blank slate" (Brooks & Brooks, 1993, in Palloff & Pratt, 2001) notion of students being empty blackboards waiting to be written upon. In assessing the use of multimedia tools to build collaborative virtual[2] communities, Goldman-Segall (1992, p. 260) offers a study contradictory to "the traditional school curriculum [that] is based on the attendance of empiricism, rationalism, and pragmatism" (Scheffler, 1965). Goldman-Segall's ethnographic research demonstrates how multimedia educational tools not only are mechanisms for cultural reflection/taking "the other" perspective, but moreover reveal what "the virtual community feeds back into the real community" (p. 293). The outcome is a negotiated understanding reflexive of participants' intentions and actions as collaborators in an educational project. Knowledge is constructed as an interaction between learner and environment, which subsequently reconfigures both (Semple, 2000). Applying a constructivist epistemology (Vygotsky, 1986), learning can be understood as a dialectical process infused by culture where meaning is constructed from a negotiation of cognitive thoughts within specific environments. Termed "electronic pedagogy" (Palloff & Pratt, 2001), this alternative view argues that when individuals work independently on subject matter and then engage in reflexive discussions about what fellow participants contributed, critical thinking skills are exercised. This chapter presents research supportive of Goldman-Segall's observation that multimedia, and particularly VC, enable individuals to reflect and view world events from others' perspectives in ways unique and different from face-to-face interactions.

In the past decade, much has been written about the pros and cons of DE from an educational framework. The main contributors are from education, technology, and administration disciplines. Additional disciplines beginning to address core cultural dimensions include human-computer interaction, usability, and technical communication, and the field of rhetoric, which now includes discussions of culture and online issues. However, each admittedly has been slow to contribute in meaningful ways. Although researchers in these paradigms are well equipped to analyze the effectiveness of DE, discussion of cultural issues is less rigorous and sparse, even when the imperative for including culture is acknowledged (Jorgensen, 2002). Jorgensen's (2002) review suggests that issues surrounding successful "community building" are a crucial component of culture in online communities (Borthick & Jones, 2000; Wegerif, 1998; Davis, 1997). Culture has also attributed great importance to the building of social capital within sociological theory (Putnam, 2005; Coleman, 1988) and society's general functioning (Durkheim, 1951; Merton, 1968). To understand how communities[3] function successfully, some traditional functionalists (Durkheim, 1951; Parsons, 1954) emphasize the establishment of common social norms. While functionalism may be useful to understand macrostructural organization of communities, those connecting macro- and micro-level analysis (Bourdieu, 1977; Giddens, 1979), and particularly some feminist analyses (Collins, 1990; Smith, 1990), reveal that power dynamics differ by unit of analysis. Within the education literature, questions of how to create the best virtual community reflect the challenge of how to create a social presence in an online environment (Lynch, 2002).

Australian market research attributes variation in cultural attitudes, communication, infrastructure, and government policy (Bowles, 2004) with responsibility for the current nature and climate of DE. Despite the vast majority of research being imported to Australia from the U.S. and the UK, there exists an absence of reliable Australian data on electronic learning (otherwise known as "e-learning") trends, as governmental indicators and Bowles (2004) claim. These implications challenge the establishment of benchmarks and expectations as "the exponential growth of contacts and networks among educators in an increasingly multinational market exists in a context of local and global stratification" (Ragusa & Atweh, 2004). As the example ethnomathematics reveals, "Research has failed to develop an ability to produce knowledge about people from within. Moreover, the knowledges generated have failed to assist in the transformation of reality, leading not to social change in justice but rather confirmation of the status quo" (Ragusa & Atweh, 2003). According to theories within STS, "Developments in transportation communication as well as the crisis of world ecology have created the so-called global society" (Hess, 1995, p. vii). In turn, the "people of diverse nationalities find themselves in increasing contact with each other. In many countries women, underrepresented ethnic groups, gays and lesbians, and other previously excluded groups have gained a greater voice" which results in "public debates on diversity, pluralism, oppression, exclusion, inclusion, colonialisms, identity politics and other issues that can be glossed as multicultural" (Hess, 1995, p. vii).

Social-psychological research shows variation exists in comfort and preference for VC (Lynch, 2004). Introverts tend to be more comfortable with electronic communication and reflection than extroverts (Palloff & Pratt, 1999). By applying this knowledge to a cultural critique, a Western/non-Western divide emerges. For example, research in Hong Kong shows students prefer to passively receive instruction rather than partake

in active pedagogy heralded by new technology and distance learning communication strategies of the 21st century (Au-Yeung et al., 2004). It is crucial to be cognizant of such cultural variation, especially with increasing student numbers and class size.

The "Australian experience" with DE shows the limitation of research and recommendations which fail to include (Monolescu et al., 2004; Palloff & Pratt, 2001; Brooks et al., 2001) or give cursory attention to (Albalooshi, 2003; Lynch, 2002, 2004), culture as a fundamental variable of focus. This is not acceptable in increasingly global educational environments, of which DE perhaps leads the way by containing potentially the highest levels of multinational participants. Lynch (2002) cites the impact of cultural values which "are reflected in informal rules and reward structure of the organization" (p. 71) at the bottom of the list of Sherry and Wilson's (1997) indicators of transformative communication. However, as this chapter reveals, ignoring and/or sidelining the impact of culture on VC environments may be both costly and damaging.

Distance Education in Australia

In 2003, the Australian National Training Authority published two volumes detailing the expectations and delivery of online/computer-based education in Australia. As part of a strategic plan to meet national goals for delivering flexible learning educational products, the ability to meet policy objectives remains hampered by the lack of procedures for data collection, institutional variation, and limited coordination between states and the federal government. Changes in the delivery of education are forewarned by the former Minister for Education, Science and Training, Brendan Nelson MP, as crucial:

Globalization, massification of higher education, a revolution in communications and the need for lifelong learning, leave Australian universi-

ties nowhere to hide from the winds of change. (Nelson, 2005)

However, this call for change is at least 13 years old. In 1992, the Minister for Employment, Education and Training, Kim Beasley, Member of Parliament, commissioned a report which provided "formal advise from the Higher Education Council [HEC] on DE in Australia," according to Peter Laver's letter to the Minister. HEC wrote: "The potential is there…both for use of DE materials and for alternative modes of delivery … the council's preferred position is consistent with the consultants: mixed mode should refer to flexible learning arrangements that can be made available to all students in all institutions" (HEC, 1992, p. 5). However, although "the potential exists technically in Australia for every higher education student to work in mixed mode format…for DE … usage is still not great. This wider use can be attributed more to enterprising teachers then to the influence of DECs [DE Centers]" (HEC, 1992, p. 6). As articulated by the federal government, the problem lies not within technological limitations but within cultural and business norms. From the cultural side:

One major problem is cultural. Australian material has generally been produced for Australian cultural conditions and for use in Australian universities ... simply making courseware available to an overseas user on a 'take it or leave it' basis, leaving unattended a host of difficulties ranging from aptness of content to the cultural appropriateness of particular forms of examination questioning, could not suffice as an approach in the medium or long-term. (HEC, 1992, p. 7)

Clearly, cultural and business norms overlap. This is evident by the government's following statement:

The other problem is the current fragmentary approach to the business enterprise of delivering higher education overseas. Although the start-up costs are likely to be heavy, the prospective return is great for institutions and for Australia, both in terms of fees won and in terms of generating an ethos on campus towards more flexible approaches to learning. Yet, one of the certainties that Australian institutions must face is competition from other (Asian) nations already active in developing higher education services for delivery overseas. (HEC, 1992, p. 8)

Although the report may seem philanthropic in its discussion of culture, further elaboration negates construing the Australian government's interest as anything but economic:

To be sensitive and responsive to the cultural needs of overseas students, who are to be engaged through DE materials and modes of delivery, may make the difference between developing an overseas market worth a few million dollars annually and a truly significant enterprise. (p. 8)

Hence, technological solutions alone are problematic.[4] For example, research on global collaborations among mathematics educators reveals:

Increased technological capability does not translate into changes in the equitability of global knowledge sharing practices. Even as computer networks facilitate collaborative research, those from the periphery 'will experience pressure against working in native languages, or on questions different from those attracting attention in the main centers. They will be measured against their peers in the centers, not against those in their own institution or region' (Gibbons et al., p. 131). Ultimately, 'globalization destroys local cultures and organizations' (Gibbons et al., p. 131) and fosters standardization over plurality, contributing towards Western imperialism. (Ragusa & Atweh, 2003)

Increasingly, when it comes to knowledge production, global interdependence among developed countries is total, while developing countries are left with "starvation and handouts from the developed parts of the world" (Winchester, 2005, p. 1). Furthermore, although we may like to think the Internet enables us to live in a "global village," nation-state boundaries and ethnic prejudices, not to mention global disparities in world indicator statistics on health, mortality, education, wealth, and so forth (The World Bank, 2005), can bring firsthand accounts of some very large social problems right into your "own backyard." This is particularly likely when global citizens come together to learn, as "globalization of the world's economies is leading to increased emphasis on internationalization of the curriculum" (Barjis, 2003).

Increasingly mobile and transient societies, fuelled by knowledge-overload in the Information Age, require new methods of communication. International competition, technological proficiency, multiple careers in renewed emphasis on productivity and quality are realities industries and businesses worldwide face (Barjis, 2003). Technology has irrevocably altered business models and policies, and higher education is no exception, in Australia and worldwide (Stein, 2003). VC presents an unprecedented opportunity for learning, dialogue, and social change. As we journey into the virtual horizon, however, it is necessary to take practical steps as businessmen/women, politicians, educators, technocrats, and general voyagers, to prepare for the journey with knowledge and cultural sensitivies of our fellow travelers, our virtual environment, and ourselves.

Case Study: Secondary Data Analysis of Virtual Communication

In Western countries, such as America and Australia, student evaluation typically takes the form of quantitative student questionnaires distributed either electronically or via the postal service. In Asia (Au-Yeung et al., 2004) and the UK (Hawkey, 2004), even when case study methodology is applied to assess collaborative online learning communities, analysis remains quantitative. Critical analysis of quantitative studies reveals quantitative surveys' subjective recall of past events can be problematic.[5] Another problematic methodological issue of international studies (Au-Yeung et al., 2004; Hawkey, 2004) of VC environments in higher education is their impossibility to analyze communication that never entails face-to-face interaction. This complexity is also evident within Australia:

'Pure' e-learning delivery—that is, learning that relies entirely on information and communication technologies—can be hard to isolate, as the technology is often used to enable other forms of communication, such as face-to-face meetings between learners and facilitators, video or telephonic conferencing or exchange of materials.' The National Centre for Vocational Education and Research believes that pure e-learning is rare in Australia. (Bowles, 2004, pp. 25-26)

This situation makes the current study unique because the only formal interactions students had were virtual, mediated by a computer. The present study enhances the literature by addressing this situational challenge, in addition to foregrounding culture. Qualitative, secondary data/discourse analysis conducted via a case study[6] approach is used to analyze communicative situations in my teaching experiences with two large DE subjects over two consecutive six-month periods in 2005-2006 at a rural Australian university[7] known for its leadership as a DE provider. This research adds to the understanding of how structure impacts the effectiveness of virtual dialogue. Moreover, it provides insight and strategic ideas regarding the development of successful VC in global environments.

Environment and Demographics

The structure of the two learning environments was similar in the provision of material (everyone received a hardcopy DE "package" containing a subject outline, reading book, and study guide), yet differed greatly in level of VC required. "VG1" (Virtual Group 1) contained nearly 300 participants and "VG2" approximately 140. Both contained individuals from across Australia and abroad, representing a range of ethnicities, nationalities, ages, disabilities, academic aptitudes, and life situations.

However, unlike VG2, which was led using a constructivist pedagogy, understanding the process of education as a socially constructed, reflexive practice characterized by collaboration, group projects, and praxis (Johnson & Johnson, 1994; Schon, 1991), VG1 contained only one asynchronous[8] general virtual forum which participants were asked to visit weekly for announcements. Students were left to be individual distance learners, with the added dimension of having access to the voluntary, general forum. In contrast, VG2 participated in multiple asynchronous electronic forums: a general forum for announcements, working group sub-forums for group virtual presentation preparation, and topic sub-forums for student discussion leadership. All students in VG2 were required to participate weekly in virtual discussions run by group leaders.

Outcomes

The constructivist and collaborative learning environment of VG2 is upheld by some as a key to virtual success. Jorgensen's (2002) literature review lends support to this conception. "When students are actively involved in collaborative (group) learning online, the outcomes can be as good as or better than those for traditional classes, but when individuals are simply receiving posted material and sending back individual work, the results are poorer then [sic] in tradi-

tional classrooms" (Jorgensen, 2002, p. 9). This quote epitomizes the difference between the two subjects. While both are defined equally as "DE," the correspondence[9] learning experience of VG1, supplemented by virtual chat and announcements, revealed minimal student satisfaction. In contrast, those in VG2 reported much learning of both subject content and life skills, such as team management.

Despite variation in the quantity and quality of VC, both cohorts expressed learning resulted from their electronic dialogue. Although VG1 was active on the general forum (1,540 postings for 335 members and 103,802 "distinct reads"), its designation as an auxiliary learning tool resulted in little dialogue relating to subject content. Despite formal encouragement, rather than use the electronic forum to ask specific content-related questions, VG1 member primarily used it to vent grievances and assuage discontent/frustration with their learning experiences. This does not mean learning did not ensue. To the contrary, students learned much about the politics of communication using (post)modern technology. In contrast, VG2 produced 765 postings from 81 users, and 25,360 "distinct reads" on the general forum and multiple other communications not reviewed in the 11 topical discussion forums. To highlight some challenges and nuances involved in VC, this chapter proceeds with qualitative discourse analysis of virtual communicative text.

Qualitative analysis reveals three key characteristics resulting from multicultural VC experiences:

1. Intergenerational Negotiation
2. 'Real-World' Impact of Ethnic Culture and Racism
3. The Impact of Technology and Systemic Practices

Intergenerational Negotiation

Although both VGs contained mature-age and traditional students, perhaps because VG1 was not structured as task-focused/topical (like VG2), introductions differed in their revelation of personal details. This impacted future communications in three ways. First, as those in VG1 disclosed their age and geographical location, allegiances formed. Participants self-segregated into "oldies," "crusties," "dinosaurs," and "late starters," with several 40-something-year-olds sharing their fears and excitement about starting university at this point in their life. As middle-agers became more active in the virtual dialogue, some younger participants, particularly those in their teens, expressed shock. For example, a student born in 1985 found it incredulous to study with others who left high school that same year. Soon, it became a competition among the young not to be the youngest and to be the oldest among the old. Some simply looked forward to graduating in the same year as one of their children.

Second, although initially a topic of much conversation, age quickly took a backseat to the establishment of commonality, particularly by level of role-overload, which continued throughout the semester. All ages lamented the struggle to balance work, family, and study. Self-initiated disclosure of life situations fostered impromptu allegiances, most commonly family status (mothers/fathers, grandparents, etc.), school leavers, and geographical location.

A third outcome of informally structured virtual dialogue among a group of 288 "strangers" was the formation of informal mentoring. Younger participants reading descriptions of life circumstances of older participants actively sought out mentoring from those "more mature" and "handling the stress better." Younger ones perceived older generations to have the advantage of wisdom, along with better-developed stress management techniques. However, even though the requests were met with encouragement, older participants perceived younger ones to be advantaged because of their familiarity with technology, recent studying skills, and belief that stress is not correlated with age. Regardless of

any extrinsic "truth," the experience of being in this VC situation together led to the development of a collective consciousness expressed by such sentiments as "being in the same boat" and able to "fall in a heap together." These conversations raised awareness of subjectivity, as discussions made it apparent that what constitutes maturity, old/young, privileged, and so forth, largely depends on one's perspective and position relative to others.

In contrast, although an equally varied range of student ages, experiences, and locations existed in VG2, the formality of the structure seemed to inhibit the formation of bonds based on demographic data. While some disclosed personal details and chatted occasionally, being assigned to a specific discussion group and work tasks had the effect of focusing virtual conversations. This led to discussions of team/task organization and learning, rather than primarily emotional support. Furthermore, VG2 infrequently left the structure of the "virtual classroom," whereas in VG1 some asked others to continue the discussion via personal e-mail.

What can be learned from this comparison, among other things, is the impact structure and management can have on the quantity and type of VC. Providing a group-work structure, facilitated by electronic sub-forums,[10] resulted in role clarity and alleviated anxiety associated with the uncertainties of DE. As the exclamation of two in VG2 reveal, combining effective technology and "human" management can relieve stress associated with working in virtual groups: "Thank god for Angela! I think this will make things heaps easier rather than using our own personal e-mails, as that way no one misses out on whats going on etc." "I agree with you and will go straight to our subforum once I have finished here. Great work!"

It is important to realize although similar group dynamics exist in face-to-face and virtual groups (Lynch, 2004), virtual groups remain significantly different in structure. VC restricted to written form may be more tedious, time consuming, interrupted by unanticipated events, and subject to a host of considerations that differ from face-to-face interactions. Consequently, although some research indicates the effectiveness of electronic discussions is greater than for face-to-face discussions (Brooks et al., 2001), attenuating an exhaustive list of structural issues identified in the literature (Bowles, 2004; Lynch, 2002; Brooks et al., 2001), such as resolving issues of time management, discussion leadership, technological complications, authoritative control, and dialogue ground rules, is essential for effective VC.

'Real-World' Impact of Ethnic Culture and Racism

The second important feature of VC is anticipating and managing the impact of 'real-world' events. The use of reflection in virtual learning environments, which is facilitated by the structure and reality of electronic learning technologies and VC practices, has caused a shift in pedagogy:

Constructive knowledge involves the opportunity to critically analyze information, converse with others about its meaning, reflect upon how information fits within your personal belief in value structures, and arrive at a meaningful understanding of that information ... this method is projected important, and lends itself well, to the online learning environment because learning online supports dialogue and the collaborative development of understandings. (Lynch, 2004, p. 109)

As it becomes common practice for DE to bridge individuals' roles as students and other life roles (Lynch, 2004), external factors may become increasingly influential. When dialogue can occur 24 hours/7 days a week from the comfort of one's own preferred environment, under the influence of substances or not, within a structure that does not require communications to be pre-reviewed,

boundaries that usually govern face-to-face interaction are removed. This creates heightened potential for unmediated conflict, posing a greater risk to VC breakdown.

It is imperative managers and administrators conduct risk assessment prior to commencement and build coping mechanisms within the structure to ensure that high-quality service delivery is not undermined. To minimize undesirable outcomes and maximize communicative action, risk assessment cannot be an entirely top-down strategy. VC requires negotiation on the part of each contributor. If equity in legitimacy of voice is granted to uphold democratic/pluralist ideology, be aware it will engender diversity, and thus conflict resolution/minimization may require equal plurality in approach.

Knowledge production and true communication necessitates "we have to learn from the painful experiences and the irreparable suffering of those who have been humiliated, insulted, injured, and brutalized that nobody may be excluded in the name of moral universalism—neither underprivileged classes nor exploited nations, neither domesticated women nor marginalized minorities"(Habermas, 1993, p. 15). When the public partakes in a VC discussion, traditional statues (gender, class, race, etc.) responsible for enforcing social norms remain covert. This is simultaneously liberating and constricting, as those accustomed to social privilege may find themselves lacking power they may ordinarily take for granted. In contrast, VCs grant traditionally marginalized social groups' power to participate without the restrictions master statuses typically impose in face-to-face interactions.

Analysis of virtual dialogue reveals it is not so easy to remove social identity and status that years of socialization have firmly entrenched via ideology. Even if social cleavages are not immediately recognizable through written prose, expressed value systems and the cultural relativity of social standpoints (Harding, 1991; Smith, 1987) become readily exposed when debate ensues, as the following case example illustrates. The result is twofold. On one hand, VC traverses boundaries (geographical, social, and economic), facilitating intimate dialogue among sectors of the public which otherwise may isolated. This poses a unique opportunity for education, as individual life stories and experiences work to dispel (or uphold) stereotypes. On the other hand, the threat exists for larger groups to divide along traditional nation-state, age, and other boundaries in the quest for validation of moral superiority. For instance, as Butler (1990) uses the category of gender to argue, gender is not some intrinsic state of being, but rather a negotiated performance reproduced and re-enacted daily. So, too, is culture a socially constructed product reinvented via VC.

The informality of VC fosters an increasingly more intimate type of dialogue than face-to-face classroom interactions. This encourages deeper reflection on cultural norms and beliefs. The disclosure of "taboo" prejudices too politically incorrect to reveal beyond the safe environment of one's computer terminal becomes commonplace as individuals' biases are identified by others. Asynchronous VC is unique because it provides a written account of one's own thoughts and dialogue which continue to exist even when one's current opinions may no longer be reflected in past writings. In this study, the institutionalized VC structure made viewing all prior correspondence continuously available. The impact re-reading past communications had is noticeable. Perhaps due to the fractured nature of asynchronous VC, the expression of self-identities, while seeming reflexive of "real-life" realities, metamorphosed over the six months of virtual dialogue. Several who entered the dialogue espousing rigid, clear boundaries and belief systems revealed in later communication how their interactions, both within and outside the learning environment, changed. For some, this caused a discrepancy between their "old" and "new" selves, while for others virtual interactions served to preserve preconceived notions. To explore this phenomenon further, two case examples will be drawn upon.

- *Case Example 1.* **The impact of multiculturalism on VC:** VG1 dialogue regarding racism and immigrants emerged in response to the Macquarie Fields[11] Riots in Sydney. What ended up being a nine-day virtual conversation among 35 participants was initiated by a 34-year-old who wrote how she was disgusted and appalled at the rape of a pregnant woman abducted by three men in Macquarie, Sydney. She reveals the incident caused her mental anguish and conflict because although she attended a highly multicultural school in inner-city Sydney, such incidents as racial riots in the media cause her to feel she's becoming racist. She identifies that this is at odds with her identity as a "typical" Australian and notes how infuriating it is that the more Australia lets immigrants into the country, the more ethnic fights are imported from immigrants' country of origin.

The ensuing VC reveals three challenges technology poses to discussions of social problems. First, initial responses highlighted the complexity of dealing with heated emotional and sociocultural issues. A primary concern was how to communicate and define national/cultural identity in an environment where value systems and beliefs varied widely, and where individual characteristics remained unknown. For example, the very first response used the well-known history of Australia's rape and decimation of thousands of aboriginals, and the years of aboriginal assimilation into white British culture, to question who counts as immigrants. Yet, because another student failed to read the discussion closely, s/he challenged the respondent's justification of aboriginal men raping and murdering white women, arguing many ethnicities share a country and need to stop blaming each other for past actions.

The discussion that followed reveals the second challenge virtual reality poses to effective communication—the complexity of articulating any universal meaning/intention using subjective cultural symbols (words). When the original initiator reflected/re-read her initial words, she articulated how she did not explain herself properly, tried to qualify what she meant by "typical," and backpedaled about her intended meaning. Responses to her clarification shows effort to clarify VC sometimes does little to change/retract original statements and may not assuage others' discontent. For example, a fourth contributor challenged her "typical" Australian comment, noting that indigenous Australians are as typical as you can get and that noted accusations and judgments make matters worse.

This virtual dialogue continued, as individuals debated concepts of race, racism, nationality/nationalism, immigration, hate, prejudice, Eastern vs. Western cultures, terrorism, rape and violence, power, control, and dominance. Arguments about ability to transcend culture led to standpoint/point-of-view discussions, escalating until the physical reality of seeing such dialogue alive as text on the computer screen inspired one to reflect how the very act of dialogue occurring among multicultural individuals was in and of itself inspiring. This participant found it empowering to note as a cultural artifact, a product of democratic societies. Although the reflection offset spiraling cynicism, uncertainty of being heard among competing cyberspace voices remained a reality, as the preface "whoever else cares to read this response" implied. Perhaps luckily for this communicator, the "reality" of the conversation itself was used by others to evidence cultural pride as the tide of conversation flowed to embrace multiculturalism. Haraway's (1991) concept of cyborgs captures the symbiotic relationship between humans and machines, and is increasingly

manifested through social analysis of VC. "Technology is beginning to mediate our social relationships, our self-identities and our wider sense of social life to an extent we are only just beginning to grasp" (Featerstone & Burrows, 1995, p. 13). Although the racism example confirms the similarity of virtual asynchronous and synchronous face-to-face communication whereby inclusion of an alternative point of view shifts both focus and climate, it also reveals difference. What differs between the two communication styles (perhaps more synchronous vs. asynchronous) remains the quantity of time to devote to reflection. Synchronous dialogue demands an immediate response, often with little time to analyze the evidence previously provided. Yet, in asynchronous environments, a communicator can do considerable research before responding, as another contributor did when s/he noted the paucity of information provided to evidence claims of the influence culture has on events and ideas. Hence, the examples reveal asynchronous dialogue using computers as a medium alter the meaning, flow, and outcome of communication.

This brings us to the third challenge VC poses: negotiating definitions of authority. In the classical Weberian tradition, power can be defined as the ability to achieve desired ends in the face of resistance. In this case, the power both the rapists and rioters exerted in Sydney demonstrates traditional power. Traditional power often lacks legitimization, as reflected in the conversation. The difference between power and authority lies within perception. Authority is power others perceive as legitimate, not coercive. When authoritative voices enter a dialogue, opposition is minimized. This occurred in this case when two police officers, one in Sydney, the other in Melbourne, added their perspectives. However, for VC, authority poses unique challenges: (a) there may be several authoritative voices competing for power in the dialogue, (b) it may be harder to verify whether one's identity/position is indeed true, and (c) control over the direction of communication may be relinquished to persuasive writers, due to written dialogue's uni-dimensionality.

In this example, the Sydney police officer decided he had heard enough from what he defined as "armchair critics," telling them it was time to "get real and listen to how it really is!!" As he described leading a riot team of police during the Macquarie Fields Riots, his authoritative prose left little room for further discussion. Emotionally charged, and backed by years of experience and hardships, he made a charismatic plea for hard-core justice, where all individuals are treated the same under the law, irrespective of ethnicity or politics.

These insights were met with cries of joy from many, with thanks for the officer "set[ting] us straight on the subject." The authority commanded by the police officer and role as expert were repeatedly asserted. Another added, "you have expressed how a lot of my family, friends & I feel about the Macq fields riots but you have the evidence to back it up." The disadvantage of such discussions is the dichotomy that quickly is established between the knowers (those with the right to speak, who are identified as "absolutely right and are coming from a position of experience and knowledge") vs. those with less worthy ideas. The impact of position to grant communicative authority is notable, and was acknowledged by many who stated they were glad to "have someone in a position of experience who can shed light on this subject" and "always find it hard to form and express an opinion on these types of matters because I never know the real situation."

Who has the right to speak (and be heard) has been a topic of interest in feminist epistemology (Roof & Wiegman, 1995; Garry & Pearsall, 1989) and of critical political theorists, such as Antonio Gramsci. However, deciding whose perspective deserves legitimization is a contentious issue, and in this case, continues to fuel deep-seated prejudices. "Those who have developed these lovely theories do so from an educated persons perspective. These people have little knowledge of the type of individual that has no regard for the laws we are all expected to live by and for the safety, property and well-being of others." Such was the sentiment of a self-identified Victorian police officer, who added he worked in disadvantaged and culturally diverse areas. He proceeded to use his status to express dissatisfaction with Australia's welfare state "where we make excuses for poor (and even criminal) behavior."

Once again, this led to a flood of bigoted, culturally insensitive exchanges, such as a response from a participant who has a police officer as her partner. What began as agreement with the Victorian officer, regarding those who see situations firsthand, and everyday having more right to speak than others without such knowledge, digressed into disclosure of how, although she could "respect and appreciate poverty, youth issues and disadvantaged groups," she was "tired of systems protecting these people to the detriment of others." Her tirade ended with a revelation about how much better off her sister on "government handouts" is than she who owns a business.

VG participants, equipped with all their identities and subsequent bodies of knowledge (as professionals in various fields, occupants of various neighborhoods and countries, situational knowledge from interpersonal relationships, etc.) acted out real-world battles in cyberspace. With each passing communication, participants divided more firmly along political lines, varying in expressions of sympathy vs. critique of police officers and level of open-mindedness. After nine days, interest subsided and new issues were up taken. However, unlike verbal dialogue, which lives in our memories alone, months later every detail of the communication remained intact—as a "real" artifact for all to view, if desired.

Unlike face-to-face communications, VCs appear to foster a unique combination of emotive and rationalized thoughts about world events. Although it may be impossible to anticipate every response in a debate, written responses tend to be more personal and reflexive than face-to-face discussions and exhibit less inhibition. In large groups, the geospacial/physical constraints imposed by size, where individuals may not get to discuss ideas one on one, is vastly altered by VC. VC enables multiple one-on-one conversations, which may result in a ratio of one to hundreds. However, it is questionable whether individuals consciously think about what it means to express deeply personal thoughts in a public forum.

- *Case Example 2.* **The subjectivity of electronic communication:** Research exploring communication norms in virtual environments in education (Palloff & Pratt, 2001) has drawn particularly from stage and systems theory to explain the organization and development of electronic group dynamics, including conflict and resolution (McClure, 1998; Tuckman & Jensen, 1977). The second case example provides support for the need of task clarity, focused collaboration, and quick leadership intervention when conflict arises for successful group functioning (McClure, 1998). It also gives credence to Palloff and Pratt's (2001) warning of the heightened potential for misinterpreted communica-

tion, due to lack of face-to-face interaction rituals and less adherence to social norms based on the work of Schopler, Abell, and Galinsky (1998). Adding to Thomas' (1923) "definition of the situation," as articulated in classic symbolic interactionism theory, the case illustrates how subjective meanings individuals attach to a situation have real-world consequences, which may be independent of any "objective" reality. As Lynch (2004) articulates, "when reading a typed message, there is a strong tendency to project—consciously or not—your own expectations, wishes, anxieties, and fears into what the person wrote. This may lead to further conflict and, because it is written, sometimes builds a feeling of resentment that lasts longer" (p. 13).

Long before the instance occurred, during the first weeks of communicating virtually, a participant described the complexities a later example would reveal: "Sorry if the 'tone' of my post to the forum provoked you. Thing about cyberspace communication is that it lacks tone—or one has to work harder at communicating—something I'm still adjusting too." Although this instance does not reveal miscommunication, there is agreement VC is indeed subject to misinterpretation: "No, didn't provoke me as such and I agree with the lack of tone thing. Perhaps my messages are being misread also…pros and cons of technology!"

Applying the once groundbreaking insights of Cooley (1922), whose "looking-glass self"[12] concept revolutionized classical social-psychological theory, the computer may be understood as a mirror reflecting our self-image back to us. As we view this reflection, communicative uncertainty prevails: Is this indeed who I am? Have I expressed myself in a way that enables others to understand me as I wish them to? When an artifact—a computer—is added to the complex process of communication among humans, situational dynamics change. Let us consider the following example.[13]

In my role as lecturer, it is common practice to produce a final grade distribution chart so students can see their performance relative to others. To convey this data virtually, I wrote the following message:

While I cannot offer you confirmation of your final grades, I have created a chart for you to see how the class did as a whole, which I am attaching as a word file. I think you will be happy to see that out of the xx of you who completed all 3 assessment items, only xx of you failed, which is just x%.

While initially this received expressions of thanks, such was not the case for one failing student in VG1. This participant wrote how my note expressed an insensitivity to students' feelings, contained "unsupportive comments" by confirming some failed, and would make those who failed feel worse. The correspondence ended with exclamations of how I do not know what damage I might be causing and how she found "this behavior quite disgusting, egotistical, and unethical." This spurred 23 further communications, including a handful charging to my defense, telling her not to "tough talk behind a computer," how failing is a reality of life, how her response demonstrates "unacceptable behavior from an adult," and since they "are no longer children" university is preparing them for the "real world." Others pointed to the "danger of technology" where instant thoughts can be "fired off" in the heat of the moment, whereas in the past, emotions would subside prior to mailing a letter. Noting the difference VC makes. One asks: "Would you have spoken to the person that way, face to face, in front of the class of 170 people? You might say 'Yes', but I

suggest embarrassment would result." In this case, older students took on mentoring roles, outlining strategies to effectively deal with disturbing electronic information.

With painstaking effort, I responded by clarifying my intentions. However, no amount of preparation could have prepared me for her reply. From the apology and confession, I and the other approximately 200 virtual community members learned she just suffered the death of her daughter. Concluding communications displayed a range of emotions—empathy, sorrow for actions based upon imperfect knowledge, even resentment, as one noted although she "felt" for her situation, the group member only contributed once to the virtual dialogue. The armchair philosophers implored others to be nonjudgmental and reflected how "the answers to problems are not always as apparent as they appear on the surface." In sum, all seemed to learn an invaluable life lesson that may not have been possible without participating in VC.

The Impact of Technology and Systemic Practices

The third broad lesson to be learned from this case study is: when using technology to communicate, all aspects of communication can (and will!) be affected—from the hardware making it possible, or impossible, to the even slight confusion over definitions.[14] VC depends on high-quality technical delivery for success, which is contingent on geographical location,[15] resources, politics, and user ability—all beyond the scope of this work. However, it is worth noting that technological failure impacts communication. When technology fails, for any reason, confidence in the system wanes and anxiety rises. As the following experiences reveal, technological failure itself does not often cause the most customer dissatisfaction. Humans seem to expect machines, and technological systems, to fail. Many exhibit great distrust of technology. As the next example reveals, what humans are least forgiving of is other humans.

A useful, yet fallible, electronic assessment submission system is the institutional means available to students to electronically submit their work in this case. At times, students submit work only to find out later it was received as unreadable due to computer format. When their work is returned as "unreadable," some students get incited. In VG2, one student found that even though the Web site noted the submission as successful, her hard copy returned via the postal service saying "unreadable" led to her feeling "disappointed" to see hours of work done for naught. Rightly so, she wished to receive such advice weeks earlier, upon submission. Yet, when computers are not set up to properly "talk" to humans, errors in the system remain invisible.

This single experience was exacerbated by another's inflated perception of the event. Noting "what a horror story I really feel for you," another student extrapolated the instance to her fear of taking the virtual exam. Student panic, resulting in questions about what happens if the Internet service provider "decides to disconnect during the exam," led to continued fret and pleads for help to "eliminate this extreme worry." If such communication was conducted by telephone or e-mail, the result would have been a one-on-one conversation where each concern was subsequently addressed. However, because it occurred in a public arena, it provided fuel for the entire virtual community to read and reflect upon. Hence, the very structure of "public" VC—whereby individuals post messages for all to read—appears to encourage not only disclosure of individual fears, but moreover generates chaos among others[16] potentially impervious to such ideas.

Perceptions, and perception management, are often all that exists in VC. Therefore, it is crucial that strong management exists to intervene and curtail escalated fears where necessary, taking proactive steps to negotiate positive outcomes. In

VG2, far greater usage of educational technology (CD-ROM readings, sub-forums, electronic lectures, and student presentations in addition to electronic exams and assignment submission) existed. Hence, it is unsurprising that more technological difficulties, including elevated apprehension and student stress relating to inadequate technological knowledge, manifested. When two participants vented frustration at the inconveniences caused (babysitters planned, work schedules rearranged) due to Web site failure making their exam available, another participant mediated discontent by articulating faith in management. After confirming how everyone held such concerns about balancing "work, children, home and study," she expressed faith in the lecturer's management of the situation and ability "to give us the time we need to re-organize our schedules."

For global virtual communities, time is relative. The technical problem above occurred outside standard business hours, leaving management unaware until the next day. Thus, mechanisms for dealing with failure are best built into the system. Although every technological failure cannot be anticipated, it is most important to create a "humanistic side," through consistent dialogue to encourage confidence that crises will be attended as quickly and professionally as possible.

Specifically for DE, the establishment of reliable technological systems is synonymous with quality performance. For all its imperfections, technology is arguably a more viable alternative than solving geographical inadequacies of rural infrastructure and communication issues relating to distance. Both groups identified discrepancies in the privileges Australian urban residents experience compared to rural and international residents. Compounded by outdated policies, such as mandated use of the postal service to return assignments and grades, institutional rules can be inconsistent with efforts at technological leadership. Systemic inconsistencies lead to customer frustration. As new students in Saudi Arabia and Pipalyatjara communicated via e-mail, the delivery of mail varied widely (i.e., in Pipalyatjara, because of no rain in two years, "the mail plane [was] having some trouble landing," and in Sudan, mail delivery by camel was said to be slow). Hence, university policies can add to student frustration, such as when individuals receive material for one subject, yet not others.[17]

CONCLUSION

From the many examples discussed, three broad future recommendations can be put forth to encourage successful VC. VC should be: (a) culturally responsible, (b) flexible in time and style, and (c) mandatory, if group cohesion is desirable.

When electronic communication is actively managed and made routine, it becomes part of the skill set—another tool in the toolkit of the global learner. Participants learn a new set of social and communication norms that differ in type and kind from face-to-face interaction. Without physical and verbal cues, interaction—indeed communication—becomes subject to hyperanalysis by participants. As analysis reveals, this can lead to heightened sensitivity and subjectivity of interpretation for content and intent. When participation is optional, the "free rider" phenomenon (Olson, 1965), commonly associated with social movements and collective behavior, ensues. It becomes all too easy, indeed even rational, for many to sit back and benefit from the contributions of a few hard workers. Hence, crucial to successful creation of an active virtual community is the participation of members. To achieve this, and simultaneously preserve the flexibility that makes DE so popular among mature-age and international students, it is recommended that learning materials be structured to enable participants to self-select into a set number of virtual discussions. Not only does this teach effective time management skills, but moreover it gives individuals the option to not partake in discussions that, at least in the social sciences, may be cultural hot buttons. For example, although lecturers might be eager to hear the opinions and reflections on personal experiences regarding issues such as abortion, refugees, terrorism, and so forth, as distance educators we must realize our capacity to intervene/counsel/educate is mediated by our *distance.* The realities of our students' lives (and the impact a disturbing virtual conversation may have) must take precedence.

The virtual community analyzed in this chapter makes explicit cultural norms operating when individuals construct meaning and make sense of their everyday world—wherever that is. Fostering dialogue among individuals holding varied statuses within the social hierarchy (that is, our global society) challenges cultural (and class, gender, age, ethnic, etc.) norms "...from different standpoints different aspects of the ruling apparatus and of class come into view" (Smith, 1987, p. 107). Applied as a methodological tool to VC, critical analysis—infused with phenomenological sensibilities that lend insight into how micro-level internalization of sociocultural values and norms (Berger & Luckmann, 1966) impact communication—provides knowledge of how cultural awareness and individual belief systems result from systemic socialization. This subsequently creates a foundation for future analyses of global systems composed of nation-state citizens. Societies are not merely aggregations of individuals. As Hess (1995) theorizes, multicultural spaces can be understood as stages whose very existence predispose its participants to conflict as they negotiate meanings of nationalities, ethnicities, classes, genders, histories, and so forth.

REFERENCES

Albalooshi, F. (Ed.). (2003). *Virtual education: Cases in learning and teaching technologies.* Hershey, PA: IRM Press.

Australian National Training Authority. (2005). *Our universities: Backing Australia's future.*

Retrieved February 15, 2006, from http://www.backingaustraliasfuture.gov.au/ministers_message.htm

Au-Yeung, L. H., Ha, T., & Au, G. (2004). The experience of new WBI-adopters in Hong Kong. *Journal of Educational Technology Systems, 31,* 411-422.

Barjis, J. (2003). An overview of virtual university studies: Issues, concepts, trends. In F. Albalooshi (Ed), *Virtual education: Cases in learning and teaching technologies* (pp. 1-20). Hershey, PA: IRM Press.

Berger, P., & Luckmann, T. (1966). *The social construction of reality.* New York: Doubleday.

Borthick, A. F., & Jones, D. R. (2000). The motivation for collaborative discovery learning online and its application in an information systems assurance course. *Issues in Accounting Education, 15,* 181-211.

Bourdieu, P. (1977). *Outline of a theory of practice.* Cambridge, MA: Cambridge University Press.

Bowles, M. S. (2004). *Relearning to e- learn: Strategies for electronic learning and knowledge.* Carlton, Victoria: Melbourne University Press.

Brooks, D. W., Nolan, D. E., & Gallagher, S. M. (2001). *Web-teaching: A guide to designing interactive teaching for the World Wide Web* (2nd ed.). New York: Kluwer Academic/Plenum.

Brooks, J., & Brooks, M. (1993). *In search of understanding: The case for constructivist classrooms.* Alexandria, VA: Association for Supervision and Curriculum Development.

Butler, J. (1990). *Gender trouble: Feminism and the subversion of identity.* New York: Routledge.

Coleman, J. S. (1988). Social capital in the creation of human capital. *American Journal of Sociology, 94,* 95-120.

Collins, P. (1990). *Black feminist thought: Knowledge, consciousness and the politics of empowerment.* Boston: Unwin Hyman.

Cooley, C. H. (1922). *Human nature and the social order.* New York: Scribner.

Davis, M. (1997). Fragmented by technologies: A community in cyberspace. *Interpersonal Computing and Technology, 5*(1-2), 7-18.

De Freitas, S., & Oliver, M. (2005). Does e-learning policy drive change in higher education?: A case study relating models of organizational change to e-learning implementation. *Journal of Higher Education Policy and Management, 27*(1), 81-95.

Dewey, J. (1938). *Experience and education.* New York: Macmillan.

Dukheim, E. (1951). *Suicide.* Glencoe, IL: The Free Press.

Falk, I., Grady, N., Ruscoe, J., & Wallace, R. (2003). *Designing effective e-learning interventions, learning to e-learn research.* Center for Teaching and Learning in Diverse Educational Contexts. Hobart, TAS: Northern Territory University & Unitas Company, Ltd.

Featherstone, M., & Burrows, R. (Eds.). (1995). *Cyberspace, cyberbodies, cyberpunk.* London: Sage.

Gary, A., & Pearsall, M. (Eds.). (1989). *Women, knowledge and reality: Explorations in feminist philosophy.* Boston: Unwin Hyman.

Gibbons, M., Limoges, C., Nowotny, H., Schwartzman, S., Scott, P., & Trow, M. (Eds.). (1996). *The new production of knowledge.* London: Sage.

Giddens, A. (1979). *Central problems in social theory.* Berkeley, CA: University of California Press.

Goldman-Segall, R. (1992). Collaborative virtual communication: Using learning-constellations, a multimedia ethnographic research tool. In E. Barrett (Ed.), *Sociomedia* (pp. 257-296). Cambridge, MA: The MIT Press.

Habermas, J. (1993). *Justification and application: Remarks on discourse ethics.* Cambridge, MA: The MIT Press.

Haraway, D. (1991). *Simians, cyborgs, and women.* New York: Routledge.

Harding, S. (1991). *Whose science? whose knowledge?* New York: Cornell University Press.

Hawkey, K. (2004). Assessing online discussions working 'along the grain' of current technology and educational culture. *Education and Information Technologies, 9*(4), 377-386.

Herring, S. C. (2004). Slouching towards the ordinary: Current trends in computer-mediated communication. *New Media and Society, 6*(1), 26-36.

Hess, D. (1995). *Science and technology in a multicultural world.* New York: Columbia University Press.

Higher Education Council. (1992). *Response to the ministerial reference on distance education.* Canberra, ACT: Higher Education Council.

Johnson, D. W., & Johnson, R. T. (1994). Cooperative learning in the culturally diverse classroom. In R. A. DeVillar, C. T. Faltis, & J. P. Cummings (Eds.), *Cultural diversity in schools* (pp. 57-73). Albany, NY: State University of New York Press.

Jorgensen, D. (2002). The challenges and benefits of asynchronous learning networks. In H. Iyer (Ed.), *Distance learning: Information access and services for virtual users* (pp. 3-17). New York: Haworth Information Press.

Kreuger, L. W., & Neuman, W. L. (2006). *Social work research methods: Qualitative and quantitative applications.* Boston: Pearson Education.

Lash, S. (2002). *Critique of information.* London: Sage.

Leebron, E. J. (2004). Media entrepreneurship as an online course: A case study. In D. Monolescu, C. C. Schifter, & L. Greenwood (Eds.), *The distance education evolution: Issues and case studies* (pp. 240-257). Hershey, PA: Information Science Publishing.

Little, A. (2004). *The politics of community: Theory and practice.* Edinburgh: Edinburgh University Press.

Lynch, M. (2002). *The online educator: A guide creating to virtual classroom.* London: Routledge Falmer.

Lynch, M. (2004). *Learning online: A guide to success in the virtual classroom.* New York: Routledge Falmer.

Merton, R. (1968). *Social theory and social structure.* New York: The Free Press.

McClure, B. (1998). *Putting a new spin on groups.* Hillsdale, NJ: Lawrence Erlbaum.

Monolescu, D., Schifter, C.C., & Greenwood, L. (Eds.). (2004). *The distance education evolution: Issues and case studies.* Hershey, PA: Information Science Publishing.

Olson, M. (1965). *The logic of collective action: Public goods and the theory of groups.* Cambridge, MA: Harvard University Press.

Palloff, R. M., & Pratt, K. (1999). *Building learning communities in cyberspace: Effective strategies for the online classroom.* San Francisco: Jossey-Bass.

Palloff, R. M., & Pratt, K. (2001). *Lessons from the cyberspace classroom: The realities of online teaching.* San Francisco: Jossey-Bass.

Parsons, T. (1954). *Essays in sociological theory.* New York: The Free Press.

Piaget, J. (1927). *The child's conception of time.* New York: Ballantine Books.

Putnam, R. D. (Ed.). (2005). *Democracies in flux: The evolution of social capital in contemporary societies.* Oxford: Oxford University Press.

Ragusa, A., & Atweh, B. (2003, November). Analysing global collaborations using a post-structuralist model of social justice and social change. In *The Centre for Social Change Research 2003 Conference Proceedings.* Brisbane: Queensland University of Technology.

Ragusa, A., & Atweh, B. (2004, August). Social justice, social change and higher education: Analyzing global collaborations among higher education researchers. In *Proceedings of the Society for the Study of Social Problems Conference,* San Francisco.

Ritzer, G. (2004). *The globalization of nothing.* Thousand Oakes, CA: Pine Forge Press.

Robinson, J. (1999). The time diary method: Structure and uses. In W. Pentland, A. Harvey, M. Lawton, & M. McColl (Eds.), *Time use research in the social sciences* (pp. 47-88). New York: Kluwer Academic/Plenum.

Roof, J., & Wiegman, R. (Eds.). (1995). *Who can speak? Authority and critical identity.* Chicago: University of Illinois Press.

Royse, D. (1999). *Research methods in social work* (3rd ed.). Chicago: Nelson-Hall.

Scheffler, I. (1965). *Conditions of knowledge.* Chicago: Scott, Foresman & Company. Cited in Goldman-Segall (1992).

Schifter, C. (2004). Faculty participation in DE programs: Practices and plans. In D. Monolescu, C. C. Schifter, & L. Greenwood (Eds.), *The distance education evolution: Issues and case studies* (pp. 1-21). Hershey, PA: Information Science Publishing.

Schon, D. (1991). *The reflective turn.* New York: Teachers College Columbia University.

Schopler, J., Abell, M., & Galinsky, M. (1998). Technology-based groups: A reviewed conceptual framework for practice. *Social Work, 4*(3), 254-269.

Semple, A. (2000). Learning series and the influence on the development and use of educational technologies. *Australian Science Teachers Journal, 46*(3), 21-28.

Sherry, L., & Wilson, B. (1997). Transformative communication as a stimulus to Web innovations. In B. Khan (Ed.), *Web-based instruction.* Englewood Cliffs, NJ: Educational Technology Publications.

Shields, S. F., Gil-Egui, G., & Stewart, C. M. (2004). Certain about uncertainty: Strategies and practices for virtual teamwork in online classrooms. In D. Monolescu, C.C. Schifter, & L. Greenwood (Eds.), *The distance education evolution: Issues and case studies* (pp. 116-141). Hershey, PA: Information Science Publishing.

Smith, D. (1987). *The everyday world as problematic: A feminist sociology.* Boston: Northeastern University Press.

Smith, D. (1990). *The conceptual practices of power: A feminist sociology of knowledge.* Boston: Northeastern University Press.

Stein, A. (2001). Preparation for e-learning: An Australian study. In F. Albalooshi (Ed.), *Virtual education: Cases in learning and teaching technologies* (pp. 140-155). Hershey, PA: IRM Press.

Sydney Morning Herald. (2005a, March 1). *Fatal crash: Driver's arrest imminent.* Retrieved February 8, 2006, from http://www.smh.com.au/news/National/Fatal-crash-drivers-arrest-imminent/2005/03/01/1109546829118.html

Sydney Morning Herald. (2005b, March 1). *Fourth night of riots: Nine charged.* Retrieved February 8, 2006, from http://www.smh.com.

au/news/National/Fourth-night-of-riots-nine-charged/2005/03/01/1109546826854.html

Thomas, W. (1923). *The unadjusted girl*. Boston: Little, Brown.

Tuckman, B., & Jensen, M. (1977). Stages of small group development revisited. *Group and Organizational Studies, 2*(4), 419-427.

Vygotsky, L. (1986). *Thought and language*. Cambridge, MA: Massachusetts Institute of Technology.

Wegerif, R. (1998). The social dimension of asynchronous learning networks. *Journal of Asynchronous Learning Networks, 2*(1), 34-49.

Wilson, J. M. (2002, January 11). Successful distance-education spinoffs. *Chronicle of Higher Education, 48*, 18.

Winchester, I. (2005). Globalization, diversity and education for a democratic 21st century. *Journal of Educational Thought, 39*(1), 1-5.

World Bank. (2005). *World development indicators 2005*. Retrieved February 13, 2006, from://Web.worldbank.org/WBSITE/EXTERNAL/DATASTATISTICS/0,,contentMDK:20523710~hIPK:1365919~menuPK:64133159~pagePK:641331 50~piPK:64133175~theSitePK:239419,00.html

ENDNOTES

[1]   Precisely defining what constitutes "DE" remains a contested issue. Adjectives such as "flexible delivery," "virtual," "correspondence," and "online" are found intermittently dispersed throughout the literature to describe non-face-to-face education. Although DE is not a new phenomenon, with correspondence programs existing during the 19th century, the addition of technologically driven communication systems is recent (Schifter, 2004).

[2]   The concept of "virtual" learning spaces is defined by Graves (2000) "as those not constricted by time or place" (Leebron, 2004, p. 241).

[3]   Politics surrounding the concept "community" reveals it to be highly contested terrain (Little, 2002). For the scope of this research, community encapsulates neither the classical political theories of Aristotle, Tonnies, or Paine, nor entertains arguments over communitarianism vs. individualism. In this study I conceptualize community as a system of shared commitments and social values "expressed and promoted symbolically and culturally" (Frazer, 1999, p. 209 in Little, 2004, p. 131) as Frazer articulates in discussions of the welfare state. In sum, what I termed "virtual community" draws upon recent conceptualizations, due to societal changes brought on by modernity and globalization which no longer require geographical connection to establish "community." As operationalized, community here is informed by identity politics and increasingly limited by mental and infrastructure limitations rather than geography.

[4]   Prior to 2005, academic policy governing student computer access made computer requirements minimal. This meant, for social equity reasons, educators could not require students to participate in electronic forums. When policy in 2005 changed to reflect new technological minimum standards, making computer access mandatory, this did little to eradicate existing disparity among students. Despite shifting policy, variation in student access continued, with some having ready access via employment and/or home, while others traveled to public spaces with public terminals. Hence, practical implications of social inequality remain and continue to need addressing.

[5]   For example, when trying to understand how and why individuals in specific communities spend their time, Robinson's (1999) research reveals survey respondents' estimations

are grossly unrepresentative of reality and tend to exhibit bias towards over-reporting workload commitments. Although time use varies in kind from VC participation, the activity of cognition associated with memory recall is similar. Surveys produce a qualitatively different type of reflection and selection of content than analysis of primary texts yields. While the cohort for this study completed both qualitative and quantitative surveys, only discourse analysis is used as the basis for case study.

6 As with every methodology, the inevitability of limitations must be noted. Using case study as an analytical tool means the findings are necessarily situational, contextual, and non-generalizable (Kruger & Neuman, 2006; Royse, 1999).

7 In this environment, student forums were largely informal and participation optional.

8 Discussions of DE provisions described as "asynchronous learning network (ALN)" (Wilson, 2002) and "computer-mediated communication (CMC)" (Herring, 2004) have been attributed with increasing popularity (Herring, 2004) among educators and described as "a canonical model of online education that has received wide acceptance" (Wilson, 2002). Although the ALN model, as described by the CEO of UMassOnline, contains "threaded discussions and live chat," for the Australian case study, live chat is not currently possible.

9 Traditional DE refers to learning by correspondence, whereby students are sent reading material and assessment items to complete and return by mail. The university in this study sought to enhance DE by simply creating electronic discussion forums. This approach is inadequate as unstructured electronic discussions do not necessarily translate into better learning. Even with a study guide, without the guidance of lec-

tures, many students were unable to grasp the subject material.

10 As one student defined, "sub groups are the groups we are in for our discussion groups … what every topic you are discussing is the sub group you are in."

11 The "Macquarie Fields Riots" occurred in Sydney's southwest for four nights following a fatal motor vehicle accident on February 25, 2005, when two young men, passengers in a stolen motor vehicle, died after being pursued by Sydney police, while the driver fled the scene (*Sydney Morning Herald,* 2005a, 2005b).

12 Cooley's research explored how we imagine our appearance is to others, our imagination of their judgments of our appearance, and any subsequent modification.

13 In contrast, no such situation arose in VG2. As the size, virtual structure, and assignment design differed, it is impossible to speculate why. Future studies may wish to analyze why, and under what conditions, such differences in communication arise.

14 For example, although I thought asking students to send me an e-mail "so I can figure out if it's individual accounts or the whole system which isn't working," would clearly indicate I was referring to one's e-mail account, not the subject forum, this proved to be an incorrect assumption. Distinguishing between electronic communication technologies was problematic for some who incorrectly attempted to clarify my instructions by saying by "e-mailing Angela meant this actual post on the forum she has made" (for which I responded "Actually I meant real e-mail …")Although a minor point, had students used the wrong communication device, the technological problem would have been unsolved.

15 Consider the following virtual correspondence received: "I am currently working in Sudan with the United Nations, in somewhat

remote areas ... My issue is that to date, I have not received the prescribed reading material. I wanted to test the best method of receiving goods from Australia, and decided to put 'camel mail' to the test ... To date—non arrival!"

[16] Such sentiments continue to be put forth in telephone conversations with students, some who ultimately decide to only read lecturers' forum postings to minimize distress.

[17] This is due to the university's practice of mailing out DE material by subject, instead of by student. In this case, printing failure caused delay in the publication of some subject material, yet not others.

This work was previously published in Linguistic and Cultural Online Communication Issues in the Global Age, edited by J. Wang, pp. 306-327, copyright 2007 by Information Science Reference (an imprint of IGI Global).

Chapter XIX
Adaptive Computation Paradigm in Knowledge Representation:
Traditional and Emerging Applications

Marina L. Gavrilova
University of Calgary, Canada

ABSTRACT

The constant demand for complex applications, the ever increasing complexity and size of software systems, and the inherently complicated nature of the information drive the needs for developing radically new approaches for information representation. This drive is leading to creation of new and exciting interdisciplinary fields that investigate convergence of software science and intelligence science, as well as computational sciences and their applications. This survey article discusses the new paradigm of the algorithmic models of intelligence, based on the adaptive hierarchical model of computation, and presents the algorithms and applications utilizing this paradigm in data-intensive, collaborative environment. Examples from the various areas include references to adaptive paradigm in biometric technologies, evolutionary computing, swarm intelligence, robotics, networks, e-learning, knowledge representation and information system design. Special topics related to adaptive models design and geometric computing are also included in the survey.

INTRODUCTION

Adaptive computing focuses on the methodology and implementation of algorithms and systems that can adjust to different situations and circumstances. An adaptive system may change its own behavior depending on the goals, tasks, and other features of individual users and the environment. Adaptivity is important for ubiquitous and pervasive computing, and as it will be shown in this survey, plays an important role in a variety of traditional as well as emerging areas, such as biometric technologies, evolutionary computing, swarm intelligence, robotics, networks, e-learning, knowledge representation and information system design.

The constant demand for complex applications, the ever increasing complexity and size of software systems, and the inherently complicated nature of the information drive the needs for developing radically new approaches for information representation and processing. This drive is leading to creation of new and exciting interdisciplinary fields that investigate convergence of software science and intelligence science, as well as computational sciences and their applications. As can be seen from the definition, the driving force behind the need for adaptive paradigm is variety of situations, variability in backgrounds and needs of different user groups or applications. This survey article presents the new paradigm of the algorithmic models of intelligence, based on the adaptive hierarchical model of computation, and presents the algorithms and applications utilizing this paradigm in data-intensive, collaborative environment.

ADAPTIVE METHODS IN TERRAIN MODELING

For a long time, researchers were pressed with questions on how to model real-world objects realistically, while at the same time preserving efficiency, quality and operability requirements. The examples from the area of computer graphics and terrain modeling showcase the concept perfectly. Over the past twenty years, a grid, mesh, TIN, k-d trees, and Voronoi based methods for model representation were developed (Bonnefoi and Plemenos 2000, Gold and Dakowicz 2006, Cohen-Or and Levanoni 1996, Duchaineauy et. al. 1997, Franc and Skala 2002, Iglesis 2002, Kolingerová 2002). Most of these were however static methods, not suitable for rendering dynamic scenes or preserving higher level of details (see

Figure 1.). In 1997, first methods for dynamic model representation: Real-time Optimally Adapting Mesh (ROAM) and Progressive Mesh (PM), were developed (Duchaineauy 1997). However, even with the further improvements (Li et. a. 2003), these methods were not capable of dealing with large amount of complex data or significantly varied level of details (see Figure 2.). The main difference between terrain visualized using static and adaptive methods is the size and distribution of the triangles – in Figure 1, it is clearly seen that the patches of similar triangles are used throughout the various terrain features, while Figure 2 uses adaptive methods to decide on the most appropriate triangle sizes based on the curvature and distance from the viewer. However, this method is still not sufficient for dealing with all variety of terrain features, nor it is fast enough to be used in real-time.

Recently, the adaptive multi-resolution technique for real-time terrain rendering was developed (Apu and Gavrilova 2005). The method is characterized by the efficient representation of massive underlying terrain, utilizes efficient transition between detail levels, and achieves frame rate constancy ensuring visual continuity. The method is based on the adaptive loop subdivision and recursive split operation (see Figure 3.), implemented with the use of novel S-Queue operations ordering data structure.

Furthermore, a novel approach based on adaptive dynamic viewer-dependent level of details (LOD), utilizing the above strategy, was developed for real-time terrain rendering. The approach uses mesh regularity operator and LOD control parameters to achieve fast recursive seamless patch stitching, ensure geometric regularity, improve rendering quality, provide multi-resolution storage and allow for rendering and transmission of massive data sets (see Figure 4).

More formally, the process can be described as follows. A mesh M can be viewed as a piecewise linear surface. It is defined as a pair (K, V) where $V \subset \mathbb{R}^3$ is the set of vertices and K is a simplicial

Figure 1. A static mesh (40,000 triangles)

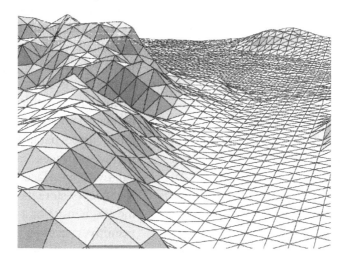

Figure 2. Real-time optimally adaptive mesh (25,000 triangles)

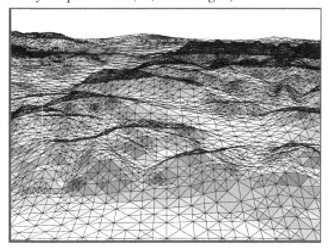

Figure 3. Adaptive loop subdivision and recursive split operations

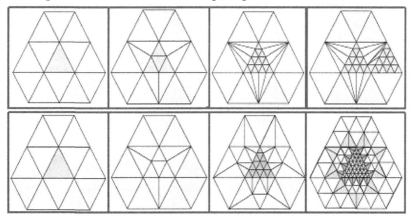

complex specifying the connectivity of the mesh simplices (the adjacency of the vertices, edges and faces). A combinatorial k-simplex of K is the ($k +$ 1) element subset of K. Therefore the 0-simplices $\{i\} \in K$ are called vertices, the 1-simpices $\{i, j\}$ $\in K$ are called edges, and the 2-simplices $\{i, j, l\}$ $\in K$ are called faces.

A mesh can be considered as higher dimensional generalization of the concept of graph used in a variety of graphics applications. For instance, a mesh $M = (K, V)$ defines a graph $G = (V, \wp)$ where V is the set of vertices in M and $\wp$ is the 1-simplices of K. Therefore G is the minimum unrestricted topological realization of M. Nevertheless, higher simplices of K (i.e. faces) could be reconstructed from G by means of a convex combinatorial relationship of the transitive closure of $\wp$. For example, a triangulation of the mesh could be obtained from the transitive closure of edges defining a mesh M.

Mesh optimization is the process of reducing a mesh M_0 to a mesh M_k, where M_k contains less number of vertices and geometric primitives (i.e. triangles) than M_0. The goal is to find M_k such that the no other mesh M'_k exists, which repre-

sent a better approximation of the mesh M_0. In practical applications, it is sufficient to converge to any of the optimal solutions. There are many variations of mesh optimization techniques. Intuitively, mesh optimization is a compression method for geometric models with large details. In computer graphics, various processes such as regular tessellations, polygonized spline surfaces, polygonized parametric surfaces, polygonized implicit surfaces, range scanned surfaces and subdivision surfaces generate polygonal meshes to render or store the object. In most cases, these meshes consist of a large number of geometric primitives. In order to render them or store them efficiently, one needs to reduce the number of primitives significantly. This process of simplification must be performed in a way such that the loss of details is minimal while conforming as much as possible to the specified criteria.

The novel approach to mesh optimization based on adaptive dynamic viewer-dependent level of detail method was developed in (Apu and Gavrilova 2005). The introduced data structure, called Adaptive Loop Subdivision (ALS), can intuitively be viewed as a special filter that

Figure 4. Varied Mesh regularity operator and LOD control parameters

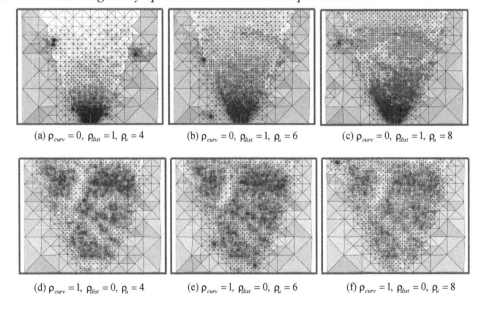

(a) $\rho_{curv} = 0$, $\rho_{dist} = 1$, $\rho_u = 4$ (b) $\rho_{curv} = 0$, $\rho_{dist} = 1$, $\rho_u = 6$ (c) $\rho_{curv} = 0$, $\rho_{dist} = 1$, $\rho_u = 8$

(d) $\rho_{curv} = 1$, $\rho_{dist} = 0$, $\rho_u = 4$ (e) $\rho_{curv} = 1$, $\rho_{dist} = 0$, $\rho_u = 6$ (f) $\rho_{curv} = 1$, $\rho_{dist} = 0$, $\rho_u = 8$

increases the details and smoothness properties of a mesh. It is a subdivision method based on triangle meshes. In general, every triangle in the base mesh M^i is split into four inner triangles (see Figure 4b). Each vertex position is adjusted according to a combinatory mask. The refined mesh M^{i+1} contains exactly four times the number of triangles than M^i. This four to one augmentation of LOD is a direct correspondent to the refinement of Haar wavelet.

Standard subdivision technique was first introduced by Loop in 1987 (Loop, 1987) in his Master's Thesis. It became widely acceptable and numerous improvements were suggested subsequently. However, the scheme does not allow local refinements. If one triangle is subdivided without the neighboring triangles, cracks will become visible. The new ALS scheme allows a way to repair those cracks without noticeable visual artifacts through the following conditions imposed on subdivision procedure:

1. If f_i are the faces adjacent to the face f in M^i and $\Im: F(M^i) \to \mathbb{Z}$ is a function corresponding to the LOD of a face ($F(M_j)$) is the set of faces of M^i) then:

    $$\forall i(\text{neighbor}(f, f_i) \to 0 \leq |\Im(f) - \Im(f_i)| \leq 1$$

2. A face f can be subdivided if and only if $\aleph(f) = 1$; $\aleph: F(M^i) \to \{0, 1\}$. Here,
    $$\aleph(f) = \begin{cases} 0; & \text{if f is a T-face} \\ 1; & \text{otherwise} \end{cases}$$

3. Let $\prod: F(M^i) \to F(M^{i-1})$ be the parent relation ship of a face. That is $f' = \prod(f)$ if and only if f in M^i has been generated by splitting f'. The following condition must hold:

    $$\forall f_i\ \forall f_j = ((\aleph(f_i) = 0) \wedge (\aleph(f_j) = 0) \wedge \text{neighbor}(f_i, f_j) \to (\Im(f_i) \neq \Im(f_j)) \vee (\prod(f_i) = \prod(f_j)))$$

These constrains are the prime directives of the developed ALS method. They enforce the regularity of the scheme and ensures that no thin triangle is introduced. Their application leads to fine results shown in Figure 4 as well as numerous other advantages. ALS scheme was subsequently successfully used not only for terrain visualization, but in geographical information systems, motion planning and computer simulation applications.

ADAPTIVE METHODOLOGY IN TRADITIONAL APPLICATIONS

Adaptive Geometric Methods

At the same time as adaptive methods were making their way in the area of terrain rendering, the renewed interest to topology-based data structures, Voronoi diagram and Delaunay triangulation in particular, has grown significantly (Okabe et.al. . 1992). The key developments on both conceptual and implementation level are regularly presented at the International Symposium on Voronoi Diagrams in Science and Engineering Conference Series. Utilization of these developments in molecular modeling, bioinformatics and robotics promotes further stimulus to research on adaptive and dynamic problems. Thus, article (Gold and Dakowicz 2006) studies dynamic ship navigation visualization system using kinetic Voronoi diagram as an underlying concept. Utilization of the dynamic Voronoi diagram for 3D robot planning and navigation is studies in (Kolingerova 2005). Adaptive Voronoi diagram based approach to swarm simulation is presented in (Apu and Gavrilova 2006). These developments lead the way toward utilization of adaptive hierarchical models in computational geometry.

Recently, some preliminary results on utilization of computational geometry techniques in biometrics began to appear, such as research on image processing using Voronoi diagrams (Asano

Figure 5. Planar Voronoi diagram representation

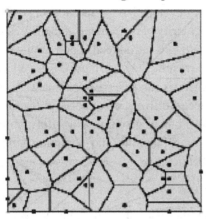

2006, Liang and Asano 2004), work on utilizing Voronoi diagram for fingerprint synthesis (Bebis 1999), and studies on 3D modeling of human faces using triangular mesh (Li and Jain 2005). Some interesting results were recently obtained in the BTLab, University of Calgary, through the development of topology-based feature extraction algorithms for fingerprint matching, 3D facial expression modeling and iris synthesis (Wang et. al. 2005, Wecker et. al. 2006, Bhattachariya and Gavrilova 2006).

Adaptive Image Processing and Visualization

Adaptive image processing is one of the most important techniques in visual information processing, especially in image restoration, filtering, enhancement, and segmentation. While existing literature presents some important aspects of the issue, there were no works that would treat the problem from a viewpoint that is directly linked to human perception – until the book "Adaptive Image Processing: A computational Intelligence Perspective Book" appeared (William et. al. 2001). This comprehensive collection of references treats adaptive image processing from a computational intelligence viewpoint, relating neural networks, fuzzy logic, and evolutionary computation to

adaptive image processing. Based on the fundamentals of human perception, this book also gives a detailed account of computational intelligence methods and algorithms for adaptive image processing in regularization, edge detection, vision and any area where intelligent visual information processing is required.

Adaptive processing has been tightly linked not only to image processing, but to computer graphics and scientific visualization. In (Lopse et.al. 2002), authors provide an algorithm for computing a *robust adaptive polygonal approximation* of an implicit curve in the plane. The approximation is adapted to the geometry of the curve because the length of the edges varies with the curvature of the curve. Robustness is achieved by combining interval arithmetic and automatic differentiation.

Another example is adaptive visualization area of research, which is often explored in connection with geographical, urban or medical applications. A variety of engineering disciplines use large high-resolution geometric models whose computational requirements exceed current computer hardware capacities. The research presented in (Lu and Hammersley 2000) describes an *adaptive visualization* solution for interactively building such models. While adaptive visualization techniques have conventionally been applied to existing complete models, their method provides adaptive visualization of models while still under construction, through a clever utilization of multiresolution methods.

A common application of adaptive paradigm can be found in the area of medical imaging. A common active contour (*snake*) model is a popular choice for medical imaging applications, however the article by (Shen and Davatzikos 2000) goes further in exploring adaptive paradigm in this context. They propose a clever approach to geometric design and the structure of the model through *adaptive method for carrying out model deformations* in the most reliable way. Specifically, authors suggest to use an attribute vector to characterize the geometric structure around each point of the snake model, which allows to deform to nearby edges with considering geometric structure. They also provide an adaptive-focus statistical model which allows the deformation of the active contour in each stage to be influenced by the most reliable matches. Finally, they propose the deformation mechanism that is robust to local minima and is based on evaluating the snake energy function on segments of the snake at a time, instead of individual points. The approach is novel and unique, and is proven to perform very well experimentally.

Adaptive Information Systems

The current fast evolution in the areas of software, hardware and networks suggests that it will be possible to offer access to information systems through variety of interactive means, including computers, notebooks, PDA's, cellular phones, game consoles, GPS devices etc. Thus, this variety of technologies and information available required creation of a flexible environment to support adaptive interaction and services according to changing requirements, interfaces, devices, communication and user needs.

One of the research initiatives that started in 2002 was devoted specifically to this problem. The *Multichannel Adaptive Information Systems* project (MAIS) was funded by Basic Research Funds of the Italian Department of Education and involved six Universities and industry collaborations. The project research areas were information systems, database systems, human computer interaction, computer networks and telecommunication, hardware design, middleware, management engineering, with the focus on adaptive computing paradigm. Adaptive e-services, adaptive portable devices and adaptive networks were at the focus of the research. The prototype applications of the methods were developed in the areas of tourism, education, and risk management in archeology.

Another relevant project is described in (Doerr 1999). Authors state that one way to increase software system adaptability is to allocate resources dynamically at run-time rather than statically at design time. For example, fine-grained run-time allocation of processor utilization and network bandwidth creates an opportunity to execute multi-modal operations. Thus, this allocation strategy enhances adaptability by combining deterministic and non-deterministic functionality. Authors next showcase that adaptability is essential to improve versatility and decrease lifecycle maintenance costs for embedded real-time systems.

Adaptive Networks

As already seen from the above applications, the driving force behind the need for adaptive paradigm is variety of situations, variability in backgrounds and needs of different user groups or applications. The further expansion of Internet communications, not only for electronic exchange of ideas, but also as a means of collecting a wide range of information, has lead to a variety of other applications besides e-learning. Thus, electronic commerce, Internet transactions, collaborative newsgroups, facebooks, on-line teleconferencing are all rapidly developing. However, one of the problems is the difference in information available to network users. Network systems and services are becoming increasingly complex and diverse, and the processes involved in accessing required information are growing ever more advanced. As a result, the information disparity that arises from the presence or absence of knowledge about networks and computers is becoming a problem that cannot be overlooked. Another problem is one that is derived from changes and increases in communications traffic.

The key to dealing with the above challenges is *user adaptability* and *adaptability to changes in communication demand*. User adaptability means that the user does not conform to the conditions of the network, but rather the network adapts instantaneously to the user environment and to service needs, which change with every passing moment. Adaptability to changes in communication demand means that the network configuration and equipment functions change dynamically to absorb the introduction of new services and macro-fluctuations in traffic. NTT Laboratories is one of the organizations that combines knowledge, expertise and application research in the area of *adaptive networks*, which constantly change their functions and configurations to respond immediately to changes in the environment, and to be the network platform of the Information Sharing Society of the future. Their key terms to describe the research in adaptive networks is Intellect, Evolution, and Simple & Seamless.

ADAPTIVE METHODS IN EMERGING AREAS

Biometrics and Adaptive Computing

Adaptive techniques have made their way in emerging scientific areas such as *biometric computing*. In information technology, biometric refers to a study of physical and behavioral characteristics with the purpose of person identification. In recent years, the area of biometrics has witnessed a tremendous growth, partly as a result of a pressing need for increased security,

and partly as a response to the new technological advances that are literally changing the way we live. Availability of much more affordable storage and the high resolution image capturing devices have contributed to accumulating very large datasets of biometric data. On the other hand, it also created significant challenges driven by the higher than ever volumes and the complexity of the data, that can no longer be resolved through acquisition of more memory, faster processors or optimization of existing algorithms. This justifies the need for the development of a new concept for biometric data storage and visualization based on adaptive paradigm.

It is obvious to anyone who works in the area of biometric computing that the problem is not trivial. It is not enough to simply fill the existing deficiency in data representation and visualization through application of advanced results from the areas of computational geometry and computer graphics. The backbone of the methodology is in the application of adaptive hierarchical data representation to achieve flexible and versatile data representation, fast data retrieval, reliable matching, easy updates and smooth and continuous data processing.

To achieve this objective, we suggest a novel way to represent complex biometric data (e.g. a bitmap, a graphics file, a set of vectors, a polygonal curve) through the organization of the data in a hierarchical tree-like structure. Such organization is similar to *Adaptive Memory Subdivision (AMS)* representation (see Figure 6).

Figure 6. Adaptive Memory Subdivision (AMS) model

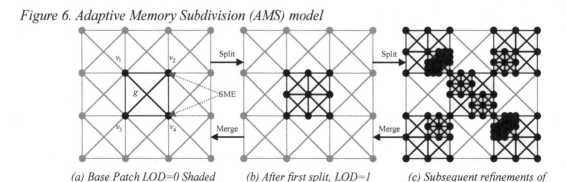

(a) Base Patch LOD=0 Shaded Region is a primitive cluster

(b) After first split, LOD=1

(c) Subsequent refinements of ASM primitive clusters

AMS is a hybrid method based on the combination of traditional hierarchical tree structure with the concept of expanding or collapsing tree nodes, depending on the amount of information and level of detail (LOD) that needs to be represented. *Spatial quad-tree* is used to hold the information about the system, as well as the instructions on how to process this information. Expansion is realized through the spatial subdivision technique that refines the data and increases LOD, and collapsing is realized through the merge operation that simplifies the data representation and makes it more compact. The greedy strategy is used to optimally adapt to the best representation based on the user requirements, amount of available data and resources, and required LOD. This powerful technique enables to achieve compact data representation with required LOD. For instance, it enables to efficiently store and retrieve minor details of the facial image (e.g. scars, wrinkles) or detailed patterns of the compared irises.

Adaptive methods have been studied for increasing hand geometry reliability while new processing algorithms, such as symmetric real Gabor filters, have been used to decrease the computational cost involved in iris pattern recognition (Sanchez-Reillo et. Al. 1999). This work explores adapting these methods to small *embedded systems*, and proposes the design of new biometric systems, where the users template is stored in a portable storage media for added security. Such media could be used to store sensitive information, for instance related to user's health records, and proposed adaptive access methods are devised to avoid the reading of this data unless the biometric verification has been performed.

While the above research is aimed at increase reliability and security of biometric data, another highly interesting direction is merging *adaptive paradigm with multimodal biometric fusion*. Multimodal biometric is intended to utilize biometric information obtained by multiple sensors and from multiple sources in order to increase authentication reliability. The paper by (Veera-machaneni 2003) introduces a new Adaptive Multimodal Biometric Fusion Algorithm(AMBF) algorithm, which is a combination of *Bayesian decision fusion* technique and a *particle swarm optimization* method. A Bayesian framework is typically used to fuse decisions received from multiple biometric sensors. The optimal rule is a function of the error cost and a priori probability of an intruder. This Bayesian framework formalizes the design of a system that can adaptively increase or reduce the security level. Particle swarm optimization searches the decision and sensor operating points (i.e. thresholds) space to achieve the desired security level. The optimization function aims to minimize the cost in a Bayesian decision fusion. The particle swarm optimization algorithm results in the fusion rule and the operating points of sensors at which the system can work. The swarm algorithm can easily handle the scalability issue as the number of sensors increases and efficiently search through the highly large fusion rule search space.

The presented method successfully merges two highly interesting and important paradigms: adaptive method based on evolutionary computing and multimodal biometric system with Beyesian decision rule. As a result, it can successfully address the varying security needs and user access requirements in a biometric system. The authors report that the adaptive algorithm allows to achieve desired security level and to seemingly switch between different rules and sensor operating points for varying user needs.

The adaptive approach can be successfully sued not only for biometric modeling but also in synthesis of the biometric data. A combination of the method with *multi-resolution approach,* suitable for extracting details of the model at different scales of resolution, is a promising new direction of research which can be used to complement the missing information or to recreate the model. The method performs the high-level detail extraction and capturing of the model characteristics, and then applies this information for synthesis of new biometric data. This novel approach has shown a high potential in a recent study on iris synthesis (Wecker et.al. 2006). Moreover, *adaptive learning method can assist in* examining extracted features, retrieval patterns, and dynamic updates with the purpose of making the model more flexible.

Adaptive Methods in Robotics

Another highly important and rapidly developing area of research, that encompasses artificial intelligence, engineering, vision, geometric processing and decision-making, is robotics. *Adaptive robots* is an area of research that studies the design of robots that function in a changing environment by using high-level cognitive abilities and/or adaptive behaviors. The Dutch AIBO team, composed by research groups from the DECIS Lab and Universities of Amsterdam, Delft, Twente and Utrecht, is the leading force behind research on collaborative robot behavior and intelligent behavior of the team of robots, through robot soccer simulation and applied studies (Wong et. al. 2001). Exploring adaptive paradigm in a variety of areas essential to success of this project, including *adaptive robot vision, adaptive navigation and adaptive learning* are just some of the examples of the current state-of-the art research related to this project. Adaptive methods to improve *self-localization* in robot soccer were devised in (Dahm and Ziegler 2003). The authors utilized adaptive strategies to improve the reliability and performance of self-localization in robot soccer with legged robots. Adaptiveness is the common feature of the presented algorithms and has proved essential to enhance the quality of localization by a new classification technique as well as to increase the confidence level of information about the environment. Cooperative strategy based on *adaptive Q-learning* for robot soccer was developed in (Hwang et.al. 2004). The strategy developed enabled robots to cooperate with each other to achieve the objectives of offense and defense. Through the mechanism of learning, the robots learned from experiences in either successes or failures, and utilized these experiences to improve the performance. The cooperative strategy is based on a hierarchical architecture. An adaptive Q-learning method showed to allow more flexibility in learning that the traditional Q-learning approach, especially in the context of cooperative strategy.

Adaptive Knowledge Representation and Learning

Adaptive Knowledge Representation and Reasoning Conference (AKRR) is one of the unique events devoted completely to the emerging paradigm of *adaptive knowledge representation*. The forum is concerned with all adaptive aspects related to knowledge representation and reasoning. Specifically, such areas as adaptive systems in economic sciences and organizational theory, new generation of semantic web, adaptive systems in medical education, research and practice, and adaptive machine translation are within the conference scope.

The idea of utilizing *adaptive methods in e-learning* is not new. One of the first articles on the subject that appeared in 1998 describes web-based educational applications that are expected to be used by very different groups of users (Brusilovsky 1998). Thus, authors argue that such a system needs to adapt to users with very different backgrounds, prior knowledge of the subject and learning goals, without human assistance. They next describe an approach for developing *adaptive electronic textbooks* and present InterBook—an authoring tool based on this approach which simplifies the development of adaptive electronic textbooks on the Web.

An extensive research in the area of adaptive learning was undertaken since that time. One example is the research on knowledge representation in the area of learning design and adaptive learning, presented in (Kravcik and Gasevic 2006). The authors deal with learning design and adaptation, and state that the procedural knowledge is highly important. They examine the degree of reusability and interoperability of procedural knowledge in the current adaptive educational hypermedia systems, and discuss several useful strategies and techniques, including informal scripts, system encoding, elicited knowledge, and standardized specifications.

Hierarchical Models in Cognitive Informatics

As it has been seen in the previous sections, adaptive computing heavily relies on hierarchical models of knowledge representing various natural and artificial phenomena. Such models can represent, for instance, complex three-dimensional terrain patterns, evolutionary behaviour of a swarm of living organisms, or an intricate structure of a web-linked virtual library. As it was recently discovered at the front line of the cognitive science and cognitive informatics research, hierarchical cognitive models can be also efficiently use to study internal information and knowledge presentation in human brains (Wang 2007).

It is commonly accepted that memory is the foundation of all forms of natural intelligence. Neural Informatics (NeI) is a branch of cognitive informatics, where memory is recognized as the foundation and platform of any natural or artificial intelligence (Wang 2003). While traditionally the Long-Term Memory (LTM) is perceived as static and fixed in adult brains, recent discoveries in neuroscience and cognitive informatics indicate that LTM is dynamically reconfiguring, particularly at the lower levels of the neural clusters (Wang 2007). The article explains the memory establishment, enhancement, and evolution, which are typical functions of the brain, are not limited to only childhood developmental stage; thus the more complex, dynamic model is necessary to represent such functions. In order to achieve this task, the pioneering theory is presented in the article that is based on the concept of the Hierarchical Neural Cluster (HNC) Model of Memory. Furthermore, the Object-Attribute-Relation (OAR) model is introduced to formally represent the structures of internal information and knowledge acquired and learned in the brain (Wang 2007). The OAR model explains the mechanisms of internal knowledge and information representation, as well as their physical and physiological meanings, and allows to better understand learning mechanisms and help to develop more powerful algorithms for a variety of complex problems faced by scientists everyday.

CONCLUSION

The article presented a comprehensive survey of the new paradigm of the algorithmic models of intelligence, based on the adaptive hierarchical model of computation. It started with the adaptive methods for terrain modeling, and presented methodically the adaptive paradigm in geometric computing, biometric, robotics, image processing and vision, knowledge representations, information systems, e-learning and networks. Illustrations were further provided to explain some concepts related to adaptive information processing and models. Aside from the areas covered in the survey, there constantly appear a variety of new and emerging applications utilizing adaptive models of computations. It is our hope that this survey inspires readers to further in-depth study of the exciting topic of adaptive computations.

REFERENCES

Apu, R. and Gavrilova, M.L. "Adaptive Spatial Memory Representation for Real-Time Motion Planning," 3IA'2005 Int. Conf. on Comp. Graphics and Artificial Intelligence, France pp.21-32, 2005

Apu, R. and Gavrilova, M.L. "Battle Swarm: An Evolutionary Approach to Complex Swarm Intelligence," 3IA Int. C. Comp. Graphics and AI, Eurographics, Limoges, France, pp. 139-150, 2006

Asano, T. "Aspect-Ratio Voronoi Diagram with Applications," ISVD 2006, IEEE, pp. 32-39, 2006

Bardis,G., Miaoulis, G. and Plemenos, D. "Learning User Preferences at the Declarative and Geometric Description Level," 3IA'2005, Limoges (France), May 11-12, 2005

Bebis G., Deaconu T. and Georiopoulous, M. "Fingerprint Identification using Delaunay Triangulation," ICIIS 99, Maryland, pp. 452-459, 1999

Bhattachariya, P. and Gavrilova, M.L.. "CRYSTAL - A new density-based fast and efficient clustering algorithm", IEEE-CS Press, ISVD 2006, pp. 102-111, Banff, AB, Canada, July 2006

Bonnefoi, P.F. and Plemenos, D. "Constraint satisfaction techniques for declarative scene modelling by hierarchical decomposition," 3IA'2000, Limoges (France), May 3-4, 2000

Brusilovsky, P., Eklund, J. and Schwarz, E., "Web-based education for all: a tool for development of adaptive courseware," Computer Networks and ISDN Systems, Volume 30, Issues 1-7, pp. 291-300, 1998

Capelli R., Maio, D. and Maltoni D. "Synthetic Fingerprint-Database Generation," ICPR 2002, Canada, vol 3, pp 369-376, 2002

Cohen-Or, D. and Levanoni, Y. "Temporal continuity of levels of detail in Delaunay triangulated terrain," Visualization'96, pp. 37-42. IEEE Press, 1996

Dahm, I. and Ziegler, J. "Adaptive Methods to Improve Self-localization in Robot Soccer," LNCS 2752, pps. 393-408, 2003

Doerr, B.S., Venturella, T., Jha, R., Gill, C.D. and Schmidt, D.C., "Adaptive Scheduling for Real-time, Embedded Information," in Proceedings of the 18th IEEE/AIAA Digital Avionics Systems Conference, 10 pages, 1999

Duchaineauy, M. et. al., "ROAMing Terrain: Real-Time Optimally Adapting Meshes," IEEE Visualization '97, pp. 81-88, 1997

Franc, M. and Skala, V. "Fast Algorithm for Triangular Mesh Simplification Based on Vertex decimation," CCGM2002 Proceedings, Lecture Notes in Computer Science, Springer, 2002

Gavrilova, M.L. Computational Intelligence: A Geometry-Based Approach, Book, in series Studies in Computational Intelligence, Springer-Verlag, to appear in 2008

Gold, C. and Dakowicz, M. "Kinetic Voronoi/Delaunay Drawing Tools", ISVD 2006, IEEE-CS, pp. 76-84, Banff, Canada, 2006

Hwang, K.S., Tan, S.W. and Chen, C.C. "Cooperative strategy based on adaptive Q-learning for robot soccer systems," IEEE Transactions on Fuzzy Systems Volume: 12, Issue: 4, pp. 569- 576, 2004

Iglesias, A. "Computer Graphics Techniques for Realistic Modeling, Rendering, and Animation of Water. Part I: 1980-88." Int. Conf. on Computational Science (2) 2002, 181-190, 2002

Kawaharada, H. and Sugihara, K. "Compression of Arbitrary Mesh Data Using Subdivision Surfaces," IMA Conference on the Mathematics of Surfaces 2003, 99-110, 2003

Kolingerova I. "Probabilistic Methods for Triangulated Models," 8th Int. Conference on Computer Graphics and Artificial Intelligence 3IA 2005, Limoges, France, 93-106, 2005

Kravcik, M. and Gasevic, D. "Knowledge Representation for Adaptive Learning Design," Proceedings of Adaptive Hypermedia. June, Dublin, Ireland, 11 pages, 2006

Li S., Liu X. and Wu E., "Feature-Based Visibility-Driven CLOD for Terrain," In Proc. Pacific Graphics 2003, pp 313-322, IEEE Press, 2003

Li, S. and Jain, A. Handbook of Face Recognition. Springer-Verlag 2005

Liang X.F. and Asano T. "A fast denoising method for binary fingerprint image," IASTED, Spain, pp. 309-313, 2004

Loop, C. T. Smooth Subdivision Surfaces Based on Triangles. Masters Thesis, University of Utah, Department of Mathematics. 1987

Lopes, H., Oliveira, J.B. and de Figueiredo, L.H. "Robust adaptive polygonal approximation of implicit curves," Computers & Graphics Volume 26, Issue 6, pp. 841-852, 2002.

Lu, H. and Hammersley, R. "Adaptive visualization for interactive geometric modeling in geoscience," the 8th International Conference in Central Europe on Computer Graphics, Visualization and Interactive Digital Media 2000, p.1, Feb. 2000

Luo, Y. and Gavrilova, M.L.. "3D Facial model synthesis using Voronoi Approach," IEEE-CS proceedings, ISVD 2006, pp. 132-137, Banff, AB, Canada, July 2006

Medioni, G. and Waupotitsch, R. "Face recognition and modeling in 3D," IEEE Int. Workshop on Analysis and Modeling of Faces and Gestures, pp. 232-233, 2003

Moriguchi, M. and Sugihara, K. "A new initialization method for constructing centroidal Voronoi Tessellations on Surface Meshes," ISVD 2006, IEEE-CS Press, pp. 159-165, 2006

Okabe, A., Boots, B. and Sugihara, K. Spatial tessellation concepts and applications of Voronoi diagrams, Wiley & Sons, Chichester, England, 1992

Perry, S.W., Wong H.S. and Guan, L. Adaptive Image Processing: A computational Intelligence Perspective, CRC Press, 9 volumes, 272 pages, 2001

Sanchez-Reillo, R., Sanchez-Avila, C. and Gonzalez-Marcos, A. "Multiresolution Analysis and Geometric Measures for Biometric Identification Systems," Secure Networking Proceedings, LNCS, Volume 1740, p. 783, 1999

Shen, S. and Davatzikos, C. "An Adaptive-Focus Deformable Model Using Statistical and Geometric Information," IEEE Transactions on Pattern Analysis and Machine Intelligence Vol. 22 No. 8 pp. 906-913 August 2000

Veeramachaneni, K., Osadciw, L.A. and Varshney, P.K. "Adaptive Multimodal Biometric Fusion Algorithm Using Particle Swarm," SPIE, vol 5099, pp. 211, Orlando, Florida, April 21- 25, 2003

Wang, Y. "Cognitive informatics: A new transdisciplinary research field." Brain and Mind: A Transdisciplinary Journal of Neuroscience and Neurophilosophy, 4(2), 115-127, 2003

Wang, Y. "The OAR Model of Neural Informatics for Internal Knowledge Representation in the Brain", Int'l Journal of Cognitive Informatics and Natural Intelligence, 1(3), 66-77, July-September, 2007

Wang, H., Gavrilova, M.L., Luo, Y. and Rokne, J. "An Efficient Algorithm for Fingerprint Matching", ICPR 2006, Int. C. on Pattern Recognition, Hong Kong, IEEE-CS , 2006

Wecker, L., Samavati, F. and Gavrilova, M.L. "Iris Synthesis: A Multi-Resolution Approach," GRAPHITE 2005, ACM Press, in association with SIGGRAPH, pp. 121-125, 2005

Wong, C.C., Chou, M.F., Hwang, C.P., Tsai, C.H. and Shyu, S.R. "A method for obstacle avoidance and shooting action of the robot soccer," Robotics and Automation, proceedings ICRA. IEEE

International Conference, pp 3778- 3782 vol.4 2001

Yanushkevich, S., Wang, P., Srihari, S. and Gavrilova, M.L. Image Pattern Recognition: Synthesis and Analysis in Biometrics, Book, World Scientific, 452 pages, 2006

Compilation of References

Abeysundara, G. (2005). *Dynamic cellular channel allocation using intelligent agents.* School of Computer Science, University of Catleton.

Abu Musa, A. (2004). *Exploring the Perceived Threats of Computerized Accounting Information Systems In Emerging Countries: An Empirical Study on Saudi Organization.* European Conference On Accounting information System, Section two.

Abu-Taieh. (2004). Computer Reservations System Auditing Headache of the Airline Industry – computerized Auditing and Accounting. *Innovations through information technology* (p. 477). Idea Group Inc (IGI).

Advanced Integration Method (AIM) Implementation Guide Card-Not-Present Transactions. (2005). *Version 1.0.* Merchant Commerce and Payment Services.

Ahmad, R. (2006). *A hybrid channel allocation algorithm using hot-spot notification for wireless cellular networks.* IEEE CCECE/CCGEI, 891-894.

Ahola, J., & Esa Rinta-Runsala. (2001). *Data mining case studies in customer profiling.* Research report TTE1-2001-29; VTT Information Technology.

AICPA Auditing Standards Board. (2001, April). *SAS No. 94: The Effect of Information Technology on the Auditor's Consideration of Internal Control in a Financial Statement Audit.*

Air Freight Market Outlook. (2007). Retrieved 5 2008, from IATA ECONOMICS BRIEFING: http://www.iata.org/NR/rdonlyres/CE373AB8-1093-4192-A892-9C559F57CA29/0/Cargo_Market_Outlook_Sep07.pdf

Al-Agha, k. (2000). Resource management in wireless networks using intelligent agents. *International Journal of Network Management, 10*(1), 29-39.

Albizu, E., & Olazaran, M. (2006). BPR implementation in Europe: the adaptation of a management concept. *New Technology, Work and Employment, 21*(1), March.

Albuquerque, A. B., & Belchior, A. D. (2002). E-Commerce Website quality evaluation. *Euromicro Conference, 2002. Proceedings.* (pp. 294 – 300).

Al-Khatib, A. M. (2008). *Mining Fraudulent Behavior in e-payment System.* Ph.D. Dissertation.

Al-Khatib, A. M., & Ezz Hattab. (2007). Mining Fraudulent Transactions in e-payment Systems. *9th international conference (iiWAS2007)* (pp. 179–189).

Al-Khatib, A. M., & Hattab, E. (2005). Credit Card Fraud Detection Techniques: A survey. *7th international conference (iiWAS2005), 1,* 505–516.

An, J., Hines, E. L., Leeson, M. S., Sun, L., Iliescu, D. D., & Wang, K. Y. (2007). Genetic algorithms and fuzzy logic for dynamic channel allocation in cellular radio networks. *IEEE Radio and Wireless Symposium,* Long Beach, California, USA.

Anderson, R. (2004). *Economics and security Resource.* Page http://www.cl.cam.ac.uk/users/rja14/econsec

Antonia, S., Michalis, X. & Stavrinoudis, D. (2003, July). *VECIMS 2003 - International Symposium on Virtual Environments, Human-Computer Interfaces, and Measurement Systems,* Lugano, Switzerland.

Antonia, S., Stavrinoudis, D., & Michalis, X. (2007). In-Depth Analysis of Selected Topics related to the Quality Assessment of E-Commerce Systems. In J. Filipe, H. Coelhas, & M. Saramago (Eds.), *e-Business and Telecommunication Networks Vol II*. (pp. 39-48). ISBN: 978-3-540-75992-8.

Aradhya, V. N. M., Kumar, G. H., & Noushath, S. (2007). Robust Unconstrained Handwritten Digit Recognition using Radon Transform. In *Proceedings of IEEE-ICSCN 2007* (pp. 626-629).

Arnold, M., Schumucker, M., & Wolthusen, S. (2003). *Techniques and Applications of Digital Watermarking and Content Protection*. Boston, MA: Artech House.

Arora, A., Krishman, R., Telang, R., & Yang, Y. (2005). *An empirical analysis of vendor response to software vulnerability disclosure*. Mimeo.

Arora, A., Nandkumar, A., Krishman, R., Telang, R., & Yang, Y. (2004). *Impact of vulnerability disclosure and patch availability: An empirical enalysis*. Presented at the Third Workshop on Economics and Information Security, Minneapolis, MN.

Arora, A., Telang, R., & Xu, H. (2004). *Optimal policy for software vulnerability disclosure*. working paper, Carnegie-Mellon.

Arquilla, J. (1999). Ethics and information warfare, In Z. Khalilzad, J. White, & A. Marsall (Eds.), *Strategic appraisal: The changing role of information in warfare* (pp. 379-401). Santa Monica, CA: Rand Corporation.

Arvish, A. (2007). *Airplane Economics: Operating and Maintennace Cost.*

August, T., & Tunca, T, (2005). *Network software security and user incentives*. Mimeo.

Auramo, J., Kauremaa, J., & Tanskanen, K. (2005). Benefits of IT in SCM: an explorative study of progressive companies. *International Journal of Physical Distribution & Logistics Management, 35*(2).

Avison, D. E., & Fitzgerald, G. (2003, January). Where Now for Development methodologies. *Communications of the ACM, 46*(1), 79-82.

Awamleh, R., Evans, J., & Mahate, A. (2000). *Internet Banking in Emergency Markets: The case of Jordon – A Note*. University of Wollongong, Dubai Campus.

Bagchi, P., & Skjoett-Larsen, T. (2005). Supply chain integration: a Europe survey. *International Journal of Logistics Management, 16*(2).

Bahli, B., & Di Tullio, D. (2003). Web Engineering: An Assessment of Empirical Research. *Communications of the Associations for Information Systems, 12*, 203-222.

Balasubramanian, P., & Tewary, A. (2005). Design of supply chains: Unrealistic expectations on Collaboration. *Sadhana, 30*(2 & 3), April/June.

Barnes and Vidgen (2002). An Integrative Approach to the Assessment of E-Commerce Quality. *Journal of Electronic Commerce Research, 3*(3), 114-127.

Barnes, S., & Vidgen, R. (2001). Assessing the Quality of Auction Web Sites. *In Proceedings of the 34th International Conference on System Sciences.*

Barrat, M. (2004). Understanding the meaning of collaboration in the supply chain. *SCM: An International Journal, 9*(1).

Bayles, W. (2001). Network attack. *Parameters, US Army War College Quarterly, 31*, 44-58.

Beck, K. (1999). Embracing Change with Extreme Programming. *IEEE Computer, 32*(10): 70–77.

Beck, K. et al., (2001, February). Manifesto for Agile Software Development. *The Agile Alliance*, http://www.agilealliance.org/

Bejar, R., Domshlak, C., Fernandez, C., Gomes, C., Krishnamachari, B., Selman, B., & Valls, M. (2005). Sensor networks and distributed CSP: Communication, computation and complexity. *Journal of Artificial Intelligence, 161*, 117–147.

Belongie, S., Malik, J., & Puzicha, J. (2002). Shape Matching and Object Recognition Using Shape Contexts. *IEEE Transactions on Pattern Analysis and Machine Intelligence, 24*(24), 509-522.

Bentz, D. P. (1997). Three Dimensional Computer Simulation of Portland Cement Hydration and Microstructure Development. *J. Am. Ceram. Soc., 80*(1), 3-21.

Berenson et. al. (2002). *Business Statistics, Concepts and Application*, Eighth Edition. Prentice Hall.

Bernal, & Mason, G. (1960). Coordination of Randomly Packed Spheres. *Nature 188*, 910.

Bernal, J. D., Cherry, I. A., Finney, J. L., & Knight, K. R. (1970). An Optical Machine for Measuring Sphere Coordinates in Random Packings. *J. Phys., E 3*, 388-90.

Bessiere, C., Maestre, A., Brito I., & Meseguer P. (2004). Asynchronous backtracking without adding links: a new member in the ABT family. *Artificial Intelligence Journal, 161*, 7-24.

Bidgoli, H, (2002). *Electronic Commerce Principles and Practice*. San Diego: Academic Press.

Bierwagen, G. P., & Saunders, T. E. (1974). Studies of the Effects of Particle Size Distribution on the Packing Efficiency of Particles. *Powder Technology 10*, 111-19.

Bissett, A. (2004). High technology war and "surgical strikes". *Computers and Society (ACM SIGCAS), 32*(7).

Boehmer, J. (2006). *DWC and MIT Study: Taxes Comprise 16% Of Typical Airfare*. Retrieved 5 12, 2008, from Business Travel News: http://www.dwc.edu/news/2006-2007/DWCMITstudyBTN.shtml

Bok, S. (1986). *Secret*. Oxford, UK: Oxford University Press.

Boumerdassi, B. (2000). An efficient reservation-based Dynamic channel assignment strategy. *IEEE 3G Mobile Communication Technologies, 1st International Conference, 471*, 352-355.

Bowen P., Cheung M., & Rohde F. (2007). Enhancing IT governance practices: A model and case study of an organization's efforts. *International Journal of Accounting Information Systems* (pp. 191-221).

Brown, C. (1997). Examining the hybrid IS governance solution: evidence from a single case study. *Information System Research,* (1), 69-94.

Brown, C., & Sambamurthy, V. (1999). *Repositioning the IT organization to enable business transformation*. Pinnaflex Educational Resource, Cincinnati,OH.

Brown, E. R., Haddock, J. E., Crawford, C., Hughes, C. S., & Lynn, T. A. (1998). "Designing Stone Matrix Asphalt Mixtures. Volume II(a). NCHRP Report 9-8/2, TRB, Washington, D.C.

Camp, L. J., & Wolfram, C. (2004). Pricing security. In L.J. Camp & S. Lewis (Eds.), *Economics of information security*, Vol. 12, *Advances in information security*, Springer-Kluwer

Cassivi, L. (2006). Collaboration planning in a supply chain. *SCM: An International Journal, 11*(3).

Cater-Steel, A. P. (2004). Low-rigour, Rapid Software Process Assessments for Small Software Development Firms. *Proceedings of the 2004 Australian Software Engineering Conference (ASWEC '04)*.

Chan, C., & Cheng, L. (2004). Hiding Data in Images by Simple LSB Substitution. *Pattern Recognition, 37*(3), 469-474.

Chang, K. (2006). Relationship Quality and Negotiation Interdependence: the Case Study of International Defect Claim. *Total Quality Management, 16*(7), September.

Chatzky, J. S. (1998). Taking time to automate. *Money Magazine, 27*(12), 196

Chen, L., Gillenson, M., & Sherrell, D. (2004). Consumer Acceptance of Virtual Stores: A Theoretical Model and Critical Success Factors for Virtual Stores. *The DATA BASE for Advances in Information Systems, 35*(2).

Cheng, E., Li, H., & Love, P. (2000). Establishment of Critical Success Factors for Construction Partnering. *Journal of Management in Engineering*, March/April.

Chin, K., Tummala, V., Leung, J., & Tang, X. (2004). A study on supply chain management practices. *International Journal of Physical Distribution & Logistics Management, 34*(6).

Chiung Moon, Kim, J., Choi, G., & Seo, Y., (2002). An efficient genetic algorithm for the traveling salesman problem with precedence constraints. European Journal of Operational Research, *140*(3), 606-617.

Choi, I.C., Kim, S.I., & Kim, H.S. (2003). A genetic algorithm with a mixed region search for the asymmetric traveling salesman problem. *Computers & Operations Research, 30*(5), 773–786

Choi, J., Fershtman, C., & Gandal, N. (2007). *Network Security: Vulnerabilities and Disclosure Policy.* (CEPR Working Paper #6134).

Choudrie, J., Ghinea, G., & Weerakkody, V.(2004). Evaluating Global e-Government Sites: A View Using Web Diagnostic Tools. *Electronic Journal of e-Government, 2*(2), 105-114.

Chu, S., & Fang, W. (2006). Exploring the Relationships of Trust and Commitment in Supply Chain Management. *The Journal of America n Academy of Business, Cambridge, 9*(1), March.

Churbuck, D. (1998). What are you waiting for? *Forbes, 161*(12)261.

Church, J., & Gandal, N. (2006). *Platform competition in telecommunications.* In M. Cave, S. Majumdar, & I. Vogelsang (Eds.), *the handbook of telecommunications, 2,* 117-153, Elsevier.

Clark, R. (1989). *Congruence between strategy, IT, and decision making at the unit level: A comparison of U.S.A and Canadian retail banks.* Unpublished dissertation, University of Massachusetts.

COBiT 4.1 Executive Summary Framework.Coen, M., & Kelly, U. (2007, January). Information management and governance in UK higher education institutions: bringing IT in from the cold. *Perspectives, 11*(1).

Colbert, J. L., & Brown, P. L. (1996). A comparison of internal controls: COBIT, SAC, COSO and SAS 55/78. *IS Audit Control J, 4,* 26-35.

Commonwealth of Australia. (2000). *The changing nature of fraud in Australia.*

Computer Emergency Response Team CERT Coordination Center (2000). *Results of the Security in ActiveX.*

Workshop, Software Engineering Institute, Carnegie Mellon University, USA.

Conference on Electronics, Communications and Computers, Veracruz, Mexico.

Constantine, L. (2001, April). Lightweights, Heavyweights and Usable Processes for Usable Software. *Keynote at Software Development 2001.*

Cooper, D., & Tracey, M. (2005). Supply chain integration via IT: strategic implications and future trends. *Int. J. Integrated Supply Management, 1*(3).

Cox, I., Miller, M., & Bloom, J. (2002). *Digital Watermarking.* CA, USA: Academic Press.

Cuitter Consortium Research Briefs (2000). http://www.cutter.com

Cundall, P. A., & Strack, O. D. L. (1979). A Discrete Numerical Model for Granular Assemblies. *Geotechnique, 29,* 47-65.

Curtis, M., & Borthick (1999). Evaluation of Internal Control from a Control Objective Narrative. *Journal of Information Systems, 13*(1), Spring.

Dantu, P. (1957). Contribution à l'étude mécanique et géométrique des milieux pulvérulents. *Proc. of the 4th Int. Conf. on Soil Mech. and Found. Eng, 1,* 144-148.

Dantzig, B.G. & Ramser, J.H. (1959). The truck dispatching problem. Management Sciences, *6*(1), 80-91.

Davis, E. (1996). Perceived Security Threats to Today's Accounting Information Systems: Survey of CISAs. *IS Audit & Control Journal, 3,* 38-41.

Davis, E. (1997, March). An Assessment of Accounting Information Security. *CPA Journal, 66*(3).

de Burca, S., Fynes, B., & Roche, E. (2004). Evaluating Relationship Quality in a Business-to-Business Context. *Irish Journal of Management, 25.*

DeCoste, D., & Schölkopf, B. (2002). Training invariant support vector machines. *Machine Learning, 46,* 161–190.

Defee, C., & Stank, T. (2005). Applying the strategy-structure performance paradigm to the supply chain environment. *The International Journal of Logistics Management, 16*(1).

Deloitte Global Security Survey (2008). *Global financial services industry.*

Delone, W., & Mclean, E. (2003). The DeLone and McLean of Information Systems Success: A Ten-Year Update. *Journal of Management Information Systems, 19*(4), 9-30.

Denning, D. (1999). *Information warfare and security.* Boston: Addison-Wesley.

Deshpande, Y., & Gaedke, M. (2005). Web Engineering: Developing Successful Web Applications In A Systematic Way. *14th International World Wide Web Conference,* 10-14 May, 2005, Chiba, Jap.

Deshpande, Y., Murugesan, S., Ginige, A., Hansen, S., Schwbe, D., Gaedke, M., & White, B. (2002). Web Engineering. *Journal of Web Engineering, 1*(1), 3-17. Santa Barbara, CA.

Dexter, A. R., & Tanner, D. W. (1972). Packing Densities of Mixtures of Spheres with Log-Normal Size Distributions. *Nature Phy. Scl. 238,* 31-32.

Diniz, E. (1998). *Web Banking in USA. Journal of Internet Banking and Commerce.* www.arraydev.com/commerce/jibc/9806-06.htm

Dowlatshahi, S. (200515 September). Strategic success factors in enterprise resource-planning design and implementation: a case-study approach. *International Journal of Production Research, 43*(18).

Duda, R. O., & Hart, P. E. (1973) *Pattern Recognition and Scene Analysis.* New York: Wiley.

Dunham, M. H. (2003). *Data Mining Introductory and Advanced Topics.* Prentice Hall.

Egger, F. (2001). Affective Design of E-Commerce User Interfaces: How to Maximise Perceived Trustworthiness. *International Conference on Affective Human Factors Design.* London: Asean Academic.

Eid, R., Trueman, M., & Ahmad, A. (2004). Factors affecting the success of business-to-business international Internet marketing (B-to-BIIM): an empirical study of UK companies. *Industrial Management & Data System, 104*(1).

Elfriede, D., & Rashka, J. (2001). *Quality Web Systems, Performance Security, and Usability.* New York: Addison – Wesley.

Elias, A. G. M. (2004). *Knowledge management.* Prentice-Hall, Inc.

Ericsson, E. (1999). Information warfare: Hype or reality? *The Nonproliferation Review, 6*(3), 57-64.

Etnoteam, S. P. A. M. (2000). *Evaluating and designing the quality of Websites (a quality model for Websites).* University of Milan.

Eze, E. (1999). *The potential use of IT for competitive advantage: An empirical examination of Nigerian commercial banks.* Unpublished dissertation, Walden University.

Faltings, B., & Yokoo, M. (2004). Introduction: Special issue on distributed constraint satisfaction. *Journal of Artificial Intelligence, 161*(1-2), 1-5.

Fawcett, T., & Provost, F. (1997). *Adaptive Fraud Detection.* Data Mining and Knowledge Discovery.

Fayad, M. E., Laitinen, M., & Ward, R. P. (2000). Software Engineering in the Small. *Communications of the ACM, 43,* 115-118.

Fayad, M. E., Laitinen, M., & Ward, R. P. (2000, March). Software Engineering in the Small. Communications of the ACM, *43*(3).

Fernandez, I., Gonzalez, A., & Sabherwal, R. (2004). *Knowledge Management, solutions, technology.* Prentice-Hall, Inc.

Forman, H., & Lippert, S. (2005). Toward the development of an integrated model of technology internalization within the supply chain context. *The International Journal of Logistics Management, 16*(1).

Fowler, M., & Highsmith J. (2001, August). The Agile Manifesto. *Software Development Magazine*. http://www.sdmagazine.com/documents/s=844/sdm0108a/0108a.htm

Franch, M., & Gaio, L. (2003). *Evaluating and designing the quality of Websites*. IEEE, Multimedia.

Freeman, H., & Davis, L. S. (1997). A corner finding algorithm for chain code curve. *IEEE Transactions on Computing, 26*, 297-303.

Funk, J. E., & Dinger, D. R. (1994). *Predictive Process control of Crowded Particulate Suspensions*. Boston: Kluwer Academic Publishers.

Furht, B., & Kirovski, D. (2006). *Encryption and Authentications: Techniques and Applications*. USA: Auerbach Publications.

Furnas, C.C. (1931). Grinding aggregates I—mathematical relations for beds of broken solids of maximum density. *Ind. Eng. Chem. 23*, 1052.

Fynes, B., de Burca, S., & Voss, C. (2005). Supply chain Relationship Quality: the competitive environment and performance. *International Journal of Production Research, 43*(16).

Galliers, R., & Leidner, D. (2003). *Strategic information management: challenges and strategies in managing information systems*. third Edi. Butterworth-Heinemann: UK.

Gandal, N. (2002). *Compatibility, standardization and network effects: Some policy implications. Oxford Review of Economic Policy, 18*, 8091.

Garboczi, J. F., & Bentz, D. P. (1992). Computer Simulation of the Diffusivity of Cement-Based Materials. *Journal of Materials Science, 27*, 2083-2092.

Garg, N. K., & Jindal, S. (2007). An Efficient Feature Set for Handwritten Digit Recognition. In *Proceedings of 15th International Conference on Advanced Computing and Communications* (pp. 540-544).

Gefen, D., Straub, D., & Boudreau, M. (2000). Structural Equation Modeling and Regression: Guidelines of Research Practice. *Communications of the Association for Information Systems, 4*(7).

Ghani, R. (1999). *Using Error-Correcting Codes for Text Classification*. Center for Automated Learning & Discovery, School of Computer Science, Carnegie Mellon University, Pittsburgh, PA.

Gledec, G. (2005). Evaluating Web Site Quality. *In Proceedings of the 7th Internet Users Conference (CUC2005)*, Croatia.

Goldberg D.E. (1989) *Genetic algorithms in search optimization and machine learning*. Addison-Wesley Publishers.

Goldberg, D. (1989). *Genetic Algorithms in Search, Optimization, and Machine Learning*. USA: Addison-Wseley Professional.

Goo, J., & Nam, K. (2007). Contract as a Source of Trust - Commitment in Successful IT Outsourcing Relationship: An Empirical Study. *Proceedings of the 40th Hawaii International Conference on System Sciences – 2007 IEEE*.

Goode, J. F. & Lufsey, L. A. (1962). A New Graphical Chart for Evaluating Aggregate Gradations. *Assoc. Asphalt Paving Technologists, 31*, 176-207.

Gopalakrishnan, K., & Shashidhar, N. (2007). Characterising the aggregate structure variations in asphalt concrete during compaction using computer automated imaging techniques. *Int. J. Computer Applications in Technology, 28*(4), 295–303.

Gorgevik, D. (2004). *Classifier Combining for Handwritten Digit Recognition*. Ph.D. dissertation, Faculty of Electrical Engineering, Skopje, Macedonia.

Gotoh, K., & Finney, J. L. (1974). Statistical Geometrical Approach to Random Packing Density of Equal Spheres. *Nature, 252*, 202-205.

Grady and Francesco, (2006). *The Law and Economics of Cyber Security: An Introduction*. Cambridge University Press.

Greenstein, M., & Vasarhelyi, M. (2000, July). The Electronization of Business Process. *European conference on AIS, Section One.*

Gresse von Wangenheim, C., Anacleto, A., & Salviano, C. F. (2006). *Helping Small Companies Assess Software Processes, IEEE Software*, (pp. 91-98).

Gunasekaran, A., & Ngai, E. (2004a, September). Information systems in supply chain integration and management. *Production Planning & Control, 15*(6).

Gunasekaran, A., & Ngaie, E. (2004b, September). Virtual supply-chain management. *Production Planning & Control, 15*(6).

Guo, H., & Georganas, N. (2002). *Multi-resolution Image Watermarking Scheme in the Spectrum Domain.* Presented at the IEEE Canadian Conference on Electrical and Computer. Engineering, Canada.

Gutman, R., & Rieff, D. (1999). *Crimes of War: What the public should know.* New York: Norton.

Guzman, V., Miyatake, M., & Meana, H. (2004). *Analysis of Wavelet –Based Watermarking Algorithm.* Paper presented at the 14th International IEEE

Haav, H., &, Lubi, T. (2007). A Survey of Concept-based Information Retrieval Tools, Institute of Cybernetics at Tallinn Technical University.

Hansmann, U., Merk, L., Nicklous, M. S., & Stober, T. (2001). *Pervasive Computing 2nd Edition.* Berlin: Springer-Verlag.

Hauptman, R. (1996). Cyberethics and social stability. *Ethics and Behavior, 6*(2), 161-163.

Hayale, T., & Abu Khadra, H. (2006). Evaluation of the Effectiveness of Control Systems in the Computerized Accounting Information Systems: An Empirical Research Applied on Jordanian Banking Sector. *Journal of Accounting – Business & Management, 13*(2006), 39-68.

Heimlich, J. (1999). Evaluating the Content of Web Sites. *Environmental Education and Training Partnership Resource Library.* Ohio State University Extension, USA.

Heimlich, J., & Wang, K. (1999). Evaluating the Structure of Web Sites. *Environmental Education and Training Partnership Resource Library*, Ohio State University Extension, USA.

Henfridsson, O., & Holmstrom, H. (2003). Developing E-Commerce in Internetworked Organizations: A Case of Customer Involvement Throughout the Computer Gaming Value Chain. *The DATA BASE for the Advances in Information Systems, 33*(4).

Henry, L. (1997). A Study of the Nature and Security of Accounting Information Systems: The Case of Hampton Roads, Virginia. *The Mid- Atlantic Journal of Business, 33*(63), 171-189.

Himma, K. (2004). The ethics of tracing hacker attacks through the machines of innocent persons. *International Journal of Information Ethics, 2*(11), 1-13, The Honeynet Project. *know your enemy* 2nd Boston: Addison-Wesley.

Ho, J., & Pardo, T. (2004). Toward the Success of eGovernment Initiatives: Mapping Known Success Factors to the Design of Practical Tools. Proceedings of the *37th Hawaii International Conference on System Sciences – 2004 IEEE.*

*Homeland Security and Personal Safely, (*2003), *Report of the joint inquiry into the terrorist attacks of* Venice, Italy.

Homeland security: Information sharing responsibilities, challenges, and key management issues [GAO- 03-715T]. (2003, May 8). Presented to Committee on Government Reform, House of Representatives.

Hsu, C., & Wu, J. (1998). Multiresolution Watermarking for Digital Images. *IEEE Transactions on Circuits and Systems- II, 45*(8),1097-1101.

Hu, Y., Zhu, F., Lv, H., & Zhang, X. (2006). Handwritten digit recognition using low rank approximation based competitive neural network. *Lecture Notes in Computer Science 3972*, 287-292.

Huang, C. & Wu, J. (2000). *A Watermark Optimization Technique Based on Genetic Algorithms.* Presented at the

2000 SPIE – Visual Communications Image Processing, Perth, Australia.

Huang, J., & Yang, C. (2004). *Image Digital Watermarking Algorithm Using Multiresolution Wavelet Transform.* Paper presented at the International IEEE Conference on Systems, Man, and Cybernetics, the Hague, the Netherlands.

Hust, A., Klink, S., Junker, M., & Dengel, A. (2004). *Query Expansion for Web Information Retrieval.*

Hust, A., Klink, S., Junker, M., & Dengel, A. (2005). *Towards Collaborative InformationRetrieval: Three Approaches.*

IATA Economics. (2007). *Airline Profitability - 2006.* Retrieved 5 2008, from IATA Economic Briefing: http://www.iata.org/NR/rdonlyres/5B3D0818-D9D0-43CB-AA65-C5548639FA85/0/Airline_2006_Profits.pdf

IATA. (2006, 6). *IATA Economic Briefing European Aviation Taxes.* Retrieved 2008, from IATA: http://www.iata.org/NR/rdonlyres/71ABA881-5E98-411A-825A-C97A12A92164/0/EU_Taxation_June_06.pdf

IATA. (2008, 3 1). *Fuel.* Retrieved 5 17, 2008, from IATA: http://www.iata.org/pressroom/facts_figures/fact_sheets/fuel.htm

Ibrahim, M., & Ribbers, P. (2006). Trust, Dependence and Global Interorganizational Systems. the *39th Hawaii International Conference on System Sciences, 2006 IEEE.*

icao. (2008). Retrieved 2008, from http://www.icao.int/icao/en/atb/Ead/Fep/forms/english/cost_en.pdf

ITGI (IT Governance Institute) Board briefing on IT Governance 2001.

Jain, A. K., Duin, R. P. W., & Mao, J. (2000). Statistical Pattern Recognition: A Review, *IEEE. Trans. Pattern Recognition and Machine Intelligence, 22*(1), 4-36.

Jarrah, F. (1999a). *Internet shoppers in the Arab world spend US$ 95 million.* www.dit.net/itnews/newsjune99/newsjune22.html

Jarrah, F. (1999b). *Internet users in the Arab world close to one million.* www.dit.net/itnews/newsmay99/newsmay77.html

Jarvenpaa, S., & Ives, B. (1991). Executive involvement and participation in the management of information technology. *MIS Quarterly, 15*(2), 205-227.

Jiang, W., Sun, Z., Yuan, B., Zheng, W., & Xu, W. (2006). User-Independent Online Handwritten Digit Recognition. In *Proceedings of the Fifth International Conference on Machine Learning and Cybernetics* (pp. 3359-3364).

Jingho Z., & Tianshun, Y. (2004). *A knowledge-based Approach to text classification.*

Joachims, T. (1999). Making large–scale SVM learning practical. In B. Scholkopf, C. J. C. Burges, and A. J.

Julian, T., & Standing, C. (2003). The value of User Participation in the E-Commerce Systems Development. *Informing and IT Education Conference*, Pori, Finland.

Jullien, R., & Meakin, P. (1987). Simple Three-Dimensional Models for Ballistic Deposition with Restructuring. *Europhysics Lett., 4*, 1385-90.

Jung, H., Cho, S., Shik, S., Koh, Chung, Y., Lee, K., Lee, S., & Kim, C. (2003). *Image Watermarking Based on Wavelet Transform Using Threshold Selection.* Paper presented at the International IEEE SICE Conference.

Kampstra, R., Ashayeri, J., & Gattorna, J. (2006). Realities of supply chain collaboration. *The International Journal of Logistics Management, 17*(3).

Kanji, G. (2002). Performance Measurement System. *Total Quality Management, 13*(5).

Kannan, K., & Telang, R. (2004). *Market for software vulnerabilities? Think again.* Working paper, Carnegie-Mellon.

Katzenbeisser, S., & Petitcolas, F. (2000). *Information Hiding: Techniques for steganography and digital watermarking.* Boston, MA: Artech House.

Ketcham, R. A., & Shashidhar, N. (2001). Quantitative Analysis of 3-D Images of Asphalt Concrete. *Proceedings, 80th Annual TRB Meeting,* Washington, D.C.

Kim, K., & Im, I. (2002). The Effects of Electronic Supply Chain Design (e-SCD) on Coordination and Knowledge Sharing: An Empirical Investigation. *35th Hawaii International Conference on System Sciences, IEEE 2002.*

King, L. (2001). The CSFs That Influence Organizations To Adopt Internet Technology. *Malaysian Journal of Library & Information Science, 6*(2).

Kirkpatrick, S., Gelatt, Jr., C.D., & Vecchi, M.P. (1983). Optimization by Simulated Annealing. *Science, 220*(4598), 671-680.

Kise, K., Junker, M., Dengel, A., & Matsumoto, K. (2001). Experimental Evaluation of Passage-Based Document Retrieval. In *Proceedings of the Sixth International Conference on Document Analysis and Recognition (ICDAR'01).*

Klapper, L., & Love, I. (2002). *Corporate Governance, Investor protection and performance in Emmerging Markets.* working paper. The World Bank.

Kokkinaki, I. A., Mylonas, S., & Mina, S. (2005, September). e-Government Initiatives in Cyprus. *e-Government Workshop (eGOV05)*, Brunel University, UK.

Kordel, L. (2004). IT Governance Hands-on Using CO-BiT to Implement IT Governance. *Information Systems Control Journal, 2.*

Kostic, Z., & Sollenberger, N. (2002). Performance and implementation of dynamic frequency hopping in limited-bandwidth cellular systems. *IEEE Transactions on Wireless Communications, 1*(1), 28-36.

Kostic, Z., Maric, I., & Wang, X. (2001). Fundamentals of dynamic frequency hopping in cellular systems. *IEEE Journal on Selected Areas in Communications, 19*(11), 2254-2266.

Kumswat, P., Attakitmongcol, K., and Striaew, A. (2005). A New Approach for Optimization in Image Watermarking by Using Genetic Algorithms. *IEEE Transactions on Signal Processing, 53*(12),4707-4719.

Lainhart, I. V., & John, W. (2000). COBIT: A Methodology for Managing and Controlling Information and Information Technology Risks and Vulnerabilities. *Journal of Information Systems, 14*(1).

Lambert, D., Knemeyer, A., & Gardner, J. (2005). Supply chain partnerships: model validation and implementation. *Journal of Business Logistics, 25*(2).

Langelaar, G., Setyawan, I., & and Lagendijk, R. (2000). Watermarking Digital Image and Video Data: A State-of-Art Overview. *IEEE Signal Processing Magazine, 17*(5), 20-46.

Lauer, F., Suen, C. Y., & Bloch, G. (2007). A trainable feature extractor for handwritten digit recognition. *Pattern Recognition 40*(6), 1816-1824.

LeCun, Y., Jackel, L. D., Bottou, L., Brunot, A., Cortes, C., Denker, J. S. et al. (1995). Comparison of learning algorithms for handwritten digit recognition. In *Proceedings of International Conference on Artificial Neural Networks* (pp. 53-60).

Lee N. H., & Bahk S. (2007). Dynamic channel allocation using the interference range in multi-cell downlink systems. *IEEE Wireless Communication and Networking Conference*, (pp. 1716-1721).

Lefebvre, E., Léger1, P., & Hadaya, P. (2003). E-collaboration within one supply chain and its impact on firms' innovativeness and performance. *Information Systems and E-Business Management, 1*(2).

Leng, R. (1994). Interstate crisis escalation and war, In M. Portegal & J. Knutson (Eds.), *the dynamics of aggression* (pp. 307-332), Hillsdale, NJ: Lawrence Erlbaum.

Lenstra, J. & Rinnooy, K.A., (1981). Complexity of vehicle routing and scheduling problems. *Networks, 11*, 221-227.

Lewis, J. (2002). *Assessing the risks of cyber-terrorism, cyber war, and other cyber threats.* Washington, DC: Center for Strategic and International Studies.

Li, C., Lim, J., & Wang Q. (2007). Internal and External influences on IT control governance. *International Journal of Accounting Information Systems*, (pp. 225-239).

Lin, F., Sung, Y., & Lo, Y. (2005). Effects of Trust Mechanisms on Supply-Chain Performance: A Multi-Agent Simulation Study. *International Journal of Electronic Commerce*, *9*(4).

Lin, O., & Joyce, D.(2004)."Critical Success Factors for Online Auction Web Sites. *In the Proceedings of the 17ʰ NACCQ.*

Lin, X., & Ng, T. T. (1997). A Three-Dimensional Discrete Element Model Using Arrays of Ellipsoids. *Geotechnique, 47*(2), 319-29.

Lin, Y., Dou, J., & Wang, H. (1992) Contour Shape Description Based on an Arch Height Function, *Pattern Recognition, 25*(1), 17 - 23.

Liu, L., Nakashima, K., Sako, H., & Fujisawa, H. (2003). Handwritten digit recognition: benchmarking of state-of-the-art techniques. *Pattern Recognition, 36*(10), 2271-2285.

Liu, Z., & Chu, W. (2004). *Knowledge-Based Query Expansion to Support Scenario-Specific Retrieval of Medical Free Text.*

Loch, D., Houston, H., & Warkentin, M. E. (1992, June). Threats to Information Systems: Today's Reality, Yesterday's Understanding. *MIS quarterly Journal*, (pp. 173–186).

Lodhi, H. (2002). *Text Classification using String Kernels*. Department of Computer Science, Royal Holloway, University of London, Egham, Surrey TW20 0EX, UK.

Loh, T., & Koh, S. (2004, September). Critical elements for a successful enterprise resource planning implementation in small- and medium-sized enterprises. *International Journal of Production Research, 42*(17).

Luftman, J. (2004). *Managing the Information Technology Resource*. Pearson.

Ma, H., & Zaphiris, P.(2003). The Usability and Content Accessibility of the e-Government in the UK. *In Proceedings of Human Computer Interaction International Conference*, Greece.

Mahdavi, M., Edwards, R. M., & Ladas, C. V. (2007). On the effect of a random access protocol on the performance of the session-based data subsystem in GSM/GPRS. *IEEE Transactions on Vehicular Technology, 56*(4), 1781-1796.

Mäkinen, T., Varkoi, T., & Lepasaar, M. (2000). A Detailed Process Assessment Method for Software SMEs. *Proc. 7th European Software Process Improvement Conf. (EuroSPI).* www.iscn.at/select_newspaper/assessments/tampere.html.

Mallat,S. (1989). A theory for multi-resolution signal decomposition: The wavelet Representation. *IEEE Transactions on Pattern Analysis And Machine Intelligence, 11*(7), 674-693.

Mandia, K., & Prosise, C. (2003. *Incident response and computer forensics.* New York: McGraw-Hill/Osborne.

Manion, M., & Goodrum, A. (2000). *Terrorism or civil disobedience: toward a hacktivist ethic. Computers and Society (ACM SIGCAS), 30*(2), 14-19.

Manning, C. D., & Sch¨utze, H. (1999). *Foundations of Natural Language Processing.* MIT Press.

Markoff, J. (2004). *Home Web Security Falls Short. Survey Shows.* available at http://www.staysafeonline.info/news/safety_study_v04.pdf

Masad, E., & Button, J. (2004). Implications of Experimental Measurements and Analyses of the Internal Structure of Hot-Mix Asphalt. *Transportation Research Record, 1891, TRB*, 212–220.

Masad, E., Muhunthan, B., Shashidhar, N., & Harman, T. (1999a). Internal Structure Characterization of Asphalt Concrete Using Image Analysis. *Journal of Computing in Civil Engineering, 13*(2), 88–95.

Masad, E., Muhunthan, B., Shashidhar, N., & Harman, T. (1999b). Quantifying Laboratory Compaction Effects on the Internal Structure of Asphalt Concrete. *Transportation Research Record, 1681, TRB*, 179–185.

Mason, J., & Lefrere, P. (2003, December). Trust, Collaboration, e-Learning and Organizational Transformation. *International Journal of Training and Development, 7*(4).

Mason-Jones, R., & Towill, D. (2000). Coping with Uncertainty: Reducing Bullwhip Behaviour in Global Supply Chains. *Supply Chain Forum: An International Journal, 1.*

McBride, J., McNurlin, A., & Sprague, R. (2005). *Information Systems Management In Practice.* 6th Edition, Prentice-Hall.

Mccollum, T., & Salierno, D. Choosing the Right Tools. *Internal Auditor Journal*, (pp. 34-43).

McDonald, A., & Welland, R. (2002).. Available at http://www.dcs.gla.ac.uk/ accessed *Evaluation of Commercial Web Engineering Processes* 20/5/2006.

Meathreal, R., & Galton, A. (2000). Qualitative Representation of Planar Outline. In *Proceeding of 14th European Conference on AI* (pp. 224-228).

MENA News_42. (2008, Jun). Industry Bids Farewell to Paper Ticket Meets deadline for 100% ET. *IATA MENA News* , (p. 3).

Mena, J. (Ed.). (2003). Investigative Data mining for Security and Criminal Detection. B. H. pub. Company.

Michael, J., Wingfield, T., & Wijiksera, D. (2003). *Measured responses to cyber attacks using Schmitt analysis: a case study of attack scenarios for a software-intensive system.* In *Proceedings of the 27th IEEE Computer Software and Applications Conference*, Dallas, TX.

Mihalcea, R. (2004). Information Retrieval and Web Search Instructor.

Miller, G. G. (2001). *The Characteristics of Agile Software Processes.*

Miller, R. (1991). *Interpretations of conflict: ethics, pacifism, and the just-war tradition.* Chicago, IL: University of Chicago Press.

Min, S., Roath, A., Daugherty, P., Genchev, S., Chen, H., & Arndt, A. (2005). Supply chain collaboration: what's happening? *The International Journal of Logistics Management, 16*(2).

Mishra, A. R. (2006). *Advanced Cellular Network Planning and Optimisation: 2G/2.5G/3G... Evolution to 4G.* John-Wiley.

MIT-Daniel Webster College. (2006, 1 30). *The Ticket Tax Project.* Retrieved 5 17, 2008, from MIT Global Airline Industry Program: http://web.mit.edu/TicketTax/

Mitra, S. (1998). *Digital Signal Processing.* Columbus, OH: McGraw –Hill.

Modi, P. J., Jung, H., Tambe, M., Shen, W. M., & Kulkarni, S. (2001). Dynamic distributed resource allocation: Distributed constraint satisfaction approach. *Proceedings of the 8th International Workshop on Intelligent Agents*, (pp. 264-276).

Molander, R., & Siang, S. (1998). *The legitimization of strategic information warfare: Ethical considerations. AAAS Professional Ethics Report, 11*(4), Retrieved November 23, 2005, from http://www.aaas.org/spp/sfrl/sfrl.htm

Mollenkopf, D., & Dapiran, P. (2005, March). The importance of developing logistics competencies: a study of Australian and New Zealand firms. *International Journal of Logistics: Research and Applications, 8*(1).

Montori, V., Wilczynski, N., Morgan, D., & Haynes, R. (2003). Systematic reviews: *A cross-sectional study of location and citation counts. BMC Medicine, 1*(2).

Murugesan, S., Deshpande, Y., Hansen, S., & Ginige, A. (1999, May). Web Engineering: A New Discipline for Development of Web-based Systems. *Proceedings of the First ICSE Workshop on Web Engineering, International Conference on Software Engineering*, Los Angeles, http://aeims.uws.edu.au/WebEhome/ICSE99-WebE-Proc/San.do

Nah, F., Lau, J., & Kuang, J. (2001). Critical factors of successful implementation of enterprise systems. *Business Process Management Journal, 7*(3).

Nah, F., Zuckweiler, K., & Lau, J. (2003). ERP Implementation: Chief Information Officers' Perceptions of CSFs. *International Journal of Human-Computer Interaction, 16*(1).

Narahari, Y., & S. Biswas. S., (2000), Supply Chain Management: Modeling and Decision Making. Invited paper. International Conference on Flexible Autonomous Manufacturing Systems, Coimbatore Institute of Technology. Coimbatore, January 2000.

Nardin, T. (Ed.), (1998). *the ethics of war and peace*. Princeton, NJ: Princeton University Press.

nasm. (2008). *Navigation in the Air*. Retrieved 2008, from National Air and Space Museum : http://www.nasm.si.edu/gps/airnav.html

Ngai, E., Cheng, T., & Ho, S. (2004). CSFs of Web-based supply-chain management systems: an exploratory study. *Production Planning & Control, 15*(6).

Nicholson, B., & Carme, E. (2002). Offshore Software Sourcing by Small Firms. *An Analysis of Risk, Trust and Control*.

Nielsen, J. (2000). *Designing Web Usability: The Practice of Simplicity*. New Riders Publishing. Indianapolis. Indiana.

Nitzberg, S. (1998). *Conflict and the computer: Information warfare and related ethical issues*. In *Proceed* Ethics of Cyber War Attac*king of the 21st National Information Systems Security Conference*, Arlington, VA (p. D7).

Niu, X., Lu, Z., & Sun, S. (2000). Digital Image Watermarking based on multi-resolution Decomposition. *IEEE Electronics Letters, 36*(13), 1108-1110.

Nizovtsev, D., & Thursby, M. (2005). *Economic analysis of incentives to disclose software vulnerabilities*. Mimeo,

Nolan, G. T., & Kavanagh, P. E. (1992). Computer Simulation of Random Packing of Hard Spheres, *Powder Technology, 72*, 149-55.

Oak Vale Fund Report , www.oakvaluefund.com, p1, July 2004.

Oger, L., Lichtenberg, M., Gervois, A., & Guyon, E. (1989). Determination of the Coordination Number in Disordered Packings of Equal Spheres. *Journal of Microscopy 156(1)*,. 65-78.

Orwant, C. (1994). *EPER ethics*. In *Proceedings of the Conference on Ethics in the Computer Age*, Gatlinburg, TN (pp. 105 -108)

Ozment, A. (2004). *Bug auctions: Vulnerability markets reconsidered*. Mimeo.

Pachter, L., & Sturmfels, B. (2005). *Algebraic Statistics for Computational Biology*, Cambridge University Press.

Paper, D., & Chang, R. (2005, January). The State of Business Process Reengineering: A Search for Success Factors. *Total Quality Management, 16*(1).

Paulk, M. C., (1998). Using the Software CMM in Small Organizations. *Joint 1998 Proc. Pacific Northwest Software Quality Conf. and 8th Int'l Conf. Software Quality, PNSQC/Pacific Agenda*, (pp. 350–361). www.pnsqc.org/proceedings/pnsqc98.pdf

Pauwels, E. (2006, August). Change governance series-Making Sense of regulations and best practices. *Copyright ©Serena Software, Inc.*

Peansupap, V., & Walker, D. (2005). Factors Enabling Information and Communication Technology Diffusion and Actual Implementation in Construction Implementation. *ITcon, 10*.

Phua, C. (n.d.). *Minority Report in Fraud Detection: Classification of Skewed Data*. Sigkdd Explorations, Vol. 6.

Plamondon, R., & Srihari, S. (2000). On-line and off-line handwriting recognition: A comprehensive survey. *IEEE Transactions on Pattern Analysis and Machine Intelligence, 22*(1), 63-84.

Plant, R., & Willcocks, L. (2007). Critical Success Factors in International ERP Implementations: A case Research Approach. *Journal of Computer Information Systems*, spring.

PolyAnalyst 4 user Manual. (2002). Megaputer Intelligence, Inc.

Potdar, V., Han, S., & Chang, E. (2005). *A Survey of Digital Image Watermarking Techniques.* Paper presented at the 3rd International IEEE Conference on Industrial Informatics, Perth, Australia.

Potvin, J.Y. (1996). Genetic Algorithms for the traveling salesman problem, *Annals of Operations Research, 63,* 339–370.

Powell, M. J. (1980). Computer-Simulated Random Packing of Spheres. *Powder Technology, 25,* 45-52.

Prakash, R., Shivaratri, N. G., & Singhal, M. (1999). Distributed dynamic fault-tolerant channel allocation for cellular networks. *IEEE Transactions on Vehicular Technology, 48*(6), 1874-1888.

Pressman, R. S. (1998, September/October). Can Internet-Based Applications Be Engineered? *IEEE Software.*

Pressman, R. S. (2003). Software Engineering: a Practitioner's Approach (4th ed.). McGraw-Hill Publishing Company.

Pringle, L. (2001). Size does matter: improvement for SMEs. *Software (SEA National),* (pp. 4-7).

Priscoli, F. D., Magnani, N. P., Palestini, V., & Sestini, F. (1997). Application of dynamic channel allocation strategies to the GSM cellular network. *IEEE Selected Areas in Communications, 15*(8), 1558-1567.

Prodromidis, A. L. (2000). *Agent-Based Distributed Learning Applied to Fraud Detection.* Columbia University.

Purdue (2002, September 10). *New simulation shows 9/11 plane crash with scientific detail.* Retrieved May 1, 2008, from Purdue News : www.purdue.edu/UNS/html4ever/020910.Sozen.Pentagon.html

Qiu, Y., & Frei, H. (1993). Concept-based query expansion. In *Proceedings of SIGIR-93, 16th ACM International Conference on Research and Development in Information Retrieval,* (pp. 160–169), Pittsburgh, US.

Quan Lau, S.(n.d.). *Domain Analysis of E-Commerce Systems Using Feature-Based Model Templates, A thesis,* Waterloo, Ontario, Canada.

Ramamurthy, K., Premkumar, G., & Crum, G. (1999). Organizational and Interorganizational Determinants of EDI Diffusion and Organizational Performance: A Causal Model. *Journal of Organizational Computing and Electronic Commerce, 9*(4).

Ranganathan. C., Dhaliwal, J., & Teo, T. (2004). Assimilation and Diffusion of Web Technologies in Supply-Chain Management: An Examination of Key Drivers and Performance Impacts. *International Journal of Electronic Commerce, 9*(1), Fall.

Ranum, M. (2004). *the myth of homeland security.* Indianapolis: Wiley

Rao, K. K., & Krishnan, R. (1994). Shape Feature Extraction from Object Corners, Image Analysis and Interpretation. In *Proceedings of the IEEE Southwest Symposium* (pp. 160–165).

Rao, K., & Yip, P. (1990). *Discrete Cosine Transform: algorithms, advantages, applications.* USA: Academic Press.

Rau, K. (2004, Fall). Effective Governance of IT: Design, objectives, roles, and relationships. *Information System Management.*

Ray, K C. (2002, August). Adopting xp The path to—and pitfalls of—implementing Extreme Programming. *STQE* (pp. 34-40). www.stqemagazine.com

Reddy, A., & Chatterji, B. (2005). A New Wavelet Based Logo-watermarking Scheme. *Pattern Recognition Letters, 26*(7), 1019-1027.

Redouane, A. (2002). Guidelines for Improving the Development of Web-Based Applications. *Proceedings of the Fourth International Workshop on Web Site Evolution (WSE'02)* 0-7695-1804-4/02 2002 IEEE.

Ricardo, B., & d Berthier, R. (1999). Addison Wesley *Modern Information Retrieval Textbook,* ACM Press.

Righini, G., & Trubian, M., (2004), A note on the approximation of the asymmetric traveling salesman problem. *European Journal of Operational Research, 153*(1), 255-265.

Rodriguez, D., Harrison, R., & Satpathy, M. (2002). A Generic Model and Tool Support for Assessing and Improving Web Processes. *Proceedings of the Eighth IEEE Symposium on Software Metrics* (METRICS.02) 0-7695-1339-5/02 © 2002 IEEE.

Rothenburg, L., & Bathurst, R. J. (1992). Micromechanical Features of Granular Assemblies with Planar Elliptical Particles. *Geotechnique, 42*(1), 79-95.

Russell, S., & Norvig, P. (2003). *Artificial Intelligence: A Modern Approach*. Prentice-Hall, 2nd Edition.

Ryan, S. D., & Bordoloi, B. (1997). Evaluating Security Threats in Mainframe and Client Server Environments. *Information & Management, 32*(3), 137-142.

Saadeh, S., Tashman, L., Masad, E., & Mogawer, W. (2002). Spatial and Directional Distributions of Aggregates in Asphalt Mixes. *Journal of Testing and Evaluation, ASTM, 30*(6), 483–491.

Sadri, J., Suen, C. Y., & Tien, D. B. (2007). A genetic framework using contextual knowledge for segmentation and recognition of handwritten numeral strings. *Pattern Recognition 40*(3), 898-919.

Saenchai, K., Benedicenti, L., & Paranjape, R. (2005). A dynamic extension of the asynchronous weak commitment search algorithm. *IEEE Canadian Conference on Electrical and Computer Engineering*, (pp. 1112-1115).

Safabakhsh, R., Zaboli, S., & Tabibiazar, A. (2004). *Digital Watermarking on Still Images Using Wavelet Transform*. Presented at the International IEEE Conference on Information Technology: Coding and Computing, Las Vegas, Nevada.

Salmenkaita, M., Gimenez, J., & Tapia, P. (2001). A practical DCA implementation for GSM networks: Dynamic frequency and channel assignment. *IEEE Vehicular Technology Conference, 4*, 2529-2533.

Salton, J. (1989). *Automatic Text Processing: The Transformation: Analysis and Retrieval of Information by Computer*. Mass: Addison-Wesley, Reading

Sanders, N., & Premus, R. (2005). Modeling the Relationship between Firm Capability, Collaboration, and Performance. *Journal of Business Logistics, 26*(1).

Santos, L. O. (1999). *Web-site Quality Evaluation Method: a Case Study on Museums*. ICSE 99 - 2nd Workshop on Software Engineering over the Internet.

Sauro, J., & Kindlund, E. (2005). A Method to Standardize Usability Metrics Into a Single Score. *CHI2005 Methods and Usability*, Portland, Oregon, USA.

Schechter, S, (2004). *Computer security, strength and risk: A quantitative approach*. Mimeo.

Scherocman, J. A. (1991). Stone Mastic Asphalt Reduces Rutting. *Better Roads, 61*(11), 26.

Schmitt, M. (1998). Bellum Americium: The U.S. view of twenty-first century war and its possible implications for the law of armed conflict. *Michigan Journal of International Law, 19*(4), 1051-1090.

Schmitt, M. (2002), Wired warfare: computer network attack and jus in bello. *International Review of the Red Cross, 84*(846), 365-399.

Schneier, B. (n.d.). At http://www.schneier.com/essays-comp

Schwarz, A., & Hirschheim, R. (n.d.). An extended platform logic perspective of IT governance: managing perception and activities of IT. *Journal of Strategic Information Systems, 12*(2003), 129-166.

ScienceDaily. (2007, September). *Airplane Design: Better Flight-control Systems, Safer, Cheaper, And Greener*. Retrieved 2008, from http://www.sciencedaily.com/releases/2007/09/070915122014.htm

Search Engine, NLTK Tutorial: Text Classification, nltk.sourceforge.net/tutorial/classifying/ (visited Jan, 2008).

Sebe, F., Domingo-Ferrer, J., & Herrera, J. (2000). *Spatial Domain Image Watermarking Robust Against Compres-*

sion, *Filtering, Cropping, and Scaling.* Paper presented at the 3rd International Workshop on Information Security, Wollongong, Australia.

Shashidhar, N. (1999). X-ray Tomography of Asphalt Concrete. *Transportation Research Record: Journal of the Transportation Research Board, 1681, TRB,* 186–192.

Shashidhar, N., Zhong, X., Shenoy, A., & Bastian, E. (2000). Investigating the role of aggregate structure in asphalt pavements. In *Proc., 8th Annual Symposium on Aggregates, Asphalt Concrete, Bases and Fines,* ICAR, Denver, Colorodo, 2000.

Shaw, N., & DeLone, W. (2002). Sources of Dissatisfaction in End- User Support: An Empirical Study. *The DATA BASE for Advances in Information Systems, 33*(2).

Sherer, S. (2003). CSFs for Manufacturing Networks as Perceived by Network Coordinators. *Journal of Small Business Management, 41*(4).

Shieh, C., Huang, H., Wang, F., & Pan, J. (2004). Genetic Watermarking Based on Transform Domain Techniques. *Pattern Recognition, 37*(3), 555-565.

Signore, O. (2005). A Comprehensive Model for Web Sites Quality. *In the Proceedings of the 7th IEEE International Symposium on Web Site Evolution (WSE'05).*

Silaghi, M. C. (2006). Framework for modeling reordering heuristics for asynchronous backtracking. *IEEE International Conference on Intelligent Agent Technology,* (pp. 529-536).

Silaghi, M. C., & Faltings B. (2004). Asynchronous aggregation and consistency in distributed constraint satisfaction. *Journal of Artificial Intelligence, 161,* 25-53.

Simatupang, T., & Sridharan, R. (2005). An integrative framework for supply chain collaboration. *The International Journal of Logistics Management, 16*(2).

Simatrupang, T., Wright, A., & Sridharan, R. (2004). Applying the theory of constraints to supply chain collaboration. *Supply Chain Management: An International Journal, 9*(1).

Sims, D. (1994). New realities in aircraft design and manufacture. *Computer Graphics and Applications, IEEE, 14*(12), 91 .

Singh, I., & Sook, A. (2002). An Evaluation of the Usability of South African University Web Sites. *In Proceedings of the 2002 CITTE Conference,* Durban, South Africa.

SITA. (2008). Baggage mistakes cost billions. *Middle East AirPort, 1*(1), 12.

Skjoett-Larsen, T., Thernoe, C., & Andresen, C. (2003). Supply chain collaboration: theoretical perspectives and empirical evidence. *International Journal of Physical Distribution & Logistics Management, 33*(6).

Smola, editors, *Advances in Kernel Methods — Support Vector Learning,* (pp. 169–184), Cambridge, MA: MIT Press.

Sohal, A., & Fitzpatrick, P. (2002). IT governance and management in large Australian organizations. *Int. J. Production Economics, 75*(2002), 97-112.

Sohn, H. Y., & Moreland, C. (1968). The Effect of Particle Size Distribution on Packing Density. *Canadian J. Chem. Eng. 46,* 162-67.

Soliman, F., Clegg, S., & Tantoush, T. (2001). CSFs for integration of CAD/CAM systems with ERP systems. *International Journal of Operations & Production Management, 21*(5/6).

Soliman, K., & Janz, B. (2001). Interorganizational Information Systems: Exploring an Internet-Based Approach. Issues in Supply Chain Management, 1.

Somers, T., & Nelson, K (2001). The Impact of Critical Success Factors across the Stages of Enterprise Resource Planning Implementations. *34th Hawaii International Conference on System Sciences - 2001 IEEE.*

Soppe, W. (1990). Computer Simulation of Random Packings of Hard Spheres. *Powder Technology, 62,.* 189-96.

Stallings, W. (2005). *Wireless Communications and Networks.* Prentice-Hall, 2nd Edition.

Standing, C. (2002, March). Methodologies for developing Web applications. *Information and Software Technology, 44*(3), 151-159.

Stein, S. (2006). *Software Process Improvements in a Small Organization.* Master Thesis ,Software Engineering Thesis no: MSE-2006:01 January 2006. Available at: http://quality.hpfsc.de/master-sstein.pdf accessed 4/6/2006.

Stein, S. (2006). Software Process Improvements in a Small Organization. Master Thesis. Software Engineering Thesis no: MSE-2006:01 January 2006. Available at: http://quality.hpfsc.de/master-sstein.pdf accessed 4/6/2006

Stolfo, S. J. (1997). *Credit Card Fraud Detection Using Meta-Learning.* Columbia University.

Stolfo, S. J., & Wei Fan. (1999). *Cost-based Modeling for Fraud and Intrusion Detection: Results from the JAM Project.* Columbia University; 0-7695-0490-6/99.

Strang, G. & Nguyen, T. (1996). *Wavelets and Filter Banks.* Wellesley, MA: Wellesley-Cambridge Press.

Suen, C. Y., & Tan, J. (2005). Analysis of errors of handwritten digits made by a multitude of classifiers. *Pattern Recognition Letters 26,* 369-379.

Syaiful, A. (2006 Jan-Apr). Effective information technology governance mechanisims: An Australian study. *Gadjah Mada International Journal of Business, 8*(1), 69-102.

Tan, F., & Tung, L.(2003, December). Exploring Website Evaluation Criteria Using the Repertory Grid Technique: A Web Designers' Perspective. *In the Proceedings of the 2nd Annual Workshop on HCI Research in MIS,* WA.

Tashman, L., Masad, E., Peterson, B., & Saleh, H. (2001). Internal Structure Analysis of Asphalt Mixes to Improve the Simulation of Superpave Gyratory Compaction to Field Conditions. *Journal of the Association of Asphalt Paving Technologists, 70,* 605–645.

Tay, P., & Havlicek, J. (2002). *Image Watermarking Using Wavelets.* Presented at the IEEE Midwest Symposium on Circuits and Systems, Tulsa, Oklahoma.

Te˘si´c, J., & Manjunath, B. (2005). *Nearest Neighbor Search for Relevance Feedback.*

Timothy, B., Knechel, W., Jeff, R. P. L., & Willingham, J. J. (1998). An Empirical Relationship between the Computerization of Accounting Systems and Incidence and Size of Audit Differences. *Auditing Journal, 17*(1),Spring 1998.

Townsend, S., Zhou, Y., & Croft, B. (2004). *A Framework for Selective Query Expansion.* Whose the editors.

Travers, T., Bideau, D., Troadec, J. P., & Messager, J. C. (1986). Uniaxial Compression Effects on 2D Mixtures of 'Hard' and 'Soft' cylinders. *J. Phys. A 19,* L1033-L1038.

Trier, O., Jain, A. K., & Taxt, T. (1996) Feature extraction methods for character recognition - A survey, *Pattern Recognition, 29*(4), 641-662.

Trkman P., & Groznik A. (2006). Measurement of Supply Chain Integration Benefits. *Interdisciplinary Journal of Information, Knowledge, and Management, 1.*

Troadec, J. P., Gervois, A., Annic, C., & Lemaître, J. (1974). A model of binary assemblies of dises and its application to segregation study. *J. Phys. (France) I 4,* 1121-1132.

Tummala, V., Phillips, C., & Johnson, M. (2006). Assessing SCM success factors: a case study. *Supply Chain Management: An International Journal, 11*(2).

Turban, E., & Aronson, J. (2001). *Decision Support Systems and Intelligent Systems.* 6th edition, Prentice Hall, Upper Saddle River, NJ.

Tuttle, B., & Vandervelde, S. (2007). An empirical examination of COBiT as an internal control framework for information technology. *International Journal of Accounting Information Systems, 8*(2007), 240-263.

Ullidtz, P. (1998). *Modelling Flexible Pavement Response and Performance.* First Edition, Lyngby: Polyteknisk Forlag.

Ulsch, M., & Bamberger, J. (2006, March). *Sound IT governance needs requires breadth and depth.* Financial Executive.

Umble, E., Haft, R., & Umble, M. (2003). Enterprise resource planning: Implementation procedures and critical success factors. *European Journal of Operational Research, 146.*

Vakola, M., & Wilson, I. (2004). The challenge of virtual organization: CSFs in dealing with constant change. *Team Performance Management, 10*(5/6).

Vavrik, W. R., Pine, W. J., Huber, G., Carpenter, S .H., & Bailey, R. (2001). The Bailey Method of Gradation Evaluation: The Influence of Aggregate Gradation and Packing Characteristics on Voids in the Mineral Aggregate. *Journal of the Association of Asphalt Paving Technologists, 70.*

Veltkamp, R., & Tanase, M. (2000). *Content-Based Image Retrieval Systems: A Survey.* Technical Report UU-CS-2000-34, Dept of Information and Computing Sciences, Utrecht University.

Vetterli, M., & Kovačević, J. (1995). *Wavelets and Subband Coding.* USA: Prentice Hall.

Vischer, W. M., & M. Bolsterli (1972). Random Packing of Equal and Unequal Spheres in Two and Three Dimensions. *Nature (London) 239*, 504.

Wang, C., Doherty, J., & Van Dyke, R. (2002). A Wavelet-Based Watermarking Algorithm for Ownership Verification of Digital Images. *IEEE Transactions on Image Processing, 11*(2), 77-78.

Wang, E., Tai, J., & Wei, H. (2006, October). A Virtual Integration Theory of Improved Supply-Chain Performance. *Journal of Management Information Systems, 23*(2).

Wang, L. B., Paul, H. S., Harman, T., & Angelo, J. D. (2004a). Characterization of Aggregates and Asphalt Concrete Using X-Ray Computerized Tomography: A State-of-The-Art Report. *Journal of the Association of Asphalt Paving Technologists,* 73, 467-500.

Wang, Z., & Mathiopoulos, P. T. (2005). On the performance analysis of dynamic channel allocation with FIFO handover queuing in LEO-MSS. *IEEE Transactions on Communications, 53*(9), 1443-1446.

Ward, R. P., Fayad, M. E., & Laitinen, M. (2001, April). Software Process Improvement in the Small. *Communications of the ACM, 44*(4).

Weaver, N., & Paxson, V, (2004). *A worst case worm.* Mimeo.

Web Document, Haav, H., &, Lubi, T. (2007). A Survey of Concept-based Information Retrieval Tools, Institute of Cybernetics at Tallinn Technical University.

Web Engineering Home Page [http://fistserv.macarthur.uws.edu.au/san/WebEhome/]

Web site of State Bank of Pakistan www.sbp.org.pk

Web site of the Banks Directory. www.bankdirectory.ws

Web Site, www.dcs.gla.ac.uk/keith/chapter.1/ch.1.html (visited Jan, 2008)

Weill, P., & Ross, J. (2004a). *IT governance: how top performers manage IT decision rights for superior results.* Boston, MA: Harvard Business School Press.

Weill, P., & Ross, J. (2004b). *IT governance on one page.* MIT Sloan Management.

Weill, P., & Ross, J. (2004c). *How Top Performers Manage IT Decision Right for Superior Results.* Harvard Business School Press.

Westerman, G. (2006, December). IT risk management: From IT necessity to strategic business value. CISR WP No.366 and MIT Sloan WP No.4658-07.

Westman, A. E. R., & H. R. Hugill (1930). The Packing of Particles. *J. Amer. Ceram. Soc. 13*, 767-79.

Westwood, C. (1997). *The future is not what it used to be: Conflict in the information age.* Fairbairn, Australia: Air Power Studies Center.

Wierer, J., & Boston, N. (2007a). A Handwritten Digit Recognition Algorithm Using Two-Dimensional Hidden Markov Models for Feature Extraction. In *Proceedings of 2007 International Conference on Acoustics, Speech and Signal Processing.*

Wilding, R., & Humphries, A. (2006). Understanding collaborative supply chain relationships through the application of the Williamson organizational failure framework. *International Journal of Physical Distribution & Logistics Management, 36*(4).

Williams, L., Espe, T., & Ozment, J. (2002). The Electronic Supply Chain: its impact on the current and future structure of strategic alliance, partnerships and logistics leadership. *International Journal of physical Distribution & Logistics Management, 32*(8).

Wolfgang, R., Podilchuk, C., & Delp, E. (1999). Perceptual Watermarks for Digital Images and Video. *Proceedings of the IEEE, 87*(7), 1108-1126.

Wong, P., Cheung, S., & Ho, P., (2005, October). Contractor as Trust Initiator in Construction Partnering - Prisoner's Dilemma Perspective. *Journal of Construction Engineering and Management.*

Xiu-fang, W., Tian, T., & Xue-song, S. (2007). Handwritten Digit Recognition Based on Nonlinear Potential Function Arithmetic. In *Proceedings of Second IEEE Conference on Industrial Electronics and Applications* (pp. 2831-2833).

Yang, C., Ting, P., & Wei, C. (2006, March). A Study of the Factors Impacting ERP System Performance from the Users' Perspectives. *The Journal of American Academy of Business, Cambridge, 8*(2).

Yang, J., & Manivannan, D. (2007). Performance comparison of two channel allocation approaches: Channel pre-allocation vs. non pre-allocation. *IEEE Proceedings of the 3rd International Conference on Wireless and Mobile Communications,* (pp. 61-61).

Yang, J., Jiang, Q., Manivannan, D., & Singhal, M. (2005). A Fault-Tolerant Distributed Channel Allocation Scheme for Cellular Networks. *IEEE Transactions on Computers, 54*(5), 616-629.

Yang, S. (2003). Filter evaluation for DWT-domain image watermarking. *Electronics Letters, 39*(24), 1723 – 1725.

Yates, R., & Ribeiro-Neto, B. (1999). *Modern Information Retrieval.* Addison-Wesley Publishing Company.

Yeh, Y. (2005). Identification of factors affecting continuity of cooperative electronic supply chain relationships: empirical case of the Taiwanese motor industry. *Supply Chain Management: An International Journal, 10*(4).

Yokoo, M. (1995). Asynchronous weak-commitment search for solving distributed constraint satisfaction problems. *Proceedings of the 1st International Conference on Principles and Practice of Constraint Programming,* (pp. 88–102).

Yokoo, M., & Hirayama, K. (2000). Algorithms for distributed constraint satisfaction: A review. *Journal of Autonomous Agents and Multi-Agent Systems, 3*(2), 198-212.

Yokoo, M., Durfee, E. H., Ishida, T., & Kuwabara, K. (1998). The distributed constraint satisfaction problem: Formalization and algorithms. *IEEE Transactions on Knowledge and Data Engineering, 10*(5), 673-685.

Yoo, S., & Jin, J. (2004). Evaluation of the Home Page of the Top 100 University Web Sites. *Academy of Information and Management Sciences, 8*(2), 57-69.

Youngsu, L. J. K. (n.d.). From Design Features to Financial Performance for Online Stock Trading Sites.

Yuan, E., & Wenzel, G. (2005). Assured counter- terrorism information sharing using: Attribute based information security. (ABIS), In *Proceedings of IEEE Aerospace Conference* (pp. 1-12).

Yubin, S., Huan, H., Hua, L., & Shaowen, Y. (2000). Performance analysis of the minimum call blocking probability for dynamic channel allocation in mobile cellular networks. *Proceedings of the IEEE International Conference on Communication Technology, 1*, 269-273.

Yusuf, M., & Haider, T. (2004). Recognition of Handwritten Urdu Digits using Shape Context. In *Proceedings of INMIC 2004* (pp. 569-572).

Zaphiris, P., Dellaporta, A., & Mohamedally, D. (2006). User needs analysis and evolution of portals. In A. Cox (Ed.), *Portals: people, processes and technology.* London, UK: Facet Publishing.

Zettel, J., et al. (2001). LIPE: A Lightweight Process for E-Business Startup Companies Based on Extreme Programming. *Proc. Third Int'l Conf. Product-Focused Software Process Improvement (PROFES 2001)*. Berlin: Springer Verlag.

Zhang, M., & Yum, T. S. P. (1989). Comparisons of channel assignment strategies in cellular mobile telephone systems. *IEEE Transactions on Vehicular Technology, 38*(4), 211-215.

Zhang, P., & Dran, G.(2001)."Expectations and Ranking of Website Quality Features: Results of Two Studies on User Perceptions. *In the Proceedings of the 34th Hawaii International Conference on System Sciences.*

Zhang, W., Wang, G., Xing, Z., & Wittenburg, L. (2005). Distributed stochastic search and distributed breakout: Properties, comparison and applications to constraint optimization problems in sensor networks. *Journal of Artificial Intelligent, 161*(1-2), 55-87.

Zheng, J., Johnson, P. F., & Reed, J. S. (1990). *J. Amer. Ceram. Soc. 73*, 1392.

Zhong, X., Shashidhar, N., & Chang, C. S. (2000). DEM Stability for Static Analysis in Aggregate Packing. *Proceedings of 14th Engineering Mechanics Conference*, Austin, Texas.

Zikmond, W. (2003). *Business Research Methods, 7th* edition. Thomson publisher.

Zou, P., & Seo, Y. (2006). Effective applications of E-commerce technologies in construction supply chain: current practice and future improvement. *ITcon, 11.*

Zwass, V. (1996). Structure and macro-level impacts of electronic commerce: from technological infrastructure to electronic marketplaces. *International Journal of Electronic Commerce, 1.*

About the Contributors

Evon Abu-Taieh is a PhD holder in simulation. A USA graduate for both her master's of science and bachelor's degrees with a total experience of 19 years. Author of many renowned research papers in the airline and IT, PM, KM, GIS, AI, simulation, security and ciphering. Editor/author of book: *Utilizing Information Technology Systems Across Disciplines: Advancements in the Application of Computer Science* (IGI, USA). Editor/author *Handbook of Research on Discrete Event Simulation Environments: Technologies and Applications*, (IGI, USA). Guest Editor, *Journal of Information Technology Research (JITR)*. Editorial board member in: *International Journal of E-Services and Mobile Applications (IJESMA)* and *International Journal of Information Technology Project Management (IJITPM)* and *International Journal of Information Systems and Social Change (IJISSC)*. Editor/author of book: *Simulation and Modeling: Current Technologies and Applications* (IGI, USA). Developed some systems like: Ministry of transport databank, auditing system for airline reservation systems and Maritime Databank among others in her capacity as head of IT department in the ministry of transport for 10 years. Furthermore worked in the Arab Academy in her capacity as assistant professor, dean's assistant and London School of Economics (LSE) director. Appointed many times as track chair, reviewer in many international conferences: IRMA, CISTA, and WMSCI. Enjoys both the academic arena as well as the hands on job. (abutaieh@gmail.com)

Asim A. El Sheikh got a BSc (honors) from University of Khartoum (Sudan),an MSc and a PhD from University of London (UK). El Sheikh worked for University of Khartoum, Philadelphia University (Jordan) and The Arab Academy for Banking & Financial Sciences (Jordan). El Sheikh is currently the dean of the faculty of information systems & technology at the Arab Academy for Banking & Financial Sciences. El Sheikh's areas of research interest are computer simulation and software engineering.

Jeihan Abu-Tayeh attend school at the Rosary School in Amman, then she acquired her bachelor's in pharmaceutical science and management from Al-Ahlyya Amman University. Furthermore, in 2002, she got her MBA with emphasis on "International Marketing & Negotiations Technique", with outstanding GPA of 3.87 out of 4 (with honors) from Saint Martin's College, State of Washington; U.S.A. Currently, Jeihan Abu-Tayeh is a head of the International Agencies & Commissions Division at the

Jordanian Ministry of Planning and International Cooperation. In her capacity, she has the opportunity to maintain sound cooperation relations with the World Bank Group, as well as the UN Agencies, in order to extend to Jordan financial and technical support for developmental projects through setting appropriate programs and plans, building and improving relations with those organizations. This is achieved through loans and aids programs, by means of designing project proposals, conducting problem & needs assessment for the concerned governmental and non-governmental Jordanian entities, followed by active participation in extensive evaluation processes, conducted by either the UN Country Team, or the World Bank Group Country Team.

* * *

Ahmad Ababneh, born in Jordan, 1979. MSc in computer science, Yarmouk University, Jordan, Irbid. 2004. He is an instructor in Computer science department, Yarmouk University, Irbid, Jordan; he had many consultancy assignments in the areas of education in Jordan and. Currently he is interested in the area of Arabic Information Retrieval Processing.

Sattar J Aboud received his Master degree in 1982 and a PhD in 1988 in the area of computing science. The two degrees were awarded from U.K. In 1990, he joined the Institute of Technical Foundation in Iraq as an assistant professor. In 1995 he joined the Philadelphia University in Jordan as a chairman of computer science department. Currently, he is a professor at the Middle East University for Graduate Studies, Amman-Jordan. His research interests include areas like public key cryptography, digital signatures, identification and authentication, and networks security. He has supervised numerous PhDs and master's degrees thesis. He has published more than 60 research papers in a multitude of international journals and conferences

Husam A. Abu Khadra is assistant professor of accounting information systems at the Arab Academy for Banking and Financial Sciences (AABFS). Abu Khadra got a bachelor's degree in accounting from Zarka University (Jordan), an MSc and PhD from the Arab Academy for Banking and Financial Sciences (Jordan). Abu Khadra worked in several international companies before joining the AABFS in October 2006. Abu Khadra's research interest is in the area of accounting information systems.

Arafat Abu Mallouh is currently a computer lab supervisor at the University of Hashemite. He earned his MSc degree in Computer Science from Amman Arab University for Graduate Studies in 2008. He received his BSc in computer science from the University of Hashemite in 2001. His primary research interest is in computer networks, artificial intelligence, experts systems, fuzzy logic, and data mining.

Aymen Abu-Errub received his BSc in applied physics - digital electronics, with a minor degree in computer science from Kuwait University in 1989; the MSc in information technology from Al-Neelain University of Sudan, in 2003. He received his PhD degree in computer information systems from the Arab academy for banking and financial sciences, Jordan, in 2008/2009. He has published conference and journal papers in image watermarking.

Khaled Saleh Al Omoush has a PhD in management information systems from The Arab Academy for Banking and Financial Sciences, Jordan. He is assistant professor at Management Information Systems Department in the Faculty of Economics and Administrative Sciences at the Al-Zaytoonh University of Jordan. Khaled's research interests lie in the field of Web systems applications, the CSFs of IT dissemination, Electronic supply chain management, and performance measurement of IT systems, e-business.

Sattam Alamro is an assistant professor in Albalqa' Applied University. He has a PhD in management information systems from the Arab Academy for Banking and Financial Sciences, His principal research interests lie in the fields of management, management information systems, knowledge management and e-commerce , he authored/coauthored more than 6 scientific papers. He is currently investigating how to implement e-commerce standards in SMEs in Jordan.

Hussein Al-Bahadili is an associate professor at the Arab Academy for Banking & Financial Sciences (AABFS). He earned his MSc and PhD from the University of London (Queen Mary College) in 1988 and 1991, respectively. He received his BSc in engineering from the University of Baghdad in 1986. He has published many papers in different fields of science and engineering in numerous leading scholarly and practitioner journals, and presented at leading world-level scholarly conferences. Dr. Al-Bahadili is also working as an IT and communication consultant in support of the IT and Wireless Communication Division of the Middle-East Advanced Semiconductor Inc. (MEASI), the leader in communications in Iraq. His research interests include parallel and distributed computing, wireless communication, data communication systems, computer networks, cryptography, network security, data compression, image processing, data acquisition, computer automation, electronic system design, computer architecture, and artificial intelligence and expert systems.

Ali Al-Haj received the BSc degree in electrical engineering from Yarmouk University, Jordan, in 1985; the MSc degree in electronics engineering from Tottori University, Japan, in 1988; and the PhD degree in electronics engineering from Osaka University, Japan, in 1993. He then worked as a research associate at ATR Advanced Telecommunications Research Laboratories in Kyoto, Japan, until 1995. He joined Princess Sumaya University, Jordan, in October 1995, where he is now an associate professor. Dr. Al-Haj has published conference and journal papers in dataflow computing, parallel information retrieval, VLSI digital signal processing, neural networks and digital watermarking.

Firas M. Alkhaldi is an associate professor of knowledge management and enterprise systems, He holds a BA and MA in applied economics from WMU, USA, and a PhD in business information systems/knowledge management from Huddersfield University, UK. He is a leading KM expert and certified e-business consultants. He is the dean of scientific research and graduate studies at the Arab Academy for Banking and Financial Sciences and a professor in the faculty of information Systems and Technology, AABFS. His research interest is in knowledge conversion and transfer, organizational knowledge theory, knowledge culture, Innovative work environment, human and social implications of enterprise systems (ERP, CRM, and SCM). His work appears in a number of international journals and conferences.

Adnan M. Al-Khatib – PhD is computer information systems faculty member - Yarmouk University - Jordan, Sept. 1994 – present. Computer information systems lecturer - University of Bahrain – Bahrain

Sept. 2005 – 2008. - Computer lecturer - Mu'tah University - Jordan, Sept. 1991 - Sept. 1994. Supervisor system programmer and system designer - Ministry of Planning - Kuwait, Feb. 1978 - Aug. 1990.

Riyad Al-Shalabi, Born in Jordan, 1964. PhD. in computer science, Illinois Institute of Technology, Chicago, IL, USA 1996. He is an associate professor of computer science, he is an instructor in computer information systems, Arab Academy for Banking & Financial Sciences, Amman, Jordan; he served in several universities where he served as a chairman in Computer Science Department at Yarmouk University, he had many consultancy assignments in the areas of education in Jordan and. Currently he is interested in the area of Arabic Natural Language Processing and Arabic Information retrieval.

Haroon Altarawneh is an assistant professor in Albalqa' Applied University. He has a PhD in Computer Information Systems from the Arab Academy for Banking and Financial Sciences, His principal research interests lie in the fields of software engineering, Web engineering (Agile Development, Extreme programming) and software process improvement, he authored/coauthored more than 14 scientific papers. He is currently investigating how to implement software process improvements standards in small software development firms.

Farrukh Amin is an MCS (master's of computer science) specialized in management information systems (MIS) from the University of Karachi, holds Masters Degree in Economics and Post Graduate Diploma in MIS. He is a certified trainer from the School of Leadership, Karachi and also certified Systems Analyst and Programmer. He received 3-month technology training from Technology Department of the Philips Academy, Boston, USA. He has over 21 years of experience of working in the software industry, manufacturing industry and educational institutions in Pakistan and abroad. He has great interest in research and publication and finished many research and conference papers. Currently he is associated with the Institute of Business Management, Karachi as assistant professor in computer science & MIS.

R. Dhanlakshmi ME, currently pursuing her PhD in computer science from Mother Teresa Women's University, Kodaikannal, TamilNadu. Her research interests are in the areas of intelligent tutoring system, networking, internet protocols, data mining and cryptography. She received her bachelor's degree in electrical and electronics engineering from Madras University, master's degree in computer science and engineering from Madurai Kamaraj University. She has published two technical papers in the referred International Journal and eight papers in national and international conferences.

Maha T. El-Mahied, a lecturer in the Balqa' University, earned her master's degree in management information system. Holds two bachelor's degrees one in interior design, and the second in business management and accounting. Worked as interior designer specialized in Islamic arts. Enjoys research in knowledge management field and management information systems. Published a paper on the reason of failure of information systems in underdeveloped countries.

K. Ganesh is currently working as assistant consultant in manufacturing industry practice at Tata Consultancy Services, Limited, Mumbai. He holds a bachelor's degree in mechanical and production engineering, a master's degree in industrial engineering and a doctorate from IIT Madras. He then joined the Supply Chain Management Department of Lakshmi Machine Works Limited, Coimbatore as research analyst and has served for two years. His research interests lie in the application of meta-heuristics and decision making tools to logistics management. He has published several papers in leading research journals such as the *European Journal of Operational Research and International Journal of Advanced Manufacturing Technology*

Sameh Ghwanmeh, born in Jordan, 1963. PhD in computer engineering, Liverpool University, UK, 1996. He is an associate professor of computer engineering, he is an instructor in computer engineering, Yarmouk University, Irbid, Jordan; Currently, he serves as a computer and information center director since 1998; he had many consultancy assignments in the areas of ICT in education in Jordan. Currently he is interested in the area of Arabic Natural Language Processing, Arabic Information retrieval and Computer networks.

Kasthurirangan Gopalakrishnan is a research assistant professor of civil engineering at Iowa State University, Ames and has over 10 years of experience in transportation infrastructure systems. Dr. Gopalakrishnan received his PhD in civil engineering from the University of Illinois at Urbana-Champaign and a master's from Louisiana State University at Baton Rouge. Dr. Gopalakrishnan is also a recipient of Dwight D. Eisenhower Transportation Research Fellowship which gave him the opportunity to work at the Turner-Fairbanks Highway Research Centre (TFHRC), Washington DC on a research project entitled "Simulation, Imaging, and Mechanics of Asphalt Pavements." His current research interests include soft computing applications in pavement analysis, mechanistic-empirical pavement design concepts, image analysis, and non-destructive evaluation of pavements and he has published over 50 peer-reviewed journal articles in these areas.

Ezz Hattab is an associate professor in e-business. He developed several software and e-commerce applications. He worked in Amman Arab University, Amman Ahliyya University, Applied Science University and Arab Academy. He is an active member of numerous professional and scientific societies, including the Arab Society of Computers (ASC), and Jordanian Society of Computers (JSC). Lately, he joined the UN/ITC component as an e-business expert. He is representing Middle East region in "Online2Export 2008/2009" project. Dr. Hattab has 25 publications and 4 books in the area of Information Technology, e-business, and web applications. He is a member of the technical committee of *The International Arab Journal of Information Technology (IAJIT)*, *EBEL*, *e-Jordan* and an associate editor of the *International Journal of Mobile Learning and Organization (IJMLO)*. He is a member of the high supervision committee of Management Information Stream at the Ministry of Education in Jordan. Dr. Hattab has been awarded a scholarship from the EU to pursue his PhD in Information Technology. His PhD research was part of the Europe research project "The Webminer", in which he proposed numerous algorithms and techniques that handle Web information retrieval and search. Dr. Hattab has held several executive positions; he worked as a head of web development at Eurobjects Co., Head of Computer Science Dept at Amman University, CIO at Albayina Co., Chair of the e-learning national committee, IT adviser to His Royal Highness Prince Aasm Bin Nayef. Dr. Hattab is a certified project manager (CPM) and a certified e-Business Consultant PME™

Shyamanta M. Hazarika is an associate professor of computer science & engineering at School of Engineering, Tezpur University, India. He received his PhD from University of Leeds, England. Prior to that, he had completed MTech from Indian Institute of Technology, Kanpur, India and bachelor's in engineering from Assam Engineering College, Guwahati, India. His research interests include knowledge representation and reasoning, cognitive robotics and intelligent assistive systems.

Ghassan Kanaan, Born in Jordan, 1962. PhD in computer science, Illinois Institute of Technology, Chicago, IL, U.S.A. 1997. He is an associate professor of computer science, he is an instructor in computer information systems, Arab Academy for Banking & Financial Sciences, Amman, Jordan; he served in several universities where he served as a chairman in Computer Information Systems Department at Yarmouk university, he had many consultancy assignments in the areas of education in Jordan and. He is interested in database systems; currently he is interested in the area of Arabic Natural Language Processing and Arabic information retrieval.

P. Parthiban belongs to the Faculty of Department of Production Engineering, National Institute of Technology (NIT), Tiruchirappalli, India. He holds a Bachelor's degree in Mechanical Engineering, a Master's degree in industrial engineering from NIT Tiruchirappalli. He is currently pursuing his doctoral research at JNT University, Hyderabad. His research interests include supply chain management, lean manufacturing, and artificial intelligence. He has published papers in leading international journal and conferences.

Naga Shashidhar is a New Business Development Manager at Corning Inc., New York. Dr. Shashidhar received his PhD in Materials Science from Alfred University. He is currently working as a Materials Scientist for Corning Inc. He has extensive experience in X-ray Computed Tomography Imaging Techniques and Micro-Mechanical Modelling of Asphalt Concrete.

Saad Yaseen has a PhD in management information systems. He is associate professor and head of MIS Department in the Faculty of Economics and Administrative Sciences at the Al-Zaytoonh University of Jordan. He had conducted over 40 specialized studies in many fields such as IT, IS, e-management, and knowledge management. He is a renowned expert in the management of IT projects and a professional academician in the Middle East.

Index